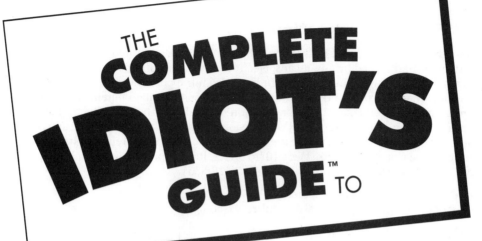

THE COMPLETE IDIOT'S GUIDE™ TO

The Internet

Fourth Edition

by Peter Kent

A Division of Macmillan Publishing
201 W.103rd Street, Indianapolis, IN 46290 USA

International Standard Book Number: 0-7897-1404-3
Library of Congress Catalog Card Number: 97-68678

99 98 97   8 7 6 5 4 3

Interpretation of the printing code: the rightmost double-digit number is the year of the book's first printing; the rightmost single-digit number is the number of the book's printing. For example, a printing code of 97-1 shows that this copy of the book was printed during the first printing of the book in 1997.

Screen reproductions in this book were created by means of the program Collage Complete from Inner Media, Inc, Hollis, NH.

Printed in the United States of America

President
Roland Elgey

Senior Vice President
Don Fowley

Publisher
Joseph B. Wikert

Publishing Manager
Jim Minatel

Manager of Publishing Operations
Linda H. Buehler

General Manager
Joe Muldoon

Director of Editorial Services
Carla Hall

Managing Editor
Thomas F. Hayes

Director of Acquisitions
Cheryl D. Willoughby

Acquisitions Editor
Jill Byus

Product Development Specialist
Henly Wolin

Production Editor
Mark Enochs

Product Marketing Manager
Kourtnaye Sturgeon

Assistant Product Marketing Manager
Gretchen Schlesinger

Acquisitions Coordinator
Michelle R. Newcomb

Software Relations Coordinator
Susan D. Gallagher

Editorial Assistant
Virginia Stoller

Book Designer
Glenn Larsen

Cover Designers
Dan Armstrong
Barbara Kordesh

Illustrator
Judd Winick

Production Team
Jenny Earhart
Julie Geeting
Laura A. Knox
Staci Somers

Indexer
Nick Schroeder

Special thanks to Christy Gleeson for ensuring the technical accuracy of this book.

We'd Like to Hear from You!

QUE Corporation has a long-standing reputation for high-quality books and products. To ensure your continued satisfaction, we also understand the importance of customer service and support.

Tech Support

If you need assistance with the information in this book or with a CD/disk accompanying the book, please access Macmillan Computer Publishing's online Knowledge Base at **http://www.superlibrary.com/general/support**. If you do not find the answer to your questions on our Web site, you may contact Macmillan Technical Support by phone at **317/581-3833** or via e-mail at **support@mcp.com**.

Also be sure to visit QUE's Web resource center for all the latest information, enhancements, errata, downloads, and more. It's located at **http://www.quecorp.com/**.

Orders, Catalogs, and Customer Service

To order other QUE or Macmillan Computer Publishing books, catalogs, or products, please contact our Customer Service Department at **800/428-5331** or fax us at **800/835-3202** (International Fax: 317/228-4400). Or visit our online bookstore at **http://www.mcp.com/**.

Comments and Suggestions

We want you to let us know what you like or dislike most about this book or other QUE products. Your comments will help us to continue publishing the best books available on computer topics in today's market.

> Henly Wolin
> Product Development Specialist
> QUE Corporation
> 201 West 103rd Street, 4B
> Indianapolis, Indiana 46290 USA
> Fax: 317/581-4663
> America Online: **hwolin**
> E-mail: *hwolin@que.mcp.com*

Please be sure to include the book's title and author as well as your name and phone or fax number. We will carefully review your comments and share them with the author. Please note that due to the high volume of mail we receive, we may not be able to reply to every message.

Thank you for choosing QUE!

Contents at a Glance

Part 1: Start at the Beginning   **1**

1 The Least You Need to Know   3
Read this to learn ten things you need to know about the Internet.

2 The Internet: What's It All About?   7
An overview of what the Internet is and what it can do for you.

3 The Premier Internet Tool: E-mail   24
Send your first e-mail message and learn what to do with messages you receive.

4 Advanced E-Mail: HTML and Encryption   43
E-mail gets fancy, e-mail get safe; how HTML Mail and public-key encryption will transform e-mail.

5 The World of the World Wide Web   55
Getting your browser started so you can surf the World Wide Web.

6 More About the Web   69
Become a Web expert: learn about saving stuff, working with the cache, and more.

7 Forms, Applets, and Other Web Weirdness   83
Things you'll run across on the Web, from Java programs to Web pages that push and pull.

8 Web Multimedia   95
Sound, video, and animations: The Web comes to life.

9 Your Very Own Web Page   109
You don't have to be an observer; you can become a participant. Here's how to publish on the Web.

Part 2: There's Plenty More   **119**

10 Push Information to Your Desktop   121
Learn how push *systems automate Web browsing, bringing information to you while you do something else.*

11 The Source of All Wisdom—Newsgroups   133
What's a newsgroup? How do you pick one from the thousands? You'll find out here.

12 Your Daily News Delivery   143
Here's how to use your newsreader to read and participate in newsgroups.

13 Yet More Discussion Groups—Mailing Lists and Web Forums   157
Thousands more discussion groups, this time based on the e-mail system.

14 The Giant Software Store FTP   171
Millions of computer files are publicly accessible through FTP sites.

15 Archie the Friendly File Librarian   187
How do you find your way through those millions of files at FTP sites? Use Archie.

16 Digging Through the Internet with Gopher   199
Gopher's simple menus were a pre-Web simplification of the Internet but they're still alive and well.

17 Yak, Yak, Yak: "Chatting" in Cyberspace   211
It's not real chatting because you type your messages; but it's a real-time discussion system you'll love (or hate).

18 Internet Phones: Talking on the Web   229
Voice comes to the Internet, and the phone companies are worried.

19 What on Earth are All Those File Types?   241
I'll explain all about download directories, dozens of file types, and compressed files.

20 Telnet: Inviting Yourself onto Other Systems   253
A little-used system that allows you to log on to computers around the world.

Part 3: Getting Things Done   **263**

21 Finding Stuff   265
Here's how to find the needle you need in the Internet haystack.

22 Staying Safe on the Internet   275
Keep your kids (and yourself) out of trouble on the Internet.

23 21 Questions: The Complete Internet FAQ   289
Questions and answers from how to get rich on the Internet to why your software won't work.

24 Ideas   303
Loads of ideas for things you can do on the Internet. It's not exhaustive just a sampler.

25 The Future of the Internet   313
The Internet changes so fast; find out about what's next.

Part 4: Resources   **325**

A All the Software You'll Ever Need   327
Visit these sites to download enough software to keep you busy for years.

B Finding a Service Provider   333
If you haven't yet got on the Internet, here's how to start.

C The E-Mail Responder   341
   Information about what you can retrieve from our mail responder.

D Speak Like a Geek: The Complete Archive   345
   You could call it a glossary.

E Online Glossary   363
   *Fifty cool, weird, useful, and interesting sites to visit on the world
   Wide WebIndex*

   Index   455

Contents

Part 1: Start at the Beginning   **1**

1 The Least You Need to Know   **3**

2 The Internet: What's It All About?   **7**

Okay, Then, What Is the Internet? 8
What Exactly Is "Information?" 9
The Internet Services 10
Getting On the Net 12
The Difference Between the Internet and
Online Services 13
What Do You Need? 14
Permanent Connections 15
Dial-In Direct Connections 16
Dial-In Terminal Connections 16
Mail Connections 18
What Do You Have? 18
I Have AOL (CompuServe, MSN, or Such),
But Where's the Internet? 19
You Want Help Setting Up? 20
That's All, Folks! 20
The Least You Need to Know 21

3 The Premier Internet Tool: E-Mail   **23**

What E-Mail System? 24
To POP or Not to POP 25
You Have a New Address! 25
A Word About Setup 27
Sending a Message 29
We Are All One—Sending E-Mail to Online Services...... 31
Write the Message 32
Where'd It Go? Incoming E-Mail 32
What Now? 33
A Word About Quoting 33
Sending Files—Getting Easier 34
Cool Things You Can Do with E-Mail 37

Caution E-Mail Can Be Dangerous! 39
Smile and Be Understood! 40
  Emoticons Galore 40
  Message Shorthand 41
The Least You Need to Know 42

4 Advanced E-Mail: HTML and Encryption   43

HTML Mail—Banish Dull E-Mail 44
  Finding an HTML Mail Program 44
  Different Programs, Different Capabilities 46
Inbox Direct—Web Pages Delivered Directly to You 46
Encryption—Keep Away Prying Eyes 47
Why Encrypt Your E-Mail? 48
Public-Key Encryption—It's Magic 49
  Public-Key Encryption and Your E-Mail 49
  Digital Signatures 51
I'm Sold...Where Do I Get My Keys? 52
  Different Size Keys 52
The Least You Need to Know 54

5 The World of the World Wide Web   55

What's the Web? 55
Let's Start 57
Getting a Browser 59
Browsing Begins at Home 59
  Moving Around on the Web 60
The Hansel and Gretel Dilemma Where Are You? 62
Bookmarks and History 62
  A Little History 63
A Direct Link, Using the URLs 63
  The URL Explained 64
What Will You Find on Your Web Journey? 66
Speeding Up Your Journey by Limiting Graphics.............. 67
There's Plenty More!... 68
The Least You Need to Know 68

6 More About the Web   69

Multiple Windows—Ambidextrous Browsing 70
Your Hard Disk as Web Server? 71

Turbo Charging with the Cache 72
   Putting the Cache to Work 73
   Decisions, Decisions 75
What Is Reload? 75
Long Documents—Finding What You Need 76
Remember to Right-Click 77
Is It Worth Saving? 77
Grabbing Files from the Web 79
   Save It 80
The Least You Need to Know 82

7 Forms, Applets, and Other Web Weirdness   83

Working with Tables 83
Interactive Web Pages—Using Forms 84
Playing It Safe—Secure Sites 85
For Your Eyes Only—Password-Protected Sites 86
Dealing with Secondary Windows 87
Panes or Frames 88
Animated Icons 89
Web Programs Java, JavaScript, and ActiveX 89
   What About JavaScript and ActiveX? 91
Just a Little Shove—Pushing and Pulling 92
The Multimedia Experience 93
The Least You Need to Know 94

8 Web Multimedia   95

What's Available? 96
Which Do You Need? Which Do You Want? 97
   Music and Voice (Very Useful) 97
   Other Document Formats (Also Very Useful) 98
   3-D Worlds (Greatly Overrated!) 99
   Video (If You Can Wait) 99
   Animations (Here and There) 101
Other Weird File Formats 101
Installing a Plug-In 102
Installing a Viewer 103
   Installing a Viewer in Netscape 103
   Setting Up Netscape Beforehand 104
   Installing a Viewer in Internet Explorer 105
The Least You Need to Know 107

9 Your Very Own Web Page   109

My Fill-in-the-Blanks Web Page 110
Make It Your Home Page 112
Your Web Page—What's It Good For? 114
First, the Basics 114
    A Word About Paragraphs 116
Don't Stop at One—Multiple Pages 116
Finding URLs 117
You and Your Service Provider 117
The Least You Need to Know 118

Part 2 There's Plenty More   119

10 Push Information to Your Desktop   121

A Lot of Choice, but Two Big Players 122
A Quick Look at Netcaster 123
    Using the Channel Finder 124
    Adding Any Web page 127
    Using Your Channels 127
Microsoft's Active Desktop 128
Other Push Systems 130
The Least You Need to Know 131

11 Newsgroups: The Source of All Wisdom   133

What's a Newsgroup? 134
So What's Out There? 135
Can You Read It? 136
Okay, Gimme a List! 136
Where Does It All Come from? 137
What's in a Name? 138
    Reaching the Next Level 139
I'm Ready; Let's Read 140
The Least You Need to Know 141

12 Your Daily News Delivery   143

A Quick Word on Setup 144
Starting and Subscribing 145
    Taking a Look 147

The Messages Are Gone! 148
Marking Your Messages 148
Moving Among the Messages 149
Saving and Printing 150
Your Turn Sending and Responding 150
What's This Gibberish? ROT13 150
Pictures (and Sounds) from Words 152
The Fancy Stuff 154
A Word of Warning 155
The Least You Need to Know 155

13 Yet More Discussion Groups: Mailing Lists and Web Forums 157

How Do Mailing Lists Work? 158
The Types of Lists 159
Using a LISTSERV Group 159
The LISTSERV Address 162
Let's Do It—Subscribing 163
Enough Already!—Unsubscribing 164
Getting Fancy with LISTSERV 165
Using Majordomo 166
Using Manually Administered Lists 166
Handling Mailing List Correspondence 167
Using the Web Forums 168
The Least You Need to Know 169

14 The Giant Software Store: FTP 171

Different Flavors of FTP 173
Hitting the FTP Trail 174
Files and Links—What's All This? 175
Finding That Pot o' Gold 177
Look for Clues 178
Getting the File 178
It's the Real Thing—Using a Genuine FTP Program 180
Which and Where 181
It's Alive! Viruses and Other Nasties 184
Where Now? 184
The Least You Need to Know 185

15 Archie, the Friendly File Librarian 187

Archie's Client/Server Stuff 188
Getting to Archie 188
Archie on the Web 189
  Searching Archie 189
  Archie's Options 191
  The Search Types 192
Getting an Archie Client 193
Mail-Order Archie 194
  "Whatis" the Descriptive Index? 196
  More E-Mail Commands 197
The Least You Need to Know 197

16 Digging Through the Internet with Gopher 199

Let There Be Gopher 200
Enough History—What Is Gopher? 201
Gopher It! 202
Archie's Friends Veronica and Jughead 204
  Jughead 205
    The Boolean Operators 206
    Any Wild Card You Want, As Long As It's * 206
    More Boolean Stuff 207
    Special Commands—Maybe 207
  Veronica 208
    Veronica Search Details 209
The Least You Need to Know 210

17 Yak, Yak, Yak: "Chatting" in Cyberspace 211

Chatting and Talking 212
  Two Types of Sessions 213
Score 1 for the Online Services 213
Chatting in AOL 214
CompuServe's Conference Rooms and CB 215
MSN's Chat System 215
Commands to Look For 217
Pick Your Avatar 218
Web Chat's Coming Up Fast 220
Internet Relay Chat—Productivity Sink Hole? 221
  Step 1 Get the Software 222
  Step 2 Connect to a Server 222

What Is It Good For? Real Uses for Chat 225
What About Talk? 226
The Least You Need to Know 227

18 Voice on the Net: Talking on the Internet   229

The Incredible Potential of Voice on the Net 229
    It Gets Better Link to the Real World 230
Phone Companies—No Imminent Danger 231
Do You Have the Hardware You Need? 231
Which Program Should I Use? 232
Working with Your Phone Program 233
    The Conference Server 235
    Now You Get to Talk 236
Your Address Is Not Always the Same 236
The Bells and Whistles 236
Internet-to-Phone Connections 238
The Future Is Video—and Other Weird Stuff 239
The Least You Need to Know 240

19 What on Earth Are All Those File Types?   241

About Download Directories 242
    Pick a Download Directory Sensibly 243
A Cornucopia of File Formats 244
    The File Extension 244
File Compression Basics 247
    Which Format? 248
    Those Self-Extracting Archives 249
Your Computer Can Get Sick, Too 250
    Tips for Safe Computing 251
    The Least You Need to Know 251

20 Telnet: Inviting Yourself onto Other Systems   253

Step 1 Find a Telnet Program 254
Making the Connection 255
HYTELNET Your Guide to the World of Telnet 255
You're In. Now What? 257
    Working in a Telnet Session 258
Special Features 259
    Keeping a Record 259
    Waving Good-Bye to the Telnet Site 259

Telnet's Ugly Sister tn3270 260
MUDs, MOOs, and MUCKs 260
The Least You Need to Know 261

Part 3: Getting Things Done   263

21 Finding Stuff   265

Finding People 266
Directories, Directories, and More Directories 266
Finding "Stuff" 268
   Finding the Search Sites 269
   How Do I Use the Search Engines? 270
   Browsing the Internet Directories 272
Finding Specific Stuff 273
Finding Out What People Are Saying 273
Set a Bookmark to Repeat the Search Later 273
FTP, Gopher, Telnet, and More 274
The Least You Need to Know 274

22 Staying Safe on the Internet   275

Your Kid Is Learning About Sex from Strangers 276
   Don't Expect the Government to Help 276
   It's Up to You; Get a Nanny 277
Your Private E-Mail Turned Up in the National Enquirer 279
Prince Charming Is a Toad! 280
She's a He, and I'm Embarrassed! 281
You Logged on Last Night, and You're Still Online
   This Morning 281
Just Because You're Paranoid Doesn't Mean Someone
   Isn't Saying Nasty Things About You 282
I Was "Researching" at Hustler Online, and Now I'm
   Unemployed 283
I Think Kevin Mitnick Stole My Credit Card Number! 283
My Wife Found My Messages in alt.sex.wanted 285
I "Borrowed" a Picture, and Now They're Suing Me! 286
I Downloaded a File, and Now My Computer's Queasy ... 286
The Least You Need to Know 287

23 21 Questions: The Complete Internet FAQ   289

What's a Shell Account? 290
How Do I Change My Password If I'm Using a PPP Connection?   290
What's a Winsock? 291
Why Won't Netscape Run in Windows 95? 291
How Do I Get Rich on the Internet? 292
How Can I Sell Stuff on the Internet? 292
If I Have a Fast Modem, Why Are Transfers So Slow? 293
Will the Internet Kill Television? 294
Why Isn't Anyone Reading My Web Page? 294
How Can I Remain Anonymous on the Internet? 294
What's finger? 295
Can Someone Forge My E-Mail? 296
What's a Flame? 296
I'm Leaving My Service Provider. How Can I Keep My
  E-Mail Address? 297
Why Can't I Get Through to That Site? 298
Why Won't This URL Work? 299
Why Do So Many People Hate AOL? 299
My Download Crashed So I Have to Start Again. Why?... 300
Should I Start My Own Service Provider Company? 300
Why Not? 300
Just One More Question… 301
The Least You Need to Know 301

24 Ideas   303

Keeping in Touch 304
Meeting Your Peers 304
Business Communications 304
Product Information 304
Product Support.. 305
Getting Software 306
Research 306
Visiting Museums 307
Finding Financial Information 307
Music 307
Magazines and 'Zines 308
Hiding from the Real World 308
Shakespeare on the Net 308

If You Can't Get Out 308
Joining a Community of People with Common Interests 309
You Don't Trust Your Doctor, So 309
Shopping 309
Cybersex 309
Political Activism 310
Subversion 310
Looking for Work (and Help) 310
Clubs and Professional-Association Information Servers . 311
Mating and Dating 311
Long-Distance Computing 311
Books 311
What Did I Miss? 311

25 The Future of the Internet   313

Progress Will Slow Down 314
High Speed Connections (Not Quite Yet) 315
The Web Comes Alive—More Multimedia 315
Intercast PC/TV 316
WebTV—A Relatively Small Niche 316
The Internet Backlash 317
The Internet Will Open Borders 317
The Internet and the Fight for Free Speech 318
Schools Use the Internet; Test Scores Continue
   to Plummet 319
$500 Internet Boxes 320
Software Over the Internet 320
On Predictions... 322
The Least You Need to Know 323

Part 4: Resources   325

Appendix A: All the Software You'll Ever Need   327

The Search Starts at Home 327
The Software Mentioned 328
The Internet's Software Libraries 328
   Plug-Ins & Viewers 331

Finding More 331
   Don't Forget Demos and Drivers 331
Looking for Something Strange? 332
The Least You Need to Know 332

Appendix B: Finding a Service Provider   333

I Want the Best! Where Do I Get It? 333
What's a Reasonable Cost? 333
Tips for Picking a Provider 334
Finding a Service Provider 335
Find a Free-Net 336
Equipment You Will Need 337
You Want Something Faster 338
   ISDN 338
   T1 Line 339
   Satellite 339
   Cable 339
   ADSL 340

Appendix C: The E-Mail Responder   341

Using the E-Mail Responder 341

Appendix D: Speak Like a Geek: The Complete Archive   345

Appendix E: Online Glossary   363

Index   455

Introduction

Welcome to *The Complete Idiot's Guide to the Internet, Fourth Edition*. That's four editions in as many years. The Internet has changed so much that constant revisions are needed to keep up. Between the second and third edition, in fact, the book had to be completely rewritten. The manner in which people used the Internet changed dramatically between 1993 and 1996. The Internet described in the first edition bears as little relation to that described in the third edition as the Pony Express does to the modern U.S. Postal Service. Things seem to be slowing down on the Internet, though. Since 1996 the changes we've seen on the Internet have been more evolutionary than revolutionary. In fact if you're just now learning about the Internet, you're lucky. Anyone who started back in 1993 or 1994 had to learn once, then learn all over again when the Internet changed. The changes are likely to be more incremental now, so you'll just have to figure it all out once and you'll easily keep up with future changes.

Back in 1993, the Internet boom hadn't begun. Sure, the Internet had been around for more than a couple of decades, but it was a secret kept from most of the world. In 1993, the average American thought the Internet was some kind of international crime conspiracy growing out of the breakup of the Soviet Union, or something to do with keeping hair in place. A few months later, though, the media started screaming about this wonderful "new" tool—about how the Internet would change the world.

Nowadays, if you have a high-tech product to sell you have to add the word "Internet" to it somehow. If you're selling a program that speeds up printing, you say that it's great for printing information from the Internet. If you're promoting a video card, you say it makes Web pages look great. If you're selling a smart washing machine, you say it cleans off the dust from the information superhighway.

The Internet's Easier Now...

More importantly, though, the Internet actually works very differently from the way it did a few years ago. Or, at least, the manner in which people use the Internet is very different now. Back in 1993, most Internet users were computer geeks. And that was okay because you needed a high degree of geekhood to get anything done on the Internet. For the average business or home computer user, getting an Internet account was like stepping into a time warp. One moment you were in your whiz-bang multimedia mouse-clicking graphical user interface—Windows, OS/2, or the Mac—and the next minute you were back in the 1970s, working on a dumb UNIX terminal (dumb being the operative word), typing in obscure and arcane, not to mention funky and strange, UNIX commands. You probably found yourself wondering, "What's this **ftp ftp.microsoft.com** thing I have to type?" or "What's **grep** all about and why do I care?" or "Why can't UNIX programmers actually *name* their programs instead of giving them two- or three-letter acronyms?" (Acronyms are so important in the UNIX world that there's even an acronym to describe acronyms: TLA, Three Letter Acronymn.)

Most Internet users these days don't need to know the answers to these ancient questions. These days the majority of new users are back in the 1990s, working in the graphical user interfaces they love (or love to hate, but that's another issue). Since 1993, thousands of fancy new Internet access programs have been written. Today, it's easier to get on the Internet, and it's easier to get around once you are there.

So Why Do You Need This Book?

Even if you've never stumbled along the information superhighway (or "infotainment superhighway," as satirist Al Franken calls it), you've almost certainly heard of it. A recent survey found that while only 2.3 percent of American high school students could tell you the name of the President of the U.S.A., 93.7 percent knew how to get to the Penthouse Online Web site—and a whopping 112 percent knew how to download bootleg copies of Hootie and the Blowfish songs.

Chances are, though, that if you've picked up this book, you are not an experienced international traveler along the highways and byways of this amazing system called the Internet. You probably need a little help. Well, you've come to the right place.

Yes, the Internet is far easier to get around now than it was in 1993. But there's still a lot to learn. The journey will be more comfortable than it was back in 1993, and you can travel much farther.

Now, I know you're not an idiot. What you do, you do well. But right now, you don't do the Internet, and you need a quick way to get up and running. You want to know what the fuss is about, or maybe you already know what the fuss is about and you want to find out how to get in on it. Well, I'm not going to teach you how to become an Internet guru, but I will tell you the things you really *need* to know, such as:

➤ How to get up and running on the Internet

➤ How to send and receive e-mail messages

➤ How to move around on the World Wide Web (and what is the Web, anyway?)

➤ How to find what you are looking for on the Internet

➤ What "push" is all about, and how to push what you want pushed, and where to push it

➤ Protecting life and limb on the information superhighway fast lane

➤ How to participate in Internet discussion groups (this could take over your life and threaten your relationships if you're not careful)

➤ How to talk to Aunt Edna in Walla Walla for $1 an hour—and bankrupt your local long-distance company

I am, however, making a few assumptions. I'm assuming that you know how to use your computer, so don't expect me to give basic lessons on using your mouse, switching between windows, working with directories and files, and all that stuff. There's enough to cover in this book without all that. If you want really basic beginner's information, check out *The Complete Idiot's Guide to PCs* (also from Que), a great book by Joe Kraynak.

How Do You Use This Book?

I've used a few conventions in this book to make it easier for you to follow. For example, when you need to type something, it will appear in bold like this:

type **this**

If I don't know exactly what you'll have to type (because you have to supply some of the information), I'll put the unknown information in italics. For example, you might see the following instructions. In this case, I don't know the file name, so I made it italic to indicate that you have to supply it.

type **this** *filename*

Also, I've used the term "Enter" throughout the book, even though your keyboard may have a "Return" key instead.

In case you want a greater understanding of the subject you are learning, you'll find some background information in boxes. You can quickly skip over this information if you want to avoid all the gory details. On the other hand, you may find something that will help you out of trouble. Here are the special icons and boxes used in this book.

Check This Out

These boxes contain notes, tips, warnings, and asides that provide you with interesting and useful (at least theoretically) tidbits of Internet information.

Techno Talk

The "Techno Talk" icon calls your attention to technical information you might spout off to impress your friends, but that you'll likely never need to know to save your life.

Acknowledgments

Thanks to the huge team at Que (see the list of people at the front of the book) who helped me put this together. There's a lot more to writing a book than just, well, writing. I'm very grateful to have people willing and able to do all the stuff that comes once the words are on the computer screen.

Part 1
Start at the Beginning

You want to start, and you want to start quickly. No problem. In Part 1 you're going to do just that. First I'll give you a quick overview of the Internet, and then I'll have you jump right in and use the two most important Internet services: e-mail and the World Wide Web. (The Web is so important these days that many people think the Internet is the Web. I'll explain the difference in Chapter 2.)

By the time you finish this part of the book, you'll be surfing around the Web like a true cybergeek—and you'll be ready to move on and learn the other Internet services.

Chapter 1

The Least You Need to Know

In This Chapter

➤ How Sound Blaster 16 is special

➤ Installing the software

➤ Making sure it works

I have some good news for you. The Internet is much easier to use today than it was three and a half or four years ago when the Internet "boom" began. The software has changed dramatically, and procedures that were a real chore just a couple of years ago are now quite simple. Still, there's a lot to learn, so we'll begin with a quick overview of these important points. You'll learn more about each of them later.

1. The Internet is a huge computer network—the world's largest—and it's open to the public. Anyone willing to spend the few dollars a month that it costs to buy access to the Internet (or who can figure out how to get a *free* account) is allowed on. What started as a tool of the U.S. military industrial complex is now a tool for everyone from senior citizens to school kids, from Communists to corporate America. You'll find a quick Internet history and summary in Chapter 2.

2. E-mail may not be glamorous, but it's the most important tool on the Internet. Millions of people zap e-mail messages across the world each day, from school kids contacting pen pals to business people communicating with colleagues and clients.

Most e-mail messages are simple text, but if you know how to use the system, you can also send computer files—pictures, spreadsheets, text, desktop publishing files, and even sounds. And now it's becoming easy to send formatted e-mail (pictures, colors, special font styles), and to encrypt your e-mail to ensure that only the recipient can read it. Read about e-mail in detail starting at Chapter 3.

3. Contrary to the impression provided by many newspapers and magazines, the World Wide Web is *not* the Internet; it's just one system running on the Internet. Basically, the Internet is the hardware, and the Web is the software (one software system among many). Still, the Web is one of the most important systems, and certainly the most popular (well, after e-mail).

   The Web is a giant hypertext system, a series of millions of electronic documents linked to each other. You view a document in a Web *browser*. You can click one linked word or picture, and another document appears; then click another *link*, and another document pops up. (You can go on like this indefinitely.) There's a lot to learn about the Web, so we'll cover it in Chapters 5 to 9.

4. A new system's appearing on the Internet, *push*. A push program automatically retrieves information from the Internet for you. All you need to do is define what information you want to see and how often you want to see it, and the program carries out your wishes. The information is generally displayed on your computer's "desktop," perhaps as a form of "desktop wallpaper." You'll learn about push in Chapter 10.

5. There are tens of thousands of discussion groups on the Internet. In Chapters 11 to 13 you'll learn about three systems for using them: newsgroups, mailing lists, and Web forums. The first system requires a special program, a *newsreader*, to display the messages. The second uses the e-mail system to distribute the group's messages. And the last method, a relatively new one, uses forms that you view and use with your Web browsers. You'll find groups about the important issues (such as events in Bosnia or Zaire), the true-but-unreported (alien visitors), the interesting (Greek archaeology), and the trivial (*Melrose Place*). Pick any subject, and somewhere you'll find a related discussion group.

6. Three services—Gopher, FTP, and Telnet—have become submerged in all the fuss about the World Wide Web. Gopher is a menu system that's similar in some ways to the Web. You select a menu option to see another menu or document somewhere else on the Internet—or maybe even somewhere on the other side of the world. Gopher's still alive, but it's not as popular as it used to be (because everyone has rushed to the Web). FTP (File Transfer Protocol) is a file-library system that contains literally millions of computer files in the form of programs, documents, sounds, clip art, and so on; again, still alive, though not used as much as before—but as you'll see, there are some very good reasons for using FTP now and again, even if the same

files are available at a Web site. And finally, Telnet is a system by which you can log on to computers all over the Internet so that you can use databases, play games, find information about jobs, and more (Telnet's used even less than Gopher and FTP, but still provides a way to access some useful and important services). Read all about these services in Chapters 14 to 16 and 20.

7. The Internet is a communications system, so what would it be without a way to really *talk* to people? There are many chat systems in cyberspace, though the best ones are actually off the Internet in the online services. On the Internet proper there's IRC (Internet Relay Chat), a system that you either love or hate (thousands seem to love it). And many new Web-based chat systems have appeared recently, too.

   You don't actually chat—not with your voice anyway. Instead, you type messages that are seen immediately by other participants, and you see their responses right away. You'll learn about these systems in Chapter 16. Then, in Chapter 17, you'll hear about the new voice-on-the-net products—the Internet's "phone" system. These are programs that allow you to literally talk to other people—yes, with your voice. Why pay 50 cents or $1 per minute to phone relatives overseas when you might be able to do so for a $1 or less per *hour*?

8. The Internet is constantly changing. Internet sites come and go, their "addresses" change, and their contents change. So some of the addresses provided in this book—the Web URLs, Gopher server addresses, and so on—might be wrong by the time you read the book. Hey, don't blame me! That's just the nature of the Internet. Things that you discover on your own or that you read about in other publications might disappear, too. But this doesn't have to be a problem. If you understand how to search for things on the Internet (see Chapter 21), you can still find what you need.

9. Okay, so you've heard about the dangers of the Internet. You've seen the articles about pornography on the Internet, you've heard Congress debate the subject, and you've been told that shopping on the Internet is dangerous. True? Well, there's no smoke without fire, but you might be surprised at just how safe the Internet really is. (After all, you can always pull the plug!) Credit card companies say that it's actually safer to use your credit card on the Internet than in the "real world." And although there is pornography on the Internet, there's not as much as some critics have claimed (*TIME* even printed a retraction after its "porn on the Internet" article), and you probably won't just stumble over it. Still, you might want to read Chapter 22 just to make sure you know what it takes to stay safe.

10. The Internet is a hardware system: computers and cables. But it's the software that really makes it run. So you'll need software, you'll need lots of it, and you'll want the latest releases. Luckily there's a lot of cheap—and even free—software ready for

the taking at a variety of software archives on the Internet. Systems like TUCOWS (The Ultimate Collection of Winsock Software), the University of Texas Macintosh Archive, and shareware.com (which has software for Windows, Macintosh, and UNIX) make it quick and easy to download new programs and have them running in minutes. In Appendix A I'll tell you where to find all kinds of software.

11. It's easy for Internet writers to focus on *how* to use the Internet. All too often, we forget a crucial question: *why*? There are thousands of reasons to use the Internet, and I've described just a few of them in Chapter 23. It's a great way for the housebound to keep in touch with the rest of the world (a paradox, perhaps, cyberspace being used as a link to the *real* world). Businesses use it as an essential business tool. Families use it to keep in touch. And people use it to contact others with similar interests. The Internet is such a diverse place that no matter what you plan to use it for now, you may eventually find that it's more important to you in a completely different way. You're on a journey of discovery... Good luck!

The Internet: What's It All About?

In This Chapter

➤ The obligatory "What is the Internet?" question answered

➤ A quick history of the Internet

➤ What sort of information flies across the Internet

➤ Internet services, from Archie to the World Wide Web

➤ Getting a connection to the Internet

➤ Four types of Internet connections

➤ The difference between the Internet and the online services

Yes, this is the "What is the Internet?" chapter. But before you skip ahead, let me tell you that we'll be covering some other subjects, too, and that I promise not to go into too much detail about Internet history. Quite frankly, most people are tired of hearing about the history of the Internet; they just want to get on the Net and get something done. However, for those of you who may have been holed up in an FBI or ATF siege for the last few years, or stuck on the *Mir* space station, here's my abbreviated history of the Internet (*very* abbreviated).

1. The Internet was created by the U.S. military industrial complex in the late '60s as a way of enabling government researchers who were working on military projects to share computer files.

2. It *wasn't* set up to figure out how computer networks could be made to survive nuclear war. Yes, yes, I said that in an earlier book, as have a gazillion other Internet authors, but then I read an article by one of the founders of the Internet and saw the light. Nuclear survivability wasn't the initial purpose of the Internet; it was, however, a consideration a few years into its life.

3. Everyone and his dog in academia jumped on the bandwagon. The Internet became a sort of secret academic communication link, connecting hundreds of academic institutions, while America went on watching *Starsky and Hutch*, not realizing what was going on.

4. Eventually, the press figured out what was happening. Granted, it took them almost a quarter of a century, but during that time they were busy being spoon-fed by our political institutions, and the Internet didn't have a public relations company.

5. In 1993, the press started talking about the Internet. In 1994 and 1995, it was about all they could talk about.

6. Ordinary Americans—and then ordinary Brits, Aussies, Frenchies, and others all around the world—began to wake up and realize that the Internet might be worth looking into. And look into it they did—by the millions.

7. The Internet today has become a haven for all the people the U.S. military industrial complex loathes: pinkos, body piercers, eco-anarchists, people who wear clothing more suited to the opposite sex, and Democrats. Along with, of course, all sorts of "ordinary" people, businesses, schools, churches, and the like.

Okay, that's it. That's my quick history of the Internet. If you want more, you'll have to look elsewhere. I want to move on to what today's Internet really is.

Okay, Then, What Is the Internet?

Let's start with the basics. What's a computer network? It's a system in which computers are connected so they can share "information." (I'll explain what I mean by that word in a moment.) There's nothing particularly unusual about this in today's world. There are millions of networks around the world. True, they are mostly in the industrialized world, but there isn't a nation in the world that doesn't have at least a few. (Okay, I don't know that for sure, but I can't think of one.)

The Internet is something special, though, for two reasons. First, it's the world's largest computer network. Second, what makes it *really* special is that it's pretty much open to anyone with the entrance fee, and the entrance fee is constantly dropping. Many users have free accounts, and many more are paying as little as $10 to $20 a month sometimes for "unlimited" usage. ("Unlimited" if you can actually connect to the service and stay connected, which is sometimes a problem with very busy services.) Consequently millions of people all over the world are getting online.

Just how big is the Internet? Well, you should first understand that many of the numbers we've heard in the last few years are complete nonsense. In 1993, people were saying 25 million. Considering that the majority of Internet users at the time were in the U.S., and that 25 million is 10 percent of the U.S. population, and that most people in this great nation thought that computer networks were something used to enslave them in the workplace—and that the Internet was some kind of hair piece sold through late-night infomercials—it's highly unlikely that anywhere near 25 million people were on the Internet. In fact, they weren't.

These days, estimates vary all over the place, ranging from 8 or 10 million to 40 million or so. Just recently I've seen advertisements claiming 65 million, probably based on the reasoning that "it was 40 million a few months ago, so it must be over 60 million by now." I don't want to get into a discussion of how many people are using the Internet. (I don't know, after all.) I do believe, however, that many of the claims are gross exaggerations. Also, it's important to remember that many users are only infrequent visitors to cyberspace, visiting just now and again, maybe once a week or so. Still, one way or another, there are a whole lot of people out there; the numbers are definitely in the tens of millions.

What Exactly Is "Information?"

What, then, do I mean by "information?" I mean anything you can send over lines of electronic communication, and that includes quite a lot these days (and seems to include more every day). I mean letters, which are called *e-mail* on the Internet. I mean reports, magazine articles, and books, which are called *word processing files* on the Internet (well, what did you expect?). I mean music, which is called *music* on the Internet.

You can even send your voice across the Internet; you'll learn how to do that in Chapter 18, but for now let me just say that you'll find it much cheaper than talking long-distance on the phone (though most certainly not as easy), as long as you can find someone to talk to.

You can also grab computer files of many kinds (programs, documents, clip art, sounds, and anything else that can be electronically encoded) from huge libraries that collectively contain literally millions of files.

Check This Out...

A Word About Numbers

When I first started writing about the Internet, I used to try to be specific; I might have said "2.5 million files." However, I've given up that practice for two reasons. First, many of the numbers were made up; no, not by me, but by Internet gurus who were trying to be specific and made "educated" guesses. Second, even if the numbers were correct when I wrote them, they were too low by the time the book got to the editor, *much* too low by the time the book got to the printer, and *ridiculously* low by the time the book got to the readers. But you can be pretty sure that there are at least a few million files available for you to copy.

But "information" could also be a type of conversation. You want to talk about Palestinian/Israeli conflict? There's a discussion group waiting for you. Do you want to meet like-minded souls with a passion for day-time soap operas? They're talking right now.

Anything that can be sent electronically is carried on the Internet, and much that can't be sent now probably will be sent in a few months. ("Such as?," you ask. Well, how about a three-dimensional image of your face? In the next year or so, special "face scanners" will appear on the scene. You'll be able to scan your face, then send a 3-D image of your face to someone, or use the image for your chat "avatar." You'll learn about avatars in Chapter 17.)

The Internet Services

Let's be a little more specific, and take a quick look at the Internet services available to you.

➤ **E-mail.** This is the most used system. Hundreds of millions of messages—some estimates go over a billion—wing their way around the world each day, between families, friends, and businesses. The electronic world's postal system is very much like the real world's postal system, except that you can't send fruit, bombs, or this month's selection from the Cheese of the Month club. (You *can*, however, send letters, spreadsheets, pictures, sounds, programs, and more.) It's much quicker, too. Cheaper, as well. And the "mailman" isn't armed. Come to think of it, it's not much like the real world's postal system, but in *principle* it's very similar, helping people communicate with others all over the world. See Chapter 3 for more information about this essential service.

➤ **Chat.** Chat's a bit of a misnomer. There's not much chatting going on here, but there is an awful lot of typing. You type a message, and it's instantly transmitted to another person, or to many other people, who can type his response right away.

If you enjoy slow and confusing conversations in which it's tough to tell who's talking to whom, and in which the level of literacy and humor is somewhere around 4th grade...you'll *love* chat! (Okay, maybe I'm being a little harsh; some people really enjoy chat. On the other hand, some people really enjoy eating monkey brains and menudo, and bungee jumping too.) You'll learn more about this in Chapter 17.

➤ **Internet "Phones."** Install a sound card and microphone, get the Internet phone software, and then talk to people across the Internet. This is not very popular today, but just wait a few months. Just think: you can make international phone calls for $1 an hour.... (Well, okay, wait a year or two. When I wrote *The Complete Idiot's Guide to the Internet, Third Edition* I said "wait a few months," and here we are a year later and Internet phone systems still haven't really "taken off." We'll discuss some of the reasons why in Chapter 18.)

➤ **FTP.** FTP is the grand old man of the Internet. The whole purpose of the Internet was to transfer files from one place to another, and for years, FTP was how it was done. FTP provides a giant electronic "library" of computer files; you'll learn how to use it in Chapter 14.

➤ **Archie.** FTP's okay, *if* you know where you are going. Archie is like the library's card catalog, telling you which file is kept where. See Chapter 15.

➤ **Gopher.** Gopher, oh, poor old gopher. If not comatose, he's at least been hobbled. Just a couple of years ago, this system (which you'll learn about in Chapter 16) was supposed to revolutionize the Internet by converting a command-line computer system to a menu system. You wouldn't have to remember and use arcane commands anymore; you could just use the arrow keys or type a number corresponding to a menu option. Then along came the World Wide Web....

➤ **World Wide Web.** It's the Web that's really driving the growth of the Internet, because it's *cool*! (Are you sick of that word yet?) Containing pictures, sounds, and animation, the Web is a giant "hypertext" system in which documents around the world are linked to one another. Click on a word in a document in, say, Sydney, Australia, and another document (which may be from Salzburg, Austria) appears. You'll learn about this amazing system in Chapters 5–9.

➤ **Telnet.** Telnet? Oh, well, may as well talk about it. Very few people use it, but it can be quite useful. Telnet provides a way for you to log onto a computer that's connected somewhere out there on the Internet—across the city or across the world. Once logged on, you'll probably be using arcane commands or a text-based menu system. You may be playing one of the many role-playing *MUD* games (that stands for Multiple User Dungeons or Multiple User Dimensions), or perusing a library catalog. Most people are too busy using the Web, but you can read about Telnet in Chapter 20.

➤ **Newsgroups.** Newsgroups are discussion groups. Want to learn all about what's going on in Zaire? (Or, at least, what the members of the discussion group say is going on?) Want to learn an unusual kite-flying technique? Want to learn about ... well, anything really. There are approximately 30,000 internationally distributed newsgroups, and you'll find out how to work with them in Chapters 11 and 12.

➤ **Mailing lists.** If 30,000 discussion groups are not enough for you, here are a 100,000 more. (Oops, there I go again, providing numbers. One large directory lists 72,000 mailing-list discussion groups. There are certainly many, many more, along with thousands of Web forums. 100,000 is just a guess; in fact there could easily be twice that number.) As you'll learn in Chapter 13, mailing lists are another form of discussion groups that work in a slightly different manner—you send and receive messages using your e-mail program. And Web forums are discussion groups located at Web sites; you'll read and submit messages using your Web browser.

➤ **Push programs.** These systems are so named because information from the Internet is "pushed" to your computer. Rather than you going out onto the Internet to find information, periodically information is sent to your computer without your direct intervention (all you need to do is state what information you want to retrieve and how often). Actually "push" is another Internet misnomer (I don't get to pick these names!); this system is really a "scheduled pull" system, as you'll see in Chapter 10.

This is not an exhaustive list. Other systems are available; these are simply the most important ones.

But these are all tools, not reasons to be on the Internet. As a wise man once said, "Nobody wants a 1/4-inch drill bit, they want a 1/4-inch hole." Nobody wants a car, either; they want comfortable, affordable transportation. And nobody wants the Web, FTP, or Telnet; they want...well, what do they want? As you read the book, you'll get ideas for how you can actually use the Internet tools for profit and pleasure (along with a good measure of incidental frustration, unfortunately). And take a look at Chapter 24, "Ideas," which gives loads of examples of how real people use the Internet.

Getting On the Net

So you think the Net sounds great. How do you get to it, though? You might get Internet access in a number of ways:

➤ Your college provides you with an Internet account.

➤ Your company has an Internet connection from its internal network.

➤ You've signed up with an online service such as America Online (AOL), CompuServe, The Microsoft Network (MSN), or Prodigy.

➤ You've signed up with a small, local Internet service provider.

➤ You've signed up with a large, national Internet service provider such as PSI.NET or SpryNet.

➤ You've signed up with one of the phone companies, such as AT&T, Sprint, or MCI.

➤ You've signed up with a Free-Net or other form of free community computer network.

The Internet is not owned by any one company. It's more like the world's telephone system—each portion is owned by someone, and the overall system hangs together because of a variety of agreements between those organizations. So there is no *Internet, Inc.* where you can go to get access to the Internet. No, you have to go to one of the tens of thousands of organizations that already have access to the Internet, and get a connection through them.

At this stage I'm going to assume that you already have some kind of Internet connection. But if you don't, or if you're considering finding another Internet account, or a replacement, you can learn more about finding a connection (and about those Free-Nets) in Appendix B.

The Difference Between the Internet and Online Services

I often hear the questions "What's the difference between the Internet and AOL, or CompuServe, or whatever?" and "If I have an AOL account, do I have an Internet account?"

Right off the bat, let me say that services such as AOL (America Online), CompuServe, Prodigy, GEnie, MSN (The Microsoft Network) and so on, are not the same as the Internet. They are known as *online services*. Although they are similar in some ways (yes, they are large computer networks), they are different in the sense that they are private "clubs."

For instance, what happens when you dial into, say, CompuServe? Your computer connects across the phone lines with CompuServe's computers, which are all sitting in a big room somewhere. All those computers belong to CompuServe (which you can buy into, if you want; the parent company, H & R Block—yes, the tax people—took the company public recently).

Now, contrast this with the Internet. When you connect to the Internet, you connect to a communications system that's linked to millions of computers, which are owned by tens of thousands of companies, schools, government departments, and individuals. If the Internet is like a giant public highway system, the online services are like small private railroads.

However, at the risk of stretching an analogy too far (I'm already mixing metaphors, so why not), I should mention that these private railroads let you get off the tracks and onto the public highway. In other words, although AOL, CompuServe, and the others are private clubs, they do provide a way for you to connect to the Internet. So, while the barbarians on the Internet are held at the gates to the private club, the private club members can get onto the Internet.

The online services view themselves as both private clubs and gateways to the Internet. As Russ Siegelman of The Microsoft Network stated, Microsoft wants MSN to be "the biggest and best content club and community on the Internet." So it's intended to be part of the Internet—but a private part. In fact, although I (and many others) call these services "online services," Microsoft now refers to MSN as an "Internet Online Service."

To summarize:

➤ The Internet is a public highway system overrun with barbarians.

➤ Online services are private railroads or exclusive clubs...or something like that.

➤ Even if you use the Internet, you can't get into the online services unless you're a member.

➤ If you are a member of the online services, you *can* get onto the Internet.

The answer to the second question I posed earlier, then, is "yes." If you have an online service account (at least with the services mentioned here), you also have an Internet account. Interestingly, these services are now being merged into the Internet. In particular, MSN is making great efforts to appear as an integral part of the Internet. Parts of MSN are already open to the public. And people on the Internet can now access the private areas in MSN if they sign up for the service. They don't have to dial into a phone number provided by Microsoft; they can get onto the Internet any way they like and then use their World Wide Web browser to get into MSN.

What Do You Need?

What does it take to get onto the infotainment superhypeway? Many of you already have Internet accounts; our high-priced research shows that most readers buy this book *after* they have access to the Internet (presumably because they got access and then got lost). However, I want to talk about the types of accounts (or connections) that are available because they all work in slightly different ways. This will help ensure that we are all on the same wavelength *before* we get going.

There are basically four types of Internet connections:

➤ Permanent connections

➤ Dial-in direct connections (PPP, SLIP, and CSLIP)

➤ Dial-in terminal connections (shell accounts)

➤ Mail connections

Generally, if you ask an online service or service provider for an account these days, you'll be given the second type, a dial-in direct connection, even though you won't hear it called that. In fact, different service providers use slightly different terms, and the terminology can become blurred. The following sections define each one, which should clarify things a little.

Service Provider

A service provider is a company that sells access to the Internet. You dial into its computer, which connects you to the Internet. The online services are an anomaly. Strictly speaking they are Internet service providers because they provide Internet access. However, they aren't normally called "service providers"; they're simply known as online services. The companies known as service providers generally provide access to the Internet and little, if anything, more. The online services, on the other hand, have all sorts of file libraries, chat services, news services, and so on, within the private areas of the services themselves.

Note, by the way, that the online services sometimes provide two types of access telephone numbers. One provides you with a dial-in direct connection to the Internet and access to the online service. The other provides access to the online service only, not to the Internet. For instance, if you use Microsoft Network you have two connection choices—**The Internet and Microsoft Network** and **The Microsoft Network**. You must pick the former if you want to use the Internet (in the Sign In dialog box click **Settings**, then click **Access Numbers**, then select **The Internet and Microsoft Network** from the **Service Type** drop-down list box). So if you're working with an online service, make sure you've set up the correct connection.

Permanent Connections

If you have a permanent connection, your computer connects directly to a TCP/IP (Transmission Control Protocol/Internet Protocol) network that is part of the Internet. Actually, what is more likely is that your organization has a large computer connected to the network, and you have a terminal or computer connected to that computer. This sort of connection is often known as a *dedicated connection*, or sometimes as a *permanent direct connection*.

What's a Protocol?

A protocol defines how computers should talk to each other. It's like a language: if a group of people agrees to speak French (or English or Spanish), they can all understand each other. Communication protocols provide a similar set of rules that define how modems, computers, and programs can communicate.

Permanent connections are often used by large organizations, such as universities, schools, and corporations. The organization has to set up special equipment to connect its network to the Internet, and it has to lease a special telephone line that can transfer data very quickly. Because that organization has a leased line, it is always connected to the Internet, which means there's no need to make a telephone call and use a modem to reach the service provider's computer. Instead, the user simply logs on to the Internet from his terminal.

Dial-In Direct Connections

Dial-in direct connections are often referred to as PPP (Point-to-Point Protocol), SLIP (Serial Line Internet Protocol), or CSLIP (Compressed SLIP) connections (PPP is the most common form these days). Like the permanent connection, this is also a TCP/IP connection, but it's designed for use over telephone lines instead of a dedicated network. This type of service is the next best thing to the permanent connection. While a permanent connection is out of the price range of most individuals and small companies, a dial-in direct connection is quite cheap (sometimes a dollar or two an hour, but often less).

This is a *dial-in* service. That is, you must have a modem, and you have to dial a telephone number given to you by the service provider or online service. The following figure shows an example of one type of software you can run while working with a dial-in direct or permanent connection. The figure shows Microsoft's FTP site, a large file library that's open to the public, displayed within Netscape Navigator 4 (a Web browser you'll learn about in Chapter 5). The main reason I'm showing you this right now is so that you can compare it to the horrible-looking dial-in terminal connection we'll talk about next. With a dial-in direct connection you can use all the nice GUI (Graphical User Interface) software that the computer industry has spent billions of dollars on over the last few years. With a dial-in terminal account you're back in the 1970s.

Dial-In Terminal Connections

With this type of connection, you also have to dial into the service provider's computer. When the connection is made, your computer simply becomes a terminal of the service provider's computer. All the programs you use are running on the service provider's computer. That means that you can transfer files across the Internet to and from your service provider's computer, but not to and from yours. You have to use a separate procedure to move files between your computer and the service provider's.

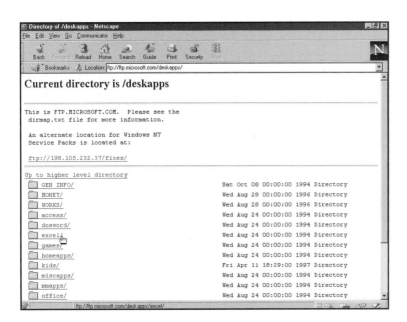

Microsoft's FTP site as viewed from a program running in a dial-in direct connection (SLIP, CSLIP, or PPP). To change directory or transfer a file, just click with the mouse.

If you want to see just how ugly this sort of connection really is, take a look at the next figure. This shows Microsoft's FTP site, the exact same service you saw in the first figure, this time shown in a simple serial communications program (specifically Windows' Hyperterminal). If you're working with a dial-in terminal connection you have to remember all the commands you need to use to get around, or you'll soon be lost.

Who uses this sort of connection? Up until 1993, and well into 1994, most Internet users did. It wasn't until the middle of 1994 that the tide began to turn, and that people began using dial-in direct accounts and the more convenient GUI software. Today few users in the industrialized world use it, unless perhaps they're using a free Internet account, or working in Podunk University. In the third world this type of account may be more common, so many users in poorer countries are still using dial-in terminal connections.

Techno Talk

Clearing Up the Confusion

This connection is often called a *dial-up connection*. But that can be confusing because you have to dial a call before connecting to a PPP or SLIP account as well. To differentiate between the two some service providers call this an *Interactive* service—which seems only slightly less ambiguous—or a *shell* account. Wherever I mention this sort of account—which isn't often—I call it a "dial-in terminal connection" because you dial the call to your service provider, and once it's connected, your computer acts as a terminal of the other computer.

Back at Microsoft's FTP site, this time with a dial-in terminal account. Now, what was the command to change directory?

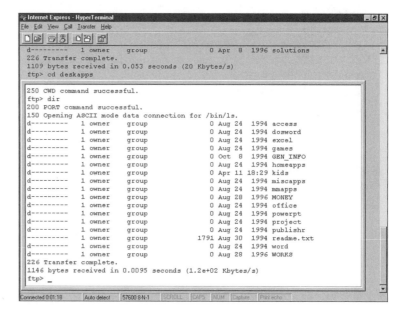

Mail Connections

A mail connection enables you to send and receive Internet e-mail and, perhaps, to read the Internet newsgroups. But you can do nothing more. This is hardly a real Internet account, so I've ignored it in this book. I'll assume you have one of the first three types of accounts.

What Do You Have?

So, where does that leave us, what do you have, and why do you care? Well, we're interested in the permanent, dial-in direct, and dial-in terminal connections. The first two are the most important because...

➤ they are easier to use

➤ you actually use both in pretty much the same way

➤ you probably have one of these connections

If you have an Internet account provided by your employer at work and you access it across your network connection, you have a permanent connection. How do you connect? Ask your system administrator. You might have to log on in some way, or you may find that you are permanently logged on. If your company has set up the network so that you can connect using your graphical user interface—Windows, the Mac, a UNIX graphical user interface, or OS/2—you can use all the fancy Internet software that's available for your particular operating system.

If you have an account through one of the major online service providers, you have a dial-in direct account—PPP, SLIP, or CSLIP (almost certainly PPP, but it makes little difference). You must use the software the online service provider gives you to dial in and connect, but once you're connected properly you can use whatever Internet software you want. (You'll learn about various programs as you go through the book.) With any of these accounts, you'll be using GUI software with windows, dialog boxes, and so on. In fact, you can use the same sort of software as the permanent connection users.

The dial-in terminal connection is the nasty "I'll use it if I absolutely have to" connection. If you are completely broke and have to use the very cheapest service you can find (perhaps a free service, one of the Free-Nets talked about in Appendix B) or if, perhaps, you are at a college that hasn't yet upgraded its Internet access, you might have to work with a dial-in terminal (shell) account. If so, you'll find yourself working at the command line, where you have to know a bunch of geeky little UNIX commands to get around.

When I first wrote this book in 1993 the book was based on this sort of account, because it was pretty much the only type of account available. These days most users are working with a graphical interface instead of the command line. So this book is based on the newest software. However, if you are still working with a command-line account (if you have a dial-in terminal account, or if your company or college has given you a dumb terminal connected to a UNIX computer connected to the Internet), you can still get help.

Almost the entire first edition of *The Complete Idiot's Guide to the Internet* is available to you using an e-mail responder, a special program that automatically sends you information when you send it an e-mail message. The first edition has all the old command-line information that's required if you're using a dial-in terminal connection. When you get to a subject in which you need more information about the UNIX command line, I'll tell you where to send an e-mail message and what to put in the body of that message. You'll automatically receive a response that includes the relevant chapter from the book. See Appendix C for more information about using the autoresponder.

I Have AOL (CompuServe, MSN, or Such), But Where's the Internet?

I've told you that the online services provide access to the Internet. But when you first install their software and connect to the service, the Internet connection might not be *enabled*. You might see a message telling you that if you want to connect to the Internet you'll have to download some more software. Follow the instructions to do so. Just in case, though, here's how to find out more about setting up an Internet connection on the three most popular online services:

➤ **America Online:** Log on, and then click the **Internet** bar in the Welcome window, or click the **Internet Connection** bar in the Channels window, or use the keyword **INTERNET**.

➤ **CompuServe:** Log on, and then click the **Internet** button in the main menu or use the GO word **INTERNET**.

➤ **The Microsoft Network:** Open the **Communicate** menu and select Internet **Community**. (If using an earlier version of the Microsoft Network software, choose **Edit**, **Go to**, **Other Service**, and then type **INTERNET**)

You Want Help Setting Up?

Unfortunately I can't help you with the initial set up of your software. There are too many different systems to cover. So here's my (very general) advice: if your service provider or online service can't help you set up, *find another one!*

Don't let me frighten you. In many cases, the initial software installation is actually quite easy. You simply run some kind of setup program and follow any instructions, and in a few minutes, you'll be up and running. (I told you in the Introduction that if you're just now learning about the Internet you're lucky. Well, here's another reason you're lucky; installing this fancy GUI Internet software back in the "early days" was a real nightmare.)

Some providers—in particular many of the small service providers—are not terribly helpful. However, things are certainly better than they were two or three years ago, when many service providers had the attitude "we give you the account to connect to, it's up to you to figure out how to do it!" These days, most are making more of an effort. But if you run into a service provider that isn't willing to explain, absolutely clearly, what you need to do to connect, you should move on. This is a very competitive business, and there are many good companies that are willing to help you.

That's All, Folks!

We don't need to talk any more about getting an Internet account. Most of you already have an account, so it's time to move on and get down to the meat of the subject: how to work with the account you have. If, on the other hand, you *don't* have an account yet, flip to Appendix B, in which I explain how to find one and tell you what computer equipment you need. In fact, even if you *do* have an account, you may want to look at this appendix because you may eventually want to swap to a cheaper or more reliable service.

Moving along, we'll assume that you have an Internet account you are completely happy with, and that you know how to log on to that account. (Check with your system administrator or look in your service documentation if you need information about logging on to the Internet.)

The Least You Need to Know

➤ The Internet is the world's largest computer network, a huge public information highway.

➤ You can do many things on the Internet: send e-mail, join discussion groups, grab files from electronic libraries, cruise the World Wide Web, and much more.

➤ There are four types of Internet connections—mail connections, which aren't much good; dial-in terminal connections, which are better, but you're working with the command line or text menus; and permanent connections and dial-in direct (SLIP and PPP) connections, both of which are much better.

➤ The Internet is a public system. The online services—America Online, CompuServe, The Microsoft Network, et al—are private services, with "gateways" to the Internet.

➤ A member of an online service can use the Internet, but an Internet user cannot use an online service unless he joins that service.

➤ You can get Internet access through your company or school, a small local Internet service provider, a giant Internet service provider (such as AT&T), or an online service.

Chapter 3

The Premier Internet Tool: E-Mail

In This Chapter

➤ Which e-mail program are you using?

➤ All about e-mail addresses

➤ Setting up your e-mail program

➤ Sending a message

➤ Retrieving your messages—then what?

➤ Sending files across the Internet

➤ Avoiding fights!

Ah, some of you think the title of this chapter is a joke. It's not. Although e-mail may not be exciting, "cool," or "compelling," it is the most popular and, in many ways, the most useful Internet service. More people use e-mail on any given day than use any other Internet service. Tens of millions of messages fly across the wires each day—five million from America Online alone (oh, there I go again, it's the number problem; it was five million last time I checked, but it's probably several times that by now).

Despite all the glitz of the Web (you'll learn about that glitz in Chapters 5–9), the potential of Internet Phone systems (Chapter 18), and the excitement—for some—of the many chat systems (Chapter 17), e-mail is probably the most productive tool there is. It's a sort of Internet workhorse, getting the work done without any great fanfare.

After spending huge sums of money polling Internet users, we've come to the conclusion that the very first thing Internet users want to do is send e-mail messages. It's not too threatening, and it's an understandable concept: you're sending a letter. The only differences are that you don't take it to the post office and that it's much faster. So that's what I'm going to start with: how to send an e-mail message.

Dial-In Terminal (Shell) Accounts

If you are working with a dial-in terminal account (also known as a shell account), this information on e-mail—beyond the basic principles—won't help you much. To learn more about working with e-mail with your type of account, you can use our autoresponder to get the mail chapters from *The Complete Idiot's Guide to the Internet*. Of course in order to use the autoresponder you need to be able to send an e-mail message! So, if necessary, ask your service provider how to send the first message. When you've got that figured out, send e-mail to **ciginternet@mcp.com**, with **allmail** in the Subject line to receive the e-mail chapters.

What E-Mail System?

Which e-mail system do you use? Well, if you are a member of an online service, you have a built-in mail system. But if you are not a member of one of the major online services...who the heck knows what you are using for e-mail! I don't. For that matter, even with an online service, there are different options; CompuServe, for instance, offers a number of different programs you can use.

Basically, it all depends what your service provider set you up with. You might be using Netscape, a World Wide Web browser (discussed in Chapter 5) that has a built-in e-mail program. Or perhaps you're using Microsoft Exchange, which comes with Windows 95. You could be using Eudora, which is one of the most popular e-mail programs on the Internet, or perhaps Pegasus. Or you might be using something else entirely.

Luckily, the e-mail concepts are all the same, regardless of the type of program you are using—even if the actual buttons you click are different.

Start with What You Were Given

I suggest you start off using the e-mail program that you were given when you set up your account. But you may be able to use something else later. If you'd like to try Eudora later, go to **http://www.qualcomm.com/**.

A free version called Eudora Light is available for the Mac and Windows. My current favorite is AK-Mail (**http://www.th-darmstadt.de/~st001295**). And you can find Pegasus at **http://www.pegasus.usa.com/**.

To POP or Not to POP

I want to make something clear about *POP*; that's Post Office Protocol, and it's a very common system used for handling Internet e-mail. A POP *server* receives e-mail that's been sent to you, and holds it until you use your mail program to retrieve it. However, POP's not ubiquitous; some online services and many companies do not use POP.

Why do you care what system is used to hold your mail? After all, all you really care about is the program you use to collect and read the mail, not what arcane system your company or service provider uses. Well, you may care if you want to change mail programs. In general the best and most advanced e-mail programs are designed to be used with POP servers. So if you need some really specific e-mail features, and have decided you want to switch to another mail program, you may find you can't do so.

Let's say, for instance, that you have an America Online or CompuServe account. The mail programs provided by these systems are really quite simple barebones programs. They lack many features that programs such as AK-Mail and Eudora have, such as advanced filtering. (Filtering allows you to automatically carry out actions on incoming e-mail depending on the characteristics of that mail. For instance, when e-mail arrives from your boss you could automatically delete it. That way you won't be lying when you tell him you didn't receive his message.) Unfortunately, you're pretty much stuck. At the time of writing you could not use a POP program with a CompuServe or America Online account, so you couldn't install Eudora or AK-mail. That may change soon, though. CompuServe, for instance, is experimenting with a POP mail system which it may make available to all its customers soon. (It's currently available to a limited few under a special beta test. For more information use GO MAILTEST.)

There's another common mail system, IMAP (Internet Message Access Protocol). This is generally used by corporate networks, not Internet service providers. If you're using a corporate network you probably won't have much choice about which mail program you can use.

You Have a New Address!

I recently discovered how you can tell an absolute beginner on the Internet; he often talks about his e-mail "number," equating e-mail with telephones. Well, they are both electronic, after all. However, you actually have an e-mail *address*. That address has three parts:

➤ Your account name

➤ The "at" sign (@)

➤ Your domain name

What's your account name? It's almost always the name you use to log on to your Internet account. For instance, when I log on to my CompuServe account, I have to type 71601,1266. That's my account name. When I log on to MSN I use PeterKent, and on AOL, I use PeKent.

After your account name, you use the @ sign. Why? Well, how would you know where the account name ends and domain name starts, eh?

Finally, you use the domain name, which is the address of your company, your service provider, or your online service. Think of it as the street address: one street address (the domain name) can be used for thousands of account names.

Account Names: They're All the Same

Actually, CompuServe calls the account name a *User ID*, MSN calls it a *Member Name*, and AOL calls it a *Screen Name*. In addition, you might hear the account name called a *user name* or *logon ID*. All of these names mean the same thing: the name by which you are identified when you log on to your account. However, I discovered that some large service providers (mainly the phone companies, for some reason, who "don't quite get it,") do something a little odd. You get some strange number as the account name, and you get *another* name to use when accessing your e-mail. Someone at AT&T's WorldNet gave me a flip answer as to *why* they do this, using a sort of "well of course we *have* to do this, but you probably wouldn't understand" tone of voice; I wasn't convinced.

Where do you get the domain name? If you haven't been told already, ask the system administrator or tech support people. (Later in this chapter you'll learn the domain names of the larger online services.)

Pronouncing Your E-Mail Address

Here's the "correct" way to say an e-mail address out loud. You say "dot" for the periods and "at" for the @ sign. Thus, pkent@arundel.net is "p kent at arundel dot net."

A Word About Setup

You *might* need to set up your e-mail system before it will work. In many cases this setup will already be done for you. If you are with one of the online services you don't need to worry—it's done for you. Some of the Internet service providers also do all this configuring stuff for you. Others, however, expect you to get into your program and enter some information. It doesn't have to be difficult. The following figure shows some of the options you can configure in Netscape Messenger, the new e-mail program that comes, along with Navigator, as part of the Netscape Communicator package, but the options will be similar in other programs.

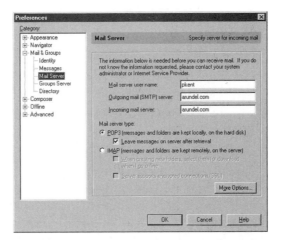

One of several mail-related panels in Netscape Messenger's Preferences dialog box, in which you can configure the mail program before you use it.

Whatever program you have, you may have to enter the following information:

Incoming Mail Server This is usually a **POP** (Post Office Protocol) account, though if you're on a corporate network it may be an **IMAP** (Internet Message Access Protocol) account. When you connect to your service provider, your e-mail program needs to check with the mail server (a program running on your service provider's system) to see if any mail has arrived. This mail server actually holds the messages that arrive for you until your mail program asks for them. Your account name is usually the same as the account name that you use to log on to your service. You might need to enter the full account name and the server host name (for instance, in Netscape Messenger I enter **pkent**, my account name, in the **Mail server user name** box, then enter the server name—**arundel.com**—in the **Incoming mail server** text box, and click the **POP** option button). On some systems, such as Eudora, you may have to enter the account name and server name all together in one box.

SMTP (Simple Mail Transfer Protocol) Server   This is another mail program. This one's used to send mail. While the POP account holds your incoming mail, the SMTP is used to transmit your messages out onto the Internet. This time you'll enter a hostname (mail.usa.net, for instance) or maybe a number (something like 192.156.196.1) that you've been given by your service provider.

Password   You'll need to enter your password so the e-mail program can check the POP for mail. This is generally the same password you use to log onto the system. Some programs, however, don't request your password until the first time you log on to retrieve your mail.

Real Name   This is, yes, your actual name. Most mail programs will send your name along with the e-mail address when you send e-mail.

Return or Reply To Address   If you want you can make the e-mail program place a different Reply To: address on your messages. For instance, if you send mail from work but want to receive responses to those messages at home, you'd use a different Reply To address. If you do this, make sure you enter the full address (such as **pkent@arundel.com**).

All Sorts of Other Stuff   There are all sorts of things you can get a good mail program to do. You can tell it how often to check the POP to see if new mail has arrived, choose the font you want the message displayed in, and get the program to automatically include the original message when you reply to a message. You can even tell it to leave messages at the POP after you retrieve them. This might be handy if you like to check your mail from work; if you configure the program to leave the messages at the POP, you can retrieve them again when you get home, using the program on your home machine. You can also define how the program will handle "attachments," but that is a complicated subject that I'll get to later in this chapter.

What Else Can I Do with My Mail Program?

You might be able to do lots of things. Check your documentation or Help files, or simply browse through the configuration dialog boxes to see what you can do. Note, however, that the online services' e-mail programs generally have a limited number of choices. E-mail programs such as Eudora, Pegasus, and AK-Mail—and those included with Netscape Navigator and Internet Explorer—have many more choices.

There are so many e-mail programs around, I can't help you configure them all. If you have trouble configuring your program, check the documentation or call the service's technical support. And as I've said before, if they don't want to help, find another service!

Sending a Message

Now that you understand addresses and have configured the mail program, you can actually send a message. So, who can you mail a message to? Well, you may already have friends and colleagues whom you can bother with your flippant "Hey, I've finally made it onto the Internet" message. On the other hand, why not send yourself a message and kill two birds with one stone: you'll learn how to send one, and then you can see what to do when you receive a message!

So start your e-mail program, and then open the window in which you are going to write the message. You may have to double-click an icon or choose a menu option that opens the mail's Compose window. For instance, in Eudora, once the program is open, you click the **New Message** button on the toolbar or choose **Message, New Message**.

Online Services

If you are working in one of the CompuServe programs, choose **Mail, Create New Mail**. In AOL choose **Mail, Compose Mail**. And in MSN you'll open the **Communicate** menu and select **Send or Read E-mail**. (If you're still working with the old version of the MSN software, click the big **E-mail** bar in MSN Central.) If you are using Netscape's e-mail program there are all sorts of ways to begin: select File, New, Message, for instance.

In all of the e-mail programs, the Compose window has certain common elements. In addition, some have a few extras. Here's what you might find:

To: This is the address of the person you are mailing to. If you are using an online service and you are sending a message to another member of that service, all you need to use is the person's account name. For instance, if you are an AOL member and you're mailing to another AOL member with the screen name of PeKent, that's all you need to enter. To mail to that member from a service *other than* AOL, however, you enter the full address: pekent@aol.com. (I'll explain more about mailing to online services in the section "We Are All One—Sending E-Mail to Online Services," later in this chapter.)

From: Not all mail programs show this, but it gives your e-mail address, which is included in the message "header" (the clutter at the top of an Internet message). It lets the recipient know who to reply to.

Reply To: Maybe you have both a From address (to show which account the message came from) and a Reply To address (to get the recipient to reply to a different address).

Subject: This is a sort of message title—a few words summarizing the contents. The recipient can scan through a list of subjects to see what each message is about. (Some mail programs won't let you send a message unless you fill in the subject line; others, perhaps most, don't mind if you leave it blank.)

Cc: You can enter an address here to send a copy to someone other than the person whose address you placed in the To: line.

Bc: This means "blind copy." As with the Cc: line, a copy of the message will be sent to the address (or addresses) you place in the Bc: (or Bcc:) line; however, the recipient of the original message won't be able to tell that the Bcc: address received a copy. (If you use Cc:, the recipient of the original message sees a Cc: line in the header.)

Attachments: This is for sending computer files along with the message. (Again, I'll get to that later in this chapter, in the section "Sending Files—Getting Easier.")

A big blank area: This is where you type your message.

E-mail programs vary greatly, and not all programs have all of these features. Again, the online service mail programs tend to be a bit limited. The following figures show the Compose window in two very different mail programs.

This is AK-Mail, my current favorite.

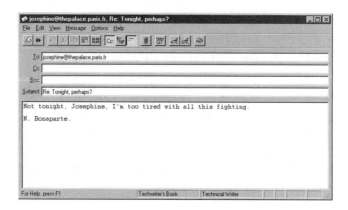

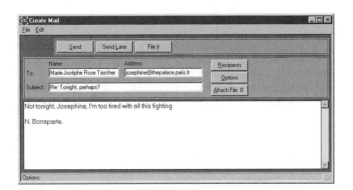

This is CompuServe's mail composition window.

Go ahead and type a To: address. Why not use your own address? If you use an online service, you might as well use the entire Internet address (for instance, on AOL type *name*@**aol.com**). The message will probably go out onto the Internet and then turn around and come back to you. I'll explain those online service addresses in the next section.

We Are All One—Sending E-Mail to Online Services

One of the especially nice things about the Internet, from an e-mail point of view, is that because all the online services are now connected to the Internet, you can send e-mail between online services. Perhaps you have an America Online account because …well, because they sent you a disk in the mail. And perhaps your brother has a CompuServe account because …well, because he's a geek, and that's where the geeks have been hanging out for years. (Before you e-mail me to complain, I've had a CompuServe account for more than a decade.) You can send e-mail to each other, using the Internet as a sort of bridge. How? Well, you just have to know the other person's account name on that service and that service's domain name.

For instance, CompuServe has this Internet domain name: compuserve.com. Say you want to send an e-mail message to someone at CompuServe who has the account name (well, User ID they call it on CompuServe) of 71601,1266. You add the two together with the @ in the middle. Then you have 71601,1266@compuserve.com. However, you can't have a comma in an Internet address. So you replace it with a period, and you end up with 71601.1266@compuserve.com. (Some CompuServe users have "proper" e-mail addresses, names instead of numbers. If you use CompuServe and want one of these real addresses, use GO REGISTER.)

The following table lists a few other services and tells you how to send e-mail to them.

Sending E-Mail to Other Services

Service	Method of Addressing
Prodigy	Add @prodigy.com to the end of the user's Prodigy address.
America Online	Add @aol.com to the end of an America Online address.
GEnie	Add @genie.geis.com to the end of a GEnie address.
MCImail	Add @mcimail.com to the end of an MCImail address.
MSN	Add @msn.com to the end of the MSN Member name.

These are quite easy. Of course, there are more complicated Internet addresses, but you'll rarely run into them. If you have trouble e-mailing someone, though, call and ask *exactly* what you must type as his or her e-mail address. (Yes, there's no rule that says you can't use the telephone anymore.)

Write the Message

Now that you have the address on-screen, write your message—whatever you want to say. Then send the message. How's that done? There's usually a big Send button, or maybe a menu option that says Send or Mail. What happens when you click the button? That depends on the program and whether or not you are logged on at the moment. Generally, if you are logged on, the mail is sent immediately. Not always, though. Some programs will put the message in a "queue," and won't send the message until told to do so. Others will send immediately, and if you are not logged on, they will try to log on first. Watch closely, and you'll usually see what's happening. A message will let you know if the message is being sent. If it hasn't been sent, look for some kind of Send Immediately menu option, or perhaps Send Queued Messages. Whether the message should be sent immediately or put in a queue is often one of the configuration options available to you.

Where'd It Go? Incoming E-Mail

Check This Out...

Fancy Fonts

Some of the online services allow you to use fancy text formatting features. For example, MSN and AOL let you use colors, indents, different fonts, bold and italic, and so on. But in general these only work in messages sent *within* the online services. Internet e-mail is plain text— nothing fancy. You might as well not bother getting fancy in your Internet e-mail because the online service's e-mail system will strip out all that attractive stuff when the message is sent out onto the Internet. However, there *is* a system you can use to send formatted e-mail, *if* both you and the recipient have the right type of mail program—HTML-Mail. This system is just now becoming popular (in 1997); we'll take a quick look at HTML-Mail in Chapter 4.

You've sent yourself an e-mail message, but where did it go? It went out into the electronic wilderness to wander around for a few seconds, or maybe a few minutes. Sometimes a few hours. Very occasionally, it even takes a few days. (Generally, the message comes back in a few minutes, unless you mistyped the address, in which case you'll get a special message telling you that it's a bad address.)

Now it's time to check for incoming e-mail. If you are using an online service, as soon as you log on you'll see a message saying that e-mail has arrived. If you are *already* online, you may see a message telling you that mail has arrived, or you may need to check; you may find a Get New Mail menu option. If you are working with an Internet service provider you generally won't be informed of incoming mail; rather, your e-mail program has to go and check. Either you can do that manually (for instance, in Eudora, there's a File, Check Mail command), or you can configure the program to check automatically every so often.

What Now?

What can you do with your incoming e-mail? All sorts of things. I think I'm pretty safe in saying that *every* e-mail program allows you to read incoming messages. Most programs also let you print and save messages (if your program doesn't, you need another). You can also delete them, forward them to someone else, and reply directly to the sender.

These commands should be easy to find. Generally you'll have toolbar buttons for the most important commands, and more options available if you dig around a little in the menus, too.

A Word About Quoting

It's a good idea to "quote" when you respond to a message. This means that you include part or all of the original message. Some programs automatically quote the original message. And different programs mark quoted messages in different ways; usually, you'll see a "greater than" symbol (>) at the beginning of each line. The following figure shows a reply message that contains a quote from the original message.

You aren't required to quote. But if you don't, the recipient might not know what you are talking about. I receive scores of messages a day, and I know people who get literally hundreds. (Of course, the radiation emitted from their computer screens is probably frying their brains.) If you respond to a message without reminding the recipient exactly which of the 200 messages he sent out last week (or which of the five he sent to you) you are responding to, he might be slightly confused.

Quoting is especially important when sending messages to mailing lists and newsgroups (discussed in Chapter 13), where your message might be read by people who didn't read the message to which you are responding.

You should quote the original message when responding, to remind the sender of what he said.

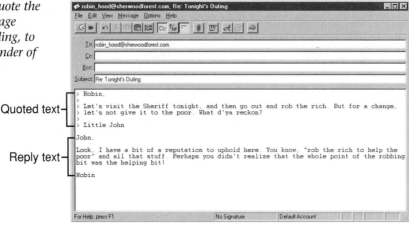

Quoted text—

Reply text—

Sending Files—Getting Easier

I used to really hate this bit. Not because it's so difficult to send files across the Internet (though it is—or at least used to be until very recently), but because it was, well, sort of embarrassing to admit how difficult it was. Now before you misunderstand, let me say that I *did* know how to send files across the Internet. However, very few other people seemed to understand, and even when they did understand they didn't seem to have software that worked properly. And unless both parties involved (the sender and the recipient) understand the process, and have the correct software, things sometimes won't work. I recall, for instance, the incredible problems I had transferring computer files to a magazine early in 1995. It didn't matter what transmission format I used (I'll discuss that in a moment), nor what program I was working with; the staff at the magazine couldn't seem to open those files—never mind that this magazine just happened to be a major *Internet* magazine. Today the situation is rapidly improving, and the problems inherent in file transfers are, for many users, a thing of the past. Still, the situation isn't perfect, and problems can still occur, so here's a quick explanation of the problem (and solutions).

Files are commonly sent across cyberspace in one of four ways:

UUENCODE   This is a system in which a computer file is converted to plain ASCII text. It may start out as a sound file or a word processing file, but once it's converted it looks like gibberish text. This is called *uuencoding*. An encoded file can be placed into an e-mail message and sent. The person at the other end must then either receive the message with a mail program that can convert uuencoded files back to their original format, or save the message as a text file and *uudecode* it—convert it back to its original format—using a special utility.

MIME   Multimedia Internet Mail Extensions is a system designed to make sending files across the Internet easier. It converts the file to text, sends it with the message, and converts it back at the other end. (You can only send text files in the Internet's e-mail system, hence the need to convert files to text.) What's the difference between UUENCODE and MIME? UUENCODE is a sort of quick fix. MIME was intended to be a nicely integrated system that works transparently so that all you have to do is select the file you want to send, and MIME does the rest. It also has a method for identifying the type of file that is being transferred. (MIME is now used on the World Wide Web to identify multimedia files linked to Web pages.) MIME is the most common method used for sending files across the Internet, these days. As with UUENCODE, the recipient must either have a compatible mail program or use a utility to convert the file back to its original format.

BinHex   This is a system used on the Macintosh, and it's very similar to UUENCODE. Files are converted into text and then converted back at the other end. It seems to be dying out, though (relatively speaking!; please don't e-mail me to tell me it's alive and well, and how the Macintosh is a better machine, and how Bill Gates should be crucified for stealing Macintosh design features). Even most Macintosh mail programs use MIME and UUENCODE.

Online Service Systems   Each of the online services has a file-transfer system. In AOL and CompuServe you can attach a file to a message and then send that message to another member of the same online service. In MSN you can insert all sorts of things directly into messages— pictures, formatted text, or computer files—then send them to other MSN members.

Now, here's the problem. If you want to send a message to another person on the Internet, you have to know which system to use. The following guidelines can help you make a good decision:

1. Check to see if the other person has an account on the same online service you do. Even if you've been given an Internet e-mail address that is obviously not an online service, ask just in case. It's far more reliable to send a file between CompuServe accounts, between AOL accounts, or between MSN accounts, for instance, than to use MIME, BinHex, or UUENCODE. (You'll find that many people—especially geeks—have accounts on two or more services.)

2. If you have to use the Internet e-mail system, check to see which system the recipient can work with (MIME, UUENCODE, or BinHex). In the past I've advised that you *don't* simply pick one and send the file because if the recipient doesn't have the right software, he won't be able to use the file. However, these days MIME is in fairly wide use, so if you're not able to check with the recipient first you could try MIME and it will probably work. (However, see the discussion of the online services

below.) The most popular POP mail programs all work with MIME: Eudora, Netscape Communicator's mail program (Messenger), Pegasus, Microsoft Internet Mail, and so on.

3. Consider which system you have built into your e-mail program. If you are lucky, the system that's built into your e-mail program is the same system the recipient uses. For example, because Eudora Light has both MIME and BinHex, you can send files to anyone using MIME or BinHex—but you cannot send to someone using UUENCODE. (At least, Eudora can't help directly. However, you'll see in a moment how to send uuencoded messages even if it's not built into your e-mail program.) Netscape Navigator has both MIME and UUENCODE, so you can use either. Many mail programs only work with MIME, though.

What if you don't have a match? Or what if the recipient has an online-service account? Or if *you* have an online-service account? There's a problem with some of the online services, because they may not work with either MIME or UUENCODE. The major online services have recently been upgrading their mail services so you can use MIME—perhaps. You can send files to and from CompuServe using MIME, though to receive them you may have to upgrade your mail system (GO NEWMAIL). AOL also allows file transfers to and from the Internet. Surprisingly MSN currently *doesn't* allow incoming and outgoing file attachments, nor do some other online services. Note, however, that even if an online service's mail system uses MIME, it may not do so *properly*. For instance, I found that when I sent a file from CompuServe to an Internet account the file was transferred correctly, but without a filename. And CompuServe had trouble accepting incoming files that had MIME attachments, too. AOL, on the other hand, may strip out the file extension on *incoming* files, yet transfer outgoing files correctly. (By the way, the online services' mail systems are very slow; I think they retype all the incoming messages, or something. Not sure what they do with attachments, but these slow down incoming mail even further.) As for The Microsoft Network, at the time of writing you can *send* messages with attachments across the Internet, but if you *receive* messages from outside MSN with attached files MSN's mail system will be unable to convert the file back to it's original format; you'll have to use a utility to do this for you, which we'll discuss next. (MSN is working on upgrading its mail system to allow it to accept incoming attachments, so perhaps by the time you read this it will be able to do so; on the other hand, it's taken them a couple of years already, so who knows how long it will be.)

There are things you can do to get around incompatibilities between your mail system and the recipient's, but they may be a hassle. Say you want to send someone a file using UUENCODE because that's the only thing he can work with. But you have a CompuServe account, which means your e-mail program won't automatically uudecode files. You can go to one of the software archives mentioned in Appendix A and download a UUENCODE program. (For instance, if you use Windows, you can use a program called Wincode.) Then you use that program to convert the file to a text file, you copy the text from the file and paste it into the message, and you send the message. (Oh, and then you cross your fingers.)

How about MIME? Say someone just sent you a MIME encoded file; what can you do, but you have a mail program that won't decode MIME attachments? Go to the software libraries and search for MIME. For instance, there are little DOS programs I use called Mpack and Munpack. You can save the message you received as a text file (virtually all e-mail programs let you do this, generally with the File, Save As command), and then use Munpack to convert that text file to the original file format. (Mpack and Munpack are also available for the Macintosh and for UNIX systems.)

If you are lucky, though, your e-mail program has MIME and UUENCODE built in, as well as some kind of command that lets you insert or attach a file. For instance, in Eudora Light, choose **Message**, **Attach File** and use the small drop-down list at the top of the Compose window to choose between **BinHex** and **MIME**. In AOL, click the **Attach** button; in CompuServe, use the **Mail**, **Send File** command in the main window, or click the **Attach File** button in the Create Mail window.

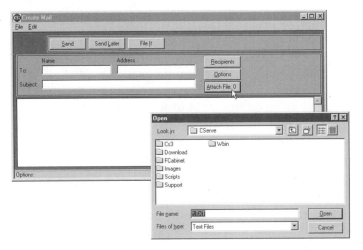

Sending a file with your e-mail is usually as simple as clicking a button and selecting the file.

Cool Things You Can Do with E-Mail

Once you understand your e-mail system and realize that it won't bite, you might actually begin to enjoy using it. The following list contains suggestions of some things you might want to do with your e-mail program.

➤ *Create a mailing list.* You can create a special mailing list that contains the e-mail addresses of many people. For instance, if you want to send a message to everyone in your department (or family, or club) at the same time, you can create a mailing list. Put all the addresses in the list, and then send the message to the list. Everyone on the list receives the message, and you save time and hassle. Some programs will have a mailing list dialog box of some sort; others let you create a "nickname" or "alias" for the mailing list and then associate the addresses with it.

➤ *Create an address book.* Virtually all e-mail systems have address books, and they're usually quite easy to use. You can store a person's complicated e-mail address and then retrieve it quickly using the person's real name.

➤ *Use aliases.* An alias, sometimes known as a *nickname*, is a simple identifier you give to someone in your address book. Instead of typing **peter kent** or **pkent@arundel.com**, for instance, you could just type a simple alias such as **pk** in order to address a message to that person.

➤ *Work with mail while you're offline.* Most programs these days let you read and write e-mail offline. This is of particular importance with services that charge you for the amount of time you are online. Figure out how to use these systems—it's worth the effort.

➤ *Forward your mail.* After being on the Internet for a while, there's a risk of attaining real geekhood—and getting multiple Internet accounts, such as one with your favorite online service, one at work, one with a cheap service provider, and so on. (Right now, I have about eight, I think.) That's a lot of trouble logging on to check for e-mail. However, some services let you forward your e-mail to another account so that if a message arrives at, say, the account you use at home, you can have it automatically sent on to you at work. Very handy. Ask your service provider how to do this; you may need to log on to your *shell* account to set this up (discussed in Chapter 21). While most Internet service providers let you do this, the online services generally *don't*, though they may soon.

➤ *Create a "vacation" message.* When you go on vacation, your e-mail doesn't stop. In fact, that's why so many cybergeeks never go on vacation, or take a laptop if they do: they can't bear the thought of missing all those messages. Still, if you manage to break away, you may be able to set a special "vacation" message, an automatic response to any incoming mail, that says basically, "I'm away, be back soon." (You get to write the response message.) Again, ask your service provider. And again, the online services generally *don't* have this service.

➤ *Filter your files.* Sophisticated e-mail programs have file-filtering capabilities. You can tell the program to look at incoming mail and carry out certain actions according to what it finds. You can place e-mail from your newsgroups into special inboxes, grab only the message subject if the message is very long, delete mail from certain people or organizations, and so on.

Caution E-Mail Can Be Dangerous!

The more I use e-mail, the more I believe that it can be a dangerous tool. There are three main problems: 1) people often don't realize the implications of what they are saying, 2) people often misinterpret what others are saying, and 3) people are comfortable typing things into a computer that they would never say to a person face to face. Consequently, online fights are common both in private (between e-mail correspondents) and in public (in the newsgroups and mailing lists).

The real problem is that when you send an e-mail message, the recipient can't see your face or hear your tone of voice. Of course, when you write a letter, you have the same problem. But e-mail is actually replacing conversations as well as letters. The U.S. Post Office is as busy as ever, so I figure e-mail is *mainly* replacing conversations. That contributes to the problem because people are writing messages in a chatty conversational style, forgetting that e-mail lacks all the visual and auditory "cues" that go along with a conversation.

In the interests of world peace, I give you these e-mail guidelines to follow:

➤ *Don't write something you will regret later.* Lawsuits have been based on the contents of electronic messages, so consider what you are writing and whether you would want it to be read by someone other than the recipient. A message can always be forwarded, read over the recipient's shoulder, printed out and passed around, backed up onto the company's archives, and so on. You don't *have* to use e-mail—there's always the telephone. (Oliver North has already learned *his* lesson!)

➤ *Consider the tone of your message.* It's easy to try to be flippant and come out as arrogant, or to try to be funny and come out as sarcastic. When you write, think about how your words will appear to the recipient.

➤ *Give the sender the benefit of the doubt.* If a person's message sounds arrogant or sarcastic, consider that he or she might be trying to be flippant or funny! If you are not sure what the person is saying, ask him or her to explain.

➤ *Read before you send.* It will give you a chance to fix embarrassing spelling and grammatical errors—and to reconsider what you've just said.

➤ *Wait a day...or three.* If you typed something in anger, wait a few days and read the message again. Give yourself a chance to reconsider.

➤ *Be nice.* Hey, there's no need for vulgarity or rudeness (except in certain newsgroups, where it seems to be a requirement for entrance).

Check This Out...

You're Being Baited Some people send rude or vicious messages because they actually *enjoy* getting into a fight like this—where they can fight from the safety of their computer terminals.

➤ *Attack the argument, not the person.* I've seen fights start when someone disagrees with another person's views and sends a message making a personal attack upon that person. (This point is more related to mailing lists and newsgroups than e-mail proper, but we are on the subject of avoiding fights) Instead of saying, "Anyone who thinks *Days of Our Lives* is not worth the electrons it's transmitted on must be a half-witted moron with all the common sense of the average pineapple," consider saying "You may think it's not very good, but clearly many other people find great enjoyment in this show."

➤ *Use smileys.* One way to add some of those missing cues is to add smileys—keep reading.

Smile and Be Understood!

Over the last few years, e-mail users have developed a number of ways to clarify the meaning of messages. You might see <g> at the end of the line, for example. This means "grin" and is shorthand for saying, "You know, of course, that what I just said was a joke, right?" You may also see :-) in the message. Turn this book sideways, so that the left column of this page is up and the right column is down, and you'll see that this is a small smiley face. It means the same as <g>, "Of course, that *was* a joke, okay?"

Emoticons Galore

Little pictures are commonly known as "smileys." But the smiley face, though by far the most common, is just one of many available symbols. You *might* see some of the emoticons in the following table, and you may want to use them. Perhaps, you can create a few of your own.

Share the Smiles

Many people simply call these character faces "smiley faces." But if you'd like to impress your friends with a bit of technobabble, you can call them *emoticons.* And if you really want to impress your colleagues, get hold of *The Smiley Dictionary* by Seth Godin. It contains hundreds of these things.

Commonly Used Emoticons

Emoticon	Meaning
:-(	Sadness, disappointment
8-)	Kinda goofy-looking smile, or wearing glasses
:->	A smile

Emoticon	Meaning
;-)	A wink
*<|:-)	Santa Claus
:-&	Tongue-tied
:-o	A look of shock
:-p	Tongue stuck out
,:-) or 7:^]	Ronald Reagan

Personally, I don't like smileys much. They strike me as being just a *tiiiny* bit too cutesy. However, I do use them now and again to make *absolutely* sure that I'm not misunderstood!

Message Shorthand

There are a couple of other ways people try to liven up their messages. One is to use obscure acronyms like the ones in this table.

Online Shorthand

Acronym	Meaning
BTW	By the way
FWIW	For what it's worth
FYI	For your information
IMO	In my opinion
IMHO	In my humble opinion
LOL	Laughing out loud (used as an aside to show your disbelief)
OTFL	On the floor, laughing (used as an aside)
PMFBI	Pardon me for butting in
PMFJI	Pardon me for jumping in
RTFM	Read the &*^%# manual
ROTFL or ROFL	Rolling on the floor laughing (used as an aside)
ROTFLMAO	Same as above, except with "laughing my a** off" added on the end. (You didn't expect me to say it, did you? This is a family book, and anyway, the editors won't let me.)
TIA	Thanks in advance
YMMV	Your mileage may vary

The real benefit of using these is that they confuse the average neophyte. I suggest that you learn them quickly, so you can pass for a long-term cybergeek.

You'll also see different ways of stressing particular words. (You can't use bold and italic in most Internet e-mail, remember?) You might see words marked with an underscore on either side (_now!_) or, perhaps less frequently, with an asterisk (*now!*).

The Least You Need to Know

➤ There are many different e-mail systems, but the basic procedures all work similarly.

➤ Even if your online service lets you use fancy text (colors, different fonts, different styles) within the service, that text won't work in Internet messages (see Chapter 4 for information on HTML-Mail, though).

➤ Sending files across the Internet is much easier now than it was just a year or so ago, but problems still arise; sending files *within* the online services is always easy.

➤ On the Internet the most common file-transfer method is MIME; UUENCODE is also used now and then. These are often built into mail programs, or you can use external utilities to convert the files.

➤ Don't send a file until you know which system the recipient is using. Or if you do, use MIME.

➤ Get to know all the neat little things your e-mail program can do for you, such as create mailing lists and carry out file-filtering.

➤ Be careful with e-mail; misunderstandings (and fights) are common.

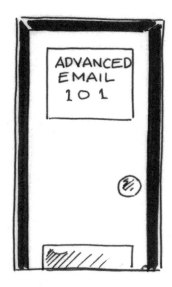

Advanced E-Mail: HTML and Encryption

E-mail has changed quite a bit over the last year or so, and will continue to change dramatically over the next year or so, thanks to two important systems: HTML Mail and encryption.

The first of these, HTML Mail, livens up e-mail a little...in some cases quite a lot. HTML Mail allows you to use different colors for the text in your messages, to work with different font sizes and styles, to create bullet lists and centered text, even to insert pictures and sounds.

As for encryption, this is actually something that has been available for a few years, but which was too complicated to catch on. Now that e-mail encryption—the ability to encrypt, or scramble, e-mail messages to make them unreadable to all but the recipient—

is being built into e-mail programs, I predict that 1997 is the Year of Encryption. Well, okay, maybe 1998 is the Year of Encryption. One way or another, though, encryption should catch on pretty soon, much to the chagrin of governments around the world.

HTML Mail—Banish Dull E-Mail

HTML Mail is a system in which HTML tags can be used within e-mail messages. HTML means HyperText Markup Language, and as you'll learn in the World Wide Web chapters of this book (Chapters 5 to 9), HTML is used to create World Wide Web pages. HTML tags are the little codes that are inserted into a Web page to tell a Web browser how to display the page. These tags can be used to modify the manner in which text appears on the page—its color, size, style, and so on—and where it appears on the page. They can be used to create tables, insert pictures and Java applications, and plenty more. Now that HTML is coming to e-mail, e-mail messages will be far more than just plain text.

In order to use HTML Mail, you need two things. First, you need an HTML Mail program. Just as important, though, you need to ensure that the recipient has an HTML Mail program. If you send an HTML-Mail message to someone who doesn't have an HTML Mail program they won't see all the formatting you've added to the message. Worse, depending on the program you've used, the message they receive may be very difficult to read, as it will be full of HTML tags, making it difficult for the recipient to find the actual text. (Some HTML Mail programs insert a plain-text version of your message at the beginning of the message, so a recipient who isn't using an HTML Mail program can still read the message.)

Finding an HTML Mail Program

So, the first step, find an HTML Mail program. Unfortunately at the time of this writing *most* e-mail programs cannot create or display HTML Mail messages. That's bound to change quickly, though, as HTML Mail becomes a new standard.

The most advanced HTML Mail program is currently Netscape Messenger, the e-mail utility within Netscape Communicator. Other programs support HTML Mail to varying degrees. For instance, AK-Mail (**http://www.akmail.com/**), E-Mail Connection (**http://www.connectsoft.com**), Opensoft ExpressMail (**http://www.opensoft.com/**), and Anawave Postmark (**http://www.anawave.com/**) support HTML Mail, and others will support it soon. (You'll see how to use an URL, one of these Web "addresses," in Chapter 5.)

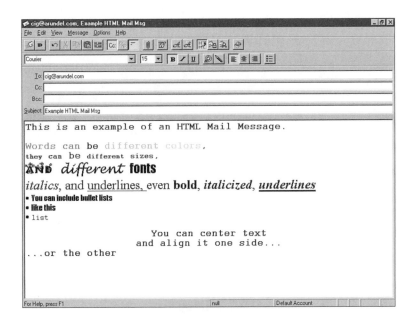

AK-Mail is one of several e-mail programs supporting HTML Mail. More will appear soon.

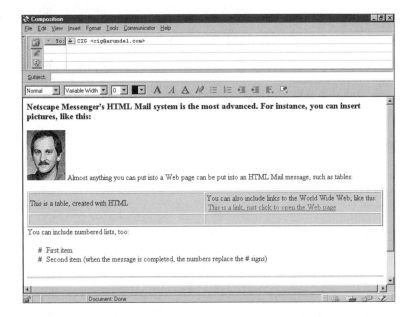

Netscape Messenger has the most advanced HTML Mail system around.

Can You Use HTML Mail?

At the time of this writing the major online services do not support HTML mail. Although these systems do allow you to use some character formatting—different colors and sizes, for instance—the system used is not HTML Mail, and when you send messages across the Internet the formatting is stripped out. In order to use HTML Mail you need a POP mail account, and a POP mail program that can work with HTML Mail. So, for the moment at least, you can't use HTML mail if you are working with one of the major online services.

If you really want HTML, you can get an e-mail account on the Internet and still keep your online-service account. For instance, Netscape provides links to several services that will give you a free mail account: **http://form.netscape.com/ibd/ html/freemail/index.html**.

Different Programs, Different Capabilities

Just because an e-mail program supports HTML Mail, it doesn't mean that it supports it well or in the best way. You'll find that some programs can handle a few simple things, but not the more complicated processes involved with HTML Mail.

Here's an example. Let's say you insert an image into a message using Netscape Messenger. That image will be transferred along with the e-mail message. If the recipient has Netscape Messenger, the image will be displayed within the message exactly where it should be. If the user has another HTML Mail program, though, the image may not be displayed in the message; it may simple be saved on the recipient's hard disk. Some HTML Mail programs won't even send the inserted image with the message. The early HTML Mail versions of Netscape's mail program (the program included with Netscape Navigator 3) simply inserted a link to the image, and didn't actually transfer the image. That caused problems, of course, because the image might be on the user's hard disk, and unavailable to the recipient.

Some HTML Mail programs may be unable to display some forms of HTML Mail messages, too. For instance, the program may be able to display simple HTML Mail messages from Netscape Messenger, but not the more complicated messages used by companies delivering Inbox Direct publications (which we'll look at next).

Inbox Direct—Web Pages Delivered Directly to You

In order to promote its new HTML Mail standard, Netscape set up a system called **Inbox Direct**. Scores of companies have signed up with Netscape to provide HTML-formatted e-mail messages to anyone who signs up at the Netscape site. These messages are in effect newsletters, all free for at least an introductory period, (and many are free for as long as you want them). You can get information from *The New York Times*, *USA Today*, *The Melbourne Age*, *Rheinische Post*, *Correo Expansión Directo*, *The Financial Times*, PlanetOut, ParentsPlace.com Gazette, National Geographic Online, PBS Previews, and many more.

To sign up for one of these publications, go to **http://home.netscape.com/** and find the Inbox Direct link, then just follow instructions. The publications have all been created using HTML Mail, so they'll be brightly colored and illustrated publications, as you can see in the following illustration. They will contain links to Web pages, pictures, tables, perhaps even JavaScript and Java applets (which you'll learn about in Chapter 7).

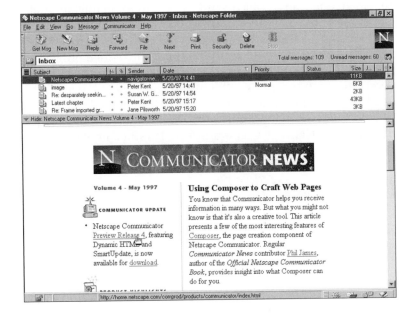

This is an Inbox Direct e-mail message, formatted with HTML Mail and displayed in Netscape Messenger.

Encryption—Keep Away Prying Eyes

The other major change coming to e-mail is the ability to encrypt messages. In other words, messages can be "scrambled" so that they can't be read if intercepted. Before a scrambled message can be read it must be decrypted, that is, converted back to its original form. Then it will be legible. Of course if all goes well, the only person who can decrypt the message is the intended recipient.

There was a great deal of interest in data encryption late in 1994 and early in 1995. Most of this interest centered around a program called PGP, Pretty Good Privacy. This program is able to encrypt a message so solidly that it's essentially unbreakable. It's almost certainly impossible to break a PGP-encrypted message using current computer technology, and even when technology improves a little breaking such a message may remain prohibitively expensive. For instance, breaking into a message to your Aunt Edna explaining when you're going to arrive for Christmas dinner would probably cost the CIA more than engineering a coup in a mid-size Central American republic. Thus your mail will likely remain completely safe. (This, of course, upsets the US Government, along with many other governments around the world.)

I know exactly when this intense interest in PGP occurred, because I made a shameless attempt to cash in on the interest by writing a book about PGP. I also know exactly when this interest subsided...about three days before my book was published. Why the sudden decline in interest in a technology that could be so useful? Because it's so hard to use.

I wrote my book based on an application called WinPGP, a Windows program that insulates the user from many of the intricacies of using PGP. Still, even using a "front end" like WinPGP, PGP remained a little complicated, and I told anyone who would listen to me that "encryption won't be popular until it's built into e-mail programs, and is as easy to use as clicking a button." I'd like to say that everyone took my advice and immediately began work on e-mail programs with built-in encryption, but actually few people listen to me (except my family, and I suspect they're just pretending). Nonetheless, such e-mail programs have begun appearing on the scene, most notably Netscape Messenger, the e-mail portion of Netscape Communicator. It's still a little more complicated than simply clicking a button, but it's certainly much simpler than it all used to be.

Why Encrypt Your E-Mail?

E-mail can get you in a lot of trouble. It got Oliver North in hot water, and ordinary people have lost their jobs or been sued over things they've said in e-mail. Several things can go wrong when you use e-mail:

➤ The recipient might pass the e-mail on to someone else.

➤ The message can be backed up to a backup system and read by someone other than the recipient later.

➤ Someone could spy on you and read your e-mail looking for incriminating comments.

➤ Your boss may decide to read your e-mail, based on the idea that if it's written on company time and company equipment, it's company property (and the courts will almost certainly back him up!)

The most likely scenario is that the recipient intentionally or thoughtlessly passes on your message to someone who you didn't count on seeing it. The second problem—that the message could be copied to a backup system—is what got Oliver North (and others) into trouble. Even if you delete a message and the recipient deletes the message, it may still exist somewhere on the network if the system administrator happened to do a backup before it was deleted. So if you are ever the subject of some kind of investigation, that message could be revived. This is more of a problem on the Internet because a message goes from your computer, to your service provider's computer, to the recipient's service provider's computer, to the recipient's computer—at least four places from which it could be copied.

Finally, someone might be out to get you. Internet e-mail is basic text, and a knowledge-able hacker with access to your service provider's system (or the recipient's service provider's system) can grab your messages and read them.

What do you do, then? The simplest solution is to avoid putting things in e-mail that you would be embarrassed to have others read. The more complicated solution is to encrypt your e-mail.

Public-Key Encryption—It's Magic

E-mail encryption systems depend on something known as **public-key encryption**. I'd like to give you a full and detailed description of exactly how it works, but I don't know exactly how it works (I'm no mathematician, and encryption is all wrapped up with the sort of math that only a geek could love), so I'll give you the simple answer: it's magic. Perhaps that's insufficient, so I'll endeavor to explain a little more, without getting more complicated than necessary.

First, let me describe **private-key encryption**, which you may have already used. A computer file can be encrypted—turned into a jumble of garbage characters that makes it useless—using a program that works with a **private key** (also known as a **secret key**, or even simply called a **password**). The private key is a sort of code word. Tell the program the name of the file you want to encrypt, tell the program the private key, and the program uses a mathematical algorithm to encrypt the file. How can you decrypt the file? You do the same thing: give the program the name of the encrypted file, give it the private key, and it uses the algorithm to reverse the process and decrypt the file. You may have used private-key encryption already, because many computer programs use it. For instance, if you use Word for Window's Protect Document command, you are using private-key encryption. The password that the program asks you for is, in effect, the private key.

Now, let's look at **public-key encryption**. This starts to get a little weird. Public-key encryption uses two keys: a private key and a public key. Through the wonders of mathematics, these keys work together. When you encrypt a file with one key (the public key, for example), the file can only be decrypted with the other key! Sounds a little odd, but that's how it works. (Okay, this is where my knowledge breaks down. Don't ask me how the mathematics work; as far as I'm concerned, it's magic!)

Public-Key Encryption and Your E-Mail

How, then, does this apply to e-mail encryption? An e-mail program with built-in encryption uses public-key encryption to encrypt your e-mail message before it sends it. When you want to send an encrypted message to someone, you have to get hold of that person's public key. These keys are often posted—yes, publicly—on the Internet. There's no need to worry about who gets hold of the public key, as it can't be used to decrypt a secret message.

Using the recipient's public key, you encrypt a message and send it off. The recipient then uses his private key (also known as the secret key because that's just what it is) to decode the message.

Where do you find someone's public key? Well, it used to be complicated; you might have to go to a **key server**, a Web or FTP site that stored thousands of public keys. Or you could ask the person to send you the key. A new system is greatly simplifying the task, though. New e-mail programs, such as Netscape Messenger, allow a user to include his public key in what's known as a **Vcard**, a special block of information that can be tacked onto the end of an e-mail message. The user can set up Messenger so that every time it sends a message, it includes the Vcard, which includes the public key. The e-mail program receiving the message can then automatically extract the public key and place it into a directory of public keys. (Assuming, of course, that the e-mail program can work with Vcards, and currently most can't.)

So, here's how it works:

1. Fred Bloggs sends you an e-mail message. He's using a Vcard-enabled program, and he has a public key in the Vcard.

2. Your e-mail program, when it receives the message from Fred, extracts Fred's public key and saves it.

3. Later, you decide that you want to send a private message to Fred, one that's so sensitive it must be encrypted. So you write the message to Fred, then click the Encrypted check box (Netscape Messenger has an Encrypted check box; other programs may have a button or menu command).

4. You click the Send button, and the mail program sees that you want to encrypt the file. So it looks through its list of public keys, searching for one that is related to Fred's e-mail address. When it finds the public key it uses it to scramble the message, then it sends it out across the Internet.

5. Fred's e-mail program receives the message, and sees that its been encrypted. It takes a closer look and sees that it's been encrypted with Fred's own public key, so it uses Fred's private key to decrypt the message. Fred can now read the message.

It's really all quite simple. What happens if someone other than Fred receives the message? Well, the recipient won't be able to decrypt the message, because the recipient won't have Fred's private key (well, we assume he won't, but that's a weakness of the system; if the private key is stolen, the security is compromised).

Click here to encrypt the
message usign the recipient's
public key

Click here to see
the encryption
options

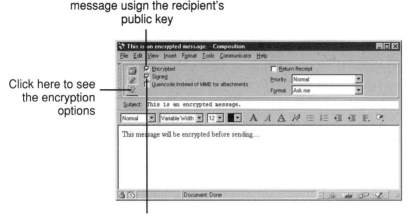

*Netscape Communi-
cator makes encrypt-
ing messages easy;
simply click the
appropriate check
boxes.*

Click here to digitally sign the
message using your private key

Digital Signatures

Remember when I said that you can encrypt messages with either key? Encrypt with one key, and only the matching key can decrypt it. Well, it wouldn't be a good idea to secure a key by encrypting it with your own private key. Remember, a message encrypted with your private key can be decrypted with your public key, and the public key is, well, public. However, if the message can be decrypted with your public key, it means that it *must* have been encrypted with the corresponding private key, your private key. And if we assume that private key is secure, and that only you have access to the private key...well, you've just signed the message.

In other words, you can sign messages by encrypting them with your private key. As long as your private key remains secure, then the recipient can be sure that the message came from you.

Just to clarify all this, remember that...

➤ To send an encrypted message to someone, you'll use their public key

➤ To send a signed message to someone, you'll use your private key

➤ To send an encrypted message to someone, and sign it, you'll use your private key and their public key.

Actually you don't have to remember all this, because an e-mail program will handle it all for you. In Netscape Messenger, for instance, if you want to sign a message simply click the Signed checkbox. The program will automatically encrypt your message using your private key.

I'm Sold...Where Do I Get My Keys?

First, you should understand that there are two types of e-mail encryption in use. Some programs use PGP encryption. In order to work with this you'll have to download PGP and create your public- and private-key pairs. Working with PGP can be complicated, though; if you want more information, search for PGP at one of the Web search sites (see Chapter 21), or go to **http://www.pgp.com/**.

Probably the most common system, the system that will win the encryption war, is the one being used by Netscape. This doesn't use PGP. Rather, you must get hold of a **personal certificate**, a special "digital" certificate that contains your private and public keys.

Where do you get your certificate? From a **key server**, a site with the necessary software to issue certificates. There are both public- and private-key servers. Right now you can get one from the public VeriSign key server (though other authorities will, presumably, be issuing them too), at **http://www.verisign.com/**. This site is set up to issue personal certificates for these mail systems:

Netscape Communicator (**http://www.netscape.com/**)

Microsoft Internet Explorer 4 (**http://www.microsoft.com/**)

E-mail Connection (**http://www.connectsoft.com/**)

Frontier Technologies Email (**http://www.frontiertech.com/**)

Opensoft ExpressMail (**http://www.opensoft.com/**)

WorldSecure Client (**http://www.worldtalk.com/**)

PreMail (**http://www.c2.net/~raph/premail.html**)

Undoubtedly many more will soon join the fray. Install the e-mail program you've chosen, then go to the Verisign site and follow the instructions for creating and installing the personal certificate in the program.

Different Size Keys

The size of the keys determine the security of the encryption system. For instance, there are actually two different versions of the Netscape Messenger security software: a 40-bit version and a 128-bit version. These numbers refer to the length of the key—the code—that is used to encrypt data. The longer the key, the more secure the transmission. The 128-bit software is built into the Netscape programs sold to customers within the United States. The 40-bit software is built into Netscape programs that are sold to customers outside the United States; it's also built into most of the systems that can be downloaded from the Netscape Web site and FTP sites and the various mirror sites.

128-Bit Netscape Communicator Versions

You can download the 128-bit software from Netscape's site (previously you could only get it by buying it at a store or having it shipped to you), but you'll have to fill out a form and provide information that Netscape can check (using the American Business Information Inc. service) to show that you are a resident of the U.S. (Only citizens and resident aliens—green-card holders—who are living in the U.S. are allowed to download the software.) You can download this software from the **http://www37.netscape.com/ eng/US-Current/index.html** page. (If this link is not working, follow the normal procedure for downloading Communicator from the Netscape site. When you get to the form where you have to select the product, operating system, language, and location look for a `Netscape Strong Encryption Software Eligibility Affida-` `vit` link. Click this link to find the U.S. version of Communicator.)

Does it really matter which version you use? In most cases, no. The 40-bit software is strong enough for all but the most critical of applications. A government department using the Web to transfer information throughout the world would probably want to use 128-bit encryption, ensuring that the message was unbreakable. But for most uses, 40-bit keys are fine. Still, 40-bit keys are much weaker, and could be broken by someone with the available computing resources. (The cost may be in the tens of thousands of dollars to break a message; if you think someone's willing to spend that to see what you're saying, then you need stronger encryption!)

Why, then, are there two versions of Netscape's software? For one reason only—ITAR, the United States Government's International Traffic in Arms Regulations. Encryption software using keys over 40-bits long is, as far as ITAR is concerned, on a par with armaments—SAM missiles and the like—and cannot be exported. Ridiculous, but true.

How Much Stronger Is 128-Bit Encryption?

Techno Talk

Much, much stronger. For instance, Pretty Good Privacy, Inc. says that the 128-bit PGP software creates messages that are 309,485,009,821,341,068,724, 781,056 times more difficult to break than 40-bit messages. They also quote a U.S. Government study that found it would take "12 million times the age of the universe, on average, to break a single 128-bit message encrypted with PGP." (That's just an average, so your mileage may vary.)

(How can you stop the export of software, something that can be exported without physically moving anything?) This situation may change soon, as a federal judge recently ruled this regulation unconstitutional, so the issue is now in the hands of the courts. The law seems to be slowly crumbling; the U.S. Department of Commerce recently allowed Pretty Good Privacy, Inc. to export 128-bit software to subsidiaries and branch offices of U.S. companies operating overseas.

Check This Out...

The Law Seems to Be Slowly Crumbling
Before we went to print the U.S. Department of Commerce began allowing some companies—including Pretty Good Privacy, Inc., Netscape, and Microsoft—to export 128-bit software in some circumstances.

Note, by the way, that some other countries have laws that are as bad or worse. France, for instance, has banned the use of even the 40-bit version of Communicator's encryption, so Netscape Communications now produces a special "security-free" Communicator for that country.

The Least You Need to Know

➤ HTML Mail allows you to create e-mail messages with colors, special fonts, pictures, tables, and more.

➤ Both the sender and recipient must have HTML Mail compatible programs, or the system won't work. For the moment, the online services don't work with HTML Mail.

➤ E-mail encryption uses a system called public-key encryption; you'll need to get a personal certificate and install it in a compatible e-mail program.

➤ E-mail programs that allow encryption also allow you to digitally sign messages, proving that they've come from you.

➤ Encryption is not legal everywhere. Some versions of the e-mail software can only be sold in the U.S.

➤ The longer the key, the safer the encryption. But even 40-bit keys are pretty safe, safe enough for most day-to-day use.

Chapter 5

The World of the World Wide Web

In This Chapter

➤ What is the Web?

➤ Which browser should you use?

➤ The home page

➤ Moving around the Web

➤ The history list and bookmarks

➤ Using the URLs

The World Wide Web is also known as *The Web*, *WWW*, and sometimes (among really geeky company) *W3*. And, in really confused company, it's called *the Internet*. I'd better clear up that little confusion about the Web and the Internet right away.

The World Wide Web is *not* the Internet. It's simply one software system running on the Internet. Still, it's one of the most interesting and exciting systems, so it has received a lot of press, to the extent that many people believe that the terms Web and Internet are synonymous. However, the Web seems to be taking over roles previously carried out by other Internet services, and at the same time Web programs—*browsers*—are including utilities to help people work with non-Web services. For instance, you can send and receive e-mail with some Web browsers, and you can read Internet newsgroups with some.

What's the Web?

Imagine that you are reading this page in electronic form, on your computer screen. Then imagine that some of the words are underlined and colored. Use your mouse to point at one of these underlined words on your screen and press the mouse button. What happens? Another document opens, a document that's related in some way to the word you clicked.

That's a simple explanation of *hypertext*. If you've ever used Apple's Hypercard or a Windows Help file, you've used hypertext. Documents are linked to each other in some way, generally by clickable words and pictures. Hypertext has been around for years, but until recently most hypertext systems were limited in both size and geographic space. Click a link, and you might see another document held by the same electronic file. Or maybe you'll see a document in another file, but one that's on the same computer's hard disk, probably the same directory.

The World Wide Web is like a hypertext system without boundaries. Click a link, and you might be shown a document in the next city, on the other side of the country, or even on another continent. Links from one document to another can be created without the permission of the owner of that second document. And nobody has complete control over those links. When you put a link in your document connecting to someone else's, you are sending your readers on a journey that you really can't predict. They will land at that other document, from which they can take another link somewhere else—another country, another subject, or another culture—from which they can follow yet another link...and on and on.

The Web has no capacity limit, either. Web pages are being added every minute of the day, all over the world. In fact, the Web is really pushing the growth of the Internet. It's so easy to create and post a Web page that thousands of people are doing it, and more are joining them each day.

If you haven't seen the Web, this may all sound a little mundane. Okay, so one document leads to another that leads to another...I try to avoid the Internet hype we've been inundated with over the last couple of years, but the Web really is a publishing revolution. It has made publishing to an international audience quick and simple. I don't mean to imply (as some Internet proponents seem to), that every Web page is a jewel that is widely read and appreciated (much of it is closer to a sow's ear than to silk). But it's a medium with which people can make their words available so that they *can* be widely read if they have some value.

Techno Talk

Dial-In Terminal (Shell) Accounts

Using the Web with a dial-in direct account is *very* different from using it with a dial-in terminal (shell) account. If you are working with a dial-in terminal account much of the information we're going to look at here won't help at all. To learn more about working with e-mail with your type of account, you can use our autoresponder to get the Web chapters from *The Complete Idiot's Guide to the Internet*. Send e-mail to **ciginternet@mcp.com**, with **web** in the Subject line to receive the e-mail chapters.

Let's Start

If you want to listen to a CD, you need a CD player. If you want to watch a video, you need a video player. And if you want to view a Web page, you need a Web player: a *Web browser*.

There are actually two parts to the Web equation. First, there's a *Web server*, a special program running on a host computer (that is, a computer connected directly to the Internet). This server administers a Web site, which is a collection of World Wide Web documents. The second part is the *browser*, a program on your PC that asks the server for the documents and then displays the documents so that you can read them.

> **Servers and Clients** If you hang around on the Internet long enough, you'll hear the terms "server" and "client" used over and over. A *server* is a program that provides information that a *client* program can use in some way.

There are really two big contenders in the Web browser war (yes, there's a war going on). One is Netscape Navigator. Right now, somewhere around 60% to 70% of all Web users are working with Netscape, though in the past Netscape has owned 80%–90% of the market. Netscape is available in versions for Windows 3.1, Windows 95 and NT, the Macintosh, and various flavors of UNIX. Netscape Navigator is now part of the Netscape Communicator suite of programs. The following figure shows the Netscape Navigator Web browser.

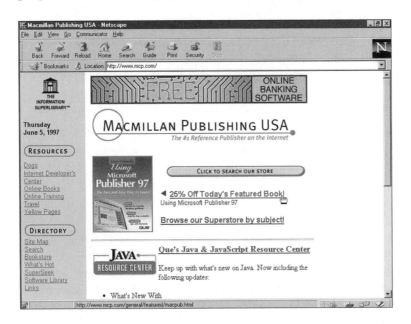

Netscape Navigator—part of the Netscape Communicator suite of programs—is currently the most popular browser on the Web.

Netscape Navigator

This browser is manufactured by Netscape Communications. You might think that it would be known as Navigator for short, but it's not. It's known as Netscape mainly for "historical" reasons. The Netscape programmers came from the NCSA (National Center for Supercomputing Applications). They originally created the first graphical Web browser, called *Mosaic*. Netscape was originally known as *Netscape Mosaic*, and the company was Mosaic Communications. Thus, the browser was known as Netscape to differentiate it from Mosaic.

The second most popular browser is Internet Explorer from Microsoft (shown in the following figure). Originally this ran only on Windows 95 and Windows NT, but now it's available for the Mac and Windows 3.1. This browser has almost all of the rest of the browser-market share, perhaps around 30%. So chances are you are using either Netscape Navigator or Internet Explorer.

MS Internet Explorer 4, Microsoft's latest weapon in the Web war with Netscape.

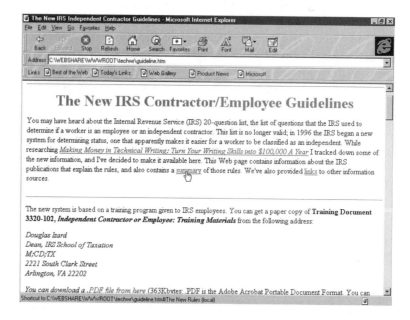

Now, I'm going to keep my head down because what I'm about to say may incite an assault by Web purists. Netscape is not the "be all and end all" of Web browsers. It is undoubtedly a good browser, but you shouldn't feel that if you don't have Netscape you're missing out on something. There are dozens of other browsers available, ranging from pretty awful to very good. Probably the best two are Netscape and Internet Explorer.

At the moment I prefer Netscape Navigator, though in the past I've prefered Internet Explorer. They seem to leapfrog each other. For a few months Netscape Navigator is better, then a new version of Explorer comes out, and it seems to be better. Then, a few weeks later, Navigator's modified again, and it has a few nice features and bug fixes that makes it better than Explorer...and so on.

Getting a Browser

Which browser should you use? If your service provider has given you one, I suggest you start with that. You'll probably be given either Netscape or Explorer...most likely Internet Explorer these days, as CompuServe, AOL, and (of course!) Microsoft Network provide that browser to their members.

If you have to pick a browser, I suggest that you try Explorer first (if you are using Windows NT or Windows 95); then try Netscape later and see if you like it. If you are using a Mac or Windows 3.1, do it the other way around: start with Netscape (even though the new Explorer for the Mac is getting good reviews). If you are using UNIX, you'll have to go with Netscape; Explorer doesn't currently have a UNIX version (though it may soon). If you want to find Netscape or Explorer, or if you want to see what other browsers are available, see Appendix A.

For now, I'm going to assume that you have a Web browser installed, and that you have opened it and are ready to start. One nice thing about Web browsers is that they all work similarly—and they look very similar, too. So whatever browser you use, you should be able to follow along with this chapter.

Browsing Begins at Home

At the *home page*, that is. When you open your browser, whatever page you see is, by definition, your home page. (I like that kind of definition; it's easy to understand.) Ideally, the home page is a page that has lots of useful links, which take you to places on the Web that you will want to go to frequently. You can create your own home page by using something called HTML, the Web document language (see Chapter 9), or even using one of the fancy new customizing systems you'll find on the Web. (Both Netscape and Microsoft have systems that automatically create customized pages for you, if you have their browsers. Go to **http://www.netscape.com/custom/index.html** for the Netscape system or **http://www.msn.com/** for the Microsoft system. (I'll explain how to use these "addresses" later in this chapter, in the section "A Direct Link—Using the URLs.")

Home Page, Start Page

Microsoft's programmers can't seem to decide whether to use the term *home page* or *start page*. The term home page originally meant the page that appeared when you opened your browser or when you used the Home button. Then all of a sudden, everybody was using the term to mean a person or company's main Web page (the page you see when you go to that Web site) such as NEC's home page, Netscape's home page, and so on. So Microsoft's programmers evidently thought it made more sense to rename the home page to "start page." Unfortunately, they're using *both* terms, so Internet Explorer 3.0 and 4.0 have a Home button on the Toolbar; Explorer 3.0 has a Go, Start Page menu option; Explorer 4.0 has a Go, Home Page menu option; and the browser's Options dialog box refers to the Start Page.

Moving Around on the Web

Let's move around a little. Whatever browser you are using, you'll almost certainly find links on the home page. These are the colored and underlined words. You may also find pictures that contain links, perhaps several different links on a picture (a different link on each part of the picture). Point at a piece of text or a picture; if the mouse pointer changes shape—probably into a pointing hand—you are pointing at a link. (Just to confuse the issue, some pictures contain links, even though the pointer doesn't change shape.)

Click one of the links—whatever looks interesting. If you are online (I'm assuming you are!), your browser sends a message to a Web server somewhere, asking for a page. If the Web server is running (it may not be) and if it's not too busy (it may be), it transmits the document back to your browser, and your browser displays it on your screen.

Where Are the Buttons? You can turn the Directory bar on and off using the **Options**, **Show Directory Buttons** menu command. These commands are also available from the Directory menu. (I'm assuming that you are using Netscape 3; earlier and later versions have different buttons.)

You've just learned the primary form of Web "navigation." When you see a link you want to follow, you click it. Simple, eh? But what about going somewhere actually useful, somewhere interesting? Most browsers these days either have toolbar buttons that take you to a useful Web page, or come with a default home page with useful links. For example, in Netscape Navigator 3 you can click one of these Directory-bar buttons:

What's New?   A selection of new and interesting Web sites from the people at Netscape.

What's Cool?   Web sites chosen for their usefulness or CQ—coolness quotient. (Personally, I'm getting tired of the word *cool*. But hey, that's my job: Internet Curmudgeon.)

Destinations   More interesting sites, this time broken down by subject—Sports, Travel, Technology, Finance, and so on.

Net Search   Web sites that help you search for a subject you are interested in. You'll be looking at these in Chapter 20.

People   Links to sites that can help you track down other Internet users.

In Netscape Navigator 4 you'll find a different toolbar setup; you can click the Guide button to open a little menu, on which you'll find similar options to those listed above.

How Does It Know Which Server?

How does your browser know which server to request the document from? What you see on your computer screen is not quite the same document that your browser sees. Open the source document—which you can probably do using the **View**, **Source** menu option—and you'll see what the Web document *really* looks like. (You'll see an example of this stuff in Chapter 9.) It's just basic ASCII text that contains all sorts of instructions. One of the instructions says, in effect, "if this guy clicks on this link, here's which document I want you to get." You don't normally see all these funky commands because the browser *renders* the page, removing the instructions and displaying only the relevant text.

Internet Explorer 3.0 has a special QuickLinks toolbar (click **QuickLinks** in the Address toolbar to open the QuickLinks toolbar). On that bar, you'll find the Services and Today's Links buttons that take you to useful starting points. The QuickLinks toolbar also has many useful links from the home page and a Search button in the main toolbar that takes you to a page from which you can search the Web—see Chapter 21.

Whatever browser you are using, take a little time to go on a journey of exploration. Go ahead…go as far as you want…get lost. Then come back here, and I'll explain how to find your way back to where you came from.

Link Colors

Some links change color after you click them. You won't see it right away, but if you return to the same page later, you'll find that the link is a different color. The color change indicates that the particular link points to a document that you've already seen. The "used-link" color does expire after a while, and the link changes back to its original color. How long it takes for this to happen is something that you can generally control with an option in the program's Preferences or Options.

The Hansel and Gretel Dilemma Where Are You?

Hypertext is a fantastic tool, but it has one huge drawback: It's easy to get lost. If you are reading a book and you flip forward a few pages, you know how to get back. You flip back, right? But with hypertext, after a few moves through the electronic library, you can become horribly lost. How, exactly, do you get back to where you came from? And *where* did you come from anyway?

Over the years, a number of systems have been developed to help a person find his way around this rather strange freeform medium. This table explains some tools you can use in most Web browsers to move through the pages and sites you've seen.

Web Page Navigation Tools

Button	Description
Back	Click the **Back** button or choose **Back** from a menu (probably the **Go** menu) to return to the previous Web page.
Forward	Click the **Forward** button or choose the **Forward** menu option to return to a page you've just come back from.
Home	Click the **Home** (or **Start**) button to go all the way back to your home page or start page.
Bookmarks	You can set bookmarks on pages you think you'll want to come back to; these can be very helpful because you don't have to struggle to find your way back the next time.
History	This is a list of pages you've seen previously. The **Back** and **Forward** commands take you back and forward through this list. But you can also go directly to a page in the history list by selecting it from the **Go** menu. (In Explorer 2.0, you select from the **File** menu.)

Bookmarks and History

The bookmark system (known as Favorites in Internet Explorer) and the history list are essential tools for finding your way around. Get to know them soon. In most browsers, you can just click a button or select a menu option to place a bookmark. Each system works a little differently, of course. In Netscape, choose **Bookmarks, Add Bookmark** (Navigator 3), or click the **Bookmarks** button and choose **Add Bookmark** (Navigator 4), and the bookmark is added to the bottom of the Bookmark menu (you can move it to a folder or submenu later). In Navigator 4 you can even select the folder into which you want to place the bookmark—click the **Bookmarks** button and then choose **File Bookmark**. In Internet Explorer, choose **Favorites, Add to Favorites**, then click the **Create In** button and select the folder into which you want to place the bookmark.

Both systems have both Bookmarks windows and an associated Bookmarks menu. (Well, okay, in Explorer they're called the Favorites window and menu.) Creating a folder in the window automatically creates a submenu in the menu.

To open Netscape's Bookmarks window choose **Bookmarks, Go to Bookmarks** (Navigator 3) or **Bookmarks, Edit Bookmarks** (Navigator 4). Or choose **Window, Bookmarks**, or **Communicator, Bookmarks** (depending on which version you have). In Explorer, choose **Favorites, Organize Favorites**.

A Little History

The history list varies tremendously. Netscape 3's history list is not very helpful. It lists some, but not all, of the pages you've visited in the current session. Other browsers—including Netscape Navigator 4— show much more, often listing pages from previous sessions. Explorer, for instance, keeps a record of up to 3,000 pages (including all the pages from the current session and earlier sessions). You can view the list in a window (see the following figure) sorted by date or by name. You can even search the list by using the Windows 95 **Find** tool on the **Start** menu, for example. Double-click an entry to open that Web page.

> **In or Out?** In Internet Explorer 2.0, the window is separate from the browser window; in versions 3.0 and 4.0 the history list is shown within the browser window.

Whatever system you have, though, using the history list is simple. Select the entry from the **Go** menu if you're using Netscape or Internet Explorer 3.0 or 4.0; in Internet Explorer 2.0, you'll find the entries on the **File** menu. You can also open the history window. In Explorer, choose **Go, Open History Folder** in version 3.0, or choose **File, More History** in version 2.0. In Netscape, choose **Window, History** (or **Communicator, History** in some 4.0 versions, depending on the operating system).

A Direct Link, Using the URLs

Earlier in this chapter I mentioned a couple of *URLs*. URLs are Web addresses, such as **http://www.msn.com/** or **http://www.netscape.com/**. These provide a direct link to a particular Web page. So instead of clicking links to try to find your way to a page, you can tell your browser the URL and say "go get this page."

> **New History List Trick** The newest versions of Explorer and Netscape Navigator (Versions 4.0) have a handy new feature that allows you to see the history list from the **Back** and **Forward** buttons. In Navigator click on the button and hold down the mouse key; in Explorer right-click on the button. In both cases you'll see a list of pages that you've visited.

Netscape Navigator
4's history list lets
you go back days or
even weeks in your
Web travels. The list
even indicates how
long it's been since
you visited the page,
and how often you've
been there.

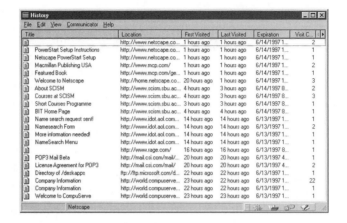

URL This
stands for Uni-
form Resource
Locator, which
is a fancy name
for "Web
address."

Most browsers have a bar near the top in which you can
type the URL of the page you want to go to. In Netscape
use the **Options**, **Show Location** or **View**, **Show Location
Toolbar** menu command is chosen to display this bar
(depending on the version you're working with); in
Internet Explorer, choose **View**, **Toolbar**. To use this box
click in the box, type the address, and press **Enter**.

If you don't want the bar there all the time (after all, it
takes up room that is sometimes better given to the Web pages themselves), you can leave
it turned off. If you keep it turned off, you can generally use a shortcut key to display a
dialog box in which you can type an URL. In Netscape, press **Ctrl+L** to open the box (or
try **Ctrl+O** if that doesn't work; it varies between versions); in Internet Explorer, choose
File, **Open** or press **Ctrl+O**. In either case, you type the URL in the box that appears, just
as you would in the text box on the toolbar.

The URL Explained

Let's take a look at an URL and see how it works. Here's a longish one:

> **http://www.microsoft.com/isapi/msdownload/new2.idc**

An URL can be broken down into certain distinct parts. Using the URL above as an
example, here's what each part means:

http://   This tells the browser that the address is for a Web page.
In addition to http://, you might see similar prefixes for
an FTP site or a Gopher menu (we'll look at those in a
moment). http:// stands for *HyperText Transfer Protocol*,
the system used on the Internet to transfer Web pages.

www.microsoft.com	This is the host name, the name of the computer holding the Web server that is administering the Web site you want to "visit."
/isapi/msdownload/	This is the directory in which the Web server has to look to find the file you want. In many cases multiple directories will be listed, so the Web server looks down the "directory tree" in subdirectories. In this example, in fact, it has to look in msdownload, which is a subdirectory of the isapi directory.
New2.html	This is the name of the file you want, the Web page. These are generally .HTM or .HTML files (that means HyperText Markup Language, the "coding" used to create Web pages). Sometimes the URL has no filename at the end; that's generally okay; the Web server will send you a "default" document for the specified directory.

The URL is really nothing complicated, just an address so your browser knows where to look for a file. However, there are different types of URLs, each of which is identified by a different *protocol* portion of the address. The Web page URLs all begin with http://. This table lists some other protocols you'll see on the Internet.

Other Internet Protocols

Protocol Prefix	Description
gopher://	The address of a Gopher site (see Chapter 16).
ftp://	The address of an FTP file library; you'll learn more in Chapter 14.
news:	The address of a newsgroup, discussed in Chapter 11. Note that this doesn't have the // after the name; neither does mailto: (below).
mailto:	When you use this URL, the browser's e-mail program opens so you can send mail. Web authors often create links using the mailto: URL so that when someone clicks the link he or she can quickly send a message to the author.
telnet://	The address of a Telnet site (see Chapter 20).
tn3270://	The address of a tn3270 site. This is very similar to Telnet and is also covered in Chapter 20.
wais://	The address of a WAIS site; WAIS is a little used database-search tool, and you probably won't run into many WAIS links. And in anycase the wais:// URL is not recognized by most browsers.

Forget http://

In most browsers these days (including Netscape and Internet Explorer), you don't need to type the full URL. You can omit the http:// piece, and the browser will assume that the http:// piece should be added. And if you type something beginning with gopher (as in gopher.usa.net, for instance) or ftp (as in ftp.microsoft.com), you can omit the gopher:// or ftp:// part, too. Also, in some browsers you can even drop the www. and .com bits. For instance, in Netscape Navigator you can type simply **mcp** and press Enter to get to the **http://www. mcp.com/** Web site (this only works if the domain ends with .com). And the newest browsers, Navigator and Explorer 4.0, have an auto-fill-in feature, something you may have seen in personal-finance programs—start typing an URL and if the browser recognizes that you've entered it before, it will fill in the rest for you.

What Will You Find on Your Web Journey?

When you travel around the Web, you'll find a lot of text documents of course. However, there is much, much more than that. As a system administrator at a Free-Net once said to me, "The Web is for people who can't read!" It was a slight exaggeration, perhaps, but his point was that on the Web, the nontext stuff is often more important than the actual words.

While traveling around the Web, you'll find these sorts of things:

➤ **Pictures:** You'll find these both inside the text documents and on their own. Sometimes, when you click a link (at a museum site, for example), a picture—not a document—is transferred to your browser.

➤ **Forms:** These days most browsers are forms compatible (Navigator and Explorer have always been forms compatible). In other words, you can use forms to interact with the Web site to send information about yourself (to subscribe to a service, for instance), to search for information, or to play a game, for example.

➤ **Sounds:** Most browsers can play sounds such as voices and music. Many Web sites contain sounds. For instance, IUMA (the Internet Underground Music Archive) has song clips from many new bands.

➤ **Files:** You'll find many Web sites that have files you can download, such as shareware, demos of new programs, and documents of many kinds. When you click a link, your browser begins the file transfer.

➤ **Multimedia of other kinds:** There are all sorts of strange things on the Web: 3-D images, animations, Adobe Acrobat .PDF hypertext files, videos, slide shows, 2-D and 3-D chemical images, and plenty more. Click a link, and the file starts transferring. If you have the right software installed, it automatically displays or plays the file. For instance, in the following figure you can see a Bubbleviewer image. (See **http://www.omniview.com/** for information about the Bubbleviewer, and Chapters 7 and 8 to learn more about multimedia.)

Where Do I Find What I Want on the Web?

You can follow any interesting links you find, as discussed earlier in this chapter. You can also search for particular subjects and Web pages by using a Web search site, as discussed in Chapter 21.

A BubbleViewer image in Netscape. You can move around inside the car, viewing up, down, and all around.

Speeding Up Your Journey by Limiting Graphics

The Web used to be a very fast place to move around. The first Web browsers could display nothing but text, and text transfers across the Internet very quickly. These days, though, things move more slowly. The things I just mentioned—pictures, video, sounds, and so on— really slow down the process. While video is the slowest thing on the Web (moving at an almost glacial pace in most cases), it's actually the pictures that are more of a nuisance; very few sites use video, but *most* use static pictures.

Most browsers provide a way for you to turn off the display of pictures. In Netscape Navigator, for instance, choose **Options**, **Auto Load Images**, and remove the check mark from the menu option to turn off images. Or in Netscape Navigator 4 choose **Edit**, **Preferences**, then click the **Advanced** category and clear the **Automatically Load Images**. Because the images are no longer transmitted to your browser, you see the pages much more quickly.

Of course you often need or want to see those images. Many images have links built into them, and while some Web pages have both graphic links and corresponding text links (for people using a browser that can't display pictures), other Web pages are totally unusable unless you can see the pictures. However, you can usually grab the picture you need quickly. Where there *should* be a picture, you'll see a little icon that functions as a sort of placeholder.

In Netscape, you can right-click the placeholder and choose **Load Image** (**Show Image** in some versions) from the shortcut menu that appears. Or you can click the **Images** button in the toolbar to see all of them. In Internet Explorer you can turn off images in the Options dialog box, *and* you can turn off sounds and video, too. Choose **View**, **Options** and click the **General** tab to see the options that are available. To view an image when you have images turned off, right-click the placeholder and choose **Show Picture** from the shortcut menu.

There's Plenty More!

There's a lot more to say about the Web than I've said in this chapter. In fact, one could write a book about it (actually, I already have: *Using Netscape 3.0* and *Using Netscape Communicator 4*). In the next couple of chapters you'll learn a few advanced Web-travel tips and a little bit about creating your own Web pages.

The Least You Need to Know

➤ The World Wide Web is a giant hypertext system running on the Internet.

➤ The two best browsers available are probably Netscape Navigator and MS Internet Explorer.

➤ The home page (sometimes called the start page in Internet Explorer) is the page that appears when you open your browser.

➤ Click a link in a document to see another document. To find your way back, use the **Back** or **Home** button.

➤ The history list shows where you've been. In Netscape Navigator 3, it includes just some of the pages you've seen in the current session; in some other browsers—including Netscape Navigator 4—it includes all of the pages from the current session and many pages from previous sessions.

➤ An URL is a Web "address." You can use the URL to go directly to a particular Web page.

Chapter 6

More About the Web

In This Chapter

➤ Running multiple Web sessions

➤ Opening files from your hard disk

➤ All about the cache and reloading

➤ Searching documents and using the pop-up menu

➤ Copying things you find to the Clipboard

➤ Saving images, documents, and files

You've seen the basic moves, now you are ready to learn more techniques to help you find your way around the Web. In the last chapter you learned how to move around on the Web using a Web browser such as Netscape Navigtor or Internet Explorer. In this chapter you'll find out how to run multiple Web sessions at the same time, how to deal with the cache, how to save what you find, and so on. You need to know these advanced moves to work efficiently on the Web.

Multiple Windows—Ambidextrous Browsing

These days, most browsers allow you to run more than one Web session at the same time. Why would you want to do that? Well, there could be many reasons. Everyone's in such a hurry these days.... While you wait for an image to load in one window, you can read something in another window. Or maybe you need to find information at another Web site but don't want to "lose your place" at the current one. (Yes, you have bookmarks and the history list, but sometimes it's just easier to open another window.) You can open one or more new browser windows, as shown in the following figure, so that you can run multiple Web sessions.

Opening multiple windows is a good way to keep from getting lost, or to do more than one thing at a time.

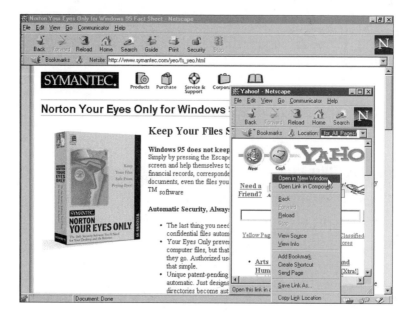

Exactly how you open a new window varies between browsers; however, you'll probably find that most are similar. Here's how various versions of the two most popular browsers, Netscape Navigator and Internet Explorer, let you open windows.

In Netscape Navigator try these procedures:

➤ Right-click the link that you want to "follow" in a new window, and then choose **Open in New Window**. A new Netscape window opens, and the referenced document opens in that window.

➤ Choose **File**, **New Web Browser**, or **File**, **New**, **Navigator Window**, or press **Ctrl+N** to open a new window displaying the home page.

Internet Explorer gives you several options:

➤ Right-click the link you want to follow, and then choose **Open in New Window**. A new window opens, displaying the referenced document.

➤ Press **Tab** until the link becomes highlighted, and then press **Shift+Enter**.

➤ Choose **File**, **New Window** (or, in some versions, **File**, **New**, **Window**) or press **Ctrl+N** to open a new window that displays the same document as the one you've just viewed.

➤ Type an URL into the Address text box, and then press **Shift+Enter** to display that document in a new window.

As you might guess, you could encounter some problems when running multiple sessions. First, there's the memory problem. Web browsers are turning into real memory hogs, so you may find that you simply don't have enough memory to run multiple sessions or to run more than one additional session. And remember that there's only so much work your modem can do. If you have several Web windows open and each is transferring things at the same time, every transfer will be slower than if it were the only thing the modem had to do.

Automatic Multiple Sessions

Now and then you'll find windows opening automatically. In fact, if you are working in Netscape and suddenly notice that the Back button is "disabled," it may be that when you clicked a link, a secondary window opened and you didn't notice. Web authors can create codes in their Web pages that force browsers to open "secondary" or "targeted" windows.

Your Hard Disk as Web Server?

If you enjoy working on the Web and spend most of your waking hours there, eventually, you'll end up with .HTM or .HTML files on your hard disk. You'll have them in your cache (discussed next), you may save documents using the **File**, **Save As** command, and perhaps you'll even create your own Web pages (see Chapter 9). Your browser provides a way to open these HTML files.

In Internet Explorer choose **File**, **Open**. Then, in the dialog box that appears, click the **Browse** button. You'll see a typical Open box from which you can select the file you want to open.

HTM or HTML?

Depending to some degree on the operating system you use, the file extension of the HTML Web files might be .HTM or .HTML. Originally, the Web was developed using UNIX computers, and Web files had the extension .HTML. Later, when Windows 3.1 machines started appearing on the Web, the .HTM extension came into use because Windows 3.1 could work only with three-character file extensions. Today, you'll see both extensions; even though Windows 95 can accept three-letter extensions, not all Windows HTML-editing programs can. And many Windows 3.1 machines are still being used to create Web pages.

Here's a geek trick for you. If you know the exact path to the file you want to open, and if you can type quickly, click in the **Address** or **Location** text box. Then type the entire path and file name, such as **C:/Program Files/Netscape/Navigator/ownweb.htm**. This should work in both Netscape and Internet Explorer. In some browsers, however, you may need to use the more formal (and older) method by entering the file path in this format: **file:///C|/Program Files/Netscape/Navigator/ownweb.htm**. Notice that in the second format, you precede the path with **file:///** and replace the colon after the disk letter (in this case C) with a pipe symbol (|).

Turbo Charging with the Cache

You need to know about a critical feature of a Web browser—one that seems to make it work really fast. Have you noticed that when you return to a Web document that you've previously viewed, it appears much more quickly? That's because your browser isn't taking it from the Internet; instead, it's getting it from the *cache*, an area on your hard disk or in your computer's RAM (memory) in which it saves pages. This capability is really handy because it greatly speeds up the process of working on the Web. After all, why bother to reload a file from the Internet when it's already sitting on your hard drive? (Okay, you may think of some reasons to do so, but we'll come back to those when we talk about the Reload command.)

Forward Slash or Backslash

UNIX computers use a forward slash (/) between directory names. DOS computers use a backslash(\). As the Web was developed on UNIX computers, URLs use forward slashes. Thus C:/Program Files/Netscape/Navigator/ownweb.htm is correct, even though in normal DOS notation this would appear as C:\Program Files\Netscape\Navigator\ownweb.htm. However, you can type it whichever way you please when you're opening a file on your hard disk or a page on the Web; both Internet Explorer and Netscape will figure it out.

Here's how this all works. When the browser loads a Web page, it places it in the cache. You can generally control the size of the cache. Not all browsers let you do so, but Netscape, Internet Explorer, and many others do. When the cache fills up, the oldest files are removed to make room for newer ones.

Each time the browser tries to load a page, it *might* look in the cache first to see if it has the page stored. (Whether or not it does depends on how you set up the cache.) If it finds that the page is available, it can retrieve the page from the cache.

Putting the Cache to Work

You'll probably want to take advantage of the cache's benefits. To configure the cache in Netscape Navigator 2 or 3, choose **Options**, **Network Preferences**, and then click the **Cache** tab. In Navigator 4 select **Edit**, **Preferences**, then open the **Advanced** category and click the **Cache** subcategory. The following figure shows Netscape's cache information.

Configure any of the available settings to meet your needs:

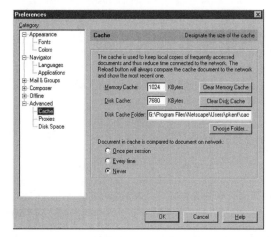

Here's where you set up Netscape's cache.

Memory Cache   You can tell Netscape how much of your computer's memory you want to assign to the cache. Netscape stores a few documents in the memory so that it can retrieve them extremely quickly. The button to the right of this option enables you to remove all the pages from the memory cache.

Disk Cache   You can also tell Netscape how large the disk cache should be—that is, how much of your disk space you want to give to Netscape. How much should you give? That all depends on how much disk space you have free. (I always say that you can never have too much hard-disk space, money, or beer; I've been proven wrong once or twice, though.) The button to the right of this option enables you to clear out the disk cache, which is handy when you finally run out of disk space.

Disk Cache Directory   You can tell Netscape *where* to place the disk cache. If you

73

have several hard disks, put it on the fastest disk or the one with most room.

Verify Documents   Now for the complicated one. This tells Netscape when to verify documents. When you request a document (by clicking a link or entering a URL), Netscape can send a message to the Web server saying (basically) "Has this document changed since the last time I grabbed it?" If it has changed, Netscape downloads a new copy. If it hasn't changed, Netscape grabs the page from the cache. You can configure Netscape to ask the Web server to verify documents **Once per Session** (in which case, it checks the first time you try to retrieve a document, but it doesn't bother after that); **Every Time** (so that it checks every time you try to get a document, regardless of how many times you view that document in a session); or **Never** (in which case, Netscape doesn't even bother to check to see if it's been updated, unless you use the Reload command).

Allow Persistent Caching of Pages Retrieved Through SSL   This is a feature of older versions of Netscape (it's not in the latest version), and it's related to Internet security. SSL stands for "secure sockets level" (which probably means no more to you than SSL, so I'm not really sure why I told you that). An SSL Web browser can use secure transmission of information; the information is encrypted before being transmitted. (See Chapter 22 for a discussion of encryption.) This feature simply tells the browser to cache pages that were sent in a secure manner.

Techno Talk

blah blah blah bla bla b

The Hard Disk Cache   Note that you are not reserving an area of your hard disk for the cache. For instance, if you have a 30,000K (almost 30MB) disk cache, your browser doesn't create a 30,000K file that prevents other programs from using that disk space. You're just telling the browser that it can use up to that much disk space for the cache *if it's available*—if other programs don't use up the space first.

Internet Explorer uses a very similar system. Choose **View**, **Options**, and click the **Advanced** tab (in Explorer 4 you must then click the **Settings** button), to see the cache information. The following figure shows Explorer 4.0's settings. Although Explorer's programmers—ever the innovators—have taken to referring to the cache as Temporary Internet Files, it's the same thing.

Near the top of the box, you can tell the browser when to check to see if there's a newer version of the file. You can tell it to check **Once per Session** in Explorer 3—this is ambiguously labelled **Every Time You Start Internet Explorer** in Explorer 4, but they're the same thing. Or you can turn it off altogether (select **Never**). In Explorer 4 you also have the option to check **Every Visit to the Page**.

Notice also that you can modify the size of the cache, this time by dragging a slider to set the percentage of the drive you want to use (instead of by entering an actual MB value). You can clear the cache using the **Empty Folder** button and select the cache directory using the **Move Folder** button. But notice that Explorer offers something extra: a **View Files** button. Click the **View Files** button to display a list of the files stored in the cache; then you can double-click a file to open it in the browser.

Internet Explorer allows you to modify the cache and view its contents directly.

Decisions, Decisions

Which of the cache options should you use? I prefer **Never** because it makes my Web sessions *much* quicker. Whenever I tell a browser to go to a Web page that's already in the cache, it loads the page from the hard disk right away, without sending a verification message to the server first. Even if the browser doesn't have to retrieve the page again—because the page hasn't changed—simply checking with the Web server can slow you down noticeably.

On the other hand, I have to remember to keep using the **Reload** command to make sure I'm viewing the latest version of the Web pages. Some people may prefer to use the **Once Per Session** option to ensure that they're always looking at the latest page—or, at least, that it's a fairly recent page.

What Is Reload?

Sometimes you *do* want to get a file from the Web again. Reload is a "cure" for the cache. If you get a page from the cache, you are not getting the latest document. Sometimes getting the most recent document doesn't matter, but in a few cases, it *does*.

For instance, say you want to return to a site you visited several weeks ago. If you have a very large cache, that document may still be available. If you have the **Never** option button selected in the Preferences dialog box, your browser displays the *old* document, without checking to see if the corresponding document stored on the Web has changed. Or perhaps, you are viewing a Web document that changes rapidly, such as a stock-quote page. Even if you viewed the page only a few minutes ago, it could already be out of date.

The cure for replacing those old, stale Web pages is to reload them. Click the **Reload** button or choose **View**, **Reload**. Internet Explorer's programmers, in their attempt to rename everything they can, use the term **Refresh** instead of Reload. (The fact that Reload is a term the Web's been using for several years and that Refresh has a different meaning—Netscape has a Refresh command that simply "repaints" the display using the contents of the memory cache—doesn't seem to matter.) Anyway, The Reload command (Refresh in Explorer) tells the browser "throw away the copy held in the cache and go get the latest version."

You'll sometimes see a **Reload Frame** command, which reloads just one frame in a framed document. We'll look at frames later in Chapter 7. And Netscape Navigator has a "super reload" command that few people know about. Holding the Shift key down and then selecting the Reload command says to Netscape Navigator "make absolutely sure you really do reload the page!" Navigator's Reload command has had a bug living in it for a couple of years, and in some cases *doesn't* reload the page. (This problem seems to be related to forms and scripts not being reloaded correctly.) Holding Shift ensures that the page really is reloaded.

Long Documents—Finding What You Need

Some Web pages are large. In fact, some are very large—thousands of lines long—with links at the top of the document that take the user to "sections" lower on the same page. Many Web authors prefer to create one large page than to create lots of small linked ones, the advantage being that once the page has been transferred to your browser you can use links to move to different parts of the page very quickly.

Virtually all browsers have some kind of Find command—generally **Edit**, **Find** or a **Find** button on the toolbar. Internet Explorer's programmers (as you might guess), have a command called **Edit**, **Find (on this page)**, which I must admit is a very good idea. This command tells the browser to search the current page instead of the Web itself; I'm sure some new users get confused about that issue. (On the other hand, Explorer's Search toolbar button is *not* the same as the Find command; it's for searching the Web.) You'll learn how to search the Web in Chapter 21.

Don't Forget Find Don't forget the Find command. It can come in very handy for searching long Gopher menus (see Chapter 16) and FTP file listings (Chapter 14), as well as large Web documents.

The **Find** command works in a way that's very similar to what you've probably used in other programs (in particular, in word processors). Click the **Find** button, or choose **Edit**, **Find**, and the Find dialog box opens. Type the word or words you are looking for, choose **Match Case** (if necessary), and then click **Find Next**. The browser moves the document so that the first line containing the word or words you are searching for is at the top of the window.

Remember to Right-Click

Remember to use the shortcut menus that appear when you right-click on items. Both Netscape and Internet Explorer use them, as do some other browsers. The shortcut menu is a new toy in the programmer's toy box—and a very nice one at that. (The Macintosh mouse has only one button; on Mac browsers you may be able to access a pop-up menu by pressing the button and holding it down.) Experiment by right-clicking links, pictures, and the background, and you'll find all sorts of useful commands, such as those listed here:

Copy Shortcut or **Copy Link Location**:   Copies the URL from the link to the Clipboard.

Open: Opens the related document, just as if you clicked the link.

Open in New Window: Opens a new window and loads the document referenced by the link you clicked.

Save Target As or **Save Link As**:   Transfers the referenced document and saves it on your hard disk without bothering to display it in the browser first.

Add Bookmark or **Add to Favorites**:   Places an entry for the document referenced by the link in the bookmark or Favorites system.

That's not all, of course. Look to see what else is available. You'll find commands for moving back through framed documents, saving image files, saving background images as your desktop wallpaper, adding wallpaper, sending the Web page in an e-mail message, and so on. Oh, which reminds me: maybe you should learn how to save such things from the Web, eh?

Is It Worth Saving?

A lot of it really is. Yes, I know that multimedia consultant and author William Horton has called the Web a "GITSO" system. You've heard of GIGO, haven't you? Garbage In, Garbage Out. Well, the Web is a Garbage In, Toxic Sludge Out system.

There really is a lot of sludge out there. But it's not *all* sludge. Much of it really is worth saving. And now and then that's just what you'll want to do: save some of it to your hard disk. Let's look at two aspects in particular: how to save and what you can save.

You can save many, many things from the Web. Most browsers work in much the same way, though one or two have a few nice little extra "save" features. Here's what you can save:

➤ **Save the document text.** You can copy text from a browser to the Clipboard and then paste the text into another application. Or you can use the **File**, **Save As** command, which enables you to choose to save the document as plain text (that is, without all the little codes used to create a Web document; you'll look at those in Chapter 9).

77

➤ **Save the HTML *source* document.** The source document is the HTML (HyperText Markup Language) document used to create the document that you actually see in your browser. The source document has lots of funky little codes, which you'll understand completely after you read Chapter 9. (Well, perhaps not completely, but at least you'll understand the basic codes.) Once you begin creating your own Web pages (you were planning to do that, weren't you?; everyone else and his dog is), you may want to save source documents so you can "borrow" bits of them. Use **File**, **Save As** and choose to save as HTML.

> **It's Not Yours** Remember that much of what you come across on the Web is copyrighted material. Unless you are sure that what you are viewing is not copyrighted, you should assume that it *is*.

➤ **Save the text or HTML source for documents you haven't even viewed.** You don't have to view a page before you save it (though to be honest, I haven't yet figured out why you would want to save it if you haven't seen it). Simply right-click the link and choose **Save Target As** or **Save Link As** from the shortcut menu.

➤ **Save inline images in graphics files.** You can copy images you see in Web pages directly to your hard drive. Right-click an image and choose **Save Image As** or **Save Picture As**.

➤ **Save the document background.** Internet Explorer even lets you save the small image that is used to put the background color or pattern in many documents. Right-click the background and choose **Save Background As**.

➤ **Create Windows wallpaper.** Internet Explorer also lets you quickly take an image or background from a document and use it as your Windows wallpaper image. Right-click the picture or the background and choose **Set as Wallpaper**.

➤ **Copy images to the Clipboard.** With this neat Explorer feature you can copy images and background images directly to the Clipboard. Right-click, and then choose **Copy** or **Copy Background** from the shortcut menu.

➤ **Print the document.** Most browsers have a **File**, **Print** command and maybe even a Print button. Likewise, you'll often find a Page Setup command that lets you set margins and create headers and footers.

➤ **Save URLs to the Clipboard.** You can save URLs to the Clipboard, so you can copy them into another program. Copy the URL directly from the Address or Location text box, or right-click a link and choose **Copy Shortcut** or **Copy Link Location**. Some browsers' versions of Netscape also allow you to drag a link onto a document in another program; the link's URL will appear in the document.

➤ **Grab files directly from the cache.** Remember that the cache is dynamic; the browser is constantly adding files to and removing files from it. If you have something you want to save, you can copy it directly from the cache. Internet Explorer makes this easy; you simply click the **View Files** button in the Options dialog box. With Netscape, you can view the directory holding the files. However, Netscape renames files, making them hard to identify. Explorer names each file with its URL. You can also find special programs that will help you view and manage files in your cache; see Appendix A for information about tracking down software.

➤ **Save computer files referenced by links.** Many links do not point to other Web documents; they point to files of other formats—which opens a whole can of worms that we'll explore right now.

Grabbing Files from the Web

I like to group these nondocument files into the two following types:

➤ **Files that you want to transfer to your hard disk.** A link might point to an .EXE or .ZIP file (a program file or a .ZIP archive file) that contains a program you want to install on your computer. We'll be talking about file formats in Chapter 19. (and see Appendix A for a list of sources of shareware programs, which would fall into this category.)

➤ **Files that you want to play or view.** Other files are not things you want to keep; instead, they are files containing items such as sounds (music and speech), video, graphics of many kinds, word processing documents, and so on, that are part of the Web site you are viewing.

Both types of files are the same in one way: whatever you want to do with them—whether you want to save them or simply play them—you *must* transfer them to your computer. However, the purpose of the transfer is different, and the way it's carried out is different.

In the second case (when you want to play or display a file), you might have to configure a special viewer, helper application, or plug-in, so that when the browser transfers the file it knows how to play or display it. We'll look at such things in detail in Chapter 8. For now, we're only interested in the first type of file—a file that you want to transfer and save on your hard disk.

Web authors can distribute computer files directly from their Web documents. Several years ago, pretty much the only file libraries were FTP sites (covered in Chapter 14). Now, though, many Web sites have links to files. Companies that want to distribute their programs (shareware, freeware, or demo programs) and authors who want to distribute non-Web documents (PostScript, Word for Windows, Adobe Acrobat, and Windows Help documents, for example) can use Web sites to provide a convenient way to transfer files.

But Files Can Be in Both Categories

Files can be in both the first and second categories. What counts is not so much the type of file, but what you want to do with the file, and how your browser is configured. If you simply want to view the file right now, it would fall into the second category: view in a viewer or plug-in. If you want to save the file on your hard disk, perhaps for later use, it would fall into the first category: save on your hard disk.

Which category a file fits also depends on the manner in which the file has been saved. In its normal format, for instance, an Adobe Acrobat file (a .PDF file), could fall into either category. In some compressed formats, it would fall into the first category only because you'd have to save it to your hard disk and decompress it before you could view it. (Compressed formats are explained in Chapter 19.)

Save It

To see how you can save a file, go to TUCOWS (The Ultimate Collection of Winsock Software at **http://www.tucows.com/**). (Its logo is, as you may have guessed by now, two cows.) This site contains a fantastic library of Internet software for Windows computers.

Suppose you find a link to a program that you want to transfer. You click it as usual, and what happens? Well, if you're using Netscape, and if the file is an .exe or .com file, you'll probably see a File Save box. If so, choose the directory into which you want to save the file (by the way, we'll discuss download directories in Chapter 19). However, you might see the Unknown File Type dialog box (shown in the next figure). This box appears whenever Netscape tries to transfer a file that it doesn't recognize; Netscape wants you to tell it what to do. You can click the **Save File** button to get to the Save As dialog box, and then you can proceed to tell it where you want to save the file.

Winsock?
What's this Winsock thing? Winsock is a contraction of *Windows Sockets*, the name of the TCP/IP "driver" used to connect Windows programs to the Internet's TCP/IP system. Just as you need a print driver to connect a Windows program to a printer, you also need a special driver to connect a program to the Internet. The term Winsock refers to programs that can connect to a TCP/IP network.

Netscape doesn't know what to do with this file type, so you have to tell it.

Explorer uses a slightly different method. First it displays a dialog box showing that a file is being transferred. After a moment or two, you'll see another dialog box (you can see both in the following figure).

Internet Explorer uses a slightly different method for managing file transfers.

You now have two choices:

➤ You can tell Explorer to **Open it**, in which case Explorer transfers the file to your desktop and runs the file. This is actually a pretty lousy idea, for a couple of reasons. First, if it's a compressed archive file, you'll be expanding all files held by the archive onto the desktop, making a huge mess and mixing them in with all the other files already there. Second, the file may be a program file that will run automatically. If, by chance it contains a virus, you could be in trouble. You should check program files with virus-check software before running them. (You'll learn more about that subject in Chapter 22.)

➤ You can **Save it to disk**. This is the preferable option. Choose this and click **OK**, and the transfer will continue. Once the file has been transferred to your hard disk, you'll see a Save As dialog box in which you can choose where to place the file.

Notice the check box entitled "Always ask before opening this type of file." If you clear the check box, the next time you download a file, Explorer will automatically transfer it and open it, even if you chose the Save it to disk option button the first time. (To recheck this check box, choose **View**, **Options** and click the **File Types** tab. Then click on the file type in the list box, click **Edit**, click **Confirm Open After Download**, and click **OK**.)

The Least You Need to Know

➤ If your computer has enough memory, you can open a second Web document in a new window and keep the current window open.

➤ You'll probably end up saving Web documents on your hard disk; you can reopen them using the **File**, **Open** command.

➤ The cache stores documents you've seen on your hard disk. The browser can get those documents from the cache the next time you want to see them, which speeds up work tremendously.

➤ Reload (or Refresh in Internet Explorer) throws away the version of the page held in the cache and grabs a new one from the Web site. You can configure the cache to do this automatically once every session.

➤ You can copy, print, and save all sorts of things: document text, the document source file, images, background images, and more.

➤ If you click a link to a nondocument file, your browser may ask you what to do with it. You can save it to your hard drive if you want.

Chapter 7

Forms, Applets, and Other Web Weirdness

> **In This Chapter**
>
> ➤ Unexpected things you'll run into on the Web
> ➤ Using tables and forms
> ➤ Getting into password-protected sites
> ➤ Using frames and secondary windows
> ➤ Web programming: Java, JavaScript, and ActiveX
> ➤ Pushing, pulling, and multimedia

A couple of years ago, you wouldn't have needed this chapter. You would have understood the Web by now. That's because a couple of years ago, the Web was filled with static documents that contained pictures and text. But the Web has changed and is still changing; it's "come alive." You'll find all sorts of things that make the Web active; no longer is it just a static medium that you view.

In this chapter, you're going to take a quick look at some weird and wonderful things you might find on the Web, such as tables, forms, password-protected sites, "secondary" or "targeted" windows, and frames. You'll also learn about Java, JavaScript, and ActiveX applets, as well as push and pull commands and multimedia.

Working with Tables

A *table* is...well, you know, a table. It's a set of columns and rows in which you organize text and (sometimes) pictures. Most browsers these days can display tables. So if you are using a recent one (such as Netscape or Internet Explorer), you'll have no problems. Tables are often used to display, well, tabular data. But they can also be used as a simple page layout tool, to get pictures and text to sit in the correct places. (The following figure shows a table being used in this way.) And recent improvements to the way that browsers handle tables allow authors to use different background colors in each cell, and different border colors.

*The Discovery Channel (**http:// www.discovery .com/**) page formatted using the table feature.*

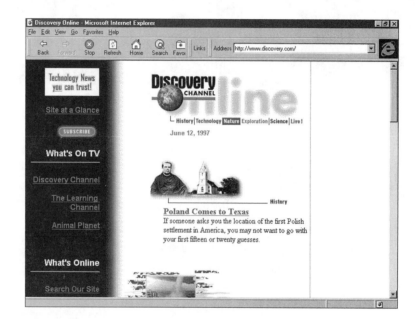

Interactive Web Pages—Using Forms

A *form* is a special *interactive* Web document. It contains the sorts of components that you've become familiar with while working in today's graphical user interfaces: text boxes, option buttons (also known as radio buttons), command buttons, check boxes, list boxes, drop-down list boxes, and so on. You'll find forms at the search sites (see Chapter 21). You use them just like you would a Windows or Macintosh dialog box: you type a search word into a text box, select any necessary options by clicking option buttons and check boxes, and then click a command button.

Forms are also used to collect information (you might have to enter your name and address when downloading demo software, for instance) and make sales. You can choose the products you want to buy and enter your credit-card information into a form. The next figure shows an order form used at the Netscape Store (**http://www.netscape.com**).

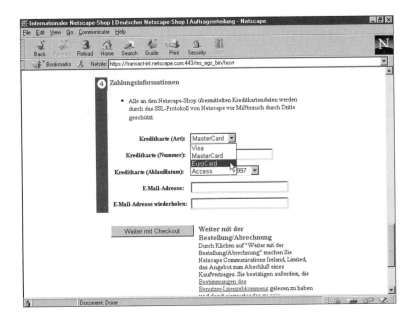

Enter all the required information, select options from the drop-down list boxes, and then click the Checkout button. (This is, of course, at the German Netscape store.)

Playing It Safe—Secure Sites

When you enter information into a form and send that information back to the Web server, there is a slight chance that it could be intercepted by someone and read. (It's not very *likely* that your information will be intercepted, but that's another story—which I'll get to in Chapter 22). Netscape, Internet Explorer, and some other browsers, provide a way to send information *securely*. If the form you are viewing comes from a special https:// server (a secure server), the information is *encrypted* before it's sent back from the form to the server. When the server receives the information, it decrypts the information. While the encrypted data is between your computer and the server, the information is useless; anyone who intercepted the information would end up with a load of garbled rubbish.

> **Just a Little Different** Forms in Web pages do function just a little differently from forms in other programs. For a start, you must click directly on an option button or check box to select it, not just on the label; in some operating systems—Windows, for instance—clicking the label will select the option or box. And while you can press Tab to move to the next field in a form in most browsers (or Shift-Tab to move to the last), this doesn't work in all browsers.

In most browsers, you know when you are at a secure site. In Internet Explorer, the little padlock icon in the lower-right corner is locked (in some versions of Explorer there is no lock until you're displaying a secure page; in others, the lock's always there, but it's open when you're at an insecure page). In some versions of Netscape Navigator there's a key in the lower-left corner of the window; the key is whole at a secure page (it's broken on non-secure pages). These versions of Navigator also display a blue bar just below the toolbars when the site is secure. Newer versions of Navigator (Version 4), don't have the blue bar or the key. Instead they use a padlock icon which is closed. You'll see the padlock icon in the lower-left corner of the browser, *and* in the toolbar; the Security button is a padlock which changes according to the type of document displayed. Other browsers use similar but slightly different methods to indicate that you are at a secure page.

One indicator of a secure site is visible in any Web browser. As you can see in the following figure, the URL of a secure Web page begins with **https://** instead of **http://**. If you send information to this site or receive information from it, you can be sure that the information will be transmitted in a secure, encrypted manner.

The https:// URL, shown on all browsers

Navigator 4 has a Security button; the padlock's locked at a secure page

Browsers use various indicators to show that a site is secure.

Navigator 2 and 3 have a blue bar

Navigator 2 and 3 have an unbroken key

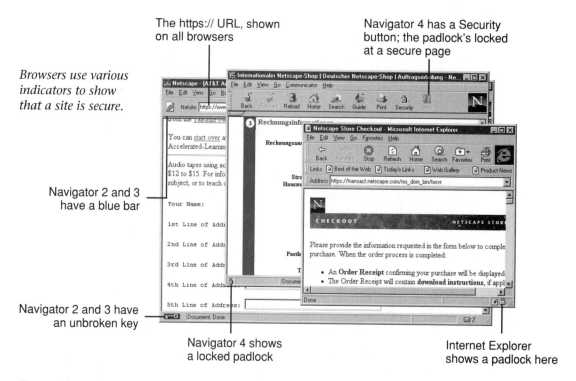

Navigator 4 shows a locked padlock

Internet Explorer shows a padlock here

For Your Eyes Only—Password-Protected Sites

One day people will actually start spending money online. Right now, however, people seem to want everything to be free. If you've paid your service provider, you don't want to pay *again* when you get where you are going, right?

Because of this, you may not find a huge number of password-protected sites right now. These are Web sites that you can't view unless you enter a password, which is given to you when you go through a registration process (which probably includes some form of wallet surgery).

You *will* find password-protected sites, however, if you enjoy Web sites with, um, lewd and lascivious content. Many adult-oriented sites use password protection as a way to keep out underage users and to force people to pay for what they want to view.

These aren't the only password-protected sites, of course. The following figure shows the Netscape Development Partners site, which is only accessible to people who have coughed up some huge sum for the privilege. In this case, you have to enter your User ID and password into a form; in other cases, the browser opens a dialog box into which you type the information. Many Webs sites use password protection to allow you to set up an account (often for free), so that when you visit you can quickly access your "user profile."

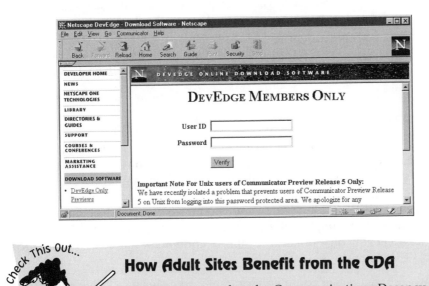

The Netscape Development Partners site; you'd better have a password if you want to get in.

How Adult Sites Benefit from the CDA

I find it amusing that the Communications Decency Act (discussed in Chapter 22) led to higher profits for the owners of porn sites. Because all but the softest of softcore moved into password-protected sites when the CDA was passed, anyone looking for these materials must pay. Before CDA many porn sites had to provide "teasers" to get people in. Now they often just say, "Sorry, you'll have to join if you want to view." (Since the CDA was declared unconstitutional this situation has been reversed to some degree.)

Dealing with Secondary Windows

I should know better, but once or twice I've been confused when I've suddenly discovered that Netscape's history list has disappeared. What happened? I clicked a link and then looked away for a moment. While my eyes were averted, another browser window opened automatically. I continued, unaware of what had happened.

Check This Out...

Public Letter to Web Authors
Dear Web authors: it's bad interface design to open a secondary window full-screen. Please open your windows slightly less than full screen, so it's obvious to your users what's going on! Signed, Confused in Denver.

If they want to, Web authors can set up a link so that when you click it a new window opens, and the referenced document appears in that window. It's a very handy feature when used properly. These windows are called *targeted* windows. (I prefer to use an older hypertext term: *secondary* windows.)

When a targeted window opens in Netscape Navigator, the history list disappears from the previous window because Netscape's history list is linked to a particular window. In newer versions of Navigator you *can* still use the history list, from the Go menu, though the Back button won't work. And that's how it works in all versions of Internet Explorer—while the Back and Forward commands stop working in that browser, you can still access the full history list and get back to a previous page.

Panes or Frames

Another new feature you may find while browsing on the Web is *frames*. (In other earlier hypertext systems, these were sometimes known as *panes*). The following figure shows an example of frames. When you open a framed document, you find that it displays two or more documents, each within its own pane. The frames around each document may be moveable (if the author set them up that way), and you may have scroll bars in each pane. Why put documents in frames? Well, for example, you might find a table of contents in one frame; clicking on a link in the table of contents would load the specified document into the other frame.

Some browsers have a special reload command for frames: click inside a frame and then choose **View**, **Reload Frame** to reload the contents of that one frame. Some versions of the Netscape browser also have a **Back in Frame** command with which you can move back to the previously viewed document within the frame. Navigator Version 2 had a real problem with frames, though; using the Back command took you all the way out of the frames, perhaps many steps back, rather than showing you the previous document you viewed within the frames. Internet Explorer and the more recent versions of Navigator (Navigator Version 4) have no Back in Frame command; instead they assume that if you're using the Back command you want to go back step by step, not all the way out of the frames.

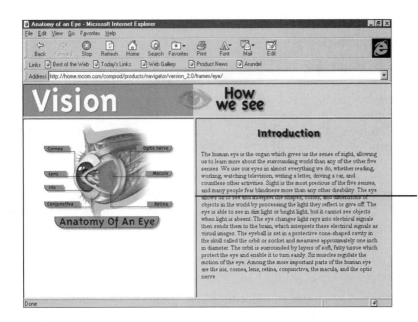

The How We See demo shows a good use of framed documents. Click parts of the eye in the left frame to see information in the right frame.

This bar divides the frames

Animated Icons

Animated icons are becoming popular these days. These are little pictures embedded into Web documents that appear to be in motion. They are relatively easy for Web authors to create, so you can expect to see many more of them appearing on the Web. They add a little motion to a page (this is known in Web jargon as "making a page more compelling"), without causing a lot of extra stuff to be transmitted to your computer.

If you find large and complicated things in motion, you've stumbled across some kind of video or animation file format (see Chapter 8) or perhaps an actual Web program created in Java or ActiveX, which we'll look at next.

Web Programs Java, JavaScript, and ActiveX

You may have heard of Java by now. I'm not talking about a chain of coffee bars; I'm talking about a new programming language that will (if you believe the hype) make the Web more exciting, make every appliance from toasters to dishwashers talk to you in Swahili, bring about world peace, and lead to a complete and total eradication of body odor.

That may be true, but for the moment Java is to a great extent a programmer's toy. It may take over the world one day, but right now you'll find that Java applications on the Web (sorry, "Java applets") are mostly fairly small programs that do nothing more extravagant than add some life to an otherwise-dull Web page. Still, you may be surprised when you arrive at a Web site and see a moving text banner or bouncing heads. That's often (though not always) Java at work. In a few cases you'll find something more ambitious, but at the moment not very often.

Java Interpreters

Java-compatible browsers are Java "interpreters." In effect, an interpreter is a program that can run another program, coordinating between the computer's operating system and the program. So a Java applet can run on any operating system (Windows 3.1, Windows 95, Macintosh System 7, and UNIX of various flavors) as long as there is an interpreter created for that operating system. Both Netscape Navigator and Internet Explorer are Java interpreters.

In order for these programs to work, you must be using a Java-compatible Web browser—and even then they may not work. Netscape 2.0 and later versions, and Internet Explorer 3.0 and later versions, are Java-compatible. The later the version, the more likely that the Java applet will function (Netscape Navigator 2, for instance, really doesn't handle Java applets very well). But even if you have the very latest browser, you may still run into problems.

When you reach a Web page that has an embedded Java applet, the Java program is transmitted to your computer, and the browser then runs the program. The program may be a game of some sort, a multimedia display, a financial calculator of some kind, or just about anything else. The following figure shows one of the better and more advanced applets, a "chat" program (we'll look at chat in detail in Chapter 17). You can find links to Java apps at Gamelan (**http://www.gamelan.com/**).

TalkCity's new chat program is a Java applet.

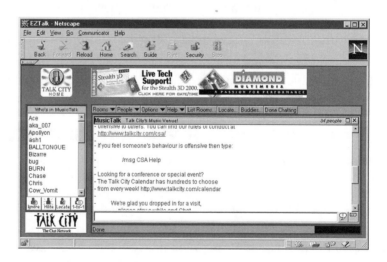

I think Java has been greatly over-hyped (can you tell?). For all the overblown projections, Java applets remain rarely used, unreliable, and slow. (And, in many cases, pointless.) Quite frankly, I don't really see the point of using Java to turn your Web browser into a command-line interface, as one Java applet I saw does. (You have Telnet for that; see Chapter 20.) Searching for interesting or useful Java applets is an experience in frustration and disappointment, with only an occasional surprise. Maybe someday Java will fulfill its promise. But it won't be soon, so don't hold your breath.

Applications Across the Net

You may have heard the theory that pretty soon, instead of buying software and installing it on your hard drive, you'll "rent" programs across the Internet, paying for the time you use. If this *ever* happens (and there are good reasons to suspect it won't), it will be a very long time from now. Internet connections are currently about as reliable and efficient as a drunk at a beer tasting, and until they are as reliable as the electricity supply, this system simply won't work. I've added this projection to my "yeah, right, don't hold your breath" list.

What About JavaScript and ActiveX?

JavaScript is Java's baby brother. It's a scripting language in which programs are written within the Web page. In other words, a JavaScript-compatible browser reads the Web page, extracts the JavaScript commands, and runs them. JavaScript is not as powerful a programming language as Java, but it's easier to create programs using JavaScript, so it's more common. You can find loads of JavaScript programs at Gamelan (**http:// www.gamelan.com/pages/Gamelan.related.javascript.html**) and The JavaScript Index (**http://www.sapphire.co.uk/javascript/**). The following figure shows an example of a JavaScript application, taken from a book I wrote on the subject.

Finally, there's ActiveX. A competitor to Java, ActiveX is a new system from Microsoft, designed to allow Web authors to easily incorporate multimedia and programs into their Web pages. Currently the only ActiveX browser is Internet Explorer, and you can probably expect it to stay that way for a while. With Netscape as the most popular browser, there's not much incentive for Netscape Communications to add ActiveX to Netscape and help their major competitor! (On the other hand, as Internet Explorer gains Web share—which it seems to be doing fairly steadily—that situation may change.)

My Area Code program, written in JavaScript.

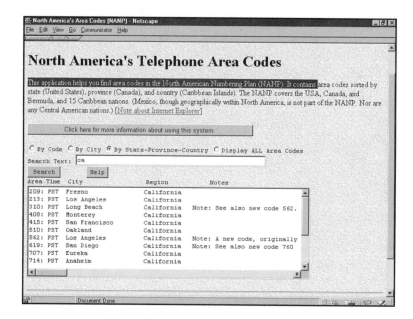

Just a Little Shove—Pushing and Pulling

Web authors can set up their Web pages to do things by themselves. Currently, information arrives at your screen because you've directly requested it—by clicking a link or entering a URL. However, Web pages will soon be using *server push* and *client pull*.

The first of these, *server push*, occurs when the Web server continues sending information even though you haven't requested it. For instance, suppose you click a link to display a Web page, and just a few minutes later, the Web page changes. Even if you don't request more information, the server sends updated information and continues to send periodic updates until you close the page.

Client pull is similar, except that the request for updates comes from the browser. For instance, suppose that you open a page. At the same time the server sends the page, it sends a special program (you don't see this; it all happens in the "background"). This program tells the browser when to request updates. After the defined interval, the browser sends a request to the server asking for the information. Again, this will continue until you leave the page.

These systems work so similarly that you usually won't know which method is being used. They are very useful when you're viewing information that changes rapidly, such as stock quotes, weather reports, news headlines, or auctions.

The Web Gets More Complicated

As you'll see in Chapter 9, creating a simple Web page is really quite easy. And even many of the more advanced Web-authoring techniques are not particularly complicated. Sure, there are special codes to learn, but it's all reasonably straightforward.

But now we're seeing the introduction of things that the average Web author will find much more complicated to use. Technologies such as Java, JavaScript, ActiveX, and push and pull require some programming skills. As a result, it's becoming harder for Web authors to keep up with the Joneses (technologically speaking), which may be a good thing. Now they can concentrate on function instead of form, forget about the glitz, and compete by making their Web sites interesting and content-rich instead of just trying to be "cool."

The Multimedia Experience

You'll find all sorts of file formats on the World Wide Web. You'll find a variety of still pictures, video and animations, sounds, electronic documents, 3-D images, and so on. Any file format that you can play or display on your computer can be linked to a Web page.

When you click a link that takes you to one of these file formats, Netscape handles the file itself, if it can. It displays the document or picture in the window in the normal way. But if the file is a format that Netscape can't handle, it has two options. It may send the file directly to a program that *can* handle it (known as a *plug-in, viewer,* or *helper*), or it may ask you what to do. We'll take a look at this subject in Chapter 8.

Before we move on, though, a quick thought related to this issue:

The Internet is not a multimedia system!

Remember that, and you'll be saved a lot of frustration. This statement may seem a little strange, after you've been bombarded by several years of advertising and media hype about the Internet. We've all seen the TV ads in which video rolls across a computer screen, within a Web browser, as quickly as if it were being displayed on...well, on a TV screen. But the Internet does *not* work that quickly, and many of its problems seem to arise from people trying to treat it as if it does.

As a multimedia forum the Internet is primitive, mainly because it's so slow. If it's "lights, cameras, action" that you're after, use the TV or go see a movie; the Internet simply can't compete. The Web, for instance, is primarily a *text based system!* All the hype in the world won't change that. What will change that is much faster connections from people's homes to the Internet, faster Web servers, and faster and more reliable "backbone" connections across the Internet. But don't hold your breath, because you'll turn blue before these things appear on the scene (see Chapter 25 for a discussion of that issue).

The Least You Need to Know

➤ The Web is far more diverse than it was a year or two ago; it's much more than just text with pictures.

➤ You'll find lots of tables and forms.

➤ Framed documents allow an author to split a document into multiple pieces, each of which is displayed in its own frame.

➤ Java, JavaScript, and ActiveX are Web programming languages that let authors bring their pages to life.

➤ Client pull is a system by which a browser automatically requests updates to a page. Server push is a system by which a server automatically sends updates.

➤ A wide range of multimedia formats must be displayed in viewers or plug-ins; you'll learn about those in Chapter 8.

Web Multimedia

In This Chapter

➤ How does a browser handle different file formats?

➤ Finding plug-ins and viewers

➤ Types of plug-ins and viewers you may want

➤ Installing plug-ins

➤ Installing viewers in Netscape

➤ Installing viewers in Internet Explorer

As the Web gets older, and as people start using it more, it's storing more and more types of computer files. You'll find animations, videos, pictures of various formats, sounds that play once they've transferred to your computer, sounds that play *as* they transfer to your computer, "slide" presentations, and all sorts of other weird and wonderful things. Think of this as the *multimedia* content of the Web—literally "multiple media." But remember that, as I explained in the previous chapter, the Internet is not a *true* multimedia system. Yes, it has many types of media. But they tend to move rather slowly!

Today's Web browsers are designed to handle *any* computer-file format. So when you click a link to a file, that file is transferred to your computer and your browser can then use it in one of three ways:

➤ **On its own**   The file format may be one that the browser can handle directly. Web browsers can play or display Web pages (.HTM or .HTML), text documents (.TXT), some graphics formats (.GIF, .XBM, .JPG, and .JPEG), and some sound formats.

➤ **With a plug-in**   The browser may open a *plug-in*, a special add-on program that plays or displays the file within the browser window.

➤ **With a viewer (or helper)**   The browser may send the file to a *viewer* or *helper*—a separate program that recognizes the file format. That program then opens a window in which the file is played or displayed.

When you first get your browser, it probably *won't* recognize all of the file formats you'll encounter. When the browser comes across a file format that it doesn't recognize, it will ask you what to do; you can then install a new plug-in or viewer to handle that file type.

Two Types of Multimedia Inclusions

There are basically two ways to include a multimedia file in a Web page. The author may include the file as a *live* or *embedded object* (a file that is automatically transferred to your computer along with the Web page). For instance, an embedded file may play a background sound or display a video within the Web page. On the other hand, the author can include the file as an *external* file; you click a link and that file alone (without a Web page) is transferred to your computer.

What's Available?

Which Plug-Ins Are Installed?
In Netscape Navigator you can quickly find out which plug-ins are installed by choosing **Help, About Plug-ins**. You'll see a page showing you each plug-in and its file name. You'll also find a link to the Inline Plug-Ins page where you can download more.

Scores of plug-ins and viewers are available; you just have to know where to find them. A good starting point for Netscape Navigator plug-ins is the Netscape Navigator Components page, at **http://home.netscape.com/ comprod/mirror/navcomponents_download.html**. You can find links to viewers and plug-ins that will work in Internet Explorer at **http://www.microsoft.com/ie/ addons/**. You can also find many viewers at the sites discussed in Appendix A.

About now you're probably wondering whether you should use a plug-in or a viewer. In general you'll probably prefer working with plug-ins because they allow the browser itself to display or play the file. In effect, a plug-in extends the capabilities of the browser, allowing it to work with a file type that it couldn't use before. A viewer, on the other hand, is a completely separate program; the Web browser remains at the previous Web page, while the multimedia file is sent to the viewer.

Of course, there may be cases in which a viewer is actually a better program and has more features than the equivalent plug-in. You may want to experiment and find the most capable of the two.

Which Do You Need? Which Do You Want?

You really don't need all the viewers and plug-ins available. There are literally hundreds already—over 150 plug-ins for Netscape Navigator alone—and more are being added all the time. So unless you are independently wealthy and don't need to waste time working, you probably won't have time to install them all (and you probably don't have the disk space you'd need). To help you determine which plug-ins and viewers you should get, I've broken them down into a few categories and the most common file formats. You may not want to get them until you really need them, though.

Music and Voice (Very Useful)

Some of the most useful plug-ins and viewers are those for music and voice. In particular, you may want RealAudio, TrueSpeech, and StreamWorks, three different systems that allow a sound file to play as it is being transferred. (RealAudio is the most popular, and so the most useful, of these sound formats.)

Most sound formats can't play until they have been completely transferred to your disk drive (you twiddle your thumbs for ten minutes—and then listen). The RealAudio, TrueSpeech, and StreamWorks formats play sounds as they are being transferred, though. They're used by radio stations and music libraries, for example, so you can listen to the news from National Public Radio (**http://www.npr.org**) or music from the Internet Underground Music Archives (**http://www.iuma.com**). The following illustration shows Netscape Navigatorusing RealAudio to play a file from the NPR site.

During your Internet travels, you are likely to come across these other sound formats:

.AU, .AIF, .AIFF, .AIFC, and .SND   A variety of common sound formats, used on UNIX and on the Mac. Your browser can probably play these without an additional plug-in or viewer.

.WAV   The Windows sound format. Your browser can probably play these without an additional plug-in or viewer.

.MID and .RMI   These are MIDI (Musical Instrument Digital Interface) formats. You may need to add a plug-in or viewer for these. (Netscape Navigator 3 and 4 come with a pre-installed plug-in that will work with MIDI files.)

The RealAudio viewer playing the newscast from NPR.

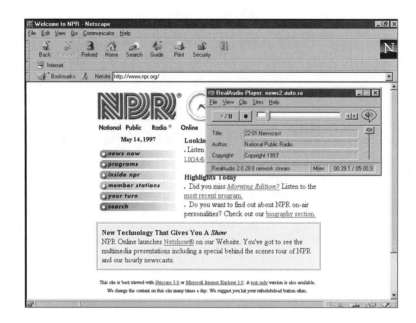

The MIDI formats are not common, but they are of interest to people who, well, are interested in MIDI. Many MIDI sites on the Web have sound clips. (MIDI is a system used to create music using computers and other electronic toys.)

You Already Have Viewers In many cases, you may already have viewers for certain file formats. For instance, if you use Windows, you can use the Windows Media Player as a viewer for MIDI files. If you use the Macintosh and have Word, you can use Word as the viewer for Word .DOC files.

Other Document Formats (Also Very Useful)

Viewers and plug-ins are also available for a number of document formats that you'll find on the Web. In particular, the Adobe Acrobat Reader is useful. Adobe Acrobat is a hypertext format that actually predates the Web. It allows an author to create a multipage hypertext document that is contained in a single file, and which can be read by any Acrobat reader, regardless of the operating system it is running on. Many authors like to use Acrobat because it gives them more control over the layout than they get when creating Web pages. You'll often find documents in Acrobat format linked to Web pages. You can see an example of an Acrobat file in the following figure.

You'll also find viewers and plug-ins that display Microsoft Word, Envoy, and PostScript documents.

An Adobe Acrobat file from the New York Times, displayed in the Adobe Acrobat viewer.

3-D Worlds (Greatly Overrated!)

Netscape Navigator has a plug-in called Live3D that you can use to view 3-D images on the Web (see the next figure). Live3D may have been installed when you installed Netscape, depending on which version you have. You can download other 3-D plug-ins or viewers, too.

Do you really want a 3-D plug-in or viewer? Probably not. Once you've seen a couple of 3-D sites, the novelty will quickly wear off. This is another of those much-touted technologies that hasn't yet lived up to the hype. 3-D images load slowly and move slowly. They are, in my opinion, an unnecessary gimmick. Perhaps one day they'll be an integral part of the Web, but for now they're little more than a toy.

> **Check This Out...**
>
> **VRML** These 3-D images are in a format known as VRML: Virtual Reality Modeling Language.

Video (If You Can Wait)

Video is fairly popular on the Web, but it has serious drawbacks. The main problem is speed. It can take literally hours for anything big to transfer, and if it's small, well, what's the point? After waiting an eternity to watch a five-second cut from a movie, I was left with the question "was that really worth it?" ringing in my head.

Video is another of those things that really requires a fast connection. If you are on a corporate network you are probably okay—assuming the video clip is stored on a fast server and the Internet itself is not as sluggish as mollasses on a cold day—but if you are using a modem to connect to a service provider you'll find it rather slow.

You can walk around these buildings, and maybe even into them. Cute but slow (and not terribly exciting once you've done it once or twice).

Still, if you want to try it, you can find many viewers and plug-ins for video. The most common formats are the Windows .AVI and QuickTime formats (which may be built into your browser already), and MPEG. A new format, .VIV, is a compressed .AVI file that provides streaming video. The following figure shows Netscape's simple plug-in. Netscape 3.0 comes with a built-in .AVI plug-in, but other .AVI plug-ins and viewers actually have more features.

*A tornado touches down in Miami; a QuickTime video from CNN (**http:// www.cnn.com/**).*

Streaming Video

I mentioned RealAudio earlier; RealAudio is a "streaming" audio format, which means it plays as it transmits. That's the new thing in video, too. Not too long ago you'd have to wait for a video file to transfer completely before you could play it. Now streaming video viewers and plug-ins are turning up; these play the video as it transmits.

Animations (Here and There)

You'll find many animation plug-ins and viewers, but only a few different formats are commonly used on the Web. It's popular these days for any software company with a proprietary file format to create a plug-in for it. But very few Web authors are actually using animation, and only a few of the available formats are commonly used. Probably the most common animation formats are Macromedia's Authorware and Directory animations, which can be viewed using the Shockwave plug-in. (What do I mean by animation, as opposed to video? Think of video as a film; think of animation as a cartoon.)

Other Weird File Formats

You'll find plug-ins and viewers available for all sorts of unusual file formats. And some plug-ins are not really programs designed for handling particular file formats that you may come across while cruising the Web; they are more like special utilities designed to extend the features of the Web browser. For instance, there are Netscape plug-ins available for these:

➤ **Carbon Copy**   A Netscape plug-in that lets you control a PC across the Internet.

➤ **Chemscape Chime**   A plug-in for 2-D and 3-D chemical models.

➤ **EarthTime**   A plug-in that displays eight different times from cities around the world.

➤ **ISYS Hindsight**   A plug-in that keeps a record of every Web page you've seen and even allows you to search the text in those pages.

➤ **Look@Me**   Allows you to view another user's computer screen across the Web and see what's going on. (Assuming they *want* you to see what's going on, of course.)

➤ **Net-Install**   A plug-in designed to automate the transfer and installation of software across the Internet.

Looking for Samples? A good place to find samples of these various multimedia formats is the Netscape plug-ins page that I mentioned earlier. For each plug-in or viewer you'll find links to Web sites using the file format handled by that program.

As I mentioned earlier, though, any file type can be sent to a viewer of some kind. However, there are only a handful that are commonly used (the ones I mentioned earlier as the common formats). You'll only want to install other plug-ins and viewers if the particular file type happens to be used at the Web sites that you frequent.

You don't necessarily need to install these plug-ins or viewers right away. You can wait until you stumble across a link to one of the file formats. If your browser doesn't recognize the format, it will ask you what to do with the file. We'll look at installing viewers and plug-ins next.

Installing a Plug-In

Installing a plug-in is very easy. Simply transfer the installation file from the Web and place it in a download directory (see Chapter 19). Then run the file (double-click it, for instance) to run the installation program. The installation program may run immediately, or you may find that a series of files are extracted from the one you downloaded, in which case you have to run a setup.exe file to start the installation program.

Follow the instructions to install the file. When it's finished, your browser will be able to automatically call the plug-in anytime it needs it.

By the way, your browser may sometimes tell you when you need a plug-in. For instance, if you see the dialog box shown in the following figure (or something similar), you have displayed a Web page with an embedded file format that requires a plug-in. You can simply click the **Get the Plugin** button, and the browser will open another window and take you to a page with information about plug-ins.

This Netscape dialog box opens when you click a link that loads a file requiring a plug-in you don't have.

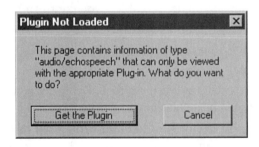

Installing a Viewer

Installing a viewer is a little more complicated than installing a plug-in, but it's still not rocket science. There are actually two different types of viewer installations. One is the type used by the early versions of Netscape, and the Macintosh and UNIX versions of Netscape, where you tell the browser which viewer to work with for each file type. The other is the type used by the Windows versions of Internet Explorer, and by the Windows versions of Netscape Navigator 4. These use the Windows file associations to set up viewers. For instance, by default Windows associates .WAV files with the Sound Recorder program. That means if you double-click a .WAV file in File Manager, Sound Recorder opens and plays the file. Internet Explorer and Navigator 4 use the same system-wide file association system to determine which program should be used when it comes across a file type.

The next section gives you a look at installing a viewer in an Netscape Navigator 3 (which is very similar to the system used in many other browsers). The section after that covers installing a viewer in Internet Explorer.

Installing a Viewer in Netscape

We're going to take a look at how to configure a viewer in the Windows version of Netscape Navigator. The process is similar in other versions of Netscape, and even in some other browsers. Note, however, that all the process is the same in Navigator 4; if you're using a Windows version of Navigator 4, you are actually going to modify the Windows file-association settings. In earlier versions Navigator stored its own list of associations, rather than using the Windows list.

Let's say you've came across a link that looked interesting, and you clicked it. Netscape displayed the Unknown File Type dialog box, shown here. This means that Netscape doesn't recognize the file…so you have to tell it what to do.

The Unknown File Type dialog box opens if you click a link to a file that Netscape doesn't recognize.

If you want, you can click the **More Info** button. Netscape will open another browser window and display an information document with a link to a page from which you can download a plug-in. Let's assume that you already know there is no plug-in for this particular file type, or that for some other reason you want to configure a viewer. Click the **Pick App** button, and you'll see the dialog box in the following figure.

*The Configure
External Viewer
dialog box lets you
define which viewer
should handle the file
type.*

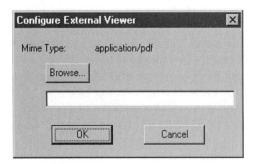

Click the **Browse** button and then find the program that you know can handle this type of file. (Remember, you can find viewers at the sites listed in Appendix A.) Double-click the program, and it is placed into the Configure External Viewer dialog box. Then click **OK**. That's it! You've just configured the viewer.

The file referenced by the link you clicked will now be transferred to your computer and sent to the program you defined as the viewer. The viewer will then display the file (assuming, of course, that you picked the right viewer).

Setting Up Netscape Beforehand

You can also set up Netscape's viewers before you ever get to a site that uses unusual file formats. Choose **Options**, **General Preferences**, and then click the **Helpers** tab. You'll see the dialog box shown here. (In Navigator 4 you'll choose **Edit**, **Preferences**, then open the Navigator category and click on the Applications subcategory; the process is similar to what I'm going to describe here.)

What's That Button For? In case you're wondering, the Unknown: Prompt User option button is the default setting for formats that haven't been set up with a viewer. If you click a file for which you've configured this setting, Netscape will ask you what to do with the files of this type when they are transferred to your browser.

The big list shows all of the different file types (well, most of them; you can add more using the **Create New Type** button). To configure a viewer for one, click it in the list and then click one of the **Actions**. You can tell Netscape to **Save to Disk** if you want, but if you intend to configure a viewer, click **Launch the Application** instead. Then click the **Browse** button to find the application you want to use as the viewer.

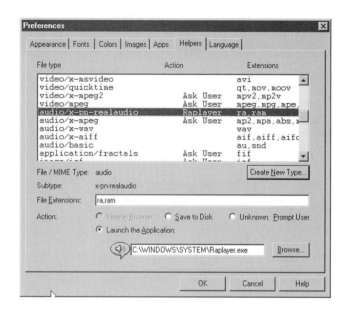

You can preconfigure viewers in Netscape's Preferences dialog box.

Installing a Viewer in Internet Explorer

Internet Explorer uses a similar system to that used by Netscape Navigator. However, instead of simply modifying Internet Explorer's internal settings, you are actually modifying the Windows file-association settings.

When you click a file type that Explorer doesn't recognize, it opens the dialog box shown in the following figure. (This is similar to what you saw from Netscape.) Because Explorer doesn't recognize the file type, you have to tell it what to do. Click the **Open it using an application on your computer** option button, and then click **OK.** Explorer transfers the file and then tries to open it.

You'll then see the Open With dialog box, shown next. Type a name for this type of file into the text box at the top. Then, if you can find the viewer you want to use in this list, click it and click **OK.** If you can't find it, click the **Other** button. In the Open dialog box that appears, select the viewer you want to use.

As with Netscape, you can always install an Internet Explorer viewer before you need it. You do this using the File Types system, which you can access from the Windows Explorer file management utility or from within Internet Explorer itself. Within Internet Explorer, choose **View**, **Options**, and then click the **File Types** tab. You'll see the Options dialog box shown in the following figure.

If Explorer doesn't recognize a file, you will see this dialog box.

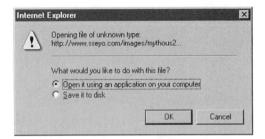

Enter a name for the file type, and then choose the application you want to use as a viewer.

To add a new viewer, click the **New Type** button, and then fill in all the information in the dialog box that appears. Enter the description (whatever you want to call it), the file extensions used by that file type, and the MIME type. Click the **New** button and type **open** in the first text box you see. Then click the **Browse** button and find the application you want to use as the viewer.

What's MIME?

MIME stands for Multipurpose Internet Mail Extensions. Though originally intended for e-mail transmission of files, it's used on the Web to identify file formats. You can find detailed information about MIME and a large list of MIME types at **http://sd-www.jsc.nasa.gov/mime-types/** or at **http:// home.netscape.com/assist/helper_apps/mime.html.**

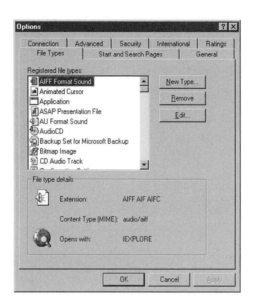

You can add viewers to Internet Explorer using the Options dialog box.

The Least You Need to Know

➤ A browser can handle many file formats: HTML, text, graphics, and sounds of various kinds. If it encounters a file format that it can't handle, it tries to pass the file to a viewer or plug-in.

➤ Viewers and plug-ins are designed to play or display file types that browsers can't handle. The difference between the two is that a plug-in temporarily converts the browser window into a viewer, while a viewer is a completely separate program that opens without changing the browser window in any way.

➤ There are literally hundreds of viewers and plug-ins, for scores of file types. Most of these file types are rarely used, however.

➤ Plug-ins are more convenient than viewers are. However, if you find a viewer that has more features than the plug-in, use it.

➤ If your browser comes across a file type that it can't recognize, it asks what to do. You can then install a plug-in or specify a viewer.

Chapter 9

Your Very Own Web Page

In This Chapter

➤ Your 10-minute Web page

➤ Setting a page as your home page

➤ Why create your own Web pages?

➤ All about HTML

➤ Adding links

➤ Creating a hierarchy of pages linked to the home page

➤ Shortcuts to grabbing links

When we first sat down to discuss what should go in the third edition of this book, someone mentioned that people were asking for information about creating their own Web pages. Quite frankly, I was skeptical. "This is an introduction to the Internet," I said. "That's a bit advanced, isn't it?" Indeed, it may seem a bit advanced to you, too. After all, you've barely learned how to get onto the Internet, and all of a sudden you can *contribute* to the Internet? Not likely!

Well, actually it's very likely. And more importantly, it's very easy. Creating a Web page is quite simple...so simple that I'm betting I can teach you to create a simple Web page in, oh, one chapter. No, I take that back! I'll bet you can create a very simple customized Web page in about 10 minutes. I'll cheat a little, though by giving you a template, in which you can fill in the "blanks."

My Fill-in-the-Blanks Web Page

I've created a Web page for you; you can get it from the e-mail responder. Send an e-mail message to **ciginternet@mcp.com**, with **ownweb** in the subject line of the message. When you receive the message, save it as a text file with the .HTM extension. Then open the file in a text editor, such as SimpleText (on the Mac) or Notepad (in Windows). Remove all of the text *before* the <HTML> text. (*Don't* remove the <HTML> part; just remove all of the text prior to it.) And remove any text that appears after </BODY>, near the bottom of the message. For more information about using the mail responder, see Appendix C.

You can use a word processor if you wish, but when you finish you'll have to remember to save the file as a text file instead of as a normal word processing file. As you'll learn later in this chapter, Web pages are simple text files. And although you *could* use a word processor, in many cases it's not a great idea because they often automatically insert special characters such as curly quotation marks and em dashes, characters that can't be converted to plain text. Therefore, you're better using a text editor.

For the impatient among you, those who don't wish to wait for the mail to arrive, I've included the text from that file here. You can type the following lines into your text editor if you want, but you must make sure you type it exactly the same as it appears here.

```
<HTML>
<HEAD>
<TITLE>My Very Own Web Page—Replace if You Want</TITLE>
</HEAD>
<BODY>
<H1>Replace This Title With Whatever You Want</H1>
Put whatever text you want here.<P>
This is another paragraph; use whatever text you want.
<H2>First Subcategory: Replace this With Whatever Title You Want</H2>
<A HREF="http://www.mcp.com">The Macmillan Web Site</A><P>
<A HREF="url_here">Another link: replace this text</A><P>
<A HREF="url_here">Another link: replace this text</A><P>
<A HREF="url_here">Another link: replace this text</A><P>
<A HREF="url_here">Another link: replace this text</A>
<H2>Second Subcategory: Replace this With Whatever Title You Want</H2>
Put more text and links here.
<H2>Third Subcategory: Replace this With Whatever Title You Want</H2>
Put more text and links here.
<H2>Fourth Subcategory: Replace this With Whatever Title You Want</H2>
Put more text and links here.
</BODY>
</HTML>
```

The following figure shows you what this file looks like when displayed in a Web browser.

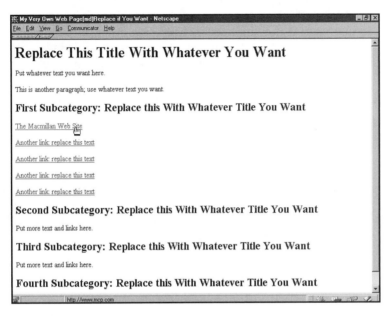

This is what the Web page template looks like in a Web browser.

For now, don't worry if you don't *understand* what is going on here; you're trying to break a speed record, not actually learn right now. In a few moments, I'll explain how this whole Web-creation thing works.

Before I get to that, though, I want you to replace some things. You can start with the text between the <TITLE> and </TITLE> *tags*. Whatever text you type between those tags will appear in the browser's title bar (as you can see in the figure), so replace the text that's there by typing your name, or **My Home Page**, or whatever you want. When you finish doing that, replace the text between the <H1> and </H1> tags. The text you type here will be a heading—the *top level* heading, as a matter of fact. You can use the same text that you entered as the title if you want (that's what Web authors often do).

What's a Tag? Text that has a less than symbol (<) in front of it and a greater than symbol (>) after it is known as a *tag*. The tags tell your Web browser how to display the text in an HTML file.

Check This Out...

Now, save your work—but don't close the text file. Use your Web browser to open the file; you can double-click on the file in Windows File Manager or Windows Explorer, or use the browser's **File**, **Open** command. You can see the changes you've made.

Next, add some text to the file if you want. Replace the text immediately below the <H1></H1> heading, or simply remove it if you don't want it. (Notice, by the way, that you must end each paragraph with the <P> tag.) After that, replace the next headings with names of categories that describe the sort of links you want in your page. If you have favorite music sites that you visit, you might make the first heading **Music**. Another heading might be **Financial**, and another might be **Goofing Around**. It's your page. Use whatever categories you want. You can quickly see your changes by saving the file and clicking the browser's **Reload** (Netscape Navigator) or **Refresh** (Internet Explorer) button.

Before you change the "Another link..." lines, take a close look at the links I've created. The first one is a link to the Macmillan Web site. (This book is published by Que, a division of Macmillan.)

```
<A HREF="http://www.mcp.com">The Macmillan Web Site</A><P>
```

The words *The Macmillan Web Site* appear on the Web page as the actual link text; you can see those words in the figure. The URL for the linked page goes between the quotation marks, as in **"http://www.mcp.com"**. Keeping that in mind, go ahead and modify the links I've provided. For instance, you might change this:

```
<A HREF="url_here">Another link: replace this text</A><P>
```

to this:

```
<A HREF="http://www.iuma.com">Internet Underground Music Archive</A><P>
```

Check This Out...

Be Careful Make sure that you don't remove any of the < or > symbols. If you do, it can really mess up your page.

Replace all the generic links with links to Web sites you like to visit. As a shortcut, you can copy a link, paste it a few times below each category heading, and then modify each of the copied links so that they point to more Web sites. When you finish making your changes, save the page and click the browser's Reload or **Refresh** button. Right before your very eyes, you'll see your brand new 10-minute Web page. Didn't I tell you it was easy?

Make It Your Home Page

Once you've created a home page, you need to tell your browser to use it as the home page. In Internet Explorer, begin by displaying your new page in the browser window. Then choose **View**, **Options** and click the **Start and Search Pages** tab (Explorer 3) or the **Navigator** tab (Explorer 4)—see the following figure. Choose **Start Page** from the drop-down list box. (Remember, Internet Explorer uses the term *Start Page* instead of home page.) Then click the **Use Current** button.

In Internet Explorer you can click the Use Current button to select the currently displayed page as the home (start).

To make your Web page the home page in Netscape Navigator 4, load the page into the browser, then choose **Edit, Preferences**, click the **Navigator** category, and click the **Use Current Page** button. In Navigator 3 choose **Options, General Preferences**, and click the **Appearance** tab. Look for the **Browser Starts With** text box. You have to type the path and file name of the page you want to open. (For instance, in Windows 95 you would type c:\program files\netscape\navigator\ownweb.htm for a file named ownweb.htm that's in the \program files\netscape\navigator\ directory on drive C:.) Then click the **OK** button.

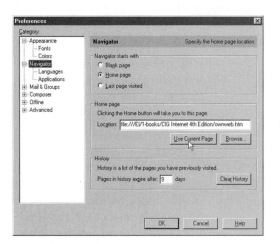

Setting the home page in Netscape Navigator 4 is similar to doing so in Internet Explorer (and much easier than in Netscape Navigator 3).

The next time you start your browser, you'll see your very own home page. And the next time you click the **Home** button, up pops your home page.

Your Web Page—What's It Good For?

Why bother creating your own page? There are a few reasons. First, telling your browser to view a home page on your hard drive will speed up loading the program. Most browsers these days are configured to use a home page at the browser publisher's Web site, but It's much quicker to load from a "local" drive than to transfer it from across the Internet. If that were the only reason, though, you could just copy an HTML document from the Web somewhere and put it on your hard drive.

The second reason has to do with the fact that everyone uses the Internet in a different way. The home page someone else has created won't have all the links you want and will contain plenty of links that you don't want. So you might as well customize your home page to work the way you want it to work and include links to sites you want to go to. You can also create a home page that has a series of documents linked to it (such as one for work, one for music, one for newsgroups, and so on).

And another reason (if you still need coaxing) is that you might want to put information about yourself or your business on the World Wide Web. You're not limited to creating a Web page for your own use and saving it on your hard drive. You can create a Web page that the world can read, saving it on your service provider's system so that it's available to the Internet at large.

First, the Basics

You've already seen how simple Web authoring can be. Now you're going to learn a bit more theory about *HTML* (Hypertext Markup Language). HTML is the "language" of the Web, and all those <xxx> tags you looked at are HTML tags.

Check This Out...

Rendering This term is used to describe the action carried out by the browser when it looks at the HTML codes and formats the text according to the instructions within those codes. It strips the codes out of the text and displays the resulting text in the browser.

HTML files are really not very complicated. They're in a simple text format. The nice thing about a simple text file is that it's widely recognized by thousands of programs and many different types of computers.

It's important to understand that while text editors (such as Notepad and SimpleText) create text files, word processors do not. A word processor is like an advanced text editor. It formats the text in many ways that simple text files cannot. It adds character formatting (italic, bold, underlines, and so on), adds special characters (curly quotation marks, copyright symbols, em and en dashes, and many others), and formats paragraph spacing, for example. That's why you have to be careful when creating HTML files in a word processor; you must save the file as text instead of in the word processor's file format.

HTML files are special text files that have been specially designed to be read by Web browsers. They use the same characters as any other text file, but they use a special convention that all Web browsers understand. That convention is this: "If you see anything in brackets like these < >, you know it's a special code." So when Web browsers are rendering the HTML document into normal text so that they can display the document on the screen, they look for these brackets and follow the instructions inside them.

You've already created a Web page, so you know what tags look like. But take a minute to go back and examine the tags you used.

<TITLE> </TITLE>   The text between these tags is the title of the document. You won't see this text in the document itself; it's simply an identifier that the browsers use. For instance, Netscape and Internet Explorer would put the text in the title bar. In addition, this title is used in bookmark and history lists.

<H1> </H1>   These particular tags mark the first level heading. You can include up to six different levels using the tags **<H2>**, **<H3>**, **<H4>**, **<H5>**, and **<H6>**. Experiment with these in your own Web page.

<P>   This tag is used at the end of a paragraph. Simply typing a carriage return in your HTML file will *not* create a new paragraph in the final document that appears in the browser. You must use the **<P>** tag instead. Without the tag, you will find that the paragraphs run together.

Notice that, in most cases, tags are paired. There's an opening and a closing tag, and the closing tag is the same as the opening tag with the exception of the forward slash after the left angle bracket. **<H1>** and **</H1>** form a pair, for instance. The **<P>** tag is one exception to this. You use only one **<P>** tag, and it appears after the paragraph.

Finally, there's an *anchor* tag, which is used to create a link:

```
<A HREF="http://www.mcp.com">The Macmillan Web Site</A><P>
```

This is simple enough. Notice that the URL is included within the angle brackets and within quotation marks. A *link tag* (a tag that you use to create a hypertext link in your document) consists of **<A**, followed by a space, followed by **HREF="**. After that tag, you enter the URL. You've looked at URLs before; these are the same URLs that you can use to tell a browser to go to a particular Web site. At the end of the URL, you add **">**, followed by some kind of text—anything you want. (That text is going to appear on the finished Web page as the link text.) Following the text, you use the closing tag **</A>**. In the example above, I also used the **<P>** tag to start a new paragraph; I wanted to make sure that the link would appear on its own line.

Does It Have to Be Upper-Case? Don't worry about the case of the tags. You can type title, TITLE, Title, TItlE, or TiTlE—whatever tickles your fancy.

A Word About Paragraphs

Check This Out...

Anchors The **A HREF "url"** tags are often called anchors. For this reason, many people refer to the actual links in the Web documents as anchors.

Web browsers don't deal with paragraphs in the same way that word processors do. If the browser finds several spaces, including blank lines, it will compress all the space into a single paragraph unless it sees the <P> tag somewhere. When it finds the <P> tag, it ends that paragraph and starts a new one below it, generally leaving a blank line between the two.

If for some reason you want to move text down to the next line but you don't want a blank line between the two lines of text, you can use the <BR> tag instead of <P>. The <BR> tag inserts a line break without starting a new paragraph.

Check This Out...

<P> and </P>

You've already learned that the <P> tag doesn't have to have a matching code to make a pair. Actually, you can use <P> and </P> as a pair if you want. <P> marks the beginning of a paragraph, and </P> marks the end. However, this is not necessary, and few Web authors do so.

Don't Stop at One—Multiple Pages

You can easily create a hierarchy of documents. Why not have a document that appears when you open the browser, with a table of contents linked to several other documents? In each of those documents you can then have links related to a particular subject.

Say, for instance, you want to set up a document for the music sites you are interested in. Call it RNR.HTM, or MUSIC.HTM, or whatever you want. Create that document in the same way you did the first one, and put it in the same directory. You can then create a link from your home page to the Rock n' Roll document, like this:

```
<A HREF="RNR.HTM">Rock n' Roll</A>
```

Although RNR.HTM is a file name, you can use it in place of the URL. In fact, RNR.HTM is a URL: it's what's known as a *relative URL*. This link tells a Web browser to "look for the RNR.HTM file." Although it doesn't tell the browser where to look for the file, the browser makes a basic assumption. Because the URL doesn't include the host name or directory, the only place the browser can look is in the same directory as the original file. (And that's just fine because you are going to place the RNR.HTM file in the same directory, right?)

This is really simple, isn't it? You create a home page (called HOME.HTM) with links to any number of other documents in the same directory. You might have links to Rock n' Roll, art, music, conspiracy theories, or whatever sort of information you are interested in and can find on the Web. Then you fill those documents up with more links to all those interesting sites. Whad'ya know! You're a Web publisher!

Finding URLs

There are shortcuts to creating the links in your home page. Who wants to type all those URLs, after all? Well, one way to grab the URLs is to visit the Web page you are interested in and copy the text from the Location or Address text box at the top of the browser window. To do that, you can highlight the text, and then press **Ctrl+C** or select **Edit, Copy.** (Most browsers have some method for copying the URL.) Then you can just paste it into your home page.

You can also grab URLs from links on a document. Point at a link and right-click to see a pop-up menu (if you're using a Macintosh, try clicking and holding the mouse button down for a second or two). Click the **Copy Shortcut** option in Internet Explorer, or click the **Copy Link Location** option in Netscape.

You can also grab information from the bookmark or, in some cases, the history list. In Internet Explorer, you can open Favorites (that's the name it uses for its bookmark system). Choose **Favorites, Open Favorites Folder** (or **Favorites, Organize Favorites**), right-click an item, and choose **Properties.** Then click the **Internet Shortcut** tab and copy the URL from the **Target URL** text box.

In Netscape, you can open the Bookmarks window (**Window, Bookmarks,** or perhaps **Communicator, Bookmarks, Edit Bookmarks**) and do much the same thing. Right-click an item, select **Properties,** and then copy the URL from the box that appears. (Or click on the item and select **Edit, Properties.**) You can also choose **File, Save As** to save the entire bookmark system in an HTML file. Then you can open that file in a text editor and pick and choose which URLs you want.

You and Your Service Provider

If you actually want to publish on the Web, you have a two-step process to go through. First, you create the page. But then you have to place it somewhere that is accessible to the Internet. It has to be put on a Web server.

Most online services and Internet service providers allow their subscribers to post their own Web pages. Some of these services even allow each subscriber to post a megabyte or two of Web pages, graphics, and so on. Check with your service to find out how much data you can post and where to put it.

117

How do you get it where it needs to go? Generally, you'll have to use FTP, which you'll learn about in Chapter 14. This is a system that allows you to transfer files from your computer to another computer on the Internet. Some of the online services use a different system, though; check with your online service for more information.

Just a Little Help

The online services have Web-authoring programs to help you create Web pages and automatically post them to the service's Web site. Dig around a little in your online service to see what's available.

The Least You Need to Know

➤ Creating a home page is very simple; you can use the template provided to create one in as few as 10 minutes.

➤ Enclose HTML tags within brackets < >.

➤ In most cases, you need an opening tag and a closing tag, such as <TITLE>My Home Page</TITLE>.

➤ You use tags to tell your browser which text you want displayed as titles, headings, links, and so on.

➤ To create a link, type <A HREF="URL">Your Link Text</A>, replacing "URL" and "Your Link Text" with those you actually want to use.

➤ If you use a file name in place of the URL in the link, the browser will look in the same directory as the current document.

➤ You can replace your browser's default home page with your new one.

➤ Once you've created a page, you can post it at your service provider's site so the whole world can see it!

Part 2
There's Plenty More

The Internet is far more than just the Web, although you might not be able to tell that from the media coverage. Of course there's push, a system that's like an automated Web browser. But the Internet also offers hundreds of thousands of discussion groups (newsgroups and mailing lists), a file-library system called FTP, a "librarian" called Archie, and a once-popular menu system known as Gopher. And, of course, there's chat. No, it's not really chat—instead of talking, you type—but many people find it to be a great way to while away an hour or ten. And how about Voice on the Net? You'll learn about a system that enables you to make international phone calls for just pennies an hour!

You might even use Telnet, a relatively little-used system that allows you to log on to computers around the world—to play games, for instance. Even if you don't use all of the services covered in this part of the book, you're almost certain to find something useful.

Chapter 10

Push Information to Your Desktop

In This Chapter

➤ Push, bringing data to your desktop in a scheduled flood.

➤ The two big push players: Netscape Netcaster and Microsoft Active Desktop.

➤ Adding channels to your desktop.

➤ Finding more

➤ Finding more push programs: PointCast, BackWeb, Websprite, and more.

In this chapter we're going to take a look at a relatively new Internet service, *push* technology. The term push is really a misnomer, but nobody asks me to come up with these names; think of push as scheduled pull. People talk of information being "pushed" to your computer, rather than you having to go get the information using your Web browser. But in fact a push system is really like an automated Web browser; the program goes and retrieves the information for you automatically.

Here's how it works. You install a push program on your computer, then configure the program to carry out certain tasks—to periodically retrieve information. For instance, you can tell the program that you want to see the latest news headlines from CNN every ten minutes, that you want to check the weather forecast before you leave work each evening, and that you want to see the latest version of the corporate Web site when you come in each morning.

As long as the program has been started—and you can set up the program to start automatically every time you start your computer—the program will automatically grab information from the Internet for you. Because information arrives on your computer's desktop automatically, without your direct intervention, it appears that the information is being pushed to your desktop—thus the term *push*.

Webcasting

There's another term you'll hear related to push systems: Webcasting. A company can set up information that it plans to distribute to people using push technology. This is Webcasting, the "broadcasting" of data through push channels. Of course this is the computer business, in which terms can have multiple meanings! Microsoft uses the term Webcasting to refer to the transmission of streaming video or audio across the Internet, not "push."

New Productivity Tool, or Great Futzing Opportunity?

The companies making push programs claim that these systems provide a fantastic way to boost productivity...I figure they're often great "futzing" opportunities. The Gartner Group, which did a study of computers and their effect on productivity, defines futzing as the things people do with their computers that waste time, as opposed to things they do that are productive. (Each employee wastes $5,590 of futzing time each year, The Gartner Group claims.) Push programs have got a lot of criticism for clogging up networks with scheduled retrievals of information, information that users may not even read (it's so easy to schedule that you may end up getting far more information than you can handle). And anyway, how does reading the latest news headlines or sports scores increase productivity?

Every computer product enhances productivity—or so you'd believe if you take everything that computer-industry PR departments claim. In fact there are very few technologies that are clearly productivity boosters, and I personally doubt whether push technology is one of them.

A Lot of Choice, but Two Big Players

There are a number of push systems available, but there will soon be just two big players: Netscape and Microsoft, of course. Both companies already have "beta" systems available for download (that is, systems that are still in development, but available if you want to try them out and see where they're headed). By the time you read this Netscape's system (**Netcaster**, part of the **Communicator** suite of programs) will almost certainly be released, and Microsoft's (**Active Desktop**) may be out, too. (Microsoft's version will be released with the next version of Windows—probably named Windows 98—due out late in 1997, perhaps early in 1998. Or maybe the middle of 1998. Or maybe late in 1998; I've given up trying to figure out Microsoft's release schedules.)

There are many other players in this game, though. There's PointCast, the first really popular push program on the Internet. There's BackWeb and Castanet, two other systems that have received a lot of attention, and there are a number of smaller and less well known systems such as Websprite. So it hardly seems fair to say that the two big players are Netscape and Microsoft. But the fact is that both companies have sufficient influence to ensure that they will be the big players. Rather than having to go somewhere on the Internet and find a push program, download it and install it, you'll get the program automatically when you install your latest browser.

Note also that these other companies realize that there will be just two big players. Marimba, the company that owns the Castanet system, is going into business with Netscape to provide 100 of its Castanet information "channels" to be distributed through Netcaster.

A Quick Look at Netcaster

Let's take a quick look at Netcaster, the push system that you're most likely to be using (at least until Active Desktop arrives on the scene). You can start Netcaster by selecting **Communicator, Netcaster** from within Netscape Navigator, or using the Netcaster icon or Start-menu option.

Netcaster has **channels**; each information source you define is known as a channel, and they're all stored in the My Channels area of the Netcaster **drawer** (Netcaster's "control panel). You can see a picture of the drawer in the following illustration. Notice the little tab on the left side of the drawer; click this to open or close the drawer. (The drawer, when open, obscures everything underneath it on your computer screen, so you'll have to close it when working in other programs.)

What Can You Put in a Channel?

In the early days of push, you could only choose from a predefined set of information channels. These days some push systems, such as Netcaster and Microsoft Active Desktop, allow you to define any Web page as an information source. You can choose to get your best friend's paintball Web site delivered to you automatically, for instance. You might choose to see the latest driveway at the Driveways of the Rich and Famous site, or check on today's Dilbert cartoon. The choice is yours.

Netscape Netcaster's drawer, the system's "control panel."

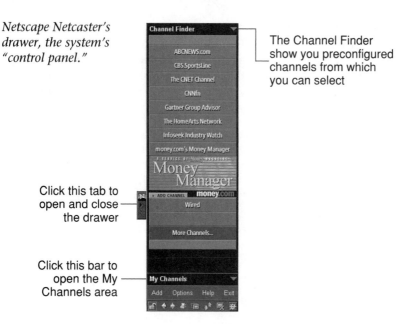

The Channel Finder show you preconfigured channels from which you can select

Click this tab to open and close the drawer

Click this bar to open the My Channels area

There are two ways to add a channel, that is, to tell the program which information sources you want to use. You can select a channel from the predefined set (the ones listed in the Channel Finder area), or you can specify a particular Web site.

Using the Channel Finder

Click the **Channel Finder** bar to see all the preselected channels. If you'd like more information about a channel that is listed, click that entry and it will open up to display a logo and an **+Add Channel button**. Click that button, and a Window opens, displaying information about that channel (as you can see in the following illustration).

If you decide that you definitely do want this channel, click the **Add Channel** button that you'll see near the top of the window; otherwise, click Cancel.

When you click the **Add Channel** button a dialog box opens, as you can see in the following illustration (you may see a window in which you must register Netcaster first). This box shows you the name of the channel (you can change the name if you wish), and the Location—the URL of the Web page. Note that you can also define how often the page is updated, that is, how often information is retrieved from this site. If you clear the **Update this channel or site every** check box, the channels is, in effect, turned off; it will not be updated. Leave the box checked, though, and select an option from the drop-down list box to define how often the channel will be updated, from once every 30 minutes to once a week.

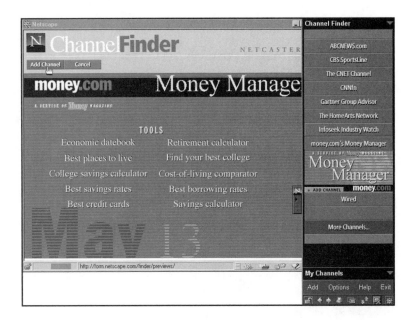

Click a channel button, then click +ADD CHANNEL to add the channel to your collection.

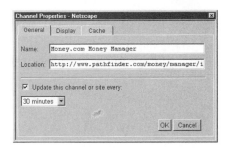

Tell Netcaster how often you want to update the information in this channel.

You now have two ways to display this channel. Click the **Display** tab, then select either **Default Window** or **Webtop Window** (see the following illustration). The Default Window is a normal browser window. But the Webtop Window is a special window; the information will appear on your computer's "desktop," as a sort of desktop wallpaper. (I'll show you the difference in a moment.)

Now click the Cache tab to see the information in the following illustration. This pane allows you to set the size of Netcaster's special cache, in which it stores channel data—it's separate from the cache used by Navigator (see Chapter 6 for information about browser's caches). But it also allows you to define how many "levels" deep the channel should go.

For instance, if the channel goes one level deep, it will contain the main page only. If it goes two levels deep it will contain the main page, plus all the pages linked to by that page. If it goes three levels deep it will contain the main page, all pages linked to by the main page, and all pages linked to by *those* pages. Downloading several layers can make a channel take up a *lot* of disk space, and take a long time to transfer, but it makes it quicker for you to read the pages. For instance, if you're downloading a news channel, you'll be able to see the headlines on the main page, *and* read the associated story. You'll be able to do that whether online or off-line, and even if you are offline the news stories won't have to be transferred across the Web; they'll come from the cache.

Use a normal browser window, or display the information as desktop wallpaper.

Configure the cache and the number of levels that should be transferred from the site.

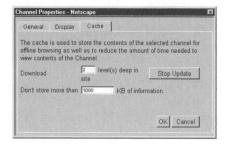

Too Many Levels Means Too Much Data Transfer

Be careful with this levels setting. The channels you see in the Channel Finder have been created especially for Netcaster, so going down three levels is probably not a problem. But if you set up your own channels (which I'll discuss next), going down three levels will be a real problem with Web pages that they contain a lot of links. Retrieving even as few as two or three levels can often take hours.

Notice also that there's a Stop Update button which can be used later to stop a channel transfer (to open a channel's Properties dialog box later, open the My Channels area of the drawer, right-click the channel name, and select Properties).

If you *don't* see a channel that interests you in the Channel Finder, click the More Channels… bar in the Channel Finder, and a browser window opens with many more channels (there should soon be over 100 channels, with plenty more on the way).

Adding Any Web page

You can specify *any* Web page you wish as a channel. In other words, you can have Netcaster automatically retrieve information from whichever of the tens of millions of Web pages are most important to you. Simply click the Add button at the bottom of the drawer, and you'll see the Channel Properties dialog box that we used before. You'll use the box in the same way as before, the only difference being that you must provide a Channel Name and the Location (the URL) of the Web page. That's all there is to it.

Using Your Channels

To work with your channels, click the My Channels bar in the drawer; you'll see a list of your channels. Click the channel you want to view, and it will open. If you defined it as a Default Window channel, then a browser window opens; this is a good setting if you have a channel from which you often need to begin a Web session. If you defined a channel as a Webtop channel, though, all your windows and icons are replaced with a Webtop window, as you can see in the following illustration.

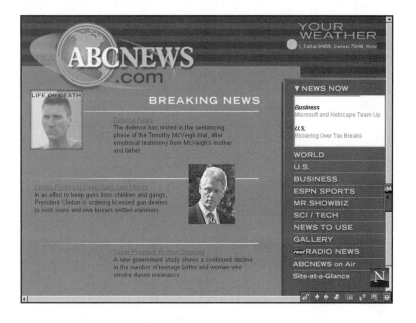

Webtop windows take over your computer desktop.

You can use the Webtop just like a Web page in the browser; it's just that this Web page has taken over your screen, with the exception of the icons you can see in the lower right part of the screen; the Netcaster tab, the Webtop toolbar, and a Netscape icon.

The Webtop toolbar contains buttons that are used to manage a Webtop session. The buttons display Security information for a page displayed on the Webtop; go Back and Forward through the Webtop "browser's" history list; print the current Webtop page; hide or display the Webtop (in effect displaying or hiding your normal desktop); move the Webtop to the front or back (in front of or behind the normal operating system desktop); close the Webtop; and open a browser window.

Play with these buttons to see their effect. For instance, you can push the Webtop to the back, so the Webtop acts almost like true desktop wallpaper. Open program windows appear above the Webtop, though the program icons that are normally shown on the desktop are not there (at least, in the current version of Netcaster; this may change later).

Microsoft's Active Desktop

Active Desktop is currently available in a rather primitive form, but it should be released sometime in 1998. It will probably be released with Windows 98, though it may appear with an earlier release of Internet Explorer 4.

Active Desktop works in a similar manner to Netcaster. Both systems are intended to take over your desktop, by the way, replacing the traditional computer desktop with a new "Web-ified" one. We're interested in the push portion of the desktops here, but suffice it to say that when you turn on Active Desktop, the desktop functions in a slightly different way from normal; you can single-click icons to start programs, for instance, instead of double-clicking.

To add channels to the Active Desktop, open your Display Properties dialog box (right-click on a blank area of the desktop and select **Properties**). Then click the **Web** tab, and you'll see something like the following illustration (remember, this is an early version of Active Desktop—what you see may differ a little).

Channels or Objects on Items

Active Desktop channels refers to these "things" on your desktop as objects on items, but they're the same thing.

To add a channel click the **New** button. You'll see a dialog box asking you if you want to select a channel (okay, an object), from a library of them at Microsoft's Web site. You can click **Yes** if you wish to do so, or **No** if you want to specify a Web site yourself. If you clicked **No** you'll see a box in which you can enter an URL. Do so, then click **OK**. Another box opens, with a **Customize** button. Use this button to open a Wizard, which asks questions about how you want to handle this channel. You can specify that the channel is updated automatically, periodically, or just that you are informed when the

Web site changes. You can also specify how often the channel is checked or updated, and , if necessary, enter a username and password.

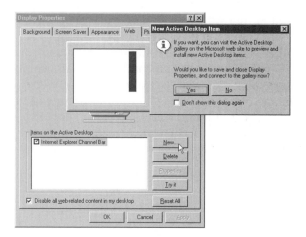

Here's where you add "channels." Click the new button to start.

These channels appear on your desktop as sizeable windows, as long as you *clear* the **Disable all web-related content in my desktop** check box in the Display Properties dialog box. (To size, point at the edge of the window and a thin border appears; when you see the double-head arrow drag the border. To move, point at the top of the window and a thick bar appears; drag this bar.) You can use the windows as if it were a normal Internet Explorer window; just click the links to move around. You can use the right-click pop-up menu to use various commands.

An early release of Active Desktop, showing a Web channel.

Other Push Systems

As I mentioned earlier, there are a number of different push systems available. While the specifics of working with other systems will vary, the basic principles remain the same: pick an information "channel," tell the program how often the information should be retrieved, then sit and wait. Most of these systems do not allow you to pick any Web site as a channel, they generally limit you to preconfigured channels. (Websprite, however, allows you to define any Web site, then tells you when that Web site changes and allows you to quickly open it in your browser.) If you want to try one of these other systems, go to one of the following sites. You'll find software you can download and install, generally for free. (This is just a small selection; there are actually many more push systems, each with its own unique twist.)

BackWeb—Around 40 channels, from JAMtv to PC Quote.
http://www.backweb.com/

Castanet—Around 100 channels, these are now available through Netscape's Netcaster. From CBS Sportsline to MapQuest.
http://www.marimba.com/

NETdelivery—"Pioneering" the concept of 'Community Marketing' - linking people with common interests and shared affinities to organizations that offer valuable information, products and services." They've just started, and their first channel is a CyberSeniors channel.
http://www.netdelivery.com/

PointCast—Perhaps the best-known of the push programs, hundreds of pre-configured channels. Newspapers, magazines, newsletters, and more. From *American Metal Market Cold-Finished Bar Supplement* to *Ekonomicke zpravodajstvi*.
http://www.pointcast.com/

Websprite—A small but very effective program that allows you to select from around 20 channels (Business Wire, Info Tech News, Sports Headlines, and so on). You can also create a Web search channel, that periodically searches for whatever you specify. You can even check on your FedEx shipments. This system also has a Delta channel, in which you can define a list of Web pages. Websprite will then tell you when those pages change. It even has an Intellispeech feature—the program speaks to you, but only when information you've defined as important arrives.
http://www.websprite.com/

Just What We Need...More Acronyms!

Microsoft has defined a new data format for push systems, CDF (Channel Data Format). A Web author can use XML (Extended Meta Language) tags to identify portions of a Web page to a push program, defining the best way for the information to be displayed, who the "broadcaster" is, and so on. Any push program that comes to the Web site "sniffing" for data will see these tags, and extract just the information it needs.

CDF has been adopted by some push-technolgy companies (such as PointCast, BackWeb, and MailBank, the owner of Websprite), while others have said they want nothing to do with it. Not surprisingly, Netscape is one of the companies that has chosen to ignore CDF.

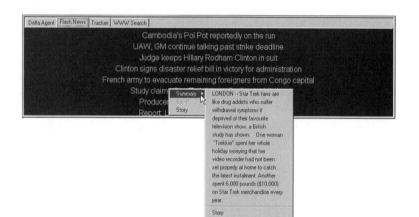

You can right-click an entry as it scrolls across Websprite to see more information; click the Story menu item to open your Web browser and see more information.

The Least You Need to Know

➤ Push programs retrieve information from the Internet for you automatically. You specify the information you want, and how often you want it, and it gets it for you.

➤ *Push* is a misnomer; these systems are really scheduled pull systems.

➤ The two big players in this game will soon be Netscape's Netcaster, and Microsoft's Active Desktop. There are many others, though, such as BackWeb, PointCast, and Websprite.

➤ Push systems generally allow you to select a channel from a list; some systems have hundreds of available channels.

➤ While most push systems don't allow you to specify any Web page you wish, several do: Netcaster, Active Desktop, and Websprite.

Chapter 11

Newsgroups: The Source of All Wisdom

In This Chapter

➤ What is a newsgroup?

➤ What you can find in newsgroups?

➤ Finding out what newsgroups exist

➤ What is Usenet?

➤ Choosing a newsreader

In this chapter I'm going to introduce you to one of the Internet's most dangerous services—newsgroups. Many people find these discussion groups to be addictive. Get involved in a few groups and, if you have an addictive personality, you'll soon find that the rest of your life is falling apart, as you spend hours each day swapping messages with people all over the world, on subjects such as bushwalking in Australia, soap operas, very tall women, or very short men.

But don't let me put you off. If you don't have an addictive personality, newsgroups can be interesting, stimulating, and extremely useful. And anyway, it's better than being addicted to booze or drugs. So read on, and in this chapter you'll find out what newsgroups are; in the next chapter, you'll find out how to use them.

What's a Newsgroup?

Let's start with the basics: *What is a newsgroup?* Well, are you familiar with bulletin board systems (BBSs)? Electronic BBSs work much like the real corkboard-and-thumbtack type of bulletin board. They're computerized systems for leaving both public and private messages. Other computer users can read your messages, and you can read theirs. There are tens of thousands of small BBSs around the world, each of which has its own area of interest. In addition, many computer companies have BBSs through which their customers get technical support, and many professional associations have BBSs so their members can leave messages for each other and take part in discussions.

An information service such as CompuServe or America Online is essentially a collection of many bulletin boards (called *forums* in CompuServe-speak, or message boards on AOL). CompuServe has a few thousand such BBSs. Instead of having to remember several thousand telephone numbers (one for each BBS), you can dial one phone number and access any number of BBSs in the series.

As you've already seen, the Internet is a collection of networks hooked together. It's huge, and consequently it has an enormous number of discussion groups. In Internet-speak, these are called *newsgroups*, and there are thousands of them on all conceivable subjects. Each Internet service provider subscribes to a selection of newsgroups—sometimes a selection as large as 3,000, 6,000, or even 15–20,000.

What do I mean by "subscribe?" Well, these newsgroups are distributed around the Internet by a service called Usenet; consequently they're often referred to as Usenet groups. Usenet distributes around 30,000 groups (the number keeps changing). But not all service providers get all of the groups. A service provider can choose which groups it wants to receive, in essence *subscribing* to just the ones it wants. Although almost 30,000 internationally distributed newsgroups exist (along with thousands more local groups), most providers get only a few thousand of them.

If your service provider subscribes to a newsgroup, you can read that group's messages and post your own messages to the group. In other words, you can work only with groups to which your service provider has subscribed. As you'll see, you read newsgroup messages by using a *newsreader*, a program that retrieves messages from your service provider's *news server*.

If you've never used a newsgroup (or another system's forum, BBS, or whatever), you may not be aware of the power of such communications. This sort of messaging system really brings computer networking to life, and it's not all computer nerds sitting around with nothing better to do. (Check out the Internet's alt.sex newsgroups; these people are not your average introverted propeller-heads!) In my Internet travels I've found work, made friends, found answers to research questions (much quicker and more cheaply than I could have by going to a library), and read people's "reviews" of tools I can use in my business. I've never found a lover or spouse online, but I know people who have (and anyway, I'm already married). Just be careful not to get addicted and start spending all your time online.

Public News Servers

If your service provider doesn't subscribe to a newsgroup you want, ask the management there to subscribe to it. If they won't, you *might* be able to find and read it at a public news server. Try looking at these sites for information about public servers:

http://www.yahoo.com/News/Usenet/Public_Access_Usenet_Sites/

http://www.reed.edu/~greaber/query.html

http://www.geocities.com/SiliconValley/Pines/3959/usenet.html

So What's Out There?

You can use newsgroups for fun or for work. You can use them to spend time "talking" with other people who share your interests—whether that happens to be algebra (see the alt.algebra.help group) or antique collecting (rec.antiques). You can even do serious work online, such as finding a job at a nuclear physics research site (hepnet.jobs), tracking down a piece of software for a biology project (bionet.software), or finding good stories about what's going on in South Africa for an article you are writing (za.events).

News? True to its UNIX heritage, the Internet uses the word "news" ambiguously. Often, when you see a reference to news in a message or an Internet document, it refers to the messages left in newsgroups (not, as most people imagine, to journalists' reports on current affairs).

The following newsgroups represent just a tiny fraction of what is available:

alt.ascii-art Pictures (such as Spock and the Simpsons) created with ASCII text characters.

alt.comedy.british Discussions on British comedy in all its wonderful forms.

alt.current-events.russia News of what's going on in Russia right now. (Some messages are in broken English, and some are in Russian, but that just adds romance.)

alt.missing-kids Information about missing kids.

bit.listserv.down-syn Discussions about Down's syndrome.

comp.research.japan Information about computer research in Japan.

misc.forsale   Lists of goods for sale.

rec.skydiving   A group for skydivers.

sci.anthropology   A group for people interested in anthropology.

sci.military   Discussions on science and the military.

soc.couples.intercultural   A group for interracial couples.

If you are looking for information on just about any subject, the question is not "Is there a newsgroup about this?" The questions you should ask are "What is the newsgroup's name?" and "Does my service provider subscribe to it?"

Can You Read It?

Check This Out...

I Want to Start One! Do you have a subject about which you want to start a newsgroup? Spend some time in the news.groups newsgroup to find out about starting a Usenet newsgroup, or talk to your service provider about starting a local newsgroup.

There are so many newsgroups out there that they take up a lot of room. A service provider getting the messages of just 3,000 newsgroups may have to set aside tens of megabytes of hard disk space to keep up with it all. So service providers have to decide which ones they will subscribe to. Nobody subscribes to all the world's newsgroups because many are simply of no interest to most Internet users, and many are not widely distributed. (Some are of regional interest only; some are of interest only to a specific organization.) So system administrators have to pick the ones they want and omit the ones they don't want. Undoubtedly some system administrators censor newsgroups, omitting those they believe have no place online.

I've given you an idea of what is available in general, but I can't specify what is available to *you*. You'll have to check with your service provider to find out what they offer. If they don't have what you want, ask them to get it. They have no way of knowing what people want unless someone tells them.

Okay, Gimme a List!

The first thing you may want to do is find out what newsgroups your service provider subscribes to. You can do that by telling your newsreader to obtain a list of groups from the news server; we'll talk more about newsreaders in a little while.

What if you don't find what you are looking for? How can you find out what's available that your provider does not subscribe to? There are lots of places to go these days to track down newsgroups. I like Liszt (**http://www.liszt.com/news/**), which currently lists over 17,000 newsgroups, and Tile.Net (**http://www.tile.net/**). Both Liszt and Tile.Net also list thousands of mailing lists (see Chapter 13); Tile.Net also lists sites (see Chapter 14). You can try the Usenet Info Center (**http://sunsite.unc.edu/usenet-i/**) or the Finding Newsgroups and Mailing Lists page (**http://www.synapse.net/~radio/finding.htm**). And of course you can search at any Web search site (which you'll learn about in Chapter 21). For instance, try Yahoo (**http://www.yahoo.com/News/Usenet/Newsgroup_Listings/**).

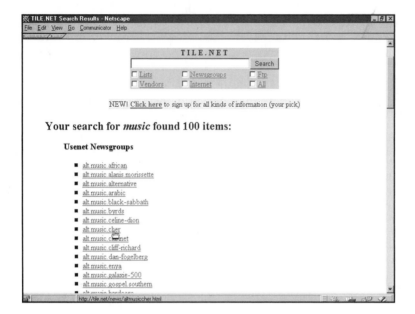

Tile.Net is a good place to find out what's available on Usenet.

Where Does It All Come from?

Where do all these newsgroups come from? People create newsgroups from their computers all over the world. Any system administrator can create a newsgroup, and many do. Each host has newsgroups of local interest—about the service provider's services, local politics, local events, and so on.

A large number of newsgroups—though not all of them—are part of the Usenet system. Like the Internet, Usenet is intangible—a network of networks. No one owns it, and it doesn't own anything itself. It is independent of any network, including the Internet (in fact, it's older than the Internet). Usenet is simply a series of voluntary agreements to swap information.

What's in a Name?

Check This Out...

Moderated Groups

As you'll see when you refer to some of the directories of newsgroups, some newsgroups are moderated, which means someone reads all the messages and decides which ones to post. The purpose is to keep the newsgroup focused and to prevent the discussions from "going astray." Of course, it may look a little like censorship—depending on what you want to say.

Now let's take a quick look at how newsgroups get their names. Newsgroup names look much like host addresses: a series of words separated by periods. This is because, like host names, they are set up in a hierarchical system (though instead of going right-to-left, they go left-to-right). The first name is the top level. These are the primary top-level Usenet groups:

comp   Computer-related subjects.

news   Information about newsgroups themselves, including software you can use to read newsgroup messages, and information about finding and using newsgroups.

rec   Recreational topics, including hobbies, sports, the arts, and so on.

sci   Discussions about research in the "hard" sciences, as well as some social sciences.

soc   A wide range of social issues, such as discussions about different types of societies and subcultures, as well as sociopolitical subjects.

talk   Debates about politics, religion, and anything else that's controversial.

misc   Stuff. Job searches, things for sale, a forum for paramedics. You know, *stuff*.

Not all newsgroups are true Usenet groups. Many are local groups that Usenet distributes internationally (don't worry about it, it doesn't matter). Such newsgroups are part of the Alternative Newsgroup Hierarchies. They have other top-level groups, such as these:

alt   "Alternative" subjects. These are often subjects that many people consider inappropriate, pornographic, or just weird. In some cases, however, it's simply interesting reading, but someone created the newsgroup in an "unauthorized" manner to save time and hassle.

bionet   Biological subjects.

bit   A variety of newsgroups from BITNET.

biz   Business subjects, including advertisements.

clari   Clarinet's newsgroups from "official" and commercial sources; mainly UPI news stories and various syndicated columns.

courts   Related to law and lawyers.

de   Various German-language newsgroups.

fj   Various Japanese-language newsgroups.

gnu   The Free Software Foundation's newsgroups.

hepnet   Discussions about high energy and nuclear physics.

ieee   The Institute of Electrical and Electronics Engineers' newsgroups.

info   A collection of mailing lists formed into newsgroups at the University of Illinois.

k12   Discussions about kindergarten through 12th-grade education.

relcom   Russian-language newsgroups, mainly distributed in the former Soviet Union.

vmsnet   Subjects of interest to VAX/VMS computer users.

You'll see other groups, too, such as the following:

brasil   Groups from Brazil (Brazil is spelled with an "s" in Portuguese).

Birmingham   Groups from Birmingham, England.

podunk   A local interest newsgroup for the town of Podunk.
thisu   This university's newsgroup.

Okay, I made up the last two, but you get the idea. You'll run into all sorts of different hierarchies, with new ones appearing all the time. If you'd like to see a list of virtually all the top-level group names in both Usenet and "Alternative" newsgroups, go to **http://www.magmacom.com/~leisen/master_list.html**.

Reaching the Next Level

The groups listed in the previous section make up the top-level groups. Below each of those groups are groups on another level. For instance, under the alt. category is a newsgroup called alt.3d that contains messages about three-dimensional imaging. It's part of the alt hierarchy because, presumably, it was put together in an unauthorized way. The people who started it didn't want to go through the hassle of setting up a Usenet group, so they created an alt group instead—where anything goes.

Another alt group is **alt.animals**, where people gather to talk about their favorite beasties. This group serves as a good example of how newsgroups can have more levels. Because it's such a diverse subject, one newsgroup isn't really enough. So instead of posting messages to the alt.animals group, you choose your particular interest. The specific areas include:

alt.animals.dolphins

alt.animals.felines.lions

alt.animals.felines.lynxes

alt.animals.felines.snowleopards

alt.animals.horses.icelandic

alt.animals.humans

And there are many more. If you're into it, chances are good there's a newsgroup for it.

All areas use the same sort of hierarchical system. For example, under the **bionet** first level, you can find the **genome** level, with such newsgroups as **bionet.genome.arabidopsis** (information about the Arabidopsis genome project), **bionet.genome.chrom22** (a discussion of Chromosome 22), and **bionet.genome.chromosomes** (for those interested in the eucaryote chromosomes).

I'm Ready; Let's Read

Now that you know what newsgroups are, you'll probably want to get in and read a few. Newsgroups store the news messages in text files—lots of text files. You'll read the messages using a *newsreader* to help you sort and filter your way through all the garbage.

If you are with an online service, you already have a built-in newsreader. These range from the good (MSN's newsreader is pretty capable), to the absolutely awful (CompuServe's was horrible last time I looked; maybe their next software upgrade will fix that). If you are with a service provider, they may give you a newsreader. For example, Netscape Navigator 2 and 3, Netscape Communicator, and Internet Explorer have built-in newsreaders, and many service providers provide one of these systems to their members (see the following figure). Or you may have one of many other newsgroup programs, such as WinVN, Gravity, or Free Agent (on Windows), or NewsWatcher and Nuntius (on the Mac). There are *loads* of commercial newsreaders around, many of which are included with products such as Internet Chameleon, SuperHighway Access, and Internet in a Box.

Netscape Communicator's built-in newsreader, Collabra.

Still Using UNIX?

If you are using a command-line interface, send e-mail to **ciginternet@mcp.com**, with **news** in the Subject line to receive the newsgroup chapters (Chapters 15 and 16) from the first edition of *The Complete Idiot's Guide to the Internet*, which explain how to use a UNIX-based newsreader.

I'm going to use the Gravity newsreader for my examples in the next chapter. If you have something different the actual commands you use will vary, but the basic principles will remain the same. Of course different programs have different features, so you might want to try out a few programs to see what you like (see Appendix A for information about finding software).

The Least You Need to Know

➤ A newsgroup is an area in which people with similar interests leave public messages—a sort of online public debate or discussion.

➤ There's a newsgroup on just about every subject you can imagine. If there isn't, there probably will be soon.

➤ Newsgroup names use a hierarchical system, and each group may have subgroups within it.

➤ The major online services have built-in newsreaders. If you are with a service provider, it may have given you a newsreader. If for any reason you're looking for a newsreader, try the software "libraries" listed in Appendix A.

➤ Some available newsreaders include Gravity, Free Agent, and WinVN on Windows, or NewsWatcher and Nuntius for the Mac.

Chapter 12

Your Daily News Delivery

In This Chapter

➤ Starting your newsreader

➤ Reading and responding to messages

➤ Marking messages as read

➤ ROT13: encoded messages

➤ Sending and receiving binary files

➤ Special newsreader features

It's time to see how to work in the newsgroups. As I mentioned in the previous chapter, I'm going to use the Gravity newsreader for my examples. (If you'd like to try this program, go to **http://www.anawave.com/**.) Of course, if you are using an online service you may be using that service's system. For instance, in MSN, you'll see icons all over the place representing collections of newsgroups. Many of MSN's BBSs—the term MSN uses for forums or subject areas—contain icons that represent links to newsgroups. Double-click the icon to go to the newsgroups, or use the Go To word **Internet** to go to the Internet BBS. In CompuServe, **GO INTERNET**, or in AOL, use the keyword **Internet** to find more information about starting the newsreaders.

There are many available newsgroup programs. Although each is a little different, they all share certain characteristics. Check your program's documentation for the specific details and to learn about any extra features it includes. Even if you don't have Gravity, I suggest that you read this information because it provides a good overview of the functions available in most newsreaders.

A Quick Word on Setup

I want to quickly discuss setup and subscribing. If you are with an online service, there's nothing to set up; it's all done for you. If you are with a service provider, though, you *may* have to set up the newsreader.

First, your newsreader must know the location of your news server. Ask your service provider the host name of the news server (the news server is the system used by the service provider to send messages to your newsreader), and check your newsreader's documentation to see where to enter this information. For instance, it may be news.big.internet.service.com, or news.zip.com, or something like that.

The other thing you may have to do is *subscribe* to the newsgroups you are interested in. I've already said that your service provider has to subscribe to newsgroups; that means that the provider makes sure the newsgroups are available to its members. However, the term subscribe has another meaning in relation to newsgroups. You may also have to subscribe to the newsgroup to make sure that the newsgroup you want to read is available to your newsreader. Not all newsreaders make you subscribe in order to read a newsgroup. For instance, you don't have to worry about this if you use MSN's newsreaders. Many newsreaders, however, require you to fetch a list of newsgroups from your service provider (the newsreader has a command you'll use to fetch and display the list) and then "subscribe" to the ones you want to read. This is no big deal, you simply choose which ones you want. Until you subscribe, though, you can't see the messages.

Check This Out...

Pick Your Own Newsreader

Some of the online services have rather weak newsreaders. But if your online service allows you to get to the Internet through a TCP/IP connection, you may be able to install another newsreader, such as Gravity, Free Agent, NewsWatcher, and Nuntius. However, in order to do so you may have to connect to one of the public news servers that we mentioned in Chapter 9. The online services often have special news servers that are not designed to be accessed by TCP/IP; they're designed to be accessed with the service's own program. Check with your service's technical support staff.

Starting and Subscribing

The following figure shows the Gravity newsreader, an excellent program designed for Windows NT and Windows 95. The first time you use the program a dialog box opens, asking for certain information.

To connect to the news server using Gravity, select **File**, **Connect** (or click the **Connect/Disconnect** toolbar button). Then select **Newsgroup**, **Get New Groups** to get the latest list of groups from your service provider's news server. The dialog box in the next figure appears, showing the newsgroups that are available on your news server. Remember that this is a list of only the newsgroups that your service provider has subscribed to, not a full list of all the groups distributed by Usenet. (For information about finding such a list, see Chapter 11.) Double-click a newsgroup name to subscribe to it, and then click **Done** to continue. (You can also use the **Search** box to search for a particular name.)

Where Are the Alt. Groups?

If you are with an online service, you may find that you can't initially read the alt. groups, and perhaps some others as well. Your online service may regard these as a trifle "naughty," in which case you have to apply for permission to read them. Go to your online service's Internet forum or BBS to find out how to activate these groups, or refer to the parental-control information.

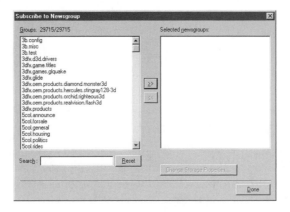

Gravity's Subscribe to Newsgroup dialog box.

When the dialog box closes, you'll see a list of the newsgroups you subscribed to. You can subscribe to more later. You just have to select **Newsgroup**, **Subscribe** to see the dialog box again. You can also select **Newsgroup**, **Get New Groups** to see only those newsgroups that have been added very recently (service providers are continually adding new ones). Or you can select **Newsgroup**, **Re-Read All Groups** to get the full list again and then display the dialog box.

Double-click one of the subscribed newsgroups, and you'll get a list of messages in that newsgroup (see the next figure). However, many newsgroups are empty, so you won't always see these message "headers." In Gravity you can see, in the **Server** column, the number of messages held in that newsgroup—if the number's 0, obviously the newsgroup is empty. (Note, however, that if there are only a few messages, it's quite possible that *all* the messages are promotional messages, completely unrelated to the subject of the newsgroup, perhaps advertising get-rich-quick schemes or pornographic Web sites.

Double-click a newsgroup, and the newsreader retrieves a list of message headers.

The list of subscribed newsgroups

Messages in the selected newsgroup

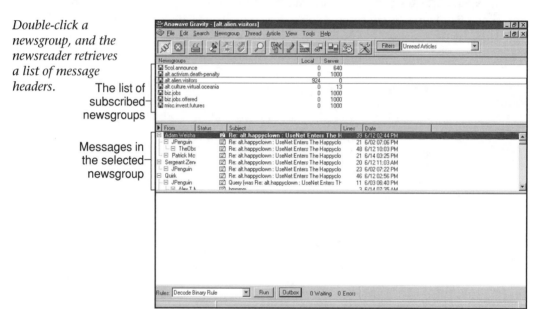

Not All the Messages

You may not see all of the messages listed at once. Some newsreaders allow you to specify a number to retrieve each time (in the program's Options or Preferences). So if it's a very busy newsgroup, you may see only a portion of the messages listed; you'll have to use another command to retrieve the rest.

Taking a Look

Notice that some messages are indented below others, and that there's a small–icon next to the messages. This indicates that the message is part of a *thread* (known as a *conversation* in some newsreaders). So what's a *thread*? Let's say you post a message to a newsgroup that isn't a response to anyone, it's just a new message. Then, a little later, someone else reads your message and replies. That message, because it's a reply, is part of the thread you began. Later, someone else sends a response to *that* message, and it becomes part of the thread. (Note, however, that there's generally a *long* lag time—a day or more— between the time someone sends a message to a newsgroup and the time that message turns up in everyone's newsreader.)

If you click the little–icon, the thread closes up, and you see only the message at the "top" of the thread. The icon changes to a + icon. Click the + icon to open the thread up again. (A message that has a–icon but does not have messages indented below it is not part of a message thread.) Most newsreaders (but not all) support threading and many other functions in a very similar manner.

To read a message, simply double-click the message's header. The newsreader retrieves the message and places it in the bottom pane of the window as you can see in the following figure.

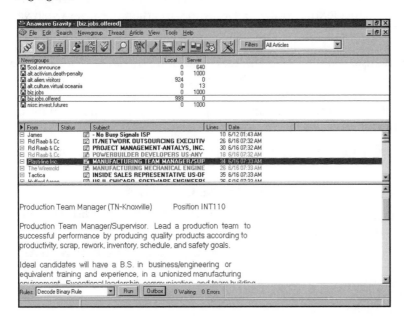

This message is from the biz.jobs.offered newsgroup.

The Messages Are Gone!

The first time you open a newsgroup, all the messages from that newsgroup currently held by your service provider are available to you. How long a message stays in the newsgroup depends on how busy that newsgroup is and how much hard-disk space the service provider allows for the newsgroup messages. Eventually all messages disappear.

You don't necessarily see all the newsgroup's messages the next time you use your newsreader, though. When you return to the newsgroup later, you may see all the messages *except* those marked as read.

Why didn't I just say "all the messages except those that you have read?" Well, there's a slight difference. The newsreader has no way of knowing which messages you've read—it can't see what you are doing. Instead it has a way of marking messages that it thinks you've read, and it generally provides you with a way to mark messages as "Read," even if you haven't read them (in effect, providing a way for you to tell it that you don't want to see the messages).

Marking Your Messages

Most newsreaders mark a message as "Read" when you open the message. They often also allow you to mark the messages as Read even if you have not read them. This might come in handy to tell the newsreader that you don't want to see certain messages when you come back to the newsgroup in a later session. For instance, say you get a couple of messages into a conversation and realize it's pure rubbish (you'll find a lot of messages that have virtually no usefulness to anyone!). Mark the entire thread as Read, and you won't see the rest of the messages the next time you open the newsgroup window. Or maybe the messages are worthwhile (to someone), but you quickly read all the messages' Subject lines and find that nothing interests you. Mark them *all* as Read so you see only new messages the next time.

You can generally also mark messages several other ways. Here's what you can do in Gravity, for instance:

➤ Click a message header and select **Article**, **Mark As, Read**.

➤ Click a message header and select **Thread**, **Mark Thread As, Read**. This marks the entire thread as read.

➤ Right-click a message header and select **Mark As, Read** or **Mark Thread As, Read** from the shortcut menu.

➤ Choose **Newsgroup**, **Mark As Read (Catchup)** to mark all the current newsgroup's messages as read.

Different newsreaders handle "Read" messages differently. Gravity actually removes them from the list. However, if you don't want the newsreader to remove them, you can change the view by choosing **Newsgroup**, **Filter Display**, **Read Articles** to see just messages you've read, or **Newsgroup**, **Filter Display**, **Read Articles** (or by selecting these from the drop-down list box in the toolbar); then Gravity shows the read-message headers in gray text. Other newsreaders might use special icons or gray text to indicate messages that you've read.

Articles In keeping with the "news" meta-phor, newsgroup messages are often known as *articles*.

I Want the Message Back!

If you need to bring a message back, you'll generally find that your newsreader has some kind of command that enables you to do so. Gravity has the **Newsgroup**, **Filter Display**, **Read Articles** command that you just looked at, for instance. But if your service provider no longer holds the message you want to see—that is, if the message has been removed from the service provider's hard disk to make more space for new messages—you're out of luck. So if you think there's a chance you may want a message later, save it using the **File**, **Save As** or equivalent command.

Many newsreaders even have commands for marking messages as Unread. Perhaps you've read a message, but want to make sure it appears the next time you open the newsgroup. You can mark it as Unread so that it will appear in the list next time you open the newsgroup.

Moving Among the Messages

You'll find a variety of ways to move around in your messages. As you already know, you can double-click the ones you want (some newsreaders use a single click). In addition, you'll find commands for moving to the next or previous message, the next or previous thread, and perhaps, the next or previous unread message or thread.

Many newsreaders also provide a way for you to search for a particular message. In Gravity, for example, select **Search**, **Search**, and you'll get a dialog box in which you can do a fairly sophisticated search. You can look for text in the From or Subject lines, or even within the text of the messages themselves; you can specify whether to search the selected newsgroup or all of the subscribed newsgroups; and you can even tell it whether to search only those messages already transferred to the newsreader or to search messages still held by the news server.

Saving and Printing

If you run across a message that you think might be useful later, you can save it or print it. Simply marking it as Unread isn't good enough because newsgroups eventually drop all messages. So sooner or later it won't be available.

Most newsreaders have a **File, Save As** (or simply **File, Save**) command and toolbar button. Most also have a **File, Print** command and button. And, of course, you can always highlight the text, copy it to the Clipboard, and then paste it into another application such as a word processing or e-mail program.

Your Turn Sending and Responding

There are several ways to send messages or to respond to messages. For example, you can use any of the techniques listed here in Gravity. (Although Gravity is typical, the commands might be different in other newsreaders.)

➤ You can send a message that isn't a response (that is, you can start a new thread). In Gravity, for instance, select **Article**, **Post** or click the **Post** toolbar button.

➤ You can reply to someone else's message (the reply is often known as a follow-up). In Gravity, you choose **Article**, **Follow Up** or click the **Follow Up** button. Other newsreaders may use a command such as **Reply to Group**.

➤ You can reply to someone privately via e-mail (that is, send a message that *doesn't* appear in the newsgroup). To do so in Gravity, select **Article**, **Reply** or click the **E-mail Author** button. Other newsreaders may use a command such as **Reply by E-mail**.

➤ You can send a copy of the message to someone else. In Gravity, select **Article**, **Forward via E-mail**.

Sending messages to a newsgroup—or via e-mail in response to a message—is much the same as working with an e-mail window. You type the message and click some kind of **Send** button.

What's This Gibberish? ROT13

Now and again, especially in the more contentious newsgroups, you'll run into messages that seem to be gibberish. Everything's messed up, each word seems to be a jumbled mix of characters, almost as if the message is encrypted. It is.

What you are seeing is *ROT13*, a very simple substitution cipher (one in which a character is substituted for another). It's actually very easy to read. ROT13 means "rotated 13." In other words, each character in the alphabet is replaced by the character 13 places further along. Instead of A you see N, instead of B you see O, instead of C you see P, and so on. Got it? So to read the message, all you need to do is substitute the correct characters. Easy. (Or *Rnfl*, as I should say.)

For those of you in a hurry, there is an easier way. Most newsreaders have a command that quickly does the ROT13 for you. For instance, in Gravity, select **Article, Unscramble (ROT13)** and, like magic, the message changes into real words. If you don't run across any ROT13 messages, and want to see what ROT13 looks like, simply use the command to take a normal message and convert it to ROT13 message (which is what I did for the following figure). How do you actually create one of these messages when sending one to a newsgroup? You'll often find a ROT13 command in the window in which you create a message. For instance, in Gravity's message composition window, there's an **Options, Scramble (ROT13)** command.

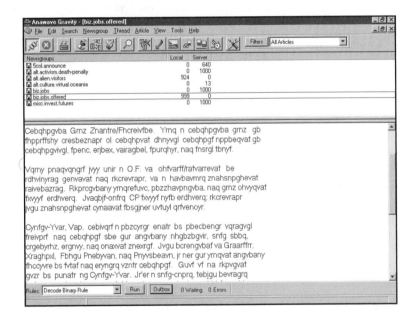

An example of a ROT13 message.

You might be wondering why a person would encode a message with a system that is so ridiculously easy to break. People don't ROT13 their messages as a security measure that's intended to make them unreadable to anyone who doesn't have the "secret key." After all, anyone with a decent newsreader has the key. No, ROT13ing (if you'll excuse my use of the term as a verb) is a way of saying "if you read this message, you may be offended; so if you are easily offended, *don't read it!*" ROT13 messages are often crude, lewd, or just plain rude. Offensive. Nasty. When a message is encoded with ROT13, the reader can decide whether or not he wants to risk being offended.

Pictures (and Sounds) from Words

The newsgroups contain simple text messages. You can't place any character into a message that is not in the standard text character set. So if you want to send a computer file in a newsgroup message—maybe you want to send a picture, a sound, or a word processing document—you must convert it to text. Some of the newer newsreaders will help you do this, either by automating the process of attaching MIME-formatted files to your messages, or by uuencoding files and inserting them into your messages. Some newsreaders will even convert such files "on-the-fly" and display pictures inside the message when they read the newsgroup messages; others will automatically convert the file to its original format.

If you were using Gravity, for example, you could follow these steps to send a file.

1. Open the message composition window using the **Post** command or the **Follow up** command.

2. Choose **Options**, **Add Attachment** or click the **Attach a file** toolbar button. You'll see a typical File Open dialog box, from which you can choose the file you want to send.

3. Select the file and click **OK**. The name of the attached file appears in the Attachments list of the message composition window (see the following figure).

Most newsreaders let you send uuencoded or MIME files to a newsgroup.

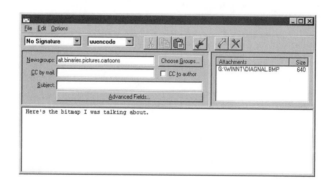

4. From the drop-down list at the top of the window, choose the form of encoding you want to use (**uuencode** or **MIME**).

5. Send the message (click the **Send** button, or select **File, Send**). The name of the file appears in the message header when you view the messages in that particular newsgroup.

When a message with an attached file is posted to a newsgroup, what do participants of that newsgroup see? Well, if the attached file is an image, as many are, some newsreaders will display the picture inside the message. Others may display the message text, something like what you see in the following illustration.

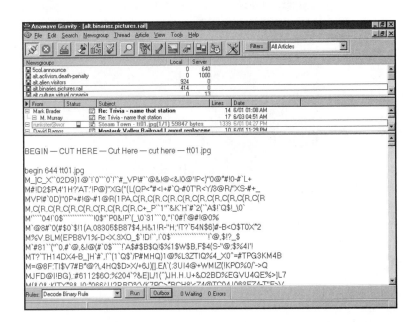

This message contains an attached file. The jumbled up text is the file, converted to text. The text must be converted back before you can view the file.

However, even if your newsreader doesn't initially display the image within the message, it may be able to convert the image file. In particular, newsreaders can often convert .GIF, .JPEG, and perhaps .BMP files to their original formats. In the case of Gravity, you can click the **View Image** button or select **Article**, **View**, and it converts the file for you and then places it in a viewer window, as shown in this figure.

No Built-In Converter?

If you are using a newsreader that doesn't have a built-in conversion system, you can save the message on your hard disk and then use a conversion program such as Wincode (a Windows program that converts UUENCODE), munpack (a DOS program that converts MIME), or Yet Another Base64 Decoder (a Macintosh program that converts both UUENCODE and MIME).

The same message after the attachment has been converted to its original format.

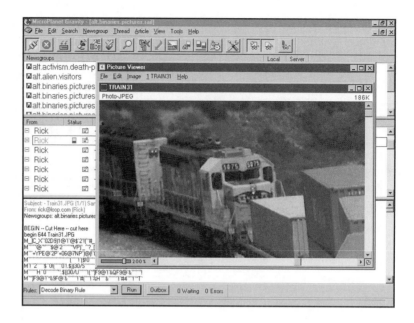

The Fancy Stuff

Some newsreaders might have nice extra features. You may be able to get the newsreader to automatically "flag" messages if the header contains a particular word. Or perhaps you can automatically remove a message if the header contains a particular word. Gravity also has a sophisticated "rules" system by which you can automatically carry out a variety of actions—throw the message away, display a special alert message, save the message in a text file, and so on—according to what appears in the header or body text. Many newsreaders let you click e-mail addresses or Web URLs that appear in messages to automatically open the mail window or your browser.

Some newsreaders will display the picture in the message window; Netscape's newsreader can do this, for instance. A few newsreaders can decode several messages together. If someone posts a large picture split into several pieces, for instance (as people often do), the newsreader may automatically retrieve all the pieces and paste them together. There are a lot of different things that newsreaders can do, so you may want to experiment to find the best for you.

A Word of Warning

Newsgroups can be *very* addictive. You can find messages about anything that interests you, angers you, or turns you on. If you are not careful you can spend half your life in the newsgroups. You sit down in the morning to check your favorite newsgroups, and the next thing you know you haven't bathed, eaten, or picked up the kids from school.

Hang around the newsgroups, and you'll find people who are obviously spending a significant amount of time writing messages. These people are usually independently wealthy (that is, they work for large corporations who don't mind paying for them to talk politics over the Internet or who don't know that they are paying them to do so). If you have a job, a family, and a life, be careful.

The Least You Need to Know

➤ Start your newsreader, and then download a list of newsgroups from the server. You may also have to subscribe to the groups you want to read; each newsreader does this a little differently.

➤ A good newsreader lets you view a "thread" or "conversation," which shows how messages relate to each other.

➤ ROT13 is a special encoding system that stops people from accidentally stumbling across offensive messages. Many newsreaders have a ROT13 command that converts the message to normal text.

➤ You can include binary files in messages using UUENCODE or MIME.

➤ Many newsreaders these days can decode UUENCODE and MIME attachments. If your newsreader doesn't, you'll need a utility such as Wincode or munpack (for Windows and DOS) or Yet Another Base64 Decoder (for the Macintosh). Or you can get another newsreader!

Chapter 13

Yet More Discussion Groups: Mailing Lists and Web Forums

In This Chapter

- ➤ More discussion groups?
- ➤ How mailing lists work
- ➤ Manual and automated lists
- ➤ LISTSERV mailing lists
- ➤ Finding lists of interesting groups
- ➤ Subscribing to mailing lists
- ➤ Working with Web Forums

Are you getting enough sleep? Are you socializing, meeting with friends and family? Do you have time to eat and bathe? Yes? Then you're clearly not spending enough time on the Internet. I've already shown you how to work with thousands of newsgroups, discussion groups on almost any subject (see Chapter 12). But obviously that's not enough. So here are thousands more discussion groups: the mailing lists and Web forums.

Mailing lists and Web forums are different types of discussion groups. The difference between these types of groups and newsgroups is simply the manner in which messages are distributed. While newsgroups are distributed through a system specifically set up for their distribution, mailing lists are distributed via e-mail, and Web forums make messages available at a Web site, through the use of Web-page forms. How many of these discussion groups are there? Well, Liszt (**http://www.liszt.com/**) currently indexes 71,618 mailing lists, though there must be many, many more. (Because there's no central distribution system it's not easy to track them all.) As for Web forums, well anyone with a little time and money, or lots of time and a few geek genes, can set up a discussion group at their Web site, so there could be many thousands of these. Again, they're hard to track, but Reference.com (**http://www.reference.com/**) estimates that there are about 25,000 Web forums.

We'll start by looking at mailing lists.

How Do Mailing Lists Work?

Each mailing list discussion group has an e-mail address. You begin by subscribing to the group you are interested in (I'll explain how in a moment). The e-mail address acts as a mail "reflector," a system that receives mail and then sends it on to a list of addresses. So every time someone sends a message to a group of which you are a member, you get a copy of the mail. And every time you send a message to a group address, everyone else on the list gets a copy.

You learned in Chapter 11 that you read newsgroups using special programs called newsreaders. However, you don't need any special program to work with a mailing list; all you need is whatever program you use for reading your e-mail. You send e-mail messages to the list in the same way that you send messages to anyone else: you enter the mailing list's address in the To box of your mail program's Compose window, type your message, and send it. And incoming messages are placed in your Inbox right along with messages from your friends and colleagues.

There are thousands of mailing lists on the Internet. Here are some suggestions of how you can go about finding the ones that interest you.

> ➤ Use your Web browser to go to the Liszt site (**http://www.liszt.com/**), probably the best directory of mailing lists. You can also try Tile.Net (**http://www.tile.net/**). You can search these lists for a particular name or by subject.

> ➤ Go to **http://www.lsoft.com/lists/listref.html**, where you'll find the Catalist, the "official catalog of LISTSERV lists." They index over 13,000 of the more than 47,000 LISTSERV lists.

> ➤ Send an e-mail message to **listserv@listserv.net**. In the message text, type **list global** **_keyword_**, where keyword is a word you want to search for within the discussion group names or subjects. For instance, you could type **list global geo** to find lists related to geography. You'll get an e-mail message back listing the matches.

> ➤ Search for mailing list at one of the Web search sites (covered in Chapter 21), or try the **http://www.yahoo.com//Computers_and_Internet/Internet/Mailing_Lists/** Web page.

➤ Go to the **news.announce.newusers** newsgroup. Sometimes you can find a list of mailing lists posted there. (See Chapters 11 and 12 for information about working with newsgroups.)

➤ Send an e-mail message to **listserv@ vm1.nodak.edu** with the command **GET NEW-LIST WOUTERS** in the body of the message. In response, you'll receive Arno Wouter's text file entitled How to Find an Interesting Mailinglist.

Peered Groups Some LISTSERV mailing lists are "peered." A peered LISTSERV group is the same as a "moderated" newsgroup: someone is checking the mail and deciding what stays and what gets trashed.

➤ Learn by word of mouth. Hang around in some newsgroups and mailing lists, and you'll hear about private mailing lists that you may be able to join by invitation.

The Types of Lists

There are two basic types of mailing lists:

➤ Manually administered

➤ Automated

Some very small mailing lists are set up to be administered by a person who will add your name to the list. Such lists are often private, with subscription by invitation only. Other lists use special mailing list programs to automatically add your name to the list when you subscribe. These are often, although not always, public lists that are open to anyone.

One of the most common and best known forms of automated list is the LISTSERV list. These are named after the LISTSERV mailing list program and are distributed through the Internet by the BITNET computer network. (Just to confuse the issue, I should state that there are now LISTSERV programs for a variety of different computer systems, which are used to run mailings lists that are *not* distributed by the BITNET computer network.)

There are other mailing list programs, too; Majordomo is one of the most common. But you don't need any fancy mailing list software to set up a small mailing list. It's actually quite easy to set up a manually administered mailing list. Some mailing lists are run from UNIX Internet accounts using a few very simple utilities to make the work easier. For instance, a UNIX user can set up a forwarding utility to automatically forward incoming e-mail to a list of e-mail addresses.

Using a LISTSERV Group

Many people think that mailing lists and LISTSERV groups are one and the same. Not quite. Although LISTSERV groups are a type of mailing list (perhaps the largest category), not all mailing lists are LISTSERV groups. The term "LISTSERV" refers to one popular mailserver program; so mailing lists administered by the LISTSERV program are known as LISTSERV groups, LISTSERV lists, or just LISTSERVs. LISTSERV originates on the BITNET network. However, many LISTSERV groups are now based on the Internet, on various UNIX hosts. There are well over 4,000 BITNET LISTSERV groups, covering subjects such as those listed in the following table:

A Sampling of BITNET LISTSERV Groups

Mailing List	Description
9NOV89-L@DB0TUI11.BITNET	Events around the Berlin Wall
AAAE@VM.CC.PURDUE.EDU	American Association for Agricultural Education
AAPOR50@USCVM.BITNET	American Association for Public Opinion Research
AATG@INDYCMS.BITNET	American Association of Teachers of German
ABSLST-L@CMUVM.BITNET	Association of Black Sociologists
ACADEMIA@TECHNION.BITNET	Academia—Forum on Higher Education in Israel
ACADEMIA@USACHVM1.BITNET	Grupo Selecto de Matematicos Chilenos
ACCESS-L@PEACH .EASE.LSOFT.COM	Microsoft Access Database Discussion List
ACCI-CHI@URIACC.BITNET	Consumer Economics and Chinese Scholars
ADA-LAW@NDSUVM1.BITNET	Americans with Disabilities Act Law
ADD-L@HUMBER.BITNET	Forum for discussion of concerns of drinking and driving
AE@SJSUVM1.BITNET	Alternative Energy Discussion List
CHRISTIA@FINHUTC	A Christian discussion group
H-RUSSIA@MSU.EDU	H-Net Russian History list
H-SHGAPE@MSU.EDU	H-Net Gilded Age and Progressive Era List
HESSE-L@UCSBVM.UCSB.EDU	The Works of Hermann Hesse
ISO8859@JHUVM	A group that discusses ASCII/EBCDI Character set issues (what fun!)
L-HCAP@NDSUVM1	A group for people interested in issues related to handicapped people in education
OHA-L@UKCC.BITNET	Oral History Association Discussion List
ONO-NET@UMINN1.BITNET	Resource for those interested in the works of Yoko Ono
PALCLIME@SIVM.BITNET	Paleoclimate, Paleoecology for late Mesozoic & early Cenozoic
PFTFI-L@ICNUCEVM.BITNET	Progetto Finalizzato Telecomunicazioni– UO Firenze

Mailing List	Description
PHILOSOP@YORKVM1	The Philosophy Discussion forum
SCAN-L@UAFSYSB.BITNET	Radio Scanner Discussion forum
SCR-L@MIZZOU1.BITNET	Study of Cognitive Rehabilitation, Traumatic Brain Injury
SCREEN-L@UA1VM.UA.EDU	Film and TV Studies Discussion List
SEMLA-L@UGA.BITNET	Southeast Music Library Association Mailing List
SEXADD-L@KENTVM.BITNET	Exchange forum for sexual addiction, dependency, or compulsion
SFER-L@UCF1VM.BITNET	South Florida Environmental Reader
SHAMANS@UAFSYSB.BITNET	Shamans Impact of the Internet on Religion
SHEEP-L@LISTSERV.UU.SE	This is a list for people interested in sheep
SIEGE@MORGAN.UCS.MUN.CA	Medieval Siege Weaponry List
SKATE-IT@ULKYVM.BITNET	Skating discussion group
SKEPTIC@JHUVM.BITNET	SKEPTIC Discussion Group
SLAVERY@UHUPVM1.UH.EDU	The history of slavery, the slave trade, abolition, and emancipation
SLDRTY-L@LISTSERV.SYR.EDU	Members of Solidarity, a socialist organization, Detroit
SLLING-L@YALEVM.BITNET	Sign Language Linguistics List
SPACESCI@UGA.BITNET	sci.space.science digest
SS-L@UIUCVMD.BITNET	SS-L Sjogren's Syndrome
SWL-TR@TRITU.BITNET	Short Wave Listening in Turkiye
TECTONIC@MSU.EDU	Geology 351 Class
TEX-D-L@DEARN.BITNET	German TeX Users Communication List
TFTD-L@TAMVM1.TAMU.EDU	Thought for the day
TGIS-L@UBVM.BITNET	Temporal Topics on GIS List
THEATRE@PUCC.BITNET	The Theatre Discussion List
THYST-L@BROWNVM.BITNET	Thistle Discussion List
TIBET-L@IUBVM.BITNET	Tibet Interest List
TN-L@UAFSYSB.BITNET	Discussion of Cranial Neurolgia Disorders
TNT-L@UMAB.BITNET	TNT Discussion Group
TRANSY-L@UKCC.BITNET	Transylvania University Alumni
TREPAN-L@BROWNVM.BITNET	Weird News List
TVDIRECT@ARIZVM1.BITNET	Professional TV Directors and Producers
UBTKD-L@UBVM.BITNET	UB TaeKwonDo

continues

Continued

Mailing List	Description
UIWAGE-L@ECUVM1.BITNET	Unemployment Insurance Wage List
UNCJIN-L@ALBNYVM1.BITNET	United Nations Criminal Justice Information Network
UNIX-WIZ@NDSUVM1.BITNET	UNIX-Wizards Mailing List
UNLBIO-L@UNLVM.BITNET	UNL Center for Biotechnology List
UTOPIA-L@UBVM.BITNET	Utopias and Utopianism
VAMPYRES@GUVM.BITNET	Vampiric lore, fact, and fiction.
VEGAN-L@TEMPLEVM.BITNET	Vegan Discussion Group
VETTE-L@EMUVM1.BITNET	Corvette Discussion—Service Info, Shows, and so on.
VOEGLN-L@LSUVM.BITNET	Discussion list on Eric Voegelin's writing and philosophy
VOICES-L@ORACLE.	Voices In My Head List
VWAR-L@UBVM.BITNET	Vietnam War Discussion List
WCENTR-L@MIZZOU1.BITNET	Moderated Writing Center forum
WEIMING@ULKYVM.BITNET	Chinese Newsletter Distribution List
WHITESOX@MITVMA.BITNET	Chicago White Sox Mailing List
WHR-L@PSUVM.BITNET	Women's History in Rhetoric
WORCIV-L@UBVM.BITNET	World Civilization Committee
WVMS-L@WVNVM.BITNET	NASA Classroom of the Future: WV Mathematics and Science List
XTROPY-L@UBVM.BITNET	Extropians—discussion and development of Extropian ideas
YACHT-L@HEARN.BITNET	The Sailing and Amateur Boat Building List

Does this list give you an idea of the wild, wacky, and well-worth-reading mailing lists available to you? (I'm planning to check out the Voices in My Head List.) This is just a tiny portion of what's out there. And this is just the LISTSERV groups; there are many more non-LISTSERV groups that cover a similarly eclectic subject matter.

The LISTSERV Address

Let's take a look at the LISTSERV address. It's made up of three parts: the group name itself, the LISTSERV site, and (usually) .bitnet. For instance, the address of the group College Activism/Information List is **actnow-l@brownvm.bitnet**. Actnow-l is the name of the group, and brownvm is the name of the site. (As you can see in the previous table, some of these LISTSERV groups—such as **SLAVERY@UHUPVM1.UH.EDU**—don't have the .bitnet bit at the end.)

A site is a computer that has the LISTSERV program, and it handles one or more LISTSERV groups. In fact, a site may have dozens of groups. The brownvm site, for instance, also maintains the ACH-EC-L, AFRICA-L, and AGING-L forums, among a few dozen more.

Let's Do It—Subscribing

Once you've found a LISTSERV group to which you want to subscribe, you must send an e-mail message to the LISTSERV site (not to the group itself), asking to subscribe to the list. Don't worry, you are not going to have to pay; the vast majority of mailing lists are completely free. Send a message with the following text in the body (not the subject) of the message.

    SUBSCRIBE group *firstname lastname*

For instance, if I wanted to subscribe to the actnow-l list at the brownvm LISTSERV site, I would send a message to listserv@brownvm.bitnet, and in the body of the message, I'd write **SUBSCRIBE actnow-l Peter Kent**.

As you can see in the following figure, you send the message to **listserv@sitename** (in this case to **listserv@brownvm.bitnet**), and the SUBSCRIBE message contains only the name of the group (not the entire group address).

Don't Forget These Details

Note that you might have to put something in the Subject line; some e-mail programs won't let you send e-mail unless you include a subject. In such a case, just type something—anything (1, for instance)—in the Subject line. And if your e-mail program automatically inserts a signature (information such as your name, street address, and so on that is inserted at the end of the message), turn the signature off before sending the message, or you'll get error messages back from the LISTSERV site.

You may (or may not) receive some kind of confirmation message from the group. Such a message would tell you that you have subscribed, and would provide background information about the group and the different commands you can use. You may receive a message telling you how to confirm your subscription. If so, follow the instructions in the message. You may also receive instructions about working with the mailing list; read this carefully, as it will contain important information. Once you've subscribed, you can either sit back and wait for the messages to arrive, or you can send your own messages. To send messages, address mail to the full group address (to actnow-l@brownvm.bitnet, for example).

This is all it takes to subscribe to a LISTSERV mailing list. (This is the AK-Mail e-mail program.)

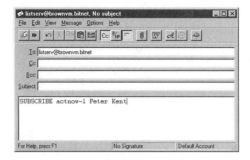

Enough Already!—Unsubscribing

When you're tired of receiving all these messages (and the volume may very well be overwhelming), you'll have to unsubscribe, which you do by sending another message to the LISTSERV address. You still send the message to listserv@sitename (such as listserv@brownvm.bitnet), but this time type **SIGNOFF** *groupname* (SIGNOFF actnow-l, for instance) in the body of the message.

The next figure shows the SIGNOFF message you use to unsubscribe. Again, make sure you address it to **listserv@sitename**, not to the group name. And make sure the group name—but not the entire group address—appears after SIGNOFF.

Message Digests

Here's a way to make your mailing lists easier to handle: get message digests. With message digests you'll receive one large message at the end of the day that contains all the messages the mailing list has received during the day—instead of receiving dozens of messages throughout the day. To request message digests, send a message to the LISTSERV server at **listserv@sitename** and type the message **set listname digest** (such as **set actnow-l digest**).

The message you receive at the end of the day has a list of Subjects at the top. You can use your e-mail program's Find command (or save the message in a text file and use your word processor's Find command) to quickly get to the messages that interest you. If you want to turn the digest off, use the command **set listname nodig**. Note, however, that not all mailing lists can provide message digests.

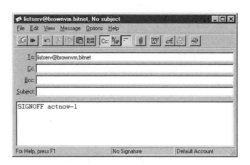

Unsubscribing to a LISTSERV mailing list is also easy.

Getting Fancy with LISTSERV

You can do a few neat things with LISTSERV. By sending e-mail messages to the LISTSERV site, you can tell the LISTSERV software how you want to handle your messages. You can ask LISTSERV to send you an acknowledgment each time you send a message (by default, most groups won't do this). You can find information about another group member, or you can tell LISTSERV not to provide information about you to other users. You can tell LISTSERV to stop sending you messages temporarily (perhaps when you go on vacation), or you can tell it to send only the message subjects instead of the entire messages. You can request a specific message, and you can even search the archives for old messages.

When you first subscribe to a mailing list, it's a good idea to send the **info** command to the **listserv@sitename address** (not the group itself). Put the word **info** in the body of the message. A document containing important information about working with the list will be returned to you.

Remember This!

Remember that when you want to send a message to be read by other group members, you must address it to the ***groupname@sitename***. For all other purposes (to subscribe, unsubscribe, change user options, get more information, and so on), send the message to ***listserv@sitename***. Send these messages to the group itself, and you may get complaints. But hey, you wouldn't be alone. Many of us (me included, several times), forget to change the address and send these commands to the wrong address! Actually, these days, some LISTSERV servers recognize a message that contains commands, intercepts it before it gets to the mailing-list group, and sends it back to you.

165

In addition, you can combine these commands. For instance, you can send an e-mail message to ***listserv@sitename*** with these lines in the body of the message:

> list
>
> query *groupname*
>
> info ?

This tells LISTSERV to send you a list of the groups handled by this site (**list**), to tell you which options you have set (**query groupname**), and to send you a list of information guides (**info ?**). It's a good idea to use this last command to find out about user documentation they have available, and then to use the **info *documentname*** command to have specific documents sent to you. (At some sites, sending e-mail to the LISTSERV address with the message **INFO REFCARD** will get you a document outlining the commands.)

Using Majordomo

Check This Out...

Mailing List Programs There are many different mailing list programs. They'll all work in a similar manner, but with a few variations. In some cases, for instance, there's no need to provide your name, just enter a **subscribe *group*** command. Or maybe the command will be **join *group***. Also, some mailing-list programs require that the command is placed in the Subject line, not the body of the message.

The other common mailing list program is Majordomo. Here's how to subscribe to a Majordomo list. It's very similar to working with LISTSERV.

To subscribe, send a message to **majordomo@*sitename***. For instance, **majordomo@usa.net**, **majordomo@ big.host.com**, and so on. In the body of the message type **subscribe *group firstname lastname***.

The same as with LISTSERV, eh? When you unsubscribe, though, you'll use a different command. Instead of SIGNOFF, use:

unsubscribe *group*

Finally, when sending messages to the group, remember to send them to ***group@sitename***.

Using Manually Administered Lists

Some lists are administered manually. That means there is no computer running the list; instead, some person actually reads the subscription requests and adds people to the list manually.

This can be administered in many ways. You may simply send e-mail to the person who administers the list and say, "hey, add me to the list please." Often, however, there's a special address associated with the list. You may have to send your subscription list to **listname-request@*hostname***. For instance, if the list is called **goodbeer**, and it's at the **bighost.com** hostname, you would send your subscription request to **goodbeer-request@bighost.com**. Once you've subscribed you can send your actual correspondence to the list to **goodbeer@bighost.com**.

Handling Mailing List Correspondence

Working with a mailing list is quite simple. When a message arrives, you find it in your e-mail inbox along with all your normal e-mail. If you read a message to which you want to reply, simply use the reply function of your e-mail program (see Chapter 3 for more information), and the new message is addressed to the correct place. At least, in most cases it is addressed correctly. Check the return address that your e-mail program enters for you. With some mailing lists, you'll find that the Return address in the header of the message you received is not the address to which you are supposed to send messages— rather, it's the address of the person who sent the message to the group. I find this rather irritating, but many groups work this way. You may be able to use a Reply To All command (not all mail programs have this, but many do), to send a message to the originator *and* to the list. Otherwise you'll simply have to type the list address into the To box in your mail-composition window.

To send a message about a new subject, simply write a new message, address it to the mailing-list address, and send it off.

In some ways, working with mailing lists is not as convenient as working with newsgroups. The newsgroup programs have a lot of features for dealing with discussions. Of course, your e-mail program will almost certainly let you print and save messages just as a newsgroup program would. What's often missing, though, are the threading functions that you get in newsgroup messages (which enable you to quickly see which messages are part of a series of responses). Some mail programs have these— Netscape's Messenger, part of the Communicator suite of programs has this—but most do not. You may also find that messages are sent to you out of order, in which case you may end up reading a response to a message that appears lower down in your e-mail inbox before you read the original message. This is all the more reason you should use the message digest (discussed earlier) to get the messages in the most convenient form possible.

Filtering Tools Learn how to use your mail program's filtering tools. That way you can quickly direct incoming mail from mailing lists into the appropriate folders, and even automatically delete messages that you're not interested in.

Using the Web Forums

Web forums are discussion groups associated with a particular Web site. They're often technical-support forums, forums set up by a company to help provide information to their customers, but you may run into forums about many different subjects and for many different purposes.

Finding Web forums is a little difficult right now; they're the sort of thing you run into, rather than go looking for. Reference.com (**http://www.reference.com/**) tracks a few Web forums, but doesn't provide a list of them...perhaps they will soon. You could search for **"web forum"** at AltaVista (see Chapter 21), and you'll find thousands, though in a very disorganized listing. I haven't yet been able to track down a good Web-forum directory.

To use a Web forum you simply click on the appropriate links at a Web site. You'll use forms to read messages and to respond to them.

One of perhaps 25,000 Web forums, in this case a discussion group related to finding accomodation in London.

The Least You Need to Know

➤ A mailing list is a discussion group in which messages are exchanged through the e-mail system.

➤ Mailing lists may be administered manually or run by a program such as LISTERV or Majordomo.

➤ Subscribe to a LISTSERV group by including the command **subscribe *groupname firstname lastname*** in the body of a message and sending the message to ***listserv@sitename***.

➤ To unsubscribe from a LISTSERV list, send the command **SIGNOFF *groupname*** in the body of a message.

➤ To subscribe to a Majordomo list, you normally send a message saying **SUBSCRIBE *groupname firstname lastname*** in the body. The message goes to the major-domo address (such as **majordomo@*bighost***), not the list name address.

➤ To unsubscribe from a Majordomo list use the **UNSUBSCRIBE** command (not SIGNOFF).

➤ To subscribe to a manually administered list, write to the person running the list and ask to join. Or you may need to e-mail to ***listname*-request@*hostname***.

➤ When you join a list, send a message with the command info in the body to find out important information about working with the list.

➤ Thousands of Web forums are available, but they're hard to track down. Search for **"web forum"** at AltaVista.

Chapter 14

The Giant Soft-ware Store: FTP

In This Chapter

➤ What is FTP?

➤ FTP may be difficult, but it can be easy

➤ Ftping with your Web browser

➤ Clues that will help you find files

➤ Ftping with true FTP programs

➤ Dealing with compressed files

➤ Protecting yourself from viruses

The Internet is a vast computer library. Virtually any type of computer file imaginable is available somewhere on the Internet. You'll find freeware (programs you can use for free) and shareware (programs you must pay a small fee to use) in almost all types of files: music, pictures, video, 3-D images, and many types of hypertext documents. You'll probably find every file type you can possibly name on the Internet.

Where are these files? You looked at the World Wide Web in Chapters 5–9, and you know that you can download plenty of files from the Web. But there's another system that predates the Web: FTP.

To give you a little bit of history, FTP is one of those quaint old UNIX-geek terms. It stands for *file transfer protocol*, and it's an old UNIX system for transferring files from one computer to another. In fact, FTP is really the original core of the Internet: the whole purpose of the Internet was to allow the transfer of computer files between research institutions. Even e-mail came later; it was reportedly slipped into the Internet by geeks who didn't keep the bureaucrats fully apprised. (The geeks feared that the managers would think e-mail would be misused; from what I've seen of electronic communications, the managers would have been right!)

Techno Talk

Using the Command Line?

Command-line users can refer to Chapters 18 and 19 of the first edition of *The Complete Idiot's Guide to the Internet* for more information. Send e-mail to **ciginternet@mcp.com** with **allftp** in the Subject line to have the chapters mailed to you. See Appendix C for more information on using the mail responder.

There are FTP sites all over the Internet, containing literally millions of computer files. And although some of these sites are private, many are open to the public. With FTP, it's very possible that you might discover a fascinating file on a computer in Austria (or Australia, or Alabama, or Anywhere). You might have checked it out because someone told you where it was, or because you saw it mentioned in an Internet directory of some kind, or because you saw a message in a newsgroup about it. The file itself could be a public domain or shareware program, a document containing information you want for some research you're working on, a picture, a book you want to read, or just about anything else.

Suppose then that you're searching for one of the files described above. You might be told to "ftp to such and such a computer to find this file." That simply means "use the FTP system to grab the file." Of course right now you probably don't know what that means either, so you'll find yourself asking, "how do I get the file from that computer to my computer?"

In some cases, you may have specific permission to get onto another computer and grab files. A researcher, for instance, may have been given permission to access files on a computer owned by an organization involved in the same sort of research—another university or government department, perhaps. (I have private FTP directories on various publishers' FTP sites, so I can upload Web pages, or chapters for a book, or whatever.) To get into a directory that requires special permission, you need to use a login name and a password.

In other cases, though, you'll just be rooting around on other systems without specific permission. Some systems are open to the public; anyone can get on and grab files that the system administrator has decided should be publicly accessible. This type of access is known as *anonymous ftp* because you don't need a unique login name to get onto the computer; you simply log in as *anonymous*, and enter your e-mail address for the password. If you are working at the UNIX command line, as many unfortunate people still do, you have to type this information. However, the rest of you are using a program that will enter this information for you.

Before you start, let me give you a word of advice about *when* you should use FTP. Many systems don't like people digging around during business hours. They would rather you come in during evenings and weekends. In fact, you may have trouble getting into many FTP sites during the day because they are so busy. You may see a message asking you to restrict your use to after-hours, or the FTP site may not let you in at all during certain hours. Of course your day may be the site's night, so you need to consider where (geographically) the site is located.

Tracking Down a File with Archie What if you know the file you want, but you have no idea where to look for it? A quick way to track down a file that's stored somewhere on an Internet FTP site is by using Archie. You'll learn about Archie in Chapter 15.

Different Flavors of FTP

FTP was originally a command-line program in which you had to type commands at a prompt and press the Enter key. Information would then scroll past on your screen, perhaps too fast for you to read (unless you knew the secret command to make it slow down or stop). You'd have to read this information and then type another command. Although UNIX geeks got some sort of strange masochistic pleasure out of that sort of thing, real people found early FTP to be a painful experience—and most people avoided it.

In the early 1990s (a year or two before the Internet boom), FTP became automated to some extent. This automation made it possible to get to some FTP sites using *Gopher*, a system we'll be looking at in Chapter 16. With Gopher, you selected files from a menu system instead of by typing commands. Yet even this was inconvenient for a number of reasons, the most important being that you could access only FTP sites for which some kindly Gopher author had created menus.

Next came graphical FTP programs. There are plenty around, but the best I've seen are CuteFTP and WS_FTP (Windows shareware programs), and Fetch, a Macintosh shareware program (a new Mac program, NetFinder, is getting very good reviews, too; see Appendix

A for information about finding all these programs). There's also Anarchie, another Macintosh shareware program (one that you'll learn more about in Chapter 15). Many others are available, particularly for Windows. Most of the graphical FTP programs allow you to see lists of files and to use your mouse to carry out the operations. Using FTP with these systems was a pleasure; all of a sudden FTP became easy.

Finally, FTP was incorporated into Web browsers. You can now go to an FTP site using your Web browser. Because the FTP site appears as a document with links in it, you can click a link to view the contents of a directory, to read a text file, or to transfer a computer file to your computer.

In this chapter we're going to look at running FTP sessions with a Web browser, for a couple of reasons. First, it's a very easy way to work with FTP. Second, you probably already have a Web browser. However, there are some very good reasons for getting hold of a true FTP program; we'll discuss this issue towards the end of this chapter.

Hitting the FTP Trail

To work through an FTP example, go to **ftp://ftp.dartmouth.edu/**. This is where you can find the Macintosh Fetch FTP program. (If you prefer to visit another FTP site, you can follow along and do so; the principles are the same.) I've given you the FTP site names, but not the directories holding the files; you can track them down when you get there.

Check This Out...

What's in a Name?

Take a minute to analyze a site name. First there's the **ftp://** part. This simply tells your browser that you want to go to an FTP site. Then there's the FTP site name (or host name): **ftp.dartmouth.edu**. It identifies the computer that contains the files you are after. That might be followed by a directory name. I haven't given you a directory name in this example, but I could have told you to go to **ftp.dartmouth.edu/pub/software/mac**. The **/pub/software/mac** bit tells the browser which directory it must change to in order to find the files you want.

To start, open your Web browser. Click inside the **Address** text box, type **ftp://ftp.dartmouth.edu** (or **ftp://** and the address of another site you want to visit), and press **Enter**. Actually, in most browsers these days, you can omit **ftp://** as long as the FTP site name begins with ftp. In other words, instead of typing out **ftp://ftp.dartmouth.edu**, you can generally get away with typing only **ftp.dartmouth.edu**.

In a few moments, with luck, you'll see something like the screen shown in the following figure. Without luck, you'll probably get a message telling you that you cannot connect to the FTP site. If that happens, check to see if you typed the name correctly. If you did, you'll have to wait and try again later; the site may be closed, or it may be very busy.

Name or Number The FTP site or host name could be a name (leo.nmc.edu) or a number (192.88.242.239).

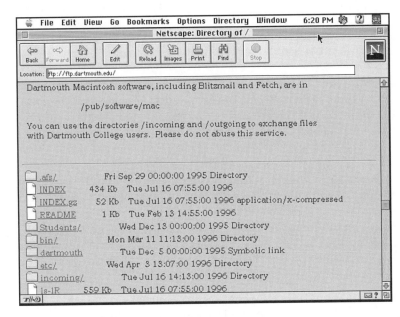

If you've used command-line FTP, you'll love working in a browser. This is the Macintosh version of Netscape Navigator 3.

Notice, by the way, that you didn't have to enter the anonymous login name or your e-mail address as a password. The browser handled all of that for you.

Incidentally, there's another way to get to an FTP site. Many Web authors create links from their Web pages to FTP sites. Click the link, and you'll go to that site.

Files and Links—What's All This?

What can you see at the FTP site? Each file and directory is shown as a link. Depending on the browser you are using, you might see information about the file or directory (refer to the previous figure). You might see a description of each item—file or directory, for instance—and the file size, so you'll know how big a file is before you transfer it.

You'll often see the file date and little icons that represent the directory or file type. In the previous figure you can see that there are both files and directories.

Private FTP Sites

If you want to enter a private FTP site, you will have to enter a login ID and a password. You can often enter the FTP site information in the format ftp://*username:password@hostname/directory/*. For example, if you enter **ftp://joeb:1234tyu@ftp.sherwoodforest.com/t1/home/joeb**, your browser connects to the ftp.sherwoodforest.com FTP site and displays the /t1/home/joeb directory; it uses the username **joeb** and the password **1234tyu** to gain access. However, in some browsers, using that method causes the browser to save your password in a drop-down list box associated with the Location text box. Therefore, if you want to be really safe, use the format ftp://*username@hostname/directory*. When the browser connects to the FTP site it opens a dialog box into which you can type your password.

Click a directory link to see the contents of that directory. The browser displays another Web document, showing the contents of that directory. In most browsers you'll also find a link back to the parent directory: in Netscape you'll see an "Up to a higher level directory" link, for instance. The following figure shows what you will find if you click the **pub** link at the **ftp.dartmouth.edu** site. Why pub? Because that's commonly used to hold publicly available files. This time you can see that there's a file in this directory, along with three more subdirectories.

How Do I Find Files? Don't
forget Archie! Archie is a system that lets you search an index of FTP sites throughout the world for just the file you need. See Chapter 15 for more information.

What happens when you click a link to a file? The same thing that would happen if you did so from a true Web document. If the browser can display or play the file type, it will. If it can't, it will try to send it to the associated application. If there is no associated application, it will ask you what to do with it, allowing you to save it on the hard disk. This all works in the same way as it does when you are at a Web site—the browser looks at the file type and acts accordingly. (See Chapters 7 and 8 for more information.)

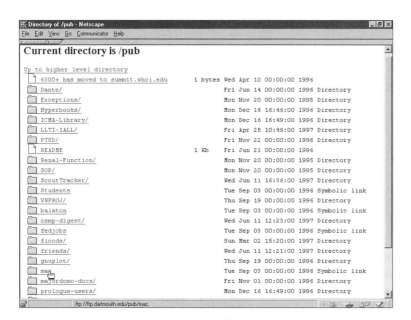

The contents of the pub directory at the FTP site. This time you're looking at a Windows version of Netscape.

Finding That Pot o' Gold

Now that you're in, you want to find the file that you know lies somewhere on this system. (In my example, you're looking for Fetch, the Macintosh FTP program.) Where do you start? Well, finding files at an FTP site is often a little difficult. There are no conventions for how such sites should be set up, so you often have to dig through directories that look like they might contain what you want, until you find what you want.

Remember, though, that your Web browser can display text files. When you first get to an FTP site, look for files called INDEX, README, DIRECTORY, and so on. These often contain information that will help you find what you need. The more organized sites even contain text files with full indexes of their contents, or at least lists of the directories and the types of files you'll find. Click one of these files to transfer the document to your Web browser, read the file, and then click the **Back** button to return to the directory.

Look for Clues

FTP Connections Through Web Pages

Many FTP sites are now accessible directly through Web documents. For instance, instead of going to ftp://ftp.winsite.com/ (a well-known shareware archive), you could go to **http://www.winsite.com/**. It's often easier to connect to and search the Web sites than it is the FTP sites.

You'll often find that directories have names that describe their contents: **slip** will probably contain SLIP software, **mac** will have Macintosh software, **xwindow** will have X Window software, **windows** will have Microsoft Windows software, **gif** will contain GIF-format graphics, and so on. If you know what you are looking for, you can often figure out what the directory names mean. In the example, you knew where to go because when you first arrived at the site you saw a message saying that Fetch was in /pub/software/ mac. So you clicked on **pub**, and then on **software**, and then on **mac**.

It Looks a Little Strange

You'll often find full FTP site and path information, which takes you straight to the directory you want (such as **ftp.dartmouth.edu/pub/ software/mac**). If you're used to working in DOS and Windows, FTP site directory names may seem strange for two reasons. First, you'll see a forward slash (/) instead of a backslash (\), separating the directories in the path. In the DOS world, you use a backslash (\), but in the UNIX world, you use the forward slash character (/) instead—and most Internet host computers still run on UNIX, so the forward slash has become a convention. Second, the directory names are often long. In DOS, you can't have directories with more than 12 characters in the name (including a period and an extension). In Windows 95, however, you can. This new operating system *and* UNIX computers allow long file and directory names.

Getting the File

When you find the file you want, simply click it, and save it in the same way you would save a file from a Web document (see Chapter 6). The following figure shows Fetch being saved from FTP.

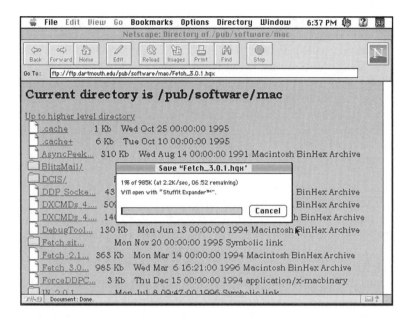

You can save files from FTP sites with a few clicks.

Many files on FTP sites are *compressed*. That is, a special program has been used to "squeeze" the information into a smaller area. You can't use a file in its compressed state, but if you store it and transmit it in that state, you'll save disk space and transmission time. You can read more about these compressed formats in Chapter 17.

In this case, we are transferring a .hqx file that contains a .sit file. A program such as StuffIt Expander can extract the .sit file (a compressed file) from within the BinHex .hqx file (a common format for transferring Mac files across the Internet).

Same Name, Different Extension

While digging around in an FTP site, you might notice that files often have the same name except for the last few characters; you might find **thisdoc.txt** and **thisdoc.zip**, for instance. The first is a simple ASCII text file, and the second is a ZIP file, which (you'll probably notice) is much smaller than the first. If you know you can decompress the file once you have it, download the compressed version. It'll save you time and money.

It's the Real Thing—Using a Genuine FTP Program

There are some very good reasons for using a genuine FTP program, instead of making do with your Web browser. First, you may run into FTP sites that won't work well through a Web browser. Also, if you need to upload files to an FTP site you may have problems; more recent browsers, such as Netscape Navigator 3 and 4, allow you to do this, but many other browsers don't. (In Navigator you can drag files from, for example, Windows Explorer, and drop them onto the FTP site displayed in the browser window to automatically upload those files.)

Here's another reason for getting hold of a true FTP program, a reason that's little understood yet very important. Some good FTP programs (such as CuteFTP) can resume interrupted transfers. For instance, let's say you've almost finished transferring the latest version of Netscape Navigator (it's over 15MB!), when the transfer stops. Why it stops is not important; perhaps your two-year-old rugrat just reached up and pressed that big red button on the front of your computer. Perhaps your service provider's system just died. Maybe lightning struck the power lines somewhere, and the power went out. Whatever the reason, if you're using a Web browser to transfer that file, you'll have to start all over again. If you were using a good FTP program, though, you could reconnect, go back to the FTP site, and begin the transfer again…and all that the program would need to do would be transfer the missing part of the file, not all the stuff that had already transferred.

Now, I've heard it said that the Internet represents in some ways a giant step *backwards* in technology. Well, okay, I've said it myself a few times. Resumed transfers is one of those cases in which the technology being used on the Internet is way behind what has been used *off* the Internet for years. (On line help is another case.) This technology is just finding its way to the Internet, but for the moment Web browsers cannot resume interrupted downloads. Some FTP programs can.

If you transfer a lot of files across the Internet, in particular large files, you'll want to use a true FTP program. (Note that not all FTP sites can resume interrupted transfers, so this won't work all the time.) You won't only want to use the FTP program when working in an actual FTP site, though. In many cases, when you think you're transferring from a Web site, the file is really coming from an FTP site. For example, look at the following illustration. This is Shareware.com, a large shareware library. Notice that underneath the links to the download files you can see little labels that tell you where each file is stored—ftp.tas.gov.au, for instance. So, in this case you can quickly see that the file is coming from an FTP site. However, most Web pages won't be this convenient. You can still figure out if the file is coming from an FTP site, though; point at the link and in the status bar you'll see the URL of the file, in this case **ftp://ftp.tas.gov.au/pub/simtelnet/win95/ inet/u2n4332f.zip**.

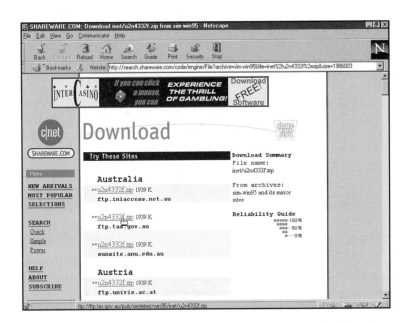

Yes, it's a Web page...but the files the page links to are actually stored at an FTP site, as you can see by pointing at a link and looking at the status bar.

You can quickly copy this information from the link using the browser's pop-up menu (in a Windows browser right-click the link and choose something like **Copy Link Location**; in a Mac browser you'll probably be able to hold the mouse button down for a moment to open the menu). Then you can paste the information into your FTP program, and use that program to download the file.

If that's not enough, here are two more reasons to use a real FTP program. It's often quicker and easier to connect to a site using an FTP program than a Web browser, and you can also set an FTP program to keep trying automatically every few minutes. So if the site's busy, the FTP program can simply try until it gets through.So you may run into cases in which the browser FTP features are not enough. For those times, you need to get a real FTP program.

Which and Where

There are lots of good FTP programs around. If you use the Mac, try Fetch or Anarchie. For Windows, try WS_FTP or CuteFTP (my personal favorite). Many good Windows FTP programs are available as freeware or shareware on the Internet. See Appendix A for ideas on where to look for the software you want. (Remember, you need a program that will allow you to resume interrupted downloads, which means you'll probably have to pay the registration fee!)

Let's take a quick look at CuteFTP. We won't go into great detail about working with this program, but it should at least give you an idea of what's going on. When you get an FTP program, go through that old familiar routine: read the documentation carefully to make sure you understand how to use it. (FTP programs are generally fairly easy to deal with.)

CuteFTP is actually very easy to use. If you've ever used UNIX FTP, you know that using it is like eating soup with a fork—not particularly satisfying. CuteFTP, on the other hand, is what FTP should be. You have all the commands at your fingertips, plus a library of FTP sites to select from. No more mistyping FTP host names!

Installing CuteFTP is simple. Just run the installation program. Then start CuteFTP by going through the Windows 95 Start menu, or double-click its Program Manager icon. CuteFTP has two ways to connect to an FTP site; you can add an entry to the Site Manager (press **F4** to open this, then click **Add Site**), or use Quick Connect (**Ctrl+C**). Use the Site Manager for FTP sites you expect to visit again (they'll be stored in the Site Manager), or use Quick Connect if you *don't* expect to be back.

For instance, in the following illustration you can see the FTP Site Edit box, the one that opens when you add a site to Site Manager. Enter the following information:

Adding FTP-site information to the Site Manager.

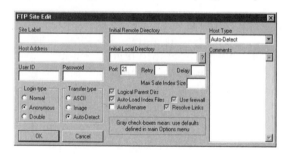

1. Type a **Site Label** (anything that helps you remember what the site contains—this name appears in the Site Manager).

2. Enter the actual FTP site **Host Address**.

3. If you are going to an "anonymous" FTP site, leave the **Anonymous** option button selected. You only need to enter a **User ID** and **Password** if you're going to a private FTP site.

4. If you know which directory you want to go to when you get to the FTP site, enter it in the **Initial Remote Directory** text box.

5. You can also enter the **Initial Local Directory**—the directory on your computer that should be displayed and into which transferred files will be placed. You can always select this later, though.

6. You can ignore most of the other settings; they're almost always okay, or represent advanced features.

7. Click the **OK** button to save the information.

8. In the Site Manager click the new entry, then click **Connect** to begin the session.

When you click OK, CuteFTP tries to connect to the FTP site. Once it's connected you'll see the FTP site's directories listed on the right, and the directories on your computer's hard disk listed on the left (see the following figure).

You can move around in the directories by double-clicking on folders or by right-clicking and selecting **Change Directory** (that's really handy, because if you know where you want to go it's a lot quicker to type it in than to go through each directory in the path to get there).

A log window, showing you the funky FTP commands that you don't have to type

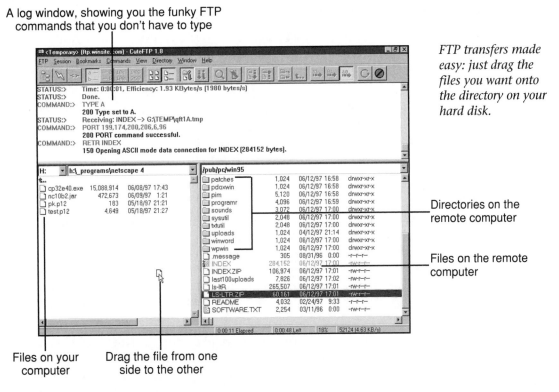

FTP transfers made easy: just drag the files you want onto the directory on your hard disk.

Directories on the remote computer

Files on the remote computer

Files on your computer

Drag the file from one side to the other

To read an index file, right-click the file and select **View**. To transfer a file to your system, just drag it from one side to the other (or, if you really prefer using menus, right-click and choose **Download**).

183

ASCII versus Binary

Notice the little **ab**, **01**, and **a0** buttons on the right side of the toolbar? These control whether the files are transferred as ASCII (the **ab** button), as Binary (the **01** button), or whether the program should decide the best way to transfer them (the **a0** button). Make sure you select the correct one before transferring a file. Select **ASCII** for files you know to be ASCII text files; select **Binary** for anything else. And remember, word processing files are not ASCII, they're binary; they contain special codes that are used to define the character formatting. You can tell the program to automatically determine a file's transfer type using the **FTP, Settings, Text File Extensions** menu option.

It's Alive! Viruses and Other Nasties

If you haven't been in a cave for the past six or seven years, you've probably heard about computer viruses. A *virus* is a computer program that can reproduce itself and even convince unknowing users to help spread it. It spreads far and wide and can do incredible amounts of damage.

As is true of real viruses, the effects of a virus on your system can range from almost-unnoticeable to fatal. A virus can do something as harmless as display a Christmas tree on your screen, or it can destroy everything on your hard disk. Viruses are real—but the threat is overstated. We'll be talking more about viruses in Chapter 22.

Where Now?

There are thousands of FTP sites all over the world. Generally, however, FTP is either a service of last resort—people go to the Web first and only use FTP if they know exactly where to go to get what they are looking for—or a service that is linked to Web pages. Perhaps you've read in a newsgroup message or a magazine article that a particular file is available at a particular FTP site. You can go directly to the site to find it, but most people don't go looking for things at FTP sites. The Web sites are far more convenient starting points.

However, you might want to see the **http://hoohoo.ncsa.uiuc.edu/ftp/** Web site—the Monster FTP Sites list—where you can find thousands of FTP sites. You can also find an FTP directory at **http://www.tile.net/**. and if you are searching for a particular file, and can't find it at the sources mentioned in Appendix A, you can try Archie, a friendly (but slow) little fellow who'll help you dig around in FTP. You'll learn about Archie in Chapter 15.

The Least You Need to Know

➤ FTP stands for file transfer protocol and refers to a system of file libraries.

➤ Anonymous FTP refers to a system that allows the public to transfer files.

➤ Start an FTP session in your Web browser using the format **ftp://*hostname*** in the Address text box (replacing *hostname* with the appropriate URL) and pressing **Enter**.

➤ Each directory and file at an FTP site is represented by a link; click the link to view the directory or transfer the file.

➤ If your browser can't connect to a particular site, or if you want the ability to resume interrupted downloads, get a true FTP program, such as WS_FTP (Windows) or Fetch (Macintosh).

➤ Protect yourself against viruses, but don't be paranoid. They're not as common as the antivirus companies want you to think.

Chapter 15

Archie, the Friendly File Librarian

In This Chapter

➤ What does Archie do?

➤ Four ways to use Archie

➤ Finding an Archie gateway on the Web

➤ Searching for files using your Web browser

➤ Using an Archie client

➤ Using Archie mail (if you don't want to wait)

➤ Doing descriptive (whatis) searches

Using FTP is okay—if you know where to go to find the file you want. And granted, you might find out about the FTP site by reading it in an e-mail message or in a document you find somewhere, or get to the file from a link in a Web page. However, that's just not helpful when you know the name of the file you are looking for you but have no idea where to find it.

Archie to the rescue! Designed by a few guys at McGill University in Canada, Archie is a system that indexes anonymous FTP sites (that is, public FTP sites), listing the files that are available at each site. Archie lists several million files at FTP sites throughout the world and provides a very useful way to find out where to go to grab a file in which you are interested. There's just one problem— Archie's extremely busy these days and can be very slow.

Archie's Client/Server Stuff

Like some other Internet systems, Archie is set up using a *client/server* system. An Archie server is a computer that periodically takes a look at all the Internet FTP sites around the world and builds a list of all their available files. Each server builds a database of those files. An Archie client program can then come along and search the server's database, using it as an index.

You may hear that it doesn't matter much which Archie server you use because they all do much the same thing; some are simply a few days more recent than others. This isn't always true. Sometimes you may get very different results from two different servers. For example, one server might find two *hits* (matches to your search request), and another might find seven.

Getting to Archie

Check This Out...

Try Archie Mail Archie has a descriptive-index search. That means you can search for a particular subject and find files related to that subject. You can't do this using a Web browser; try using Archie mail, instead. You can read more about Archie Mail later in this chapter.

To use Archie you must access an Archie server. No matter which Archie server you work with, you can choose from several methods of connecting to it:

➤ You can use Archie through the *command line*. This is unwieldy and difficult, though, and you *don't* want to do it this way if you can help it! If you absolutely can't help it, send e-mail to **ciginternet@mcp.com**, with **archie** in the Subject line to receive the Archie chapter from the first edition of *The Complete Idiot's Guide to the Internet*. (See Appendix C for more information about working with mail responder.)

➤ You can use your Web browser to go to an Archie *gateway*, a Web page containing a form that will help you search an Archie index. You enter information into the form, the information is sent to the Archie server, and the response from the server appears in another Web page.

➤ You can use a special Archie client program, such as WS_Archie (Windows) or Anarchie (Macintosh).

➤ You can use e-mail to send questions to an Archie server.

We'll start with the easiest way to use Archie: through your Web browser. Then we'll take a look at the last two methods previously listed.

Archie on the Web

Your Web browser is not a true Archie client. That is, there is no archie:// URL! Therefore, you'll have to use a "gateway" to an Archie client, of which there are dozens on the Web. Open your Web browser and go to **http://web.nexor.co.uk/archie.html** to find a list. Just in case that Web site's busy, here are several Archie sites you can try:

> http://www.lerc.nasa.gov/archieplex/
>
> http://hoohoo.ncsa.uiuc.edu/archie.html
>
> http://src.doc.ic.ac.uk/archieplexform.html

Archie? What does Archie mean? It's not an acronym (unlike Veronica and Jughead, whom you'll meet in Chapter 16). Instead it comes from the word *archive* (as in file archive). Remove the *v* and what have you got? Archie.

Most Archie sites offer both forms and nonforms search methods. Internet Explorer and Netscape Navigator are forms-capable browsers, which means that they can display forms components such as text boxes, command buttons, option buttons, and so on. If you are using one of these browsers or another forms-capable browser, select the forms search. (Most browsers can work with forms these days.)

Searching Archie

Different Gateways, Different Options

These Archie forms vary. Each Archie gateway is a little different, so if you use a different one from the one you're about to look at, you may find the options vary slightly, though they should be very similar.

The following figure shows an example of an Archie form, one at Imperial College in London (located at **http://src.doc.ic.ac.uk/archieplexform.html**). The simplest way to search is to type a file name or part of a file name into the **What would you like to search for?** text box and press **Enter** (or click the **Start Search** button). For instance, if you want to find the WS_Archie program you're going to look at later in this chapter, type **wsarchie** and press **Enter**. Why not **WS_ARCHIE**? Because even though the program name is WS_Archie, the file you need is actually called WSARCHIE.ZIP or WSARCHIE.EXE. Of course there's no way for you to know that if I hadn't told you.... If you are using a Macintosh, you might search for **anarchie** (as shown).

Archie gateways provide a link from the Web to Archie servers around the world.

Type the name of the file that you're looking for

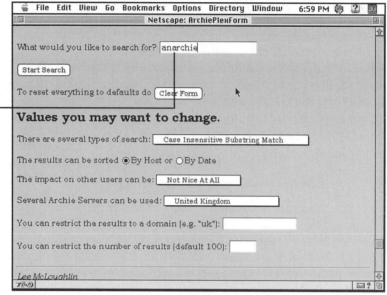

Stop! To cancel a search, click the browser's **Stop** toolbar button.

Archie searches are frequently very slow; often they simply don't work because the Archie server you selected is busy. (I'll show you how to choose another server in a moment.) If you are lucky, though, you'll eventually see a screen like the one shown next. This shows what the Archie server found: in this example, links to the WSARCHIE files. You can see that there are links to the host (the computer that contains the file you are looking for), the directory on the host that contains the file you want, and, in some cases, directly to the file you want. If you click one of the wsarchie.zip links, the browser begins transferring the file; if you click a link to a directory, your browser begins an FTP session in that directory.

Notice in the next figure that the pointer in the illustration is pointing at a directory. If you click it you'll go to that directory on the oslo-nntp.eunet.no server, which happens to be a computer in Norway. (As you can see, the directory was created in 1995.) There is, of course, a copy of the wsarchie.zip file on the ftp.cac.washington.edu host. If you look closely, though, it was created in 1994; it might not be the most recent version.

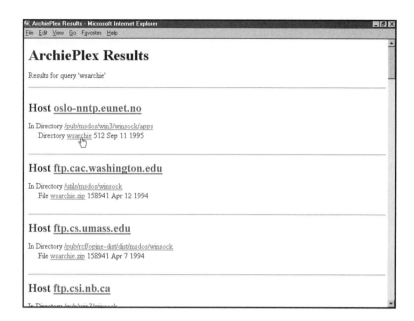

When (or if) Archie returns the result, it will be in a Web document containing links to the files.

Search the Document

Remember that you can use your browser's Find function to search the list of files once it's on-screen (in both Internet Explorer and Netscape, it's **Edit**, **Find** or **Ctrl+F**). For instance, let's say you want to download an EXE file (a self-extracting archive) instead of a ZIP file. Search for **.exe** to go directly to the file you need.

Archie's Options

Below the text box where you type what you want to search for are some more options you can use to narrow your search. Here's what you'll find:

➤ **Search type**   There are four types of searches, which I'll explain in a moment.

➤ **Sort by**   The list of files that is returned to you might be sorted by file date or according to the host containing the file. The file-date search is a good idea, as it will help you pick the latest version of the file.

➤ **Impact on other users**   You can tell Archie that you are not in a hurry (so other users can go first), or that you want the results right away. Difficult choice, huh?

➤ **Archie servers** You can select which Archie server you want to use from a list. If you find that the Archie server you tried is busy, or if it can't find what you want, try another one. You might want to try servers in countries in which the people are currently asleep; obviously those servers are likely to be less busy at night than during the day.

➤ **Restrict the results to a domain** You can tell the Archie server that you only want to see files in a particular domain (a particular host-computer type) such as UK (FTP sites in the United Kingdom), COM (commercial FTP sites), EDU (educational FTP sites) and so on.

➤ **Number of results** You can tell the Archie server how many results you want to see, but note that this setting is not always accurate.

Impact on Users

A couple of years ago people were talking seriously about how you should work on the Internet in a way that wouldn't slow down the network. For example, you should access sites that are close to you, access sites at night, and so on. However, it's hard to take that sort of thinking seriously anymore, as altruistic as it may be (and in fact you don't hear much of this kind of talk anymore). What with video, huge graphics on Web pages, Java, and so on, we're working on a whole new Internet with completely different data-transfer needs and capabilities.

The Search Types
Before you begin searching for a file name, you should determine which type of search you want to use. You have the following choices:

➤ **Exact** or **Exact Match** You must type the exact name of the file for which you are looking.

➤ **Regex** or **Regular Expression Match** You will type a UNIX regular expression. That means that Archie will regard some of the characters in the word you type as wild cards. If you don't understand regular expressions, you should just avoid this type of search altogether. (Everyone except UNIX geeks should probably avoid this option.)

➤ **Sub** or **Case Insensitive Substring Match** This tells Archie to search among file names for whatever you type. That is, it will look for all names that match what you type, as well as all names that *include* the characters you type. If you are searching for "wsarch," for example, archie finds "wsarch" and "wsarchie." Also, when you use a sub search, you don't need to worry about the case of the characters; Archie finds both "wsarch" and "WSARCH."

➤ **Subcase** or **Case Sensitive Substring Match**   This is like the sub search, except that you need to enter the case of the word correctly. If you enter "wsarch," Archie finds "wsarch" but not "WSARCH." You should generally avoid this type of search.

More often than not, you'll want to use the sub search (Case Insensitive Substring Match), and you'll probably find that sub has been set up as the default. It takes a little longer than the other types, but it's most likely to find what you are looking for.

Techno Talk
blah blah blah bla bla bl b

It Doesn't Seem to Work

The Substring Matches won't always find file names that contain what you typed. For instance, if you search for "ws_ftp" (a popular FTP program), it might not find ws_ftp32 at all, or it might find only one or two matches— even though you may know there are many files named ws_ftp32 at many FTP sites. Why does this happen? Archie shows you the ws_ftp matches before it shows you the ws_ftp32 matches; therefore, if there are a lot of ws_ftp matches, the results may exceed the find limit (controlled by the Number Of Results option). You can increase the Number Of Results and run the search again to see if there are any ws_ftp32 files, or you can make the search more specific, changing the search string to ws_ftp32.

You should realize, however, that file names are not always set in stone. With thousands of people posting millions of different files on thousands of different computers, file names sometimes get changed a little. If you have trouble finding something, try a variety of possible combinations.

Getting an Archie Client

If you use Archie a lot, you may want to get hold of a true Archie client: WS_Archie (Windows) or Anarchie (Macintosh). Of course using Archie through a Web site is very convenient, allowing you to search for a file and then click a link to download the file. But an Archie client can also automate getting the files you want by interacting with an FTP program. For instance, WS_Archie can interact with WS_FTP, ordering WS_FTP to go and get the file you select. Anarchie has a built-in FTP program, so you can search and retrieve with the same program.

Check This Out...

Looking for Shareware
Before you spend a lot of time with Archie, remember that you can often find files (particularly shareware programs) more easily at one of the Web libraries. (Appendix A gives you all the details on finding software.) You'll probably only want to use an Archie client if you have specific needs that are not met by the popular shareware sites.

You can find an Archie client at one of the software libraries mentioned in Appendix A. You also saw how to search at an Archie gateway for WS_Archie a few moments ago. Go ahead and download the client, and then install it according to the instructions you get with the program.

The following figure shows the WS_Archie screen. For this example, I searched for the Anarchie program for the Mac. I typed **anarchie** into the **Search for** text box, and then clicked **Search**—and off it went. Of course it may take a while, and sometimes it appears as if nothing is happening. But the program is really just waiting. (Read the Help file for an explanation of what the status bar messages mean.) If WS_Archie finds what I want, I can simply click the file I want to retrieve and select **File**, **Retrieve**. WS_Archie then launches WS_FTP, which downloads the file and then closes.

WS_Archie links to WS_FTP to automate downloads.

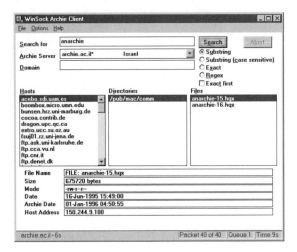

Mail-Order Archie

Archie's real downfall is time. It can take a long time to do an Archie search, and sometimes you find that you can't even get started because the Archie server is too busy to deal with your request.

For those times when you don't want to wait for Archie or spend time trying different Archies, you can use your e-mail program to send an e-mail message to an Archie server and wait for the response. You'll eventually receive a list of files and where you can find them. You then have to use your Web browser or FTP program to go to the FTP site and download the file.

How Soon Will I Get a Response?

Some responses take just a few minutes, but others (even responses to commands in the same e-mail message) can take hours. Archie says that if you wait two days without any response, there's probably a problem, and you may want to try the **set mailto *emailaddress*** command (where *emailaddress* is your e-mail address) to make sure that Archie has your correct e-mail address.

Using Archie by mail is actually quite simple. You send a message containing a command to **archie@*archieserver*** (where *archieserver* is the address of the Archie server you choose). You can choose any Archie server you want. The following table lists some possibilities.

Available Archie Servers

Archie Server Address	Location
archie.ans.net	USA, ANS
archie.internic.net	USA, AT&T (NY)
archie.rutgers.edu	USA, Rutgers University
archie.au	Australia
archie.th-darmstadt.de	Germany
archie.wide.ad.jp	Japan
archie.sogang.ac.kr	Korea

Having chosen the server, you're ready to create an e-mail message to the server. You can leave the Subject line blank if you want and put all the commands in the body of the message. (However, note that some e-mail systems don't allow blank Subject lines; if yours doesn't, you can put the first command in the Subject line).

Put the Archie commands (or the rest of them, if you put the first in the Subject line) in the body of the message. You can put as many commands as you want in a message, but each command must be on a separate line, and the first character of each

Archie List To find the latest list of Archie servers, send an e-mail message to an Archie server with the address **archie@*archieserver*** (such as **archie@archie.rutgers.edu**). In the body of the message, type *servers* on the first line. See Chapter 3 for more information about using e-mail.

command must be the first character on its line. For example, you might enter these commands:

servers
find wsarchie
whatis encryption

The **servers** command asks Archie to send you a list of Archie servers. (This list may not be complete; you may want to try several different servers to get a complete picture.) The **find** command tells Archie to search for wsarchie. And the **whatis** command enables you to do a descriptive search (in this case I'm searching for information about encryption). I'll explain **whatis** in the next section. Finally, when you finish all of this, send the e-mail message.

"Whatis" the Descriptive Index?

Archie has a **whatis** search that you might want to try. Unfortunately, this command is not currently available through the Web gateways or WS_Archie. You can use it with Archie mail, though. This command searches a *descriptive index*, an index of file descriptions.

Not all files indexed by Archie have a description, but many do. It may be worth a try if you are having trouble finding what you need. For example, you might use this command:

whatis encryption

Archie searches, and returns a list of files that meet your criteria. You may get a list of descriptions like this, for example:

codon	Simple encryption algorithm
des	Data encryption system (DES) routines and a login front-end
des-no-usa	Data encryption system (DES) code free of US restrictions

Sometimes you won't be able to figure out why the keyword you used matched some of the files listed, but that doesn't matter as long as some of them look like what you want.

Notice the word at the left end of each line. If you want to find out where the listed file is located, send e-mail back to the server with the command **find name** (where *name* is the word at the left end of the line in the preceding list). For example, if you type **find des-no-usa**, Archie will list the DES encryption files that you can download without worrying about U.S. export restrictions.

More E-Mail Commands

Here are other commands that you can use to configure your e-mail search:

➤ **set search *type***   You learned about the different search types earlier. You can send the **set search** command followed by **exact**, **regex**, **sub**, or **subcase** to tell Archie what type of search you want to do. If you don't specify a search type, the system will use **sub**.

➤ **help**   Sends a Mail Archie user's guide.

➤ **site *host***   You can enter a host IP address (the numbers that describe a host's location) or domain name, and Archie will send a list of all the files held at that FTP site.

➤ **quit**   This tells Archie to ignore everything that follows in the message. If you have a mail system that inserts a signature file automatically at the end of each message, you can use **quit** to make sure Archie doesn't think this signature information is another command. If Archie sees any command it doesn't understand, it automatically sends the help information—and you don't want to receive the help information every time you send an Archie request.

➤ **set mailto *mailaddress***   If you find that your Archie requests often go unanswered, it may be because your mail program is not inserting enough information in the From line. You can use this command (replacing *mailaddress* with your e-mail address) to enter the path to which you want Archie's response sent.

If you like the idea of working with Archie through the mail, send the **help** command to get the user's guide. There are plenty of little tricks you can use with this system.

The Least You Need to Know

➤ Archie servers index available files at thousands of FTP sites periodically. Archie clients can read the indexes.

➤ The easiest way to use Archie is through a Web page gateway on the Web. See **http://web.nexor.co.uk/archie.html** for a list of gateways.

➤ It's important to pick the correct type of search. The simplest is the **sub** search, which lets you enter part of the file name without worrying about the case you use.

➤ You may want to try WS_Archie (for Windows) or Anarchie (for the Mac). These are Archie client programs. WS_Archie works with WS_FTP to download a file you find. Anarchie has its own built-in FTP program.

➤ Using Archie by mail can be easy and convenient. You send messages to **archie@*archieserver*** (where *archieserver* is the name of the server you choose) and put the commands in the body of the message.

➤ Use the **whatis** command to search for a file description.

Chapter 16

Digging Through the Internet with Gopher

In This Chapter

➤ A bit of Gopher and Web history

➤ Why bother with Gopher?

➤ Starting a Gopher session

➤ Finding your way around Gopherspace

➤ Saving text documents and computer files

➤ Using Jughead to search a Gopher server

➤ Using Veronica to search in Gopherspace

The World Wide Web is what's "hot" on the Internet right now. Most of the growth in the Internet is occurring on the Web, and it's supposedly doubling in size every few weeks. True, that's another of those dubious Internet statistics, but regardless of the actual figures, it's certainly growing fast.

However, the Web is really quite new. At the end of 1993, even well into 1994, the World Wide Web was a sideshow on the Internet. Few people knew how to use it, and fewer still bothered. It wasn't hard to use, but there wasn't much incentive. For most Internet users there was no way to display pictures, listen to sounds, play video, or do any of the neat things you've learned to do with Internet Explorer, Netscape Navigator, or other browsers. It wasn't just that the Web was primarily text and little else; it was because the software simply wasn't available. (In fact it wasn't until the fourth quarter of 1994, soon after Netscape was released, that the Web boom really began.)

Knowing that, you're probably wondering how Internet users got around back in the distant past (okay, three years ago). What was the hot "navigation" system on the Internet in the days before Web? The answer's *Gopher*.

If you never used the Internet in the old command-line days, if Netscape and Internet Explorer and the other graphical user interface systems that abound are your only taste of the Internet, then you don't know how difficult the Internet could be. (Actually, many people are *still* using the Internet through a command-line interface—that is, typing complicated commands to get things done.) Many people who tried to use the Internet a few years ago were so turned off by the experience that they went away and never came back. FTP (which you learned about in Chapter 14) was extremely difficult. Telnet (Chapter 20) was pretty clunky—and still is. E-mail was just about bearable. All in all, the Internet was *not* a user-friendly place.

Let There Be Gopher

Command-Line Users

If you are one of the unfortunate souls still using the command-line interface, send an e-mail message to **ciginternet@mcp.com** and put the word **gopher** in the subject line. In return, you'll get the Gopher chapter from the first edition of the *Complete Idiot's Guide to the Internet*. This explains how to use Gopher if you're working from a dumb terminal.

Then along came Gopher. This tool was a revolution in simplicity, providing a nice menu system from which users could select options. Instead of remembering a variety of rather obscure and arcane commands to find what they needed, users could use the arrow keys to select options from the menu. Those options could take the user to other menus or to documents of some kind. The Gopher system is, in some ways, similar to the World Wide Web. It's a worldwide network of menu systems. Options in the menus linked to menus or other documents all over the world. These Gopher menus made the Internet much easier to use and much more accessible to people who weren't long-term cybergeeks.

For a while, Gopher looked like the future of the Internet—at least to a number of people who invested time and money in Internet software. A variety of "graphical point-and-click" Gopher programs were published commercially and were distributed as shareware and freeware. (You may have heard of WinGopher, for instance, an excellent Windows program for navigating through the Gopher system.)

Dead Before it Got Started

Gopher's days were numbered soon after it's birth. The World Wide Web actually dates back to the middle of 1992, though at that point it wasn't much more than a few documents posted by the creator of the Web, Tim Berners-Lee. Gopher began early in 1991, at the University of Minnesota, and quickly became popular thanks to its ease of use. But some people who saw the Web a year later realized that eventually the Web would usurp Gopher; even, it seems, one major proponent of Gopher understood that Gopher's popularity would be short lived. Still, Gopher hung on for another two years, until the Graphical User Interface browsers finally pushed the Web into the mainstream.

Then along came the Web. Or rather, along came the graphical Web browsers, which all of a sudden made the Web not only easy to use, but exciting, too. Interest in Gopher subsided rapidly, and everyone rushed off to learn how to create Web documents. And just where did that leave Gopher? Still alive and well (though ignored by most Internet users), for a couple of good reasons. First, there were already many Gopher systems set up, and a large number of them remain. Second, there are still millions of Internet users who don't have access to graphical Web browsers, and for them Gopher is the easiest tool available.

There's a lot of interesting information stored on Gopher servers around the world. Fortunately, you can get to it with your Web browser. That's right: your Web browser may be designed to work on the World Wide Web, but you can also use it to access Gopher.

Enough History—What Is Gopher?

The Gopher system is based on hundreds of Gopher *servers* (computers that contain the menus) and millions of Gopher *clients* (computers that are running the Gopher menu software that accesses the server's menus). Gopher servers are generally public, so any client can access the information from any server. And your Web browser is, in effect, a Gopher client.

Both commercial and shareware versions of graphical Gopher programs are available. You'll probably never use one, though. Working with Gopher through your Web browser works extremely well. Unlike FTP, which works well most (but not all) of the time, you'll find that your browser handles

Gopher

Why is it called Gopher? For three reasons. First, it was originally developed at the University of Minnesota, home of the Golden Gophers. Second, "gofer" is slang for someone who "goes fer" things—and Gopher's job is to "go fer" files and stuff. And third, the system digs its way through the Internet, like a gopher digs through a burrow. By the way, when you use Gopher you are traveling through Gopherspace.

Gopher sites just fine *all* of the time. (Okay, to be honest, there are a *few* geek things you can do with a true Gopher program that you can't do with a Web browser—such as see details about a menu option—but few people will miss these features.) So we're going to take a look at gophering through the Web.

Gopher It!

How do you get to a Gopher server? You can start a Gopher session in two ways—by clicking a link in a Web document that some kindly Web author has provided, or by typing the **gopher://** URL into the Address text box and pressing **Enter**. For instance, **gopher://wiretap.spies.com/** will take you to Internet Wiretap Gopher server, which you can see in the following figure.

The Internet Wiretap Gopher is worth a visit; you'll find loads of interesting documents here.

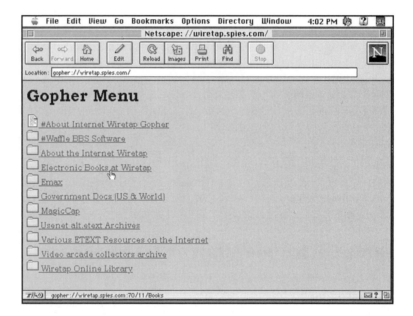

By the way, if you are using Internet Explorer or Netscape (and probably a number of other browsers), you can often ignore the gopher:// bit. If the gopher address starts with the word *gopher*, you can type the address and forget the gopher:// part. For instance, you can type **gopher.usa.net** instead of **gopher://gopher.usa.net**.

Where Can I Start?

For a list of links to Gopher servers, go to **gopher://gopher.micro. umn.edu/11/Other%20Gopher%20and%20Information%20Servers**. Or if you don't want to type all that, go to **http://www.w3.org/ hypertext/DataSources/ByAccess.html** and click the **Gopher** link.

You can also include *directories* in the URL. For instance, if you type **gopher:// earth.usa.net/00/News%20and%20Information/Ski%20Information/ A%20List%20of%20Today%27s%20SKI%20CONDITIONS** into the Address box and press Enter, you'll go to the Internet Express Gopher server, then automatically select the Colorado Ski Information and Ski Conditions menu options.

How, then, do you use a Gopher server with a Web browser? The Gopher menu options are represented by links; click the link to select that option. If the option leads to another menu, that menu appears in the window. If the option leads to a file of some kind, the file is transferred in the normal way, and your browser displays it or plays it (if it can). Files are treated just the same as they would be if you were working on a Web site.

You'll find that most of the documents at Gopher sites are text documents. But as you'll remember from the Web chapters, Web browsers can display text documents within their own windows. Of course, you won't find any links to other documents within these text documents—they're not true Web documents, after all. So when you finish, click the **Back** toolbar button to return to the Gopher menu you were just viewing. In the following figure, you can see a text document that I ran across at the Wiretap site. I selected the "Electronic Books at Wiretap" menu option and then the "Aesop: Fables, Paperless Edition" link.

Use Bookmarks

Think these addresses are too much for you to type? The next time you visit a Gopher site and find a useful Gopher menu, add it to your browser's Bookmarks (see Chapter 5) so you won't have to type it the next time.

Searching Gopher Menus

Some Gopher menus are very long. The original Gopher system had a special / command that allowed you to search a menu. Although you can't use that command, remember that your browser has a Find command. In Internet Explorer and Netscape you can use **Edit**, **Find** to perform the same function..

Aesop's fables, from the Wiretap site.

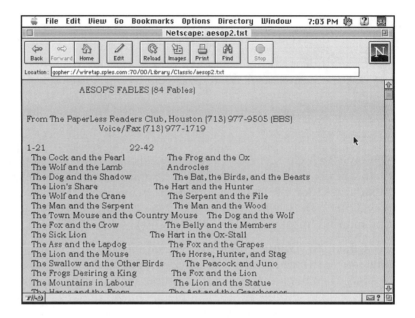

```
 🍎  File  Edit  View  Go  Bookmarks  Options  Directory  Window      7:03 PM 🕐 ❓ 📺
□                              Netscape: aesop2.txt                                    ▣
  ⇦      ⇨      ⌂       🖊       ⟳       📄      🖨       🔍       ⬤                    N
 Back  Forward  Home    Edit    Reload  Images   Print    Find     Stop

 Location: gopher://wiretap.spies.com:70/00/Library/Classic/aesop2.txt

          AESOP'S FABLES (84 Fables)


 From The PaperLess Readers Club, Houston (713) 977-9505 (BBS)
               Voice/Fax (713) 977-1719

 1-21                    22-42
   The Cock and the Pearl       The Frog and the Ox
   The Wolf and the Lamb        Androcles
   The Dog and the Shadow         The Bat, the Birds, and the Beasts
   The Lion's Share          The Hart and the Hunter
   The Wolf and the Crane        The Serpent and the File
   The Man and the Serpent        The Man and the Wood
   The Town Mouse and the Country Mouse   The Dog and the Wolf
   The Fox and the Crow          The Belly and the Members
   The Sick Lion            The Hart in the Ox-Stall
   The Ass and the Lapdog        The Fox and the Grapes
   The Lion and the Mouse        The Horse, Hunter, and Stag
   The Swallow and the Other Birds     The Peacock and Juno
   The Frogs Desiring a King       The Fox and the Lion
   The Mountains in Labour        The Lion and the Statue
   The Hares and the Frogs        The Ant and the Grasshopper
```

Archie's Friends Veronica and Jughead

Check This Out...

Cartoon Characters
Why Veronica and Jughead? They are characters in the famous Archie cartoon strip. Remember Archie, the Internet system you learned about in Chapter 15? Archie arrived on the Internet first. Then the people who created the Gopher search systems figured Archie needed company, so they named their systems Veronica and Jughead.

Gopher servers have two types of search tools—Veronica (Very Easy Rodent-Oriented Net-wide Index to Computerized Archives) and Jughead (Jonzy's Universal Gopher Hierarchy Excavation And Display). Do these acronyms mean much? No, but *you* try to create an acronym from a cartoon character's name!

Veronica lets you search Gopher servers all over the world. Jughead lets you search the Gopher server you are currently working with (though many Gopher servers don't yet have Jugheads).

If you want to search Gopherspace—this giant system of Gopher menus that spreads across the Internet—find a Veronica or Jughead menu option somewhere. For instance, at the **gopher://gopher.cc.utah.edu/** Gopher site, you'll find menu options that say "Search titles in Gopherspace using veronica" and "Search menu titles using jughead." You might have to dig around to find menus on some sites; sometimes they are several levels down the menu system. (I couldn't find Veronica or Jughead at the Wiretap site.) Although many sites don't have Jughead, virtually all have a link to Veronica.

Jughead

When you select the Jughead option, you'll see a few more links. You'll often find links to other Jughead servers at other sites, and you'll probably find a link to information telling you how to work with Jughead.

Of course, there's also a link to the actual search. For instance, go to the **gopher://gopher.cc.utah.edu** site, and you can choose **Search menu titles using jughead** and then click **Search University of Utah Menus Using Jughead**. When you click this link, you'll go to an index-server form like the one shown here. Type a word (such as **electronic books**) into the form and press **Enter**. The Gopher system searches for all menu options containing that word.

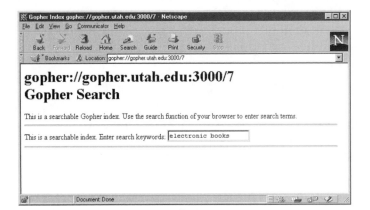

Type the word you want to search for and press Enter.

Soon (if all goes well), you'll see another Gopher menu, one that was created especially for your search and that contains a list of all the items Jughead found for you. (When you are working with Jughead, the response will probably be fairly quick. Veronica is much slower.) Click an item to see what it is, or point at it and look in your browser's status bar to see what the link "points" to.

If you don't find what you are looking for, you can click the **Back** toolbar button to return to the form and try again. This time, you might enter **book or publication**, for instance, and press **Enter** to search again.

Case Doesn't Matter You can enter the search statement in uppercase or lowercase letters; Jughead doesn't care. It considers "BOOK" to be the same as "book."

The Boolean Operators

A search in which you enter more than one term is known as a *Boolean* search. When typing your search term, you can use the Boolean operators **or**, **and**, and **not** as described here:

> **a and b**   This tells the system to search for a menu item that contains both word **a** *and* word **b**.

> **a or b**   This tells the system to search for a menu item that contains either word **a** *or* word **b**.

> **a not b**   This tells the system to search for a menu item that contains the word **a** but does *not* contain the word **b**.

When I searched for **book or publication**, I got a few more menu options. When I searched for **book or publication or publications**, I got even more.

Any Wild Card You Want, As Long As It's *

You can also use *wild cards* in your search text. A wild card is a character that takes the place of another character. So, for example, if you enter **pub*** as your search term, you're telling Jughead to search for any word beginning with "pub." The asterisk simply means "some other stuff here."

You can also combine wild cards and Boolean operators in your search. If you were to type the search term **book or pub***, Jughead would search for the word "book" *or* any words beginning with "pub." This search might find such words as "publication," "publications," "publicity," "public," and "publican."

Wild Card Rules

Jughead has only one wild card: the ***** character. You cannot use the **?** character, which is a common wild card in many other computer programs. Also, remember these basic rules: you can't start a word with the asterisk, and you can't put an asterisk within a word (it's ignored if you do).

So you can search for "book or pub*" instead of typing out "book or publication or publications." Searching like this will increase your "hit" rate dramatically—you may end up with hundreds of items. Of course, you might ask yourself, "Do I want all this extra stuff?" Well, the "publishers" and "publishing" entries that you may find could be useful, but "public" and "pubs" gives you a lot of extra stuff you didn't want (like "Title 53A - State System of Public Education, Chapter 11—Students in Public Schools, Part 3— Immunization of Students").

More Boolean Stuff

Let's take a quick look at the Boolean operators again. If you enter several words on a line without one of the Boolean operators (**and**, **or**, or **not**) between the words, Jughead assumes you mean **and**. For example, Jughead interprets the search terms **book and pub*** and **book pub*** to mean exactly the same thing: "find entries that contain both the word **book** and a word beginning with **pub**."

There are a few other things you also need to be aware of. If Jughead sees any special characters (!"#$%&'()+,-./:;<=>?@[\]^_Ô{|}~) in the search statement, it treats them as if they were spaces and replaces them with the Boolean operator **and**. For instance, if you enter the search term **This.file**, Jughead searches for **this and file**. That's not necessarily a problem, though. If I search for **Pubs_by SCERP_Researchers**, I will still find the correct menu item, because Jughead will still search for the words **Pubs**, **by**, **SCERP**, and **Researchers**.

> **Every One Is Different**
> Remember that each Gopher site is different. What you find at one site when searching with Jughead is not the same as what you'd find at another site.

Also, because you are using the words **and**, **or**, and **not** as Boolean operators, you can't actually search for these words. But then again, you'll probably never need to do so anyway.

Special Commands—Maybe

Jughead currently has four special commands you can include in a search string. Well, you *may* be able to, but some browsers won't work with these commands for some reason. Try them, and if you get a blank page returned to you, you'll know the browser can't handle them. The four special commands include:

➤ **?all** This tells Jughead to include *all* of the hits it finds. Usually, it limits the hits to 1,024, so if it finds 2,000 matching entries, you won't see 976 of them. Mind you, 1,024 is a lot—more than you are likely to need. For instance, if you search for **?all book or pub***, Jughead will search for the words **book** and **pub***, and if it finds more than 1,024 matches (it probably won't), it will display them all.

➤ **?help** This tells Jughead to create a menu option that lets you get to the Jughead Help file. You can use the **?help** command by itself, if you want, or you can do a search at the same time (for example, **?help book or pub***).

➤ **?limit=*n*** This tells Jughead to limit the number of menu items it gives you. For instance, if you used the command **?limit=10 book or pub***, Jughead would display only the first 10 items it finds.

➤ **?version** This gives you the Jughead version number. When you use this command, you'll see a menu option that reads

1. **This version of jughead is 1.0.4** (or whatever the actual version number is).

You can then click that menu option to read the Jughead Help file. You can use the **?version** command by itself, if you want, or you can do a search at the same time (for example, **?version book or pub***).

You cannot combine these commands, by the way; you can use only one for each search.

Veronica

Working with Veronica is very similar to working with Jughead, with a couple of important differences. First, when you select a Veronica menu option you'll get a choice of servers. Veronica searches *all* of Gopherspace—Gopher servers all over the world. Something called a *Veronica server* stores an index of menu options at all of these Gopher servers, so you are actually searching one of these indexes; you get to pick which one.

At the same time, you have to decide whether you want to limit your search. You can search all menu options, or only menu options that lead to other menus. Assume, for instance, that you went to **gopher://gopher.cc.utah.edu** and then chose the **Search titles in Gopherspace using Veronica** option. If you now select **Find GOPHER DIRECTORIES by Title Word(s) (via U of Manitoba)**, you will be looking for menu options that lead to other menus (often called *directories* in Gopherspeak) using the University of Manitoba Veronica server. If you select the **Search GopherSpace by Title Word(s) (via University of Pisa)**, you will be searching all menu options, both directories and options leading to files and documents, at the University of Pisa Veronica server.

When you make your selection, you'll see the same Index Search dialog box that you see when doing a Jughead search. Type the word you want to search for and press **Enter**. What happens then? Well, there's a good chance you'll get a message saying ***** Too many connections - Try again soon. ***** (or something similar). Try another server. If you don't get such a message, it may seem like your browser just waits and waits, but nothing seems to happen. These servers are very busy, so it often takes a long time to get a result. When you finally do get a result, though, you'll get a much bigger list than you did from the Jughead search. After all, you are searching the world's Gopher servers, not just one.

Veronica Search Details

Veronica searches are very similar to Jughead searches, but there are a few differences. As with Jughead, you can use Boolean operators and the * wild card, which still must appear at the end of the word—not at the beginning or within the word. With Veronica, however, if you put the * inside the word, Veronica aborts the search (whereas Jughead just ignores the asterisk).

Read the Help! For detailed information about Jughead and Veronica searches, read the Help files that you'll find in the Gopher menus near the Jughead and Veronica menu options.

Veronica also has a special -t command. This is placed within the search string (at the beginning, middle, or end—it doesn't matter) and is followed by a number that defines the *type* of item you are looking for. For instance, **book -t0** means "search for the word 'book,' but only find text documents that contain that word." Similarly, **book -t01** means "search for the word 'book,' but only find text documents and Gopher menu items that match." This list shows the numbers you can use with the -t command:

Number or Letter	Description
0	Text file
1	Directory (Gopher menu)
2	CSO name server (a searchable database used to track down other Internet users)
4	Macintosh HQX file
5	PC binary file
7	A searchable index
8	Telnet session (see Chapter 18)
9	Binary file
s	Sound file
e	Event file
I	Image file (other than GIF)
M	MIME multipart/mixed message (MIME is a system used by Internet e-mail systems to transfer binary files)
T	TN3270 Session (a similar system to Telnet)
c	Calendar
g	GIF image
h	HTML Web document

You can also use the **-m** command to specify a maximum number of items to find. For instance, the search term **-m300 book** tells the Veronica server to show up to 300 items that it finds that contain the word "book." If you don't use the **-m** command, the Veronica server searches only until it finds the default limit of 200 items. Use **-m** to tell the server to find more than the default number.

The Least You Need to Know

➤ Gopher is a text-based menu system, a real boon to Internet users working with text-based software.

➤ You can easily work with Gopher through a Web browser.

➤ Travel through Gopherspace by clicking menu options.

➤ To save a text document or file, click the link. Your browser will treat it the same way it treats any file on the World Wide Web.

➤ Use your Web browser's Bookmark system to add a bookmark to any Gopher menu you want to return to later.

➤ Many Gopher systems now use Jughead, a special search mechanism that enables you to find things on that server.

➤ Veronica is a powerful tool you can use to search through thousands of miles of Gopherspace at once. Look for a Veronica menu option somewhere in the Gopher menu.

Chapter 17

Yak, Yak, Yak: "Chatting" in Cyberspace

In This Chapter

➤ What are chat and talk?

➤ Chat sessions and public auditoriums

➤ Using the online service chat rooms

➤ Using a graphical chat program—pick your avatar

➤ Working with IRC (Internet Relay Chat)

➤ Real uses for chat

One of the most important—yet least discussed—systems in cyberspace is *chat*. It's important because its immense popularity has been a significant factor in the growth of online systems (not so much the Internet, but more the online services). It is, perhaps, the least discussed because the fact is that many people use the chat systems as a way to talk about sex and even to contact potential sexual partners.

In this chapter, you'll take a look at chatting in cyberspace—in Internet Relay Chat (the Internet's largest chat system) as well as in the online services. And you'll also learn that there's plenty more than sex-related chat.

Chatting and Talking

What is chat? Well, here's what it's *not:* a system that allows you to talk out loud to people across the Internet or an online service. That sort of system does exist (see Chapter 18), but a chat system does not use voice, it uses the typed word. Communications are carried out by typing messages to and fro.

What's the difference between chat and e-mail, then? With e-mail you send a message and then go away and do something else. You come back later—maybe later that day, maybe later that week—to see if you have a response. Chat is quite different: it takes place in *real-time*, to use a geek term. (What other kind of time is there but real-time, one wonders.) In other words, you type a message, and the other party in the chat session sees the message almost instantly. He can then respond right away, and you see the response right away. It's just like in, yes, a chat—only you are typing instead of talking.

Chat Can Have Voice

That's the problem about the Internet: you make a statement today, and tomorrow it's wrong. Right now the use of voice in chat sessions is rare. Voice *is* being added to chat, though, and you can expect chat sessions to gradually come to resemble the real thing, as people type less and talk more. However, as wonderful as that may sound it presents a problem. Many IRC (Internet Relay Chat) users are working at big companies, sitting in their little cubicles, typing away and looking busy. Their bosses may think they are working hard, but they are actually gabbing on IRC, and *voices would just give away the game!*

There's also something known as *talk,* which also isn't talking. Talk is a system in which one person can "call" another on the Internet and, once a connection has been made, can type messages to the other person. It's very similar to chat, once the two parties are connected. But the manner in which you connect is different. With chat you have to go to a chat "room" to chat with people; with talk, you simply open the talk program, enter the e-mail address of the person you want to connect to, and click a button to call that person (who may not be available, of course). To further complicate the issue, some Voice on the Net programs (discussed in Chapter 17) incorporate these talk programs—though they sometimes call them *chat* systems! For instance, Netscape Communicator's Conference program (known as CoolTalk in earlier versions of Netscape Navigator) has a little program that you can use to type messages to another person, but it's called the *Chat Tool.*

Chat is one of those "love it or hate it" kind of things. Obviously many people just love it; they even find it addictive, spending hours online each night. Personally, I can do without it. It's an awkward way to communicate. I can type faster than most people, yet I find it rather clunky. Quite frankly my experiences with chat question-and-answer sessions have not been exactly the high points of my life. I've been the guest in chat sessions in both MSN and CompuServe, and at a Web site called TalkCity; the sessions tend to be chaotic at worst, simply slow at best. You run into too many people trying to ask questions at once (though MSN has an excellent system for controlling the flow of questions, and CompuServe should have a new improved chat system soon), lots of typos, long pauses while you wait for people to type and they wait for you, and so on. No, I'm no chat fan, but I guess millions of people can't be wrong; and it certainly holds an appeal for many.

> **Sex?** Should I be talking about sex in this book? It's been suggested by my editors that I should avoid sexual subjects for fear of offending people. Chat, however, is a case in which it's hard to avoid the sexual. Certainly many people go to chat rooms for nonsexual purposes. But be warned that many (possibly most?) are there to meet members of the opposite sex...or the same sex in some cases...for sexual purposes. Cybersex may not be as much fun as the real thing, but it's very real in its own way.

Two Types of Sessions

Chat sessions are categorized into two types: private and group. Generally, what happens is that you join a chat "room," in which a lot of people are talking (okay, typing) at once. Then someone may invite you to a private room, where just the two of you can talk without the babble of the public room. These private rooms are often used for "cybersex" sessions, though of course they can also be used for more innocent purposes, such as catching up on the latest news with your brother-in-law in Paris, discussing a project with a colleague, or talking about a good scuba-diving spot in Mexico.

Often public chat rooms are used as sort of auditoriums or lecture halls. A famous or knowledgeable person responds to questions from the crowd. Michael Jackson and Buzz Aldrin, for instance, have been guest "speakers" in chat forums, as has Peter Kent and many other world famous people.

Score 1 for the Online Services

I'm going to mostly discuss the online services in this chapter because they generally have the most popular, and in some ways the best, chat systems. Chat has been extremely important to the growth of the online services, so they've made an effort to provide good chat services. Chat on the Internet, though, is still relatively little used, and in many ways not as sophisticated. (That's changing, as many new chat programs designed for the Internet, often running through the Web, are introduced.)

213

If you use CompuServe or AOL you can get to the chat rooms by using the GO or Key word **chat**. Most forums have conference rooms for chatting too, but they are often empty. If you use The Microsoft Network, you'll find chat rooms scattered all over the place; almost every forum (or BBS as they're known in MSN-speak) has a chat room. You can also go to a Chat BBS by opening the **Communicate** menu and selecting **Chat Central** (or by using the Go To word **chat** if you're using the old version of MSN). If you want to use Internet Relay Chat on the Internet, it's a little more complicated (I cover this later in the chapter).

Chatting in AOL

In AOL use the keyword **chat**, or click the **People Connection** button in the Welcome window, and you go straight to a chat window (see the next figure). Use the **List Chats** button to see all the available chat rooms. There are about a dozen categories and hundreds of individual rooms.

AOL's chat room system: lots of glitz, very busy.

AOL's system allows you to create private rooms so that you and your friends (or family or colleagues) can use that room without interference. If you want to talk to only one person, just double-click the person's name in the People Here box and click the **Message** button. If the person responds, you get your own private message window for just the two of you. You can see in the following figure that this message box has special buttons that allow you to modify the text format.

AOL provides you with a little message window in which you can carry on private conversations.

CompuServe's Conference Rooms and CB

To use a CompuServe chat room you can go to just about any forum or to the Chat forum, where you'll find loads of chat sessions. Most forums have a number of conference rooms, but unless some kind of presentation has been scheduled, they may all be empty.

You can be sure to find people to chat with in the Chat forum, though (GO **chat**, or click the big **Chat** button in the main menu). Compuserve's chat system has been completely revamped just recently, and the old "CB radio" analogy has completely gone.

You'll start by picking a chat category (General Chat, Adult Chat, Conferences and Special Events, and so on). Then click the **Chat** button to see a list of chat rooms; double-click a room to open the chat window (or click a room and then click the **Participate** or **Observe** button, to take part in the chat room's discussion or just "listen in." (See the following illustration.)

The list of rooms shows you how many people are in each room; this might be helpful if you want to pick a quiet one or get right into the action. As you can see in the figure, you can "listen" by reading other people's messages. Whenever you want to jump in, you can type your own message in the lower panel of the window; press Enter to send the message, or click the **Send** button.

You can invite people to private rooms, too; click the **Who's Here** button to see a list of members, then click the person you want to speak with and click **Private Chat**.

MSN's Chat System

While MSN's chat system is perfect for conferences in which one speaker is a guest answering questions from participants, it's not as good as some other systems when it comes to basic chat rooms. Actually it has two chat modes: the normal chat rooms, and the Comic Chat rooms. Comic Chat is a type of chat system that uses **avatars** (which we'll look at under "Pick Your Avatar," later in this chapter), little pictures to represent participants. Both systems use the same basic program, but the person creating the room can decide to make it a text-only chat or a Comic Chat (and individuals entering the room can choose to use text-only mode even if the room is a Comic Chat room).

CompuServe's chat system.

Click one of these buttons to join or listen in

Use this button to see a list of the people in the session

Click here to select a room

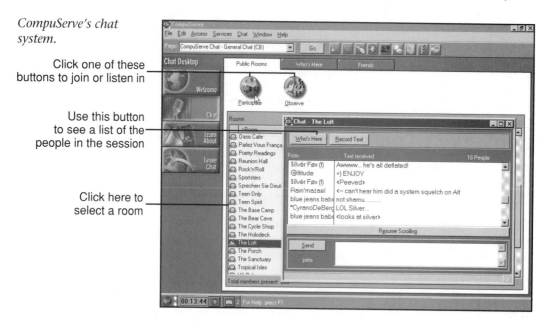

At the time of writing MSN's chat system makes setting up private conversations difficult, for instance. If you want a private chat, you have to create your own chat room, then set the chat room's properties to allow a maximum number of chat members. Then, as the creator of the room, you can kick unwanted people out of the room (using the Kick command). A little awkward—most chat systems allow you to meet a person in the chat room and go directly to a private room. The following figure shows the basic MSN chat window.

A little while ago MSN had a test chat room that allowed participants to send e-mail or chat messages to other participants, and to invite them to private rooms directly. It allowed members to leave Away From Keyboard messages when they left temporarily, and there was even a way to launch the Web browser directly from the chat window so that you can view a Web site people are talking about. These features don't seem to have been incorporated into the chat rooms yet. Perhaps they'll appear soon..

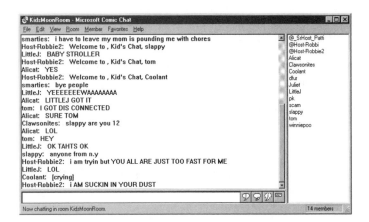

MSN's chat system can work in two modes, text only and Comic Chat.

Commands to Look For

While the details for using each chat system differ, a number of features are the same from one system to another. For example, these features are generally similar (even though the names may vary between systems):

Who or **People Here** shows a list of people currently participating in the chat session.

Invite enables you to invite a participant in the current chat to a private chat room. (On AOL you send the person an Instant Message.)

Ignore or **Squelch** enables you to tell the program to stop displaying messages from a particular user. This is very useful for getting rid of obnoxious chat-room members (you'll find a lot of them!).

Profile allows you to view information about a particular participant, including whatever information they decided to make public. Some systems allow more information than others, but the information might include a person's e-mail address, interests, real name, and even phone number and address in some systems (although most participants choose *not* to include these).

Change Profile or **Handle** gives you access to the place where you'll change your own information. Some systems let you change your profile from within the Chat program, but on others you may have to select a menu option or command elsewhere.

Record or **Log** or **Capture** usually lets you record a session. (Of course, in most cases you'll want to forget the drivel… Oh, there I go again!)

Preferences enables you to set up how the system works: whether to tell you when people enter or leave the room, for example.

Kick or **Ban** are available on some systems if you set up the chat room yourself. Kick allows you to remove someone from the chat room, while Ban stops them getting back in.

No matter which chat system you use, read the documentation carefully so you can figure out exactly how to get the most out of it.

Pick Your Avatar

The latest thing in chat is the use of graphical systems in which you select an *avatar*, an image that represents you in the chat session. The following figure shows a room with several avatars—each representing a real-life person—in Club Chat. Selecting an avatar is a simple matter of clicking a button in the top left of the window, then choosing from a drop-down list box. Then you can type a message in the text box at the bottom and click the **Send** button. You can also choose from a small selection of sounds ("Aaaah," "Joy," "Doh," and other such intellectual utterings).

So far I've heard mixed reactions to these graphical chat systems. Some people say they are awful, some say they're nothing special, and some say it's just stuff to get in the way of the chat. Others really like them. Experiment and decide for yourself!

Other Avatar chats are available, including some that are available to the public on the Web. For instance, you might try one of these:

Time Warner's Palace (**http://www.thepalace.com/**)

Club Chat (**http://www.clubchat.com/**)

WorldCHAT (**http://www.worlds.net/**)

Although you can reach these sites on the Web, you have to download a special Chat program and then reconnect using that program.

Playing with avatars in Club Chat.

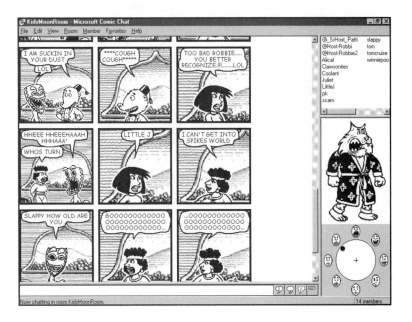

MSN's Comic Chat in action.

They're Everywhere!

These avatar chats are now sprouting on the Internet like weeds in my backyard. The Palace software, for instance, allows people to set up their own chats at their own Web sites—and many people have done so already. For more information, see the Palace site (address above) or look at Yahoo's 3D Worlds information (**http://www.yahoo.com/Recreation/Games/Internet_Games/Virtual_Worlds/3D_Worlds/**).

Web Chat's Coming Up Fast

Most chat participants are still using chat systems running on the online services, but it may not always be that way. Hundreds, perhaps thousands, of Web-based chat systems have sprung up, and in some cases are quite good. There are chat sites set up for celebrity "visits," to discuss education-related issues, gay chat sites, a skate-boarder's chat site… If you're a chat fan and have been hiding out in the online-service chat rooms, perhaps it's time to take a look at the World Wide Web and see what's available. (Here's a good place to start: **http://www.yahoo.com/Computers_and_Internet/Internet/World_Wide_Web/Chat/**).

Chat versus Discussion Group There's a little confusion on the Web about the difference between chat rooms and discussion groups. Some Web sites advertising "chat" actually have Web forums (see Chapter 13). If the discussion isn't "real time"—you type something, someone immediately responds, you type back—then it's not chat.

Web chat systems vary from the very clunky—your message is displayed within a Web page, which must be constantly rewritten in order to see the conversation—to the very good. The better sites, such as TalkCity have their own chat programs that you must download before you enter the chat room. These are true chat systems, with the same sort of features as the chat rooms in the online services. You can see an example of the Talk City chat program in the following illustration.

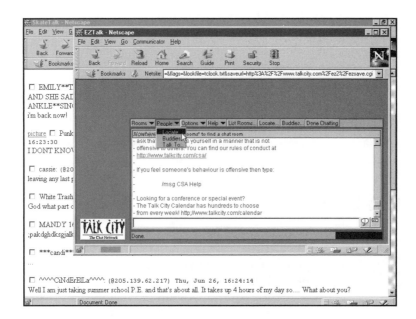

Talk City, one of the Web's more sophisticated chat sites. In the background you can see a more primitive Web-page type chat system.

Internet Relay Chat—Productivity Sink Hole?

I'll admit I haven't spent a lot of time in Internet Relay Chat. That's mainly because I've found that what few visits I *have* made have been so uninspiring that I can't think of a good reason to return. But there I go again, slamming a chat system. Actually many thousands of people really *do* like IRC (as it's known). So let's take a look at how to use it.

Techno Talk

Command-Line User?

If you don't have a graphical user interface, you cannot use the fancy IRC programs of course. You'll have to use a command-line interface to IRC, which is very awkard ...but hey, thousands of other people have managed, and you can too. For help doing this, you can get the IRC chapter from my out-of-print book *The Complete Idiot's Next Step with the Internet* by sending e-mail to **ciginternet@mcp.com** and putting the word **irc** in the Subject line (leave the message body blank). For more information, see Appendix C.

Step 1 Get the Software

The first thing you'll need is an IRC "client" program. That's the program you'll use to send and receive IRC communications. If you are using a Mac, you might try Ircle, a well-known IRC program for that operating system. On Windows, you might try mIRC or PIRCH.

So go to the software archives I discuss in Appendix A and download a copy of some kind of IRC program. Then follow the documentation's instructions to set up the program, and spend some time reading everything there is to read. Unfortunately, IRC can be a little complicated, if only because it has so many features.

Step 2 Connect to a Server

Nicknames
Your nickname is the name by which you will be identified in the chat sessions. Notice that you can remain anonymous in a chat session by entering incorrect information into the Real Name and E-mail Address boxes.

The next thing you have to do is connect to an IRC server somewhere. These are programs that run on someone's computer out on the Internet and act as "conduits," carrying information between IRC participants. These servers are the equivalent of the online services chat forums. At a server, you'll find hundreds of different IRC channels that you can choose from.

Find the command that you must use to connect to a server. With mIRC, for instance, the dialog box in the following figure opens automatically when you start the program. You can get back to it later (to select a different server, for example) by choosing **File**, **Setup**.

Here's where you choose a server to connect to and enter your personal information in mIRC.

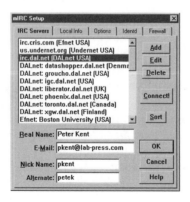

Select the server you want to use, click the **Connect** button, and away you go. You're connected to the server, and a dialog box appears, listing some of the channels (see the next figure). This is by no means all of the channels; most servers have literally hundreds.

This box holds a list of the ones you are interested in (actually it's initially a list of channels that the programmer thought you might like to start with, but you can add more). To get into one of these channels, simply double-click it.

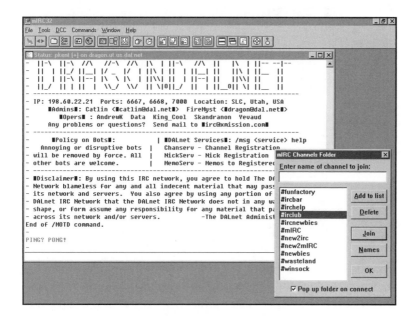

You've connected, and you're ready to join a channel.

If you'd like to see a complete listing of all the channels, close the dialog box, type /**list** in the text box at the bottom of the main window (which is where you type your messages and any IRC commands), and press **Enter**.

Know the Commands

IRC commands begin with a slash (/). There are loads of them, and most of these IRC programs hide the commands from you to some degree, providing menu commands instead. But they don't replace all of them. Some things can only be done using the original typed IRC command.

In mIRC, the /**list** command opens a window in which all the channels are listed. This may take a while because there are so many channels. As you can see in the title bar in the following figure, this server has 744 channels! If you want to enter one of these channels, all you have to do is double-click it.

mIRC's channel listing: Are 744 channels enough for you?

Once you are into a channel, just start typing; it's much like chatting in any other chat system. In the next figure, you can see a chat in progress. As usual, you type your message in the little box at the bottom, and you view what's going on in the big panel.

The participants are listed on the right side. You can invite one to a private chat by simply double-clicking a name. You can right-click to see a pop-up menu with a series of commands such as Whois (which displays information about the user in another window).

Here's where you chat in mIRC.

There's a lot to learn about IRC. These programs are a little complicated because IRC has so many features. For example, you can transmit computer files to other users; people often send pictures to each other. You can also add a special program that reads incoming messages from other chat members or that bans, kicks, and ignores users (if you open a channel, you have some control over who you let in,) and plenty more.

Spend some time playing around with the program you choose, to see what it can do, and read the documentation or help files carefully. It's complicated stuff, but once you have the feel for what one program can do, you can quickly pick up how to use one of the others.

How Many Conversations Can You Keep Going?

IRC is almost a game. People get into multiple chat sessions at once. They chat in the main window, and then they have a few private chat sessions in other windows. That's why it takes them so long to respond sometimes!

What Is It Good For? Real Uses for Chat

It could be argued that chat systems are a complete waste of perfectly good electrons. (*I wouldn't claim that, of course, but I'm sure many people would.*) The chat is often little better than gibberish. "Hey, dude, how goes it? ...Cool man, you? ...Yeah, doing well; you chatted with that babe CoolChick, yet? ...No, she cute?" ...blah ...blah ...blah.) This is neither educational nor particularly interesting.

However, I know I'm going to upset people with these comments, so I should note that not all chats are quite so inane. Chats allow people of like interests to get together in cyberspace, literally reaching across continents, across the entire globe, to discuss issues that interest them in a way that would be prohibitively expensive using any other technology. (Actually, I've proposed a *stupidity-tax* to make the totally stupid chats prohibitively expensive once again.)

There are other worthwhile uses, too. This list points out a few such scenarios:

➤ Technical support can be given using chat rooms. This will become more important as more software is distributed across the Internet. For instance, a small company that, in the past, might have provided support only within the U.S.A. can now provide support to any nation with Internet access.

➤ Companies can use chat systems for keeping in touch. An international company with salespeople throughout the world can arrange weekly "meetings" in a chat room. Families can do the same so that family members can keep in touch even when they're separated by thousands of miles.

➤ Groups that are planning international trips might want to try chat rooms. For instance, if a scout group is traveling to another country to spend the summer with another group, a chat room could provide a way for the leaders to "get together" beforehand to iron out final details.

➤ Colleges can use chat. Many colleges already provide courses over the Internet, using the Web to post lessons and using e-mail to send in completed assignments. In addition, teachers can use chat to talk with students, regardless of the geographic distance between them.

However, having said all that, you should visit Chapter 18. Chat may eventually be superseded by what's known as Voice On the Net, a system that allows you to place "phone calls" across the Internet and even have conference calls.

What About Talk?

I mentioned *talk* earlier in this chapter, then pretty much ignored it. Talk, you'll remember, is a system which allows two people to get together and chat privately online; no need to go to a chat site, you just open your talk program and begin typing.

The problem is that talk has died out; or at least is comatose for the moment. In the UNIX world—and in the early days, the Internet was firmly entrenched in the UNIX world—talk was widely available and frequently used. (There are two popular UNIX talk programs, *talk* and *ntalk*.) But very few Internet users have installed talk on their Windows or Macintosh systems…in fact most have no idea what this system is.

You can still find talk programs, though. Go to some of the sites mentioned in Appendix B and look for them. Try out a few and see which you prefer, then tell your friends to download the same one. And then you can have your own little private talk network.

Talk may be making a come back; America Online recently launched *AOL Instant Messenger*, a talk system that allows any Internet user to talk with any other Internet user. AOL members already have Instant Messenger installed (as long as they're using the latest AOL software). Other Internet users can download the software from the AOL Web site (**http://www.aol.com/**).

The Least You Need to Know

➤ A *chat* system allows participants to take part in public discussions or to move to private "rooms" if they prefer. A *talk* system is a direct link between participants in a conversation, without the need for a public chat room.

➤ Neither chat nor talk uses actual voices; you type messages and send them to and fro.

➤ Chat sessions are often very crude and sexually orientated; so if you're easily offended, pick your chat room carefully.

➤ All the online services have popular chat systems.

➤ If you want to use Internet Relay Chat, you'll have to download an IRC program from a shareware site and then connect across the Internet to a server.

➤ You can use chat rooms to keep in touch with friends, family, or colleagues— or to meet new people.

Chapter 18

Voice on the Net: Talking on the Internet

In This Chapter

➤ International calls for 5 cents/minute...

➤ Calls routed to domestic phone systems

➤ Where do you get phone software?

➤ Connecting to a "server" and finding someone to talk to

➤ Text transmission, white boards, conferencing, and more

➤ Video conferencing and other weird stuff

This chapter covers a new Internet technology that very few people are using, but that you're going to hear a *lot* about very soon—the ability to make "phone calls" on the Internet.

In the past, the word *talk* was a euphemism on the Internet. As you saw in Chapter 17, there is actually a service called *talk* that has been around for years. As you saw in that chapter, it might be more appropriately called *type*. Today, however, technology has advanced to the point that you can actually talk—yes, use your voice—across the Internet. Voice on the Net (VON) is the next big Internet application.

The Incredible Potential of Voice on the Net

I recently co-authored a book with my brother. Because he's in England and I'm in the U.S. of A., I knew we'd be spending a lot of time on the phone—and that worried me. If I had to pay 80 cents a minute, my phone bill was going to skyrocket. Luckily, I found out about Voice on the Net.

Even though you pay for online time, talking across the Internet is still much cheaper. For example, if I used one of the major online services and paid for extra hours at, say, $2.90 per hour, an Internet "phone" call would cost me 4.8 cents a minute. I wouldn't do that, though. Through a service provider I can get Internet time for $1 an hour …which breaks down to 1.7 cents a minute. I also have an "unlimited access for $19.95" account. In effect, any additional time I would spend talking on the Internet (over and above the time I would be on the Internet anyway), costs me 0 cents per minute! Beat that, AT&T!

Unlike with real phone calls, though, both parties pay for an Internet phone call. So in my case, my brother would also have to connect to his service provider and pay whatever rates he pays. But hey, that's his problem. And anyway, even if you combine what we would pay, the total's going to be much lower than the 80 cents I would pay for a traditional phone call (or even the 35 to 45 cents I might be able to get through cut-price phone services).

I can see it happening. You're starting to see the potential. Have any relatives in Russia, Australia, or France? You can cut your costs to the bone, or you can spend the same amount of money but talk for a much longer time than you ever really wanted to. Similarly, if you run a business with offices around the world, you can connect the offices' networks to the Internet, get everyone a sound card and a mike, and spend the money you save on a new Mercedes.

It Gets Better Link to the Real World

Oh, but it gets better than that. Imagine that someone created a special program that would allow phone calls across the Internet to be connected to real phone lines. A computer hooked up to the phone lines in, say, London, could accept Internet calls from anywhere in the world, connect them to the phone system, and allow Internet users to make *domestic* calls within the United Kingdom.

Such a system already exists. Although very few of these "servers" (systems that connect from the Internet to the phone system) are running, many more will soon be up and running. Imagine the potential. New telecommunications companies that are set up on a shoestring could be offering international phone service at domestic rates (plus a small fee, of course). Or international companies could be setting up phone "servers" in cities that their employees often call, virtually slashing the corporate phone bill.

And Internet phones carry more than just voice. They can also carry text and even doodles; some even allow you to transfer computer files at the same time you speak. So, while you are talking to someone, you can be transmitting the text of a memo or sketching something, or sending a photograph. Internet phones are a very powerful tool you're going to be seeing a lot of very soon.

Phone Companies—No Imminent Danger

The phone companies are not in imminent danger of going out of business, though. First, many people simply don't have computers. Fewer still have the sort of equipment required to use a system like this (you'll learn about the hardware requirements in a moment). And even fewer people want to call someone who *also* has the necessary equipment. Then consider these other problems.

➤ The calls don't provide high-quality sound. No doubt, you will *not* hear a pin dropping the other end of one of these lines!

➤ They are inconvenient. Because few people spend all day connected to the Internet, in many cases you'd have to arrange a call. (Still, in the early days of the telephone, that's just what people did. They arranged a time to go to the drugstore and rent time on the phone, and their relatives on the other side of the country, or the world, did the same. In fact in many parts of the world, that's still how people use telephones.)

➤ Currently there are still a few compatability problems; you have to make sure you're both using compatible software, and there are several different transmission systems.

Can You Hold Back Technology?

Although the phone companies will not be going out of business anytime soon, some are still worried enough to try to ban Internet phones. At the time of writing a small group of telecommunications companies was trying to get the U.S. Government to ban the use of Internet phones. Apart from the fact that this is similar to a group of horse-drawn carriage manufacturers trying to ban the newfangled automobile, it's hard to see how you can ban this kind of technology. Even if you ban it in the U.S., foreign companies will still sell it across the Internet. If we're going to do that, perhaps we should ban international credit card transactions or close our cyberborders. (For more discussion on this issue, see Chapter 25.)

Oh, here's another problem for Internet phone calls. The price for long-distance telephone calls has been dropping precipitously for several years, and seems likely to continue. Yes, I used to pay 80 cents a minute to call from the U.S. to the U.K. But now I pay 16 cents, any time of day or night. With prices going this low, VON systems are going to have to improve dramatically before people are going to use them in large numbers.

Do You Have the Hardware You Need?

The idea of working with VON might sound interesting, but there's a small hurdle you have to leap first. Do you have the right equipment?

To even consider using Internet phones, you'll need a fairly new computer. Not necessarily top of the line, but not an old piece of junk either. If you have a PC, it generally has to be a 486SX or better, perhaps even a 486DX (actual requirements will vary depending on the software you are using). If you have a Mac, you'll probably need a Quadra, Performa, or Power PC (some only run on the Power PC). On any platform, you'll also need a fair amount of RAM—probably a minimum of 8MB. But as I always say, you can never have too much money, too much time off, or too much RAM.

Next you'll need a connection to the Internet, and it should be either a fast network connection (the ideal, of course) or a dial-in direct connection (SLIP or PPP). If you have a dial-in connection, you'll want at least a 28,800bps modem; but your calls will undoubtedly sound better with a 33,600bps modem or faster.

You need a sound card, of course. Make sure it's a 16-bit card or better, and that it also allows you to record (some don't). Ideally, you need a *full-duplex* card. Check the card's specifications (on the box) when you buy it to see if it's full-duplex.

Check This Out...

Full-Duplex versus Half-Duplex If you have a full-duplex card, both you and the other person can talk at the same time. The card can record your voice at the same time it's playing incoming sounds. On the other hand, if you have only a half-duplex card you'll have to take turns talking (like the men who talked over the radios in those old war movies: "Joe, you there? Over").

You also need a microphone and speakers, or perhaps a headset. And finally, you need the software. That's easy enough to come by, but the big catch is that you have software that uses the same system for transmitting the voice signals as the software used by the person you want to call. As a result, you may end up using two or three programs. That should change soon, though, as the software companies start to settle on a standard. (That standard seems to be the H.323 standard, and these products are quickly moving toward compatibility with that standard.)

In 1996 it appeared that the use of VON software was about to increase exponentially, because the major online services claimed that they were about to provide it to their subscribers. They didn't. Perhaps, when America Online locked up entirely under the stress of millions of new users, they realized that allowing people to transmit *voice* across the network wasn't *quite* such a good idea. (Transmitting a voice signal is what could be regarded as a "high bandwidth" process; that is, it uses up a lot of network time.) If they had trouble transmitting everyone's Web pages and files and chat sessions...what would happen when eight million people started *talking*? So, for the moment, the VON revolution is on hold. Still, thousands of people are using VON, with software they find online.

Which Program Should I Use?

Some of the top products are Internet Phone (Vocaltec), TeleVox (Voxware), Netscape Communicator Conference (previously known as Netscape CoolTalk), and NetMeeting (Microsoft). Internet Phone, TeleVox, and NetMeeting have reputations as being the best products. Conference is important because it's included with Netscape Communicator, so millions of people have it available (though relatively few use it.) Follow these directions to get your hands on one or all of these products:

Netscape Conference: You can download Conference from **http://www.netscape.com/**. It's included as part of Netscape Communicator.

TeleVox: The Televox demo is available at **http://www.voxware.com/**.

Internet Phone: From an Israeli company called VocalTec, the Internet Phone demo is available for download from **http://www.vocaltec.com/**.

NetMeeting: This is Microsoft's Internet phone system, available for free download from **http://www.microsoft.com/ie/conf/**.

You can find other products by going to Yahoo and searching for *internet voice*. Or go to the Voice on the Net page at **http://www.von.com/**. Many such products are available as shareware, commercial products, and give-it-away-ware. You'll find WebPhone (NetSpeak), FreeTel, DigiPhone (Third Planet Publishing), PowWow (Tribal Voice), and so on.

Give-It-Away-Ware?

The Internet is full of stuff that is simply given away. Conference, for instance, is given away with Netscape Communicator, which is also given away. Yes, you're supposed to register Communicator, but Netscape Communications really doesn't expect many people to do so. Microsoft is currently giving away NetMeeting, too. Internet Phone and TeleVox are not free, though you can get free demo versions.

Working with Your Phone Program

Let's take a look at how to work with one of these systems. I'll assume that you have your sound card and microphone properly installed—that's one can of worms I'm *not* crawling into! I'll also assume that you've installed some sort of phone program and have run through the setup (so it already has all of your personal information that it needs, such as your name, Internet e-mail address, and so on).

The next question is, to quote Ghostbusters, *Who ya gonna call?* Yes, I know, you were so excited about the idea of making phone calls on the Internet that you went ahead and installed everything you need. But you haven't quite persuaded your siblings or your mad Aunt Edna to do the same. So you actually have *nobody* to call. Don't worry, you'll find someone.

All the software companies have set up servers to which you can connect to find someone else, just like you, who is all dressed up with nowhere to go. For instance, if you are using VocalTec's Internet Phone, you'll automatically connect to a server when you start the program. This system is based on "chat rooms," 500 of them last time I looked. (You can create your own room, so this number fluctuates.) These are not like the chat rooms we looked at in Chapter 17. Rather, they are places that people can "congregate," and then choose to "pair off" in voice conversations. You can create your own private chat room at a predefined time, for instance, in order to meet friends or colleagues.

VocalTec's Global OnLine Directory helps you find other Internet Phone users.

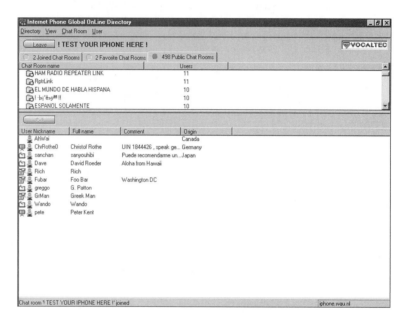

A Common Theme...Porn Raises its Ugly Head Well, what do you know? These phone servers have turned into yet another sex channel! Many of the chat rooms at the VocalTec Global OnLine Directory are set up for people who want to get involved in cybersex, enhanced with voice and video.

To connect to someone in a chat room, click a name and then click the **Call** button. Go ahead, don't be shy. Of course someone else might try to connect to you first. You'll hear a beep to inform you that someone is trying to call you. You may have the program set up to accept all incoming calls automatically (in Internet Phone, you do that using the **Phone, AutoAnswer** command), or you may have to click a button to accept a call.

Internet Phone at work; you can quickly connect with someone in a chat room and begin talking. (If you're using video, the large picture panel will show the other person.)

The Conference Server

These servers all work differently. Conference has a directory available on a Web site; just click the **Web Phonebook** button in the Conference window, or select **Communicator**, **Web Phonebook** (you can see an example of this directory in the following figure).

Find the person you want to talk to and click his name. The Conference installation program automatically configures CoolTalk as a Netscape Navigator viewer (see Chapter 8), so when you click a name in the Web page Conference opens and tries to contact the other person.

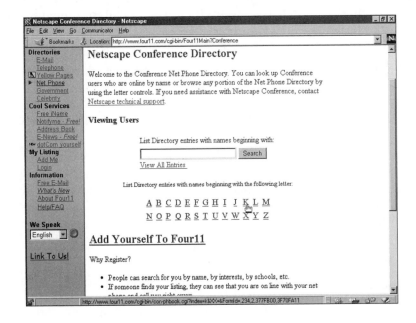

Netscape Conference's Web directory.

Now You Get to Talk

Nothing Better to Do? Connect to one of these servers (not the Conference one, but one of the servers with people actually connected) and just wait. Every now and then you'll get a call. It's a kind of a magical mystery phone session, not knowing who's going to call next. Where does he live? What does she do? Can she get her microphone working?

Some of these servers enable you to create new "rooms." You can create private rooms and use these as sort of meeting rooms for your friends and colleagues. Or perhaps you have to just click a person and then a **Call** button or something similar to connect to that person. You'll have to read the program's documentation to figure this out; there are as many different ways to do it as there are programs.

Once you are talking, you might find that the sound is a bit warbly. That's okay, though. You might be speaking with someone on the other side of the world for a tiny fraction of what you'd pay your friendly phone company. What do you want? Low cost *and* quality?

If you are both using full-duplex modems, you can probably just talk as if you are on the phone. Otherwise, you may have to take turns speaking, clicking a button to turn your mike on and off. (The button is the equivalent of saying "over.")

Your Address Is Not Always the Same

Most dial-in users don't have permanent TCP/IP host addresses. When you connect to your service provider you are assigned a temporary host address, so the next time you connect you may get a different address. That means it's often difficult to configure voice programs to call other users directly.

If a computer is connected to a network, and has a permanent TCP/IP address, then everything's fine; the TCP/IP address is used as the "telephone number." If a computer gets a different address each time it connects you have to use one of several possible methods. For instance, you can use the directories' private rooms as meeting places; you can arrange to call someone at a particular time and use the room as a way to make the connection.

With some systems you may also be able to connect using an e-mail address. The program looks up the e-mail address in an online directory, then finds the corresponding TCP/IP number and uses that to connect. Netscape Conference can use this system, for instance; each time you start Conference it connects to the directory and "registers" your e-mail address so it will be available to any callers.

The Bells and Whistles

These products offer more than just voice connections. You might want to look for some of the following features in an Internet phone system.

➤ **An answering machine.** Some products, such as Conference, have built-in answering machines. If someone tries to contact you while you are not there, your "answering machine" takes a message. Of course this works only if your computer is online. Although it's very useful for people with permanent network connections, it's not nearly as useful for people who dial into a service provider.

➤ **Type while you talk capability.** This can be a very handy feature. You can send text messages at the same time you are talking. You can send small memos or copy parts of an e-mail message you're discussing. If you are working on a project with the other person, you may find it convenient to send to-do lists or schedules back and forth. Authors working together can send materials to each other, programmers can send bits of the code they are discussing, and so on. The following figure shows one system in which you can write as you talk.

➤ **Image transmission.** Related to the business-card feature, and to the white board feature (discussed in a moment), is the capability to send a picture while you're talking. If you haven't seen Aunt Natasha in Siberia for a while, she can send a picture of the kids while you are chatting.

➤ **Conferencing.** Why speak to just one person, when you can talk to a whole crowd? Some of these programs let you set up conferences, so a whole bunch of you can gab at once.

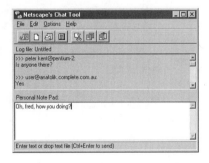

Conference's "Chat" window lets you type messages while you talk.

➤ **Group Web surfing.** This is an odd feature, though only a few programs have it. The people connected via the program, in some cases a whole bunch of people, can go on group Web surfs together. When one person clicks a Web link, the other participants' Web browsers update to show the new page. This feature is in Netscape Conference and PowWow (**http://www.tribal.com/**).

➤ **Web-page indicator.** You can automatically add an icon to your Web page showing whether you are online and able to accept calls (another neat PowWow feature).

➤ **White Boards.** A white board is one of those big white chalkboard-type things you see in conference rooms. A white board feature functions similarly to the image

237

transmission feature previously mentioned. Instead of typing something, though, you are using a sort of doodle pad thing. You can sketch something, and it's transmitted to the person at the other end. You can even use this to send graphic files; you can open the file in the white board so the person at the other end can see it. Conference's white board appears in the next figure.

➤ **Change Your Voice.** TeleVox has a "VoiceFonts" feature that allows you to completely change the way your voice sounds during a phone conversation.

➤ **Connecting voice to your Web page.** You can put links in your Web pages that, when clicked, open the user's Voice program so he can talk with you. This is for *real* geeks who rarely leave their computers. (You *do* have Web pages, don't you? See Chapter 9 to find out how to create them.)

Unfortunately, it's not a perfect world, so not all voice programs have all these neat features. You'll just have to find the features that are most important to you and go with the program that has those features.

A white board feature lets you send a picture while talking.

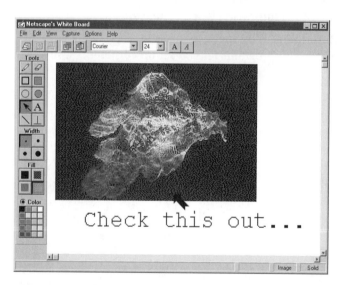

Internet-to-Phone Connections

One of the most intriguing uses of this technology is the ability to connect to a computer across the Internet and route onto the local phone service. So you might connect across the Internet from New York to Sydney and be connected to the Australian phone system—which means you can make international calls at Australian domestic rates.

A few companies are working on these products, and there are servers currently operating in Guam; Jakarta, Indonesia; Melbourne, Australia; Moscow, Russia; Vancouver and Toronto, Canada; Norwalk, CT, USA; Phoenix, AZ, USA; Los Angeles, CA, USA, and many other places. In fact one company says it will connect you to any phone anywhere in the world across the Internet (see GXC: **http://www.gxc.com**), though the rates it charges for this privelege are, in some cases, actually higher than rates available for normal phone calls.

Check the Voice on the Net page (**http://www.von.com/**) for the latest information, or see the Free World Dialup site (**http://www.pulver.com/fwd/**) as this is planned as a free service for noncommercial calls. Free World Dialup plans to allow telephone users to call a computer that is connected to the Internet, then have the call routed across the Internet to another computer somewhere connected to the phone system at the other end. So the call can be made from one phone to another, across the world, yet the call is routed across the Internet.

The Future Is Video—and Other Weird Stuff

It doesn't stop here, of course. The next step is to add video to the "phone" conversations. Finally, a true video phone; the phone companies have been talking about it for 40 years, but it took the Internet to bring it about. In fact video has already been added to some of these products. As you saw earlier, Vocaltec's Internet Phone has a video window.

Mind you, this step is a much bigger one than simply putting voice on the Internet. Voice is fairly simple. There is not too much data involved in transmitting sounds, relatively speaking. The problem with video, though, is bandwidth. The term *bandwidth* refers to the amount of information that can be transmitted across a connection. A 28,800bps connection has greater bandwidth than does a 14,400bps connection, for instance. Video images contain a lot of information, and you want the information right away. After all, video only makes sense if it's in motion. So a number compromises have to be made. The images are small, are low resolution, and have few individual images each second. Thus, video transmitted across the Internet can often be blurry and shaky. Unless you really need it, you may find that the novelty soon wears off.

Personally, I don't think video on the Internet will really catch on for a few more years—not until very high-speed connections are cheap and easily available. You also need a fast computer, of course. For now it's limited to companies with network connections. However, that hasn't stopped a variety of companies from selling video software for use on the Internet. Actually, these products are generally thought of as video-conferencing products, but the principle is the same: real-time communications across the Internet between two or more people. Go back to the Voice on the Net site (**http://www.von.com/**), and you'll find information about this, too.

The best-known product is Cu-SeeMe ("see you, see me," get it? Yeah, yeah). In fact, this product is so well known in the computer business that it's becoming a generic term, in the same way that *Hoover* is a generic term for vacuum cleaners. You can see a demo of this product at work at **http://www.wpine.com/**.

Other telecommunication systems will be added to the Internet soon. How about this idea? Have your faxes and voice mail connected to your e-mail system. If you live in the U.S. but do business in the UK, you can have a phone line set up in London. Your customers can call and leave voice mail for you or can fax you at that number, and your messages can then be compressed and attached to an e-mail message that is sent to you! In fact, you can have a number in New York, London, or Atlanta, or you can have a U.S. Toll Free number. And you'll even get the graphics in your faxes sent to you. See JFAX at **http://www.jfax.net/** for more information about this. And keep your eyes open for other weird and wonderful telecommunication/Internet hybrid services.

The Least You Need to Know

➤ You can connect to other users and actually talk on the Internet at a fraction of the cost of long distance or international calls.

➤ New Internet-to-phone system servers are being set up, which will enable you to connect across the world on the Internet, and then call someone using another country's domestic phone system.

➤ The software is plentiful and often cheap or even free. Check out the Web site **http://www.von.com/** for sources.

➤ Most companies have set up servers to which you can connect and find someone to talk to; test the system before you make the rest of your family use it.

➤ Many useful features are available in some products. You can send text or pictures while you talk, talk to a group of people, or even go on group Web trips.

➤ Video phones are available, but they require fast connections to the Internet.

Chapter 19

What on Earth Are All Those File Types?

In This Chapter

➤ About the directory (folder) system

➤ Picking a download directory

➤ File extensions and file types

➤ File types you'll run into

➤ What are compressed files?

➤ Working with compressed and archive files

➤ Avoiding viruses

It's possible to work with a computer for years without really understanding directories and file types. I know people who simply save files from their word processor (the only program they ever use) "on the disk." *Where on the disk?* Well ... you know ... on the hard disk. *Yes, but where? Which directory?* Well ... you know ... where the program saves the files.

You can get away with this lack of knowledge if you use only one program and don't use it too much. But if you plan to spend any time on the Internet and plan to make the most of your time there, you'll need to understand a bit more about files and directories. You'll come across a plethora of file types, and it helps if you understand what you are looking at.

About Download Directories

I don't want to spend a lot of time explaining what a directory is. This is very basic computing stuff, and if you don't understand it you should probably read an introduction to computing (such as *The Complete Idiot's Guide to PCs*) by Joe Kraynak. However, I'll quickly explain it, and that may be enough.

You can think of a directory as an area on your hard disk that stores computer files. You might think of it as a file folder in a filing cabinet. The hard disk is the filing cabinet, holding dozens, maybe hundreds, of folders (directories). In some graphical user interfaces, such as Windows 95 and the Macintosh, directories are actually called *folders*. (But I've been using the term *directory* too long to give it up now.)

If you look inside a filing cabinet and open a file folder, what do you find? Documents—those are the individual files. And you may also find another folder within the first folder. That's what we call a subdirectory. So directories can contain files and other directories, and those directories can contain more files and more directories (more subdirectories), and so on. Thus you have what is known as the directory tree. (The following figure shows what this "tree" looks like.) The point of this system is to help you organize your files. It's not uncommon for today's computers to have thousands of files, tens of thousands even. If you don't organize this lot logically, you'll end up with a mess that will make the Gordian Knot look simple.

Directories Are *Not* Areas of the Hard Disk!

Before you e-mail me saying that a directory is *not* an area on your hard disk, let me say *I know that!* It just *appears* to be an area on your hard disk. Actually, computer files are spread across the disk in an apparently illogical and disorganized manner—a piece of a file here, a piece there. The directory system is simply a visual way to organize the files, to make the hard disk easier to use.

The disk says, "I have a directory here that contains these files." But that's a lie, really, as the files are actually scattered willy-nilly all over the place. But it doesn't matter. It's rather like a child who *swears* that he has tidied up his room, that his socks are in the dresser and his shoes are in the closet. They're not, of course; everything's scattered over the floor. But you really don't want to look inside because it will just upset you. So you accept it and think in terms of where things *should be* within the room, without wanting to see the truth.

A *download directory* is a directory into which you download a file. For instance, let's say that you are using your Web browser to download a shareware program from one of the libraries listed in Appendix A. Where is that file saved? By definition, it's downloaded into the download directory. What is the download directory named? It may be called DOWNLOAD, but it could be anything; the download directory is simply whichever directory you tell the program to put the file in.

Folders, within folders, within folders make up the directory tree, shown here in the Norton File Manager program.

I think it's important for you to understand that the directory chosen by the browser as the download directory is not always the best place to put the file. In many cases it's a lousy choice. Internet Explorer, for instance, wants to place downloaded files on the Windows 95 *desktop*. (In Windows 95, the desktop is actually a special subdirectory of the WINDOWS directory; anything placed inside that directory will appear on the desktop— the area of your computer screen that is visible when all the programs have been closed.) That's often a bad place to put it; if you download a lot of things, your desktop will soon be as cluttered as my office. (And believe me, that's not pleasant.) Of course you can always move the file to another directory later, but in that case, why not put it where you want it in the first place?

Also, many of the files that you will download are archive files; these are sort of file "containers." Although an archive file is a single file, it has other files within it, perhaps hundreds of them. When you extract those files from inside, they are generally placed in the same directory. After you extract those files, you no longer have one easily recognized file on your desktop (or in whichever download directory the program chose). You now have dozens or more new files there. Do this with several download files and you'll soon become confused; which file came from which archive?

Pick a Download Directory Sensibly

When you download files from the Web, FTP, Gopher, your online service, or wherever, think sensibly about where you place the downloaded file. Many users create a special directory called DOWNLOAD. Some programs even do this automatically: WS_FTP, for instance, creates a DOWNLOAD directory to be used as the default location for down-loaded files. You can place all the files you download directly into that directory. Later you can decide what you want to do with the files.

I prefer to go one step further. When I download a file, I think about where I'll eventually want the file. For instance, if it's a document file related to a book I'm working on, I save it directly into one of the directories I've created to hold the book. If it's a program file, I'll have to create a directory to hold the program at some point, so why not create a directory for the program right now and download the file directly into that directory? (Depending on which operating system and program you are using, you may be able to create the directory while you are telling the program where to save the file; or you may have to use some kind of file-management program to create the directory and *then* save the file.)

Learn about directories. Make sure you understand how to find your way around the directory tree (or folder system as it's known in some operating systems). And make sure you save files in the right places, in such a manner that you can find them when you need them.

A Cornucopia of File Formats

Many computer users don't understand the concept of file formats because they never really see any files. They open their word processors, do some work, and then save the file. They may notice that when they give the file a name, the program adds a few letters such as .DOC or .WPD at the end, but they don't think much about it. If you're going to be playing on the Net, though, you need to understand just a little about file formats because you'll have to pick and choose the ones you want.

All computer files have one thing in common. They all save information in the form of zeros and ones. The difference between a file created by one word processor and another, or between a file created by a word processor and one created by a graphics program, is in what those zeros and ones actually *mean*. Just as two languages can use the same basic sounds and string them together to create different words, different programs use the zeros and ones to mean different things. One program uses zeros and ones to create words, another to create sounds, another to create pictures, and so on.

The File Extension

How, then, can a computer program identify one file from another? Well, they can often look for a familiar sequence of zeros and ones at the beginning of a file; if they find it, they know they've got the right file. But there's also something called *file extensions* that identifies files, and it has the added advantage of being visible to mere mortals. An extension is a piece of text at the end of a file name, preceded by a period, that is used to identify the file type. For example, look at this sample file name:

THISDOC.TXT

Different Extensions, Same Format

Some files are identified by two or more different file extensions. For instance, the .JPEG extension is often used on UNIX computers to identify a form of graphics file commonly used on the Web. But because Windows 3.1 and DOS can't display four-character extensions, the file is often seen with the .JPG extension; different extension, but exactly the same file format. You'll also find .HTM and .HTML files, .TXT and .TEXT files, and .AIF and .AIFF files (sound files).

The extension is the .TXT bit. This means the file is a plain text file; any program that can read what is known as ASCII text can open this file and read it.

Now, in most operating systems (including DOS and Windows), file extensions are typically three characters long, in some cases four. And normally each file has only one file extension. Some operating systems, such as UNIX and Windows 95, for example, allow multiple extensions and extensions with more than three characters such as THISDOC.NEWONE.TEXT. However, this sort of thing is becoming rare on the Internet these days, and you'll generally only run into simple three- and four-character extensions.

You might be thinking that there are probably three or four file formats you need to know about. No, not quite. Try four or five dozen. The following table gives a list to keep you going.

File Formats You Should Know

File Format	Type of File It Identifies
.ARC	A PKARC file (a DOS compression file).
.AU, .AIF, .AIFF, .AIFC, .SND	Sound files often used on Macintosh systems; Netscape and Internet Explorer can play these sounds.
.AVI	Video for Windows.
.BMP, .PCX,	Common bitmap graphics formats.
.DOC	Microsoft Word files, from Word for the Macintosh, Word for Windows, and Windows 95's WordPad.
.EPS	A PostScript image.
.EXE	A program file or a self-extracting archive file.
.FLC, .FLI, .AAS	Autodesk Animator files.
.GIF	These are graphics files often found in Web pages.
.gzip and .gz	UNIX compressed files.

continues

File Formats You Should Know   continued

File Format	Type of File It Identifies
.HLP	Windows Help files.
.HTM, .HTML	The basic Web-document format.
.hqx	A BinHex file, a format often used to archive Macintosh files. Programs such as StuffIt Expander can open these.
.JPG, .JPEG, .JPE, .JFIF, .PJPEG, .PJP	JPEG graphics files, also often found in Web pages. A few more variations of the JPEG.
.MID, .RMI	MIDI (Musical Instrument Digital Interface) sounds.
.MMM	Microsoft Multimedia Movie Player files.
.MOV, .QT	The QuickTime video format.
.MP2	An MPEG audio format.
.MPEG, .MPG, .MPE, .M1V	The MPEG (Motion Pictures Expert Group) video formats.
.PDF	The Portable Document Format, an Adobe Acrobat hypertext file. This format is becoming a very popular means of distributing electronic documents.
.pit	The Macintosh Packit archive format.
.PS	A PostScript document.
.RAM, .RA	RealAudio. This is a sound format that plays while it's being transmitted. Click a link to a RealAudio file, and it begins playing within a few seconds (you don't have to wait until the entire file is transferred).
.RTF	Rich Text Format, word processing files that work in a variety of Windows word processors.
.sea	A Macintosh self-extracting archive.
.SGML	A document format.
.shar	A UNIX shell archive file.
.sit	The Macintosh StuffIt archive format.
.tar	A UNIX tar archive file.
.TIF	A common graphics format.
.TSP	TrueSpeech, a sound format similar to RealAudio, though of a higher quality.
.TXT, .TEXT	A text file.
.WAV	The standard Windows wave file sound format.
.WRI	Windows Write word processing files.
.WRL	A VRML (Virtual Reality Modeling Language) 3-D object.

File Format	Type of File It Identifies
.XBM	Another graphics file that can be displayed by Web browsers (though it's not used very often these days).
.XDM	The StreamWorks webTV and webRadio format. This is similar to RealAudio, but it allows the real-time playing of video in addition to sound.
.Z	A UNIX compressed file.
.z	A UNIX packed file.
.ZIP	A PKZIP archive file (a DOS and Windows compression file).
.zoo	A zoo210 archive format available on various systems.

Is that all? By no means! Netscape currently claims that it has 154 plug-ins. While many duplicate the functions of other plug-ins, handling the same file types, this still represents a lot of different file formats. There are all sorts of file formats out there; to be honest, though, you'll only run across a few of them. You may never even run across a few of the ones I included in the table; for instance, the .ARC format, which used to be very common in the shareware world, is quite rare now.

File Compression Basics

As you can see from the preceding table, a number of these file formats are archive or compressed formats. These are files containing other files within them. You can use a special program to extract those files; or, in the case of a "self-extracting archive," the file can automatically extract the file.

Why do people bother to put files inside archive files? Or even, in some cases, a single file within an archive file? Two reasons. First, the programs that create these files compress the files being placed inside. So the single file is much smaller than the combined size of all the files inside.

You can reduce files down to as little as 2% of their normal size, depending on the type of file and the program you use (though 40% to 75% is probably a more normal range). Bitmap graphics, for instance, often compress to a very small size, while program files and Windows Help files can't be compressed so far. If you want to transfer a file across the Internet, it's a lot quicker to transfer a compressed file than an uncompressed file.

Check This Out...

Is It Possible? This is similar to Dr. Who's Tardis, which has much more space *inside* than would be allowed within a box of that size according to normal physics. And no, I don't plan to explain how it's done. Suffice it to say that, thanks to a little magic and nifty computing tricks, these programs make files smaller.

And the other reason to use these systems is that you can place files inside another file as a sort of packaging or container. If a shareware program has, say, 20 different files that it needs in order to run, it's better to "wrap" all these into one file than to expect people to transfer all 20 files one at a time.

Archive versus Compressed

What's the difference between an archive file and a compressed file? Well, they're often the same thing, and people (including me) tend to use the terms interchangeably. Originally, however, an archive file was a file that stored lots of other files: it archived them. An archive file doesn't have to be a compressed file, it's just a convenient place to put files that you are not using. A compressed file must, of course, be compressed. These days, archive files *are* usually compressed files, and compressed files are often used for archiving files. So there's not a lot of difference between the two anymore. There's one notable exception, though. The .tar files you may run across, UNIX tape archive files, are *not* compressed. However, they're often stored within gzip files (you'll see something like filename.tar.gz), which are compressed files.

Which Format?

You'll find that most of the compressed DOS and Windows files are in .ZIP format, a format often created by a program called PKZIP (though as the file format is not owned by anyone, other programs create .ZIP files, too). There are other compressed formats, though; you may also see .ARJ (created by a program called ARJ) and .LZH (created by LHARC) now and again, but probably not very often. PKZIP won the compression war.

In the UNIX world, .Z, .gz, and .tar files are common archive formats. And on the Macintosh, you'll find .sit (StuffIt) and .pit (Packit) compressed formats, as well as .hqx (BinHex) archive files. This table gives you a quick rundown of the compressed formats you'll see.

Common Compressed File Formats

Extension	Program That Compressed It
.arc	DOS, PKARC (an older method, predating PKZIP)
.exe	A DOS or Windows self-extracting archive
.gz	Usually a UNIX gzip compressed file (though there are versions of gzip for other operating systems, they're rarely used)
.hqx	Macintosh BinHex
.pit	Macintosh Packit
.sea	A Macintosh self-extracting archive

Extension	Program That Compressed It
.shar	UNIX shell archive
.sit	Macintosh StuffIt
.tar	UNIX tar
.Z	UNIX compress
.z	UNIX pack
.ZIP	PKZIP and others
.zoo	zoo210 (available on various systems)

It goes without saying (but I'll say it anyway, just in case) that if you see a file with an extension that is common on an operating system other than yours, it may contain files that won't be any good on your system. Macintosh and UNIX software won't run on Windows, for instance. However, that's not always true. The file may contain text files, for instance, which can be read on any system. So there are cross-platform utilities; for example, some Macintosh utilities can uncompress archive files—such as zip files—that are not common in the Macintosh world, and some zip utilities running in Windows can extract files from .gz and .tar files. For instance, some versions of Stuffit Expander, a Macintosh utility, can open .zip files, and WinZip, a Windows program, can open .gz and .tar files.

Those Self-Extracting Archives

Finally, there's something called self-extracting archives. Various programs, such as PKZIP and ARJ, can create files that can be executed (run) to extract the archived files automatically. This is very useful for sending a compressed file to someone when you're not sure if he has the program to decompress the file (or would know how to use it). For instance, PKZIP can create a file with an .EXE extension; you can run such a file directly from the DOS prompt just by typing its name and pressing Enter, or by double-clicking the file in Windows 95's Windows Explorer file-management program. When you do so, all of the compressed files pop out. In the Macintosh world .sea—Self Extracting Archive—files do the same thing. Double-click an .sea file, and the contents are automatically extracted.

If you find a file in two formats, .ZIP and .EXE for instance, you may want to take the .EXE format. The .EXE files are not much larger than the .ZIP files, and you don't need to worry about finding a program to extract the files. If you take a .ZIP file you must have a program that can read the .ZIP file and extract the archived files from within.

> **Check This Out...**
>
> **In the Meantime** How can you download and extract one of these compression utilities before you have a program that will extract an archive file? Don't worry, the programmers thought of that! These utilities are generally stored in self-extracting format, so you can download them and automatically extract them by running them.

You may already have such a program. Some Windows and Windows 95 file-management programs, for instance, can work with .ZIP files. Otherwise you'll need a program that can extract from the compressed format. See Appendix A for information about file libraries where you can download freeware and shareware that will do the job.

Your Computer Can Get Sick, Too

Downloading all these computer files can lead to problems: computer viruses. File viruses hide out in program files and copy themselves to other program files when someone runs that program. Viruses and other malevolent computer bugs are real, and they do real damage. Now and then you'll even hear of service providers having to close down temporarily after their systems become infected.

Unfortunately, security on the Internet is lax. The major online services have strict regulations about virus checks. Members generally cannot post directly to public areas, for instance; they post to an area in which the file can be checked for viruses before it's available to the public. But on the Internet it's up to each system administrator (and there are hundreds of thousands of them) to keep his own system clean. If just one administrator does a bad job, a virus can get through and be carried by FTP, the Web, or e-mail all over the world.

Viruses Under the Microscope

The term virus has become a "catch-all" for a variety of different digital organisms, such as

➤ Bacteria, which reproduce and do no direct damage except using up disk space and memory.

➤ Rabbits, which get their name because they reproduce very quickly.

➤ Trojan horses, which are viruses embedded in otherwise-useful programs.

➤ Bombs, which are programs that just sit and wait for a particular date or event (at which time they wreak destruction); these are often left deep inside programs by disgruntled employees.

➤ Worms, which are programs that copy themselves from one computer to another, independent of other executable files, and "clog" the computers by taking over memory and disk space.

However, having said all that, I've also got to say that the virus threat is also overstated—probably by companies selling antivirus software. We've reached a stage where almost any confusing computer problem is blamed on computer viruses, and technical support lines are using it as an excuse not to talk with people. "Your computer can't read your hard disk? You've been downloading files from the Internet? You must have a virus!"

Most computer users have never been "hit" by a computer virus. Many who think they have probably haven't; a lot of problems are blamed on viruses these days. So don't get overly worried about it. Take some sensible precautions, and you'll be okay.

Tips for Safe Computing

If you are just working with basic ASCII text e-mail and perhaps FTPing documents, you're okay. The problem of viruses arises when you transfer programs—including self-extracting archive files—or files that contain mini "programs." (For instance, many word processing files can now contain macros, special little programs that may run when you open the file.)

Rule of Thumb

Here's a rule of thumb to figure out if a file is dangerous. "If it does something, it can carry a virus; if it has things done to it, it's safe." Only files that can actually carry out actions (such as script files, program files, and word processing files from the fancy word processors that have built-in macro systems) can pose a threat. If a file can't do anything—it just sits waiting until a program displays or plays it—it's safe. Pictures and sounds, for instance, may offend you personally, but they won't do your computer any harm. (Can self-extracting archives carry viruses? Absolutely. They're programs, and they run—you don't know that they're self-extracting archives until they've extracted, after all.)

If you do plan to transfer programs, perhaps the best advice is to get a good antivirus program. They're available for all computer types. Each time you transmit an executable file, use your antivirus program to check it. Also, make sure you keep good backups of your data. Although backups can also become infected with viruses, if a virus hits at least you can reload your backup data and use an antivirus program to clean the files (and some backup programs check for viruses while backing up).

The Least You Need to Know

➤ Don't transfer files to your computer without thinking about *where* on your hard disk they should be. Create a download directory in a sensible place.

➤ Files are identified by the file extension, typically a three-character (sometimes four-character) "code" preceded by a period.

➤ Compressed and archive files are files containing other files within. They provide a convenient way to distribute files across the Internet.

➤ Self-extracting archives are files that don't require a special utility to extract the files from within. Just "run" the file, and the files within are extracted.

➤ Viruses are real, but the threat is exaggerated. Use an antivirus program, and then relax.

➤ The virus rule of thumb is this: "If it does something, it can carry a virus; if it has things done to it, it's safe."

Chapter 20

Telnet: Inviting Yourself onto Other Systems

In This Chapter

➤ Finding a Telnet program

➤ Four ways to start Telnet

➤ Using HYTELNET

➤ Running your Telnet session

➤ IBM tn3270 Telnet sites

➤ MUDs, MOOs, and other role-playing games

Millions of computers are connected to the Internet, and some of them contain some pretty interesting stuff. Wouldn't it be great if you could "reach out" and get onto those computers (well, some of them) to take a look at the games and databases and programs on computers around the world?

Well, you can. At least, you can get onto computers whose administrators want you to get on them, and there's a surprisingly high number of those who do. A special program called Telnet lets you turn your computer into a Telnet *client* to access data and programs on some Telnet *server*.

Many Internet users have private Telnet accounts. A researcher, for example, might have several computers he works on regularly, and he might have been given a special login name and password by the administrators of those computers. But many computers also allow "strangers" into their systems. This is completely voluntary, depending on the good will of the people who own or operate a particular computer. If a Telnet server is open to the public, anyone can get on the system and see what's available.

Step 1 Find a Telnet Program

First, you'll need a Telnet program. The selection and quality of Telnet programs are among the weakest features of the Internet. There are wonderful Web browsers around, as well as excellent e-mail and FTP programs, for instance, but the Telnet programs I've run across all seem a bit weak.

Part of the problem is that there's a limit to how much a Telnet program can help you. When telnetting, your computer becomes a terminal of the computer you've just connected to, so it has to follow the "rules" used by that computer. Because there are thousands of systems out there on the Internet, each using slightly different menu systems, command systems, and so on, it's hard to create a really good Telnet program. All the average Telnet program does is provide a window into which you can type commands and in which will appear responses. Also, because Telnet isn't a terribly exciting subject (when was the last time you saw a *TIME* or *Newsweek* article on the wonders of Telnet?), it's been ignored by most software developers.

Now I know what you're thinking…. You're thinking, "he'll probably explain how to use Telnet through the browser, and then how to use a real Telnet program." Well, you're wrong. You *can't* Telnet through your browser. Although you can *start* a Telnet program from your browser, the browser itself can't run the session. At least, none of the most popular browsers have built-in Telnet capabilities. So if you want to use Telnet, you'll need a Telnet program.

Check This Out…

A Java Telnet Application Well, maybe you *can* use Telnet through your browser. There's a new Java Telnet application (you can find it at **http://www.first.gmd.de/persons/leo/java/Telnet/**) that will run within your browser. However, it's currently rather complicated to set up.

You may already have one. If you are working with CompuServe, you'll find a Telnet program built into the CompuServe software (GO TELNET). AOL does not currently have a built-in Telnet program, but you can use the keyword **telnet** to find information about Telnet as well as a library of Telnet programs you can download (you may have to upgrade your AOL software to the latest version to be able to use one of these Telnet programs). MSN does not have a built-in Telnet program either, but you probably have Microsoft Telnet, which is usually installed when you install your Windows 95 TCP/IP network software. If you're using Windows 95 or Windows NT, open the **Start** menu, select **Run**, type **telnet**, and press **Enter**. You may find that Microsoft Telnet opens. If you are with an Internet service provider, you might have received a Telnet program with the software they gave you—but there's a good chance you didn't.

If you have to find your own Telnet program, you can do so at the software archives listed in Appendix A. You might use something like CRT for Windows or NetTerm for Windows; if you are a Macintosh user, try NCSA Telnet or dataComet. Of course you may not want to bother tracking down Telnet software until you actually find a need for it, and many people never do. If you need to access library catalogs, though, you may need Telnet, as many such systems are available via Telnet.

Making the Connection

You have a number of choices of how to begin a Telnet session.

➤ In your Web browser, click a **telnet://** link. In Web documents, you'll sometimes run across links that use the telnet:// URL (not very often, though we'll look at a site that has many such links later in this chapter). When you click the link your Telnet program opens and starts the session with the referenced Telnet site. (If this doesn't work you'll have to tell your Web browser which Telnet program to use; you enter that as the browser's **Options** or **Preferences**.)

➤ In your Web browser, type the **telnet://** URL. If your Web browser is open you can also start a Telnet session by typing **telnet://** followed by a Telnet host address and pressing **Enter**. For instance, if you type **telnet://pac.carl.org** into Internet Explorer's Address text box and press **Enter**, Windows Telnet launches and connects to the Denver Public Library's site. (Type **PAC** and press **Enter** to log on.)

➤ Open a Telnet program. You can also open Telnet directly. For instance, if you are using Windows 95, you can look in the Windows directory in Windows Explorer and double-click **telnet.exe**.

➤ Open a Telnet program from the Start menu. In Windows 95, you can also open the Windows **Start** menu, click **Run**, type **telnet://***hostname* (such as **telnet://pac.carl.org**), and press **Enter**. The Telnet program starts automatically.

A Telnet site name looks something like this: **pac.carl.org**, **freenet.sfn.saskatoon.sk.ca**, **fdabbs.fda.gov**, or sometimes a number, such as **150.148.8.48**. If you are opening a Telnet site from within your Telnet program, you'll enter the Telnet site or host name into the appropriate dialog box. For instance, to get a Telnet program to connect to a Telnet site, you might have to select **File**, **Connect** (or something similar), enter the Telnet site, and press **Enter**. If you are using CompuServe, use the **TELNET** GO word, choose **Access a Specific Site**, type the Telnet host name, and press **Enter**. You can see CompuServe's Telnet window in the following figure.

HYTELNET Your Guide to the World of Telnet

To get a taste of what's available in the world of Telnet, take a look at HYTELNET, the Telnet directory. This used to be available only through Telnet itself, but now you can view the directory at a World Wide Web site, which is much more convenient. (Ha!, what a joke, eh? No wonder nobody uses Telnet anymore, even the Telnet aficionados use the

Web because it's more convenient!) Open your Web browser and go to **http://library.usask.ca/hytelnet/**. (Alternatively, you can find other HYTELNET services at **http://www.lights.com/hytelnet/** and **http://www.cc.ukans.edu/hytelnet_html/START.TXT.html**.)

CompuServe has a built-in Telnet window that you can access using the TELNET GO word.

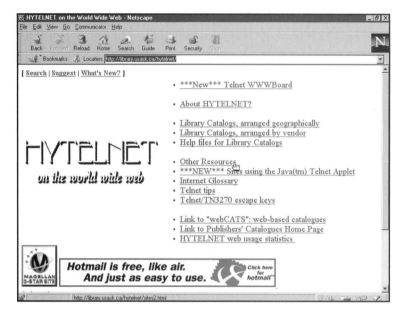

From this document you can launch Telnet sessions on computers all over the world. In the next figure, you can see the first page of HYTELNET. The most important links in this page are the Library Catalogs and Other Resources links. They take you to directories of Telnet sites (the other links just take you to information about working with Telnet).

Click the **Other Resources** link, for instance, and you'll be taken to another page with links to Databases and bibliographies, Fee-Based Services, NASA databases, and more. Travel further down the hierarchy of documents, and you'll come to information about individual Telnet services (see the next figure). This shows information about the NASA/IPAC Extragalactic Database Telnet site, where you can find information about all sorts of, well, extragalactic stuff— galaxies, quasars, and infrared and radio sources, for instance. This page shows the Telnet address (**ned.ipac.caltech.edu**), and the name you must use to log in once connected (**ned**). It also shows a list of commands you can use once connected. Note that it also has a link; the Telnet addresses are links that you can click to launch your Telnet program and begin the Telnet session.

More Directories

Your online service may also list interesting Telnet sites. For instance, in CompuServe use **GO TELNET**, then select **List of Sites** or **Telnet Site Descriptions**.

More Directories

Here are two more Web directories that will help you find Telnet and other resources:

http://www.w3.org/hypertext/DataSources/ByAccess.html
http://www.ncsa.uiuc.edu/SDG/Software/Mosaic/MetaIndex.html

You can also search for the word "telnet" at Web search sites; see Chapter 21.

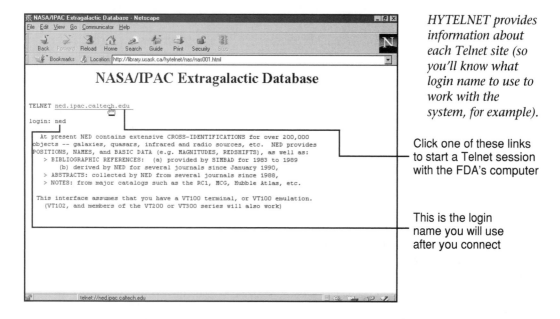

HYTELNET provides information about each Telnet site (so you'll know what login name to use to work with the system, for example).

Click one of these links to start a Telnet session with the FDA's computer

This is the login name you will use after you connect

You're In. Now What?

After your Telnet program has connected to the Telnet site, you may have to log in. To do so, you'll need to know the account name you should use. HYTELNET describes Telnet sites, including the required account names. And when you find a Telnet site described in a book or magazine, the account name is often included. In some cases, you *won't* have to log in; the computer will let you right in without asking for further information. And in other cases, the introductory screen you see when you first connect may tell you what to use. The site shown in the following figure (Saskatoon Free-Net) explains how to log on.

When you connect to a Telnet session, you often have to identify the type of computer terminal you are using. Of course, you are using a PC, but your Telnet program can *emulate* (pretend to be) a standard terminal program. By default, it's probably set to emulate a VT-100 terminal, which is good because the VT-100 setting works in most cases you'll run into. If you run into a site that doesn't like the VT-100 setting—perhaps the text on your screen isn't displayed properly during the session—you can try changing the emulation. But you don't always have many choices.

You can log on to the Saskatoon Free-Net as a guest.

Terminal Emulations

When you connect to a Telnet site you are, in effect, turning your computer into a "dumb terminal." The programs at the Telnet site will run on that site's computer, not yours. All you are using your computer for is to send text commands to the Telnet site and to view the results. And that's just what a computer "terminal" does. But there are many different kinds of terminals. Your Telnet program is pretending to be a computer terminal, but it has to be told which one to imitate (or *emulate*, in computer jargon). The VT-100 terminal is one of the most common types, and it is recognized by most Telnet sites.

Working in a Telnet Session

Every Telnet system is different. Your Telnet program functions as a means of transferring what you type on your computer to the computer you are connected to, and for that computer to send text back to you. In effect, you've turned your computer into a dumb terminal connected to another computer, so you have to follow the rules of that system.

What you see depends on what sort of system is set up on that computer. It might be a series of menus from which you select options, or it might be a prompt at which you type. Each system varies a little.

Let me warn you about one thing: Telnet can be slow—*very* slow—sometimes. On occasion, you may type something and not see what you have typed for several seconds or even several minutes. It depends on the amount of network traffic going that way as well as the number of people working on that machine at that time. If you find a particular task to be too slow, you should probably try again later. If it's always slow at that Telnet site, maybe you can find another site with the same services.

Special Features

Telnet programs vary from the absolutely awful to the quite reasonable. Many simple programs do very little but connect you to the Telnet site; once there, you're on your own. Others let you create login scripts (to speed up connecting to the site), program function keys to carry out certain actions at a particular site, modify text and background colors, and so on. Figure out what your Telnet program can do *because you're going to need all the help you can get!* Telnet is not an easy system to use; if you like the Web, you just might hate Telnet.

Keeping a Record

Many Telnet programs let you keep a record of your session. For instance, in Windows Telnet (the Telnet program that comes with Windows 95's networking software), you can select **Terminal**, **Start Logging**. In CRT, another popular Telnet program, you can choose **File**, **Log Session**. You'll generally see a dialog box, into which you can enter a file name, and everything that happens in the session is saved in the named file.

You can also usually copy text from the session. Drag the mouse pointer across the text (or choose **Edit**, **Select All** in some Telnet programs), and then choose **Edit**, **Copy**. You can then go to another program—your word processor or e-mail program, for instance— and paste in that text. CRT has a useful feature: it copies the selected text and then sends the text as if you typed it. Thus, it allows you to respond to a prompt by typing in something that appeared earlier in the session.

Waving Good-Bye to the Telnet Site

Once you log on to a Telnet site, you're in that computer's system. Because you log off differently in each system, you'll have to try a number of commands to see which one works for you. Try **quit**, **exit**, **Ctrl+d**, **bye**, and **done**, in that order. One of those will probably end the session. If none of them does the trick, look for some kind of prompt that tells you what you need to type to get out.

It's polite to end a Telnet session using the correct method. However, as a last resort you can close the connection by closing the Telnet window or by using the program's disconnect command (**Connect**, **Disconnect**, perhaps).

Telnet's Ugly Sister tn3270

Some Telnet sites are on IBM mainframes running "3270" software. If you try to telnet to a site and find that the connection is instantly closed (even before you get to the login prompt), that particular site *might* be a 3270 site (though there's no guarantee of it).

On the other hand, if you log in and see this

```
VM/XA SP ONLINE-PRESS ENTER KEY TO BEGIN SESSION
```

you've definitely reached a 3270 site. For example, if you telneted with the command **telnet vmd.cso.uiuc.edu**, you'd probably see this:

```
Trying 128.174.5.98 ...
Connected to vmd.cso.uiuc.edu.
Escape character is Ô^]'.
VM/XA SP ONLINE-PRESS ENTER KEY TO BEGIN SESSION.
```

Your Telnet program probably won't be able to handle a tn3270 session. You're welcome to try it and see, but there's a good chance it won't.

These 3270 sessions are not that common, so you may never run into them. But if you really do have to use a tn3270 site, you'll need to find a tn3270 emulator. You might try QWS3270 (a Windows tn3270 emulator), dataComet (a Macintosh program that can run both Telnet and tn3270 sessions), or tn3270 (a Mac tn3270 program). See Appendix A for information on software sites at which you can find these programs. If you have Netscape Communicator Professional, you already have a tn3270 program, IBM Host-On-Demand, which you can open from the **Communicator** menu.

MUDs, MOOs, and MUCKs

Telnet is not a very popular system right now. It's been eclipsed by the World Wide Web, and many new Internet users don't have the slightest idea what it is. However, in addition to library systems there's another popular use for Telnet: role-playing games. These are games known by such bizarre names as MUDs (Multi-User Dimensions, or maybe Multi-User Dungeons), MOOs, and MUCKs, Tiny MUDs, Teeny MUDs, UnterMUDS, and so on.

In these games, you type responses to a program running in a Telnet session. The program may describe where you are: You're in a room with a door on the West wall, a window on the East wall, and steps going down. You then tell it what to do: You might type **door** to go through the door. If this sounds exciting, these games are for you. (If it doesn't, you're not alone.)

If you are interested, check out one or more of the following options:

➤ Try **gopher://gopher.micro.umn.edu.** When you get to the Gopher menu, choose **Fun & Games** and then **Games**.

➤ Try searching for MUD at Yahoo or another search site (see Chapter 21).

➤ If you use AOL, you can find quite a bit of information about MUDS using the **telnet** keyword. You'll find that while these games have predominantly been Telnet games in the past, they are now moving onto the Web. In addition, there are special client/server programs designed for role-playing games.

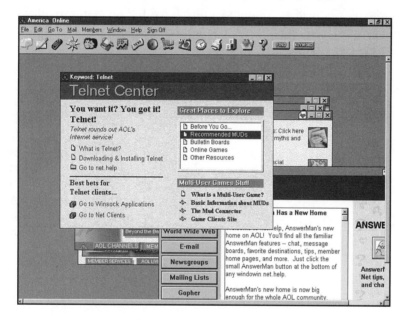

AOL's Telnet center helps you find a Telnet program and provides information about MUDs and other Telnet games.

I'm told that these games are extremely addictive—that people log on and get stuck for days at a time. Personally I don't see the excitement. But there again, I don't understand why some people become addicted to collecting string or hubcaps. Who am I to judge?

The Least You Need to Know

➤ You may already have a Telnet program; if not, you can find them in the software libraries mentioned in Appendix A.

➤ You can start your Telnet program by entering a **telnet://** URL in your Web browser or by clicking a Web link that references a Telnet site.

➤ You can also start the Telnet program and then enter the Telnet site name.

➤ Try the HYTELNET site (**http://library.usask.ca/hytelnet/**); it has links to hundreds of Telnet sites.

➤ When you connect to a Telnet site, you may have to enter a login name and password; HYTELNET tells you what to use.

➤ Once you are in, you are on your own. Each Telnet site has its own rules.

➤ Telnet sessions are often very slow.

➤ If you can't view a site, you may have entered a tn3270 site. You should get hold of a tn3270 program.

➤ If you are into role-playing games, Telnet to a MUD site. For more information, try **gopher://gopher.micro.umn.edu** (**Fun & Games**, **Games**), or search for the term **mud** at a search site (see Chapter 21).

Part 3
Getting Things Done

Now that you've learned how to use the Internet's services, it's time to learn some important general information about working on the Net. This place is so huge, you might have trouble finding what you need; I'll show you where to look. And you'll also need to learn how to stay safe on the Internet. You've heard about the problems that go along with using credit cards on the Internet, about kids finding pornography, and so on—we'll examine the truth and the lies.

In addition to covering all of those issues, I'll answer all sorts of questions I've heard from Internet users, from how to get rich on the Internet to why those $500 Internet boxes may not be such a great buy. I'll also tell you about a couple of dozen different ways that people use the Internet. Maybe, you'll find something worth pursuing or you'll think of an idea of your own. And you'll even find out where the Internet is going in the future.

Chapter 21

Finding Stuff

In This Chapter

➤ Finding people

➤ Searching the Internet with search engines

➤ Using Internet directories

➤ Searching newsgroups

➤ Other Internet services

By now you must have realized that the Internet is rather large: tens of millions of users, millions of files in FTP sites, millions and millions of Web pages, Telnet sites, Gopher servers, newsgroups, mailing lists, and so forth. This thing is huge. How on earth are you ever going to find your way around?

Finding what you need on the Internet is surprisingly easy these days. Dozens of services are available to you to find your way around. And that's what this chapter is about, finding what you need and where you need to go.

Finding People

We might as well start with the most complicated task: finding people on the Internet. There are millions of Internet users, and no single Internet directory. That's right. Unlike the online services, which have directories you can search to find someone you want to contact, there's no one place to search on the Internet. But that's not so surprising, really. After all, there's no single directory for the world's telephone system, and the Internet is comparable—it's thousands of connected networks that span the world. So how are you going to find someone?

Still Working at a Command Line?

If you are using the command-line interface, send an e-mail message to **ciginternet@mcp.com** and type who in the Subject line of the message (leave the body blank). In return, you'll receive the chapters on finding people from the first edition of *The Complete Idiot's Guide to the Internet*. For more information, see Appendix C.

Quite frankly, the easiest way to find someone's e-mail address is, if possible, talk to that person, or talk to (or e-mail) a mutual acquaintance. You can spend hours looking for someone in the Internet's various directories. If you know of someone else who might have the information, or know the person's telephone number, you can save yourself some time and trouble by tracking down the e-mail address that way. If you can't contact the person directly, or can't think of someone else who knows the person you're after, you'll have to dig a little deeper.

Directories, Directories, and More Directories

There are a lot of directories on the Web. (No, I don't mean directories on a computer's hard disk this time; now when I say "directories," I mean it as in "the telephone directory" or "directory assistance.") A good place to start is at your browser's people-search page. For instance, if you're using Netscape Navigator 4, click the Guide button and select People from the drop-down menu. In Navigator 3, click the **People** button in the Directory Buttons bar. If you're not using that browser you can go directly to Netscape's People page (**http://guide.netscape.com/guide/people.html**). Each time you go to this page, Netscape displays one of several directories (WhoWhere?, Four11, IAF, Bigfoot, InfoSpace, and Switchboard). The following illustration shows the Bigfoot directory. You can search the directory Netscape displays, or you can choose one of the others.

Another good directory to use is Yahoo! People Search (go to **http://www.yahoo. com/ search/people/**), which you can see in the following illustration. This is Yahoo's directory of people on the Internet, and it's surprisingly good. I searched for my own name and found myself , along with about 90 other Peter Kents. (I hadn't realized there were so many of us.) You can search for a name and narrow the search by including a city and state, or you can search for a telephone number.

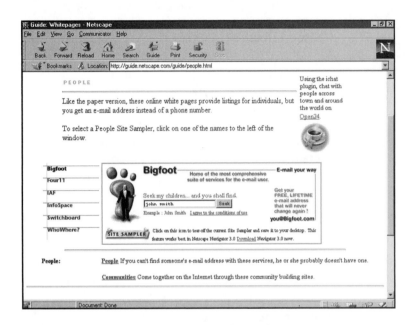

Netscape's People page automatically picks a directly for you.

Yahoo!'s People Search form.

Other Search Engines, Too Yahoo! is not the only *search engine* you can use to find directories. We'll look at more search engines later in this chapter, and you'll find that many of them will have links to directories you can use to find people, too.

If you don't find the person you need in Yahoo!'s People Search, don't worry; there's still a chance you'll find him. There are links to literally dozens more directories at Yahoo!'s **http://www.yahoo.com/Reference/ White_Pages/** page; when I looked a moment ago I found links to 115 different directories, some of which had links to dozens more, including directories at colleges.

I'm not going to go into more detail about these directories. A year or two ago it was quite difficult to find people on the Internet (when I searched for myself for the first edition of this book, I had a lot of trouble finding myself— and I knew where I was!). These days there are so many of these things that, with a bit of time and trouble, you have a good chance of finding the person you need (assuming he or she has Internet access, of course).

Before you begin your search, here are a couple of other useful Web pages to start you off:

➤ **The Directory of Directories (http://www.procd.com/hl/direct.htm)**

Links to all sorts of directories: museums, local government, universities, and companies. This may be useful if you are trying to track someone down in a specific institution.

➤ **Flip's Search Resources (http://aa.net/~flip/search.html)**

A Web page set up by someone who did an adoption search, with links to useful sites he found, such as databases of Vietnam War casualties, genealogy records, and so on.

Finding "Stuff"

Now for the more general "stuff" category. You want to find information about, well, something or other. Where do you start? The best place is probably on the Web, at the Web search sites. There are dozens of these sites, and I'm always surprised what I can turn up in just a few minutes of searching. There are basically three ways to use these search sites:

➤ View a directory from which you can select a subject category and subcategories; then you'll see a list of links to related pages.

➤ Search an index of subjects; type a keyword into a form, and then click a Search button to carry out a search. You'll see a list of links to Web pages related to the subjects you typed into the search form.

➤ Search an index of pages. Some search engines let you search for words within Web pages. AltaVista, for example, claims that it has an index of most of the words on *30 million* Web pages, at over a million Web sites! You'll see a list of pages that contain the words you typed into the form.

Which type of search should you use? The first or second method should normally be your first choice. Services such as AltaVista are very useful, but because they don't categorize the pages—they search for words within the pages instead of searching the subjects of the pages—they often give you more information than you can ever handle. The other services categorize pages (and sometimes even describe or review pages), so they are generally easier to use. Save places like AltaVista for "plan B," when you can't find what you're looking for on your first attempt.

Finding the Search Sites

Getting started is easy. Most Web browsers these days have a button that takes you straight to a search page of some kind (generally a form that lets you search a choice of search sites). For example, Netscape offers the Net Search button, Internet Explorer has a Search button, and so on.

Check This Out...

The Best?

Which is the best Web search site? There is no "best." Even though I really like Yahoo!, I sometimes use others. Each one is different and works in a different way, which means each one will give you a different result. Try a few and see which you like, or check to see how others rate them. For instance, you might try one of these pages for links to more search engines:

http://www.global-community.com/business/main.shtml

http://www.yahoo.com/Computers_and_Internet/Internet/World_Wide_Web/Searching_the_Web/

This list contains a few more URLs you can use. I've started with Yahoo because that's where I prefer to start. Of course, after you've used a few search sites, you may find that you have a different preference.

Yahoo!: **http://www.yahoo.com**

Lycos: **http://www.lycos.com/**

InfoSeek: **http://www.infoseek.com/**

HotBot: **http://www.HotBot.com/**

AltaVista: **http://www.altavista.digital.com/**

Inktomi: **http://inktomi.berkeley.edu/**

What's the difference between a Web directory and a search engine? A directory provides categorized lists of Web pages from which you can select a category, and then a subcategory, and then another subcategory, and so on until you find the site you want. A search engine lets you use a program with which you'll search a database of Web pages. With a search engine, you type a keyword and click a **Search** button or press **Enter**. The search engine then searches the database for you. Some sites such as Yahoo contain both directories and search engines.

Techno Talk

Browser Tip

Here's a really quick way to search for something; search directly from your browser's Location text box. If you're using Netscape Navigator, enter two words into the Location box. For instance, if you want to search for information about hiking in Iceland, type **iceland hiking**. (If you just want to search for one word, enter it twice, as in **iceland iceland**.) Press Enter, and Netscape picks a search engine for you from it's selection of five—Yahoo!, Magellan, InfoSeek, Lycos, and Excite—and sends the search keywords to the search engine. If you're using Internet Explorer, type **find** followed by the word you want to search for: **find iceland**, for instance.

How Do I Use the Search Engines?

Internet *search engines* allow you to search a database. Take a quick look at InfoSeek (**http://www.infoseek.com/**) in the following figure as an example.

Start by typing a search term into the text box. You can type as little as a single word, but you may want to get fancy—in which case you should read the instructions. You'll find a link at InfoSeek, probably labeled *Tips* or *Huh?*, that takes you to a document that describes exactly what you can type. Read this document; it gives you many suggestions and hints for using the search engine. (Most search engines will have a link like this to background information.)

As you will learn in the information document, you can enter these types of things at InfoSeek:

➤ **Words between quotation marks.** Tells InfoSeek to find the words in the exact order you type them: "the here and now."

➤ **Proper names.** Make sure these are capitalized correctly: Colorado, England, or Gore.

➤ **Words separated by hyphens.** Tells InfoSeek to find both words as long as they are close together in the document—diving-scuba.

➤ **Words in brackets.** Tells InfoSeek to find the search words if they appear together, but not necessarily in the order you've entered them—[diving scuba].

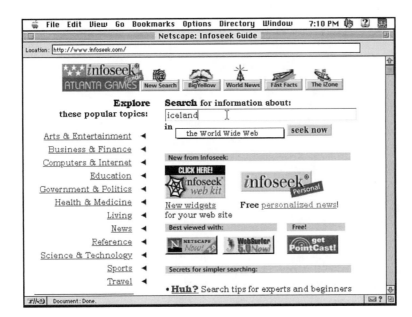

Infoseek, a Web search engine.

Each search engine is a little different and allows you to use different sorts of search terms. You can always search by simply entering a single word, but the more you know about each search engine, the more efficiently you can search. When you first go to a search engine, look around for some kind of link to a Help document.

When you finish reading the Help information, click the **Back** button to return to InfoSeek, to the page with the text box. Enter the word or phrase you want to search for, and then press **Enter** or click the **Search** button. Your browser sends the information to InfoSeek, and with a little luck you'll see a result page shortly thereafter (see the following figure). Of course you may see a message telling you that the search engine is busy. If so, try again in a few moments.

*InfoSeek found a few
links to Icelandic
subjects for me.*

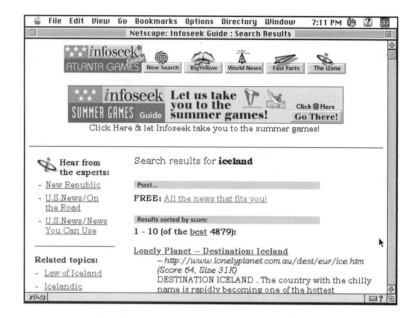

As you can see in the figure, when I searched for "iceland," InfoSeek found 4,879 links to Web sites that contain information about Iceland. The document I'm viewing doesn't show me all the links, of course. It shows me the first 10 and provides a link at the bottom of the page that I can click to see the next 10. It found links to things such as *Travel Guides to Iceland, History of Iceland, Books on Iceland, Airlines*, and plenty more. If one of these links interests me, all I have to do is click the link—and away I go, over the North Atlantic and into Iceland.

Browsing the Internet Directories

Now, let's look at the Internet directories. For a sample, we'll take a look at Yahoo!. Go to **http://www.yahoo.com/**. Yahoo has a search engine, so you can type a word into the text box if you want. But notice the category links: *Art, Education, Health, Social Science*, and so on. Each of these links points deeper into the Yahoo! system, a level lower down in the hierarchical system of document categories. To see how this works, click **Recreation**, and you see a document from Yahoo! with a list of more categories: *Amusement/ Theme Parks@, Aviation, Drugs@, Motorcycles*, and so on.

The @ sign at the end of some of these categories indicates that this entry is a sort of cross reference: you will be crossing over to another category if you select this link. For instance, click **Drugs@**, and you'll see a page from the *Health:Pharmacology:Drugs* category. This page also contains links to other drug-related categories, along with links to Web pages that are related to recreational drugs (from alcohol to XTC), political and legal issues, pharmacology, and many other subjects.

You'll also notice that some links are shown with bold text and numbers in parentheses after them—such as *Nicotine (31)*, and links that are not bolded (such as *Psychiatric Drug Therapy*). The bold links take you farther down the hierarchy, displaying another document that contains more links. The number in parentheses after the link shows how many links you'll find in that document.

The regular-text links are links across the Internet to Web documents that contain the information you're looking for. Select **WWW Drug Links**, and you'll find yourself viewing a Web document with more links to drug pages.

Finding Specific Stuff

Now that you've seen how to search for general "stuff," you're ready to learn about searching for more *specific* stuff. Instead of going to a general search site, you can go to one of many sites that help you find specific things; you might want a site where you can search for stuff about books and publications on the Internet (**http://www. alexandria-home.com/**), boat stuff (**http://boatingyellowpages.com/**), or kid stuff (**http://www.yahooligans.com/**), for example. You can find scores of these specialized search sites, with information about everything from lawyers to pets. A good place to find them is at **http://www.yahoo.com/Computers_and_Internet/Internet/ World_Wide_Web/Searching_the_Web/Web_Directories/**. You can also find them at any of the other big search sites.

Finding Out What People Are Saying

Are people talking about you (do you hear voices in your head?). If you rally want to know what people are saying about you on the Internet, you can search newsgroup messages for particular words. So you can search for your own name to find out what your friends—or enemies—are saying about you. Or you can search for a subject if you are researching a particular topic.

There are a number of places you can search newsgroups. One of the best is DejaNews (**http://www.dejanews.com/**). Or try Yahoo!; go to **http://www.yahoo.com**. At the search page, click the link—currently the **Options** link—that takes you to the advanced search. Then click the **Usenet** option button. (As another alternative, you can use InfoSeek and choose **Usenet Newsgroups** from the drop-down list before you search.) When the search site carries out the search, it displays a page of links to the matching messages. Click a link to read the message.

Set a Bookmark to Repeat the Search Later

Here's a handy little trick. If you've just done a search about a subject that you think you'll want to check back on later—to see what new information has appeared on the Internet—bookmark the search. I don't mean the search site, but the search itself.

Here's how: go to the search site, carry out the search, and when you get the page display-ing the search results, bookmark that page. The next time you want to search, all you have to do is select that bookmark. Your browser automatically sends the search state-ment to the search engine, which carries out the search and displays the result.

FTP, Gopher, Telnet, and More

No, you are not finished. You can search for much, much more. Go back to the earlier chapters on FTP, Gopher, Telnet, newsgroups, and mailing lists, and you'll see that I gave you information about how to find things on those services. For instance, you can use Archie to search FTP sites, and you can use Tile.Net and other similar services to find mailing lists and newsgroups related to subjects that interest you. You can also use Jughead and Veronica to search Gopherspace. So if you don't find what you need at any of the Web sites you learned about in this chapter, spend a little time searching the other services.

The Least You Need to Know

➤ There is no single directory of Internet users, so the easiest way to find someone is often to ask a mutual acquaintance.

➤ There are now lots of good directories. You may have to search a few, but there's a good chance that eventually you'll find the person you're looking for.

➤ A search engine is a program that searches for a word you enter.

➤ You can search indexes of keywords describing the contents of Web pages, or you can search the full text of the Web pages (millions of words in millions in pages).

➤ A directory is a categorized listing of Web links. Choose a category, then a subcat-egory, then another subcategory, and so on until you find what you want.

➤ Services such as DejaVu, Yahoo!, and InfoSeek let you search newsgroup messages. The result is a list of matching messages. Click a link to read a message.

➤ You can set a bookmark on a page that displays search results; then, to repeat the search quickly at a later date, all you have to do is select that bookmark.

Chapter 22

Staying Safe on the Internet

In This Chapter

➤ Keeping kids "safe"

➤ Protecting your e-mail

➤ The identity problem

➤ Internet addiction

➤ Protecting your credit card

➤ Keeping out of trouble with your boss or spouse

There are many dangers on the Internet—most of them imagined or exaggerated. We're led to believe that our children will become corrupted or kidnapped, our credit cards will be stolen, and we'll be arrested for copyright infringement.

Well, okay, some of these dangers are real. But remember, you're sitting in front of a computer at the end of a long cable. Just how dangerous can that be? If you use a little common sense, it doesn't have to be very dangerous at all.

Your Kid Is Learning About Sex from Strangers

Sex, sex, sex. That's all some people can think of. The media's so obsessed with sex that sometimes the only thing that our journalists really notice are stories with a little spice in them. Consequently the press has spent a lot of time over the last couple of years talking about how the Internet is awash in pornography. Well, it isn't.

I'll admit that there are pornographic images on the Internet, but in general you won't just "trip over" pornography. If you decide to take a look at the alt.binaries.pictures.erotica.pornstar newsgroup, for instance…well, just what do you expect to find?! You can hardly claim to be offended if you choose to enter such a locale. In some cases the publicly accessible sex-related Web sites are really quite "soft." Take a look at the *Hustler* or *Playboy* sites, then run down to your local magazine store and take a look at them there. You'll find that the bookstore version is far more explicit than the Web version. (Believe me, I've done this little experiment—but only in the interest of research, you understand.)

You Can Do Your Own Research Because this is a family book, I'm not going to go much further on this topic. If you care to research the subject of sex on the Internet further, check out **http://www.drv.com /hotline/hotlinx.html**, a directory of sex sites. (Don't bother checking this Web site if you're offended by sexual imagery!)

On the other hand, there *is* some very explicit stuff available. In fact since I wrote the third edition of this book, in 1996, Web sites seem to have become more explicit. In 1996 the Computer Decency Act was holding people back—much of the really explicit stuff was hidden away on private Web sites. To get in you had to subscribe by providing a credit card number. Since then the Computer Decency Act has been struck down by the courts; there are still many private sites, but there's quite a lot of very smutty stuff available at the free Web sites.

A number of newsgroups carry extremely explicit sexual images and, in a few cases, images of violent sex. (Even though most things don't particularly shock me, I have to admit that I've been disgusted by one or two things I've seen in newsgroups.)

Although the press would have you believe it's hard to get to the Smithsonian Web site or to read a newsgroup about cooking without somehow stumbling across some atrocious pornographic image, this is far from the truth. You really have to *go looking* for this stuff. The chance that you'll stumble across it is about as good as the chance that you'll run into Queen Elizabeth on your next trip to the supermarket. Of more concern, perhaps, is the access children have to explicit sites.

Don't Expect the Government to Help

If you have kids, you already know that they can be a big bundle of problems. The Internet is just one more thing to be concerned about. Still, you signed up for the job, and it's your responsibility.

Many people have suggested that somehow it's the *government's* responsibility to look after kids. (These are often the same people who talk about "getting the government off our backs" when it comes to other issues.) A couple of years ago the U.S. Congress passed the Computer Decency Act (CDA), which bans certain forms of talk and images from the Internet. This law definitely had an effect, and pornography was, for a while, harder to find on the Internet. But the CDA was sloppily written piece of overreaction; it could be construed to ban all sorts of genuine public discourse, such as discussions about abortion. Consequently the law was judged unconstitutional by a Federal court in Philadelphia, and later overturned by the U.S. Supreme Court.

The court in Philadelphia wrote that "Those responsible for minors undertake the primary obligation to prevent their exposure to such material." Hey, isn't that what I said? (I wrote most of this *before* the law was struck down. Looks like there could be a judicial career waiting for me!)

The bottom line is that the Computer Decency Act is history. And even if it's replaced by something else (various U.S. states are trying a variety of clumsy experiments), remember that the Internet is an international system. How are we going to regulate Swedish, Finnish, Dutch, or Japanese Web sites? We're not. So what are you going to do to keep your kids safe?

It's Up to You; Get a Nanny

If you want to protect your kids, I suggest you spend more time with them at the computer or get a nanny. You can't afford a nanny, you say? Of course, you can. There are now lots of programs available to help you restrict access to "inappropriate" sites. Programs such as Net Nanny (I'm not endorsing this one in particular, I just used it so I could put "Nanny" in the heading) contain a list of sites that are to be blocked; you can add sites from your own hate-that-site list, or you can periodically download updates from the Internet. Using these programs, you can block *anything* you want, not just pornography. As the Net Nanny site says, you can "screen and block anything you don't want running on your PC, like bomb-making formulas, designer drugs, hate literature, Neo-Nazi teachings, car theft tips—whatever you're concerned about."

You can find Net Nanny at **http://www.netnanny.com/**. To find other such programs, search for the word "blocking" at Yahoo or some other Web search site (or go directly to **http://msn.yahoo.com/msn/Business_and_Economy/Companies/Computers/ Software/Internet/Blocking_and_Filtering/**). You'll find programs such as SurfWatch, CyberPatrol, CYBERSitter, NetShepherd, TattleTale, Bess the Internet Retriever, and Snag. (I'm serious, all of these are names of real programs!)

If you use an online service, you'll also find that it probably offers some way of filtering out areas you don't want your kids to get to. America Online has had such filtering tools for a long time. And MSN allows you to block the Internet's alt. newsgroups and other "adult" areas.

You'll also soon find blocking tools built into most Web browsers. Internet Explorer already has blocking tools. To use them, choose **View**, **Options** and click the **Ratings** or **Security** tab. You'll find an area in which you can turn a filtering system on and off. This system is based on the Recreational Software Advisory Council's ratings (though you can add other systems when they become available), and you can turn it on and off using a password. You can set it up to completely block certain sites or to allow access with a password (just in case you don't practice what you preach!). The following figure shows a site that's blocked except for password entry..

With Internet Explorer's Ratings turned on, your kids can't get in—but you can.

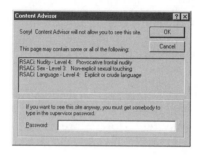

I've heard people criticize these blocking programs for two reasons: 1) because they're not perfect (of course, they're not) and 2) because they're an affront to the concept of free speech. Personally, I believe they are very useful and effective. I believe in supervising my kids, and these programs provide a supervision tool for a new era. They also provide a way for concerned parents to keep their kids away from sites they object to, without locking people up and forcing adults to read nothing more than sixth-grade materials on the Web.

What About *TIME*?

Oh, so you read *TIME* Magazine's exposé on Internet porn, did you? It was complete nonsense and widely criticized as careless and inaccurate. *TIME* based the story on a flawed study, which looked at pornographic images on BBSs (individual "adult" computer systems hooked up to the phone lines). It then used the findings to suggest that this proved somehow that the Internet was full of porn. *TIME* published a follow-up that didn't exactly apologize but that admitted the study was wrong. (It wasn't *TIME*'s fault, though; it was the fault of the "researcher," they said.) The author of the article has also publicly apologized. The original *TIME* article got front-page coverage; the follow-ups didn't, of course!

Finally, a personal viewpoint (it's *my* book, after all). This whole sex-on-the-Internet is a whole lot of fuss about almost nothing. Sure, clean up the Internet—but what are you going to do about the schoolyard? Schools are hotbeds of filthy language and talk about sex, sprinkled with the occasional pornographic magazine and actual sex. You think the *Internet's* a problem? I have the perfect solution, though. I call it "chemical supervision" and it entails giving our kids drugs to reduce certain hormonal levels. Remember, you heard it here first.

Your Private E-Mail Turned Up in the National Enquirer

E-mail can get you in a lot of trouble. It got Oliver North in hot water, and ordinary people have lost their jobs or been sued over things they've said in e-mail. Several things can go wrong when you use e-mail:

➤ The recipient might pass the e-mail on to someone else.

➤ The message can be saved on a backup system and read by someone other than the recipient later.

➤ Someone could spy on you and read your e-mail looking for incriminating comments.

The most likely scenario is that the recipient intentionally or thoughtlessly passes on your message to someone who you didn't count on seeing it. The second problem—that the message could be copied to a backup system—is what got Oliver North (and others) into trouble. Even if you delete a message and the recipient deletes the message, it may still exist somewhere on the network if the system administrator happened to do a backup before it was deleted. So if you are ever the subject of some kind of investigation, that message could be revived. A message goes from your computer, to your service provider's computer, to the recipient's service provider's computer, to the recipient's computer—at least four places from which it could be copied.

Finally, someone might be out to get you. Internet e-mail is basic text, and a knowledge-able hacker with access to your service provider's system (or the recipient's service provider's system) can grab your messages and read them.

What do you do, then? The simplest solution is to avoid putting things in e-mail that you would be embarrassed to have others read. The more complicated solution is to encrypt your e-mail. A number of encryption programs are available that scramble your message using a "public-key" encryption system, and, as discussed in Chapter 4, encryption systems are now being incorporated into e-mail programs. Figure out how they work, and use them.

Digital Signatures

You can also use this public-key encryption system to digitally sign documents. When you encrypt a message with the private key, it can only be decrypted with your public key. It's not safe; after all, your public key is public. But if it can be decrypted with your public key, it *must* have come from your private key. Therefore, it must have come from you.

If you don't have an e-mail program with built-in encryption, you can find an add-on system. A good way to start is to search for the word "encryption" at any of the Web search sites (or try **http://www.yahoo.com/msn/ Computers_and_Internet/Security_and_ Encryption/**). There's a problem with these systems, though. Right now, they're complicated to use. PGP, for instance, can be very complicated; if you want to use it, I suggest that you get one of the "front-end" programs that make it easier to use, such as WinPGP. In addition, because few people use encryption anyway, if you want to use it you'll have to arrange to use it first. Remember also that even if you encrypt your mail messages, they're not completely secure; you're still trusting the recipient not to pass on the decrypted message to someone else.

Prince Charming Is a Toad!

I'm not sure why I should have to explain this, but when you meet someone online *you don't know who that person is!* There's something about electronic communications that allows people to quickly feel as if they know the person with whom they are communicating...but they don't!

There are two problems here. First, cyberspace is not the real world. People communicate in a different way online. As another author told me recently, "I know people who seem to be real jerks online, but who are really nice people offline. And I've met people who seemed to be great online, but were complete jerks offline."

Profiles

If you are a member of an online service, be careful about what you put in your profile. Most services allow you to list information about yourself—information that is available to other members. Omit your address, phone number, and any other identifying information!

Then there's the misrepresentation problem. Some people flat out lie. A man who claims to be single may be married. A woman who claims to look like Michelle Pfeiffer may actually look like Roseanne Barr. A 35-year-old movie executive who graduated from Harvard may actually be a 21-year-old unemployed graduate of Podunk Bartending School. It's easy to lie online when nobody can see you. Couple that with a natural tendency to feel like you know the people you meet online, and you have trouble.

Not everyone lies online though. As my friend Phyllis Phlegar wrote in *Love Online* (Addison Wesley), "Even though some individuals choose to be deceptive, many others see the online world as the ultimate place in which to be totally honest, because they feel safe enough to do so." (Phyllis actually met her husband online.) But she also recognizes the dangers: "As long as the person or people you are talking to can't trace you, free-flowing communication between strangers is very safe." But if you're not careful and you give out information that can be used to trace you, Prince Charming may turn out to be the Black Prince. And if you do choose to meet someone "live" after meeting them online, be cautious.

She's a He, and I'm Embarrassed!

Chapter 18 covers chat systems, which are great places to meet people. For many they're a great place to meet people of the opposite sex (or of whatever sex you are interested in meeting). But you should know that sometimes people are not of the sex that they claim to be. I don't pretend to understand this, but some people evidently get a kick out of masquerading as a member of the opposite sex. Usually men masquerade as women, which could be construed as the ultimate compliment to womanhood or could simply be blamed on the perversity of men. Either way, there's a lot of it around, as the saying goes. (I recently heard chat systems described as being full of "14-year-old boys chatting with other 14-year-old boys claiming to be 21 year-old women." True, it's an exaggeration, but it illustrates the point well.)

So if you hook up with someone online, bear in mind that she (or he) may not be quite who he (or she) says (s)he is.

You Logged on Last Night, and You're Still Online This Morning

The Internet can be addictive. I think three particular danger areas stand out: the chat systems, the Web, and the discussion groups (mailing lists and newsgroups).

Apparently chat is extremely addictive for some people. I've heard stories of people getting stuck online for hours at a time, until early in the morning...or early in the morning after that. And I know of people who've met people online, spent hundreds of hours chatting, and finally abandoned their spouses for their new "loves."

The Web is not quite so compelling, but it's a distraction, nonetheless. There's just so much out there. If you go on a voyage of discovery, you *will* find something interesting. Start following the links, and next thing you know you've been online for hours.

Discussion groups are also a problem. You can get so involved in the ongoing "conversations" that you can end up spending half your day just reading and responding.

What's the answer to net addiction? The same as it is for any other addiction: self discipline—along with some support. It also helps if you have a life in the real world that you enjoy. Fear probably helps, too (like fear of losing your job or kids). And if you need help, why not spend a bit more time online. Do a search for "addiction," and you'll find Web sites set up to help you beat your addiction. You might also take the Internet Addiction survey at The Center for On-Line Addiction (**http://www.pitt.edu/~ksy/**), to see if you really have a problem.

Just Because You're Paranoid Doesn't Mean Someone Isn't Saying Nasty Things About You

A little while ago, someone started saying rather unpleasant things about me in a mailing list. What she didn't tell people was that she had a sort of vendetta going against me, and had for some time. (No, I'm not getting into details.) Anyway, I saw her comments in one mailing list and was struck by a thought: there are tens of thousands of internationally distributed newsgroups and thousands more mailing lists! What else is she saying? and where?!

Actually, there is a way to find out what's being said about you (or someone or something else) in newsgroups and Web pages. This is something that may be very useful for anyone who is in the public eye in any way (or for people involved in feuds).

You can read about a number of search "engines" in Chapter 21. You can search AltaVista to see what's being said about you in a Web page (this service lets you use a search engine that indexes all the words in a page, instead of just categorizing Web pages). To search a newsgroup, though, you'll need a program like Deja News (**http://www.dejanews. com/**). In Deja News, you type a name or word you want to search for, and the service searches thousands of newsgroups at once and shows you a list of matches (see the following figure). Click the message you are interested in to find out exactly what people are saying about you.

Deja News provides a great way to search newsgroup messages. (Looks like Elvis has been busy.)

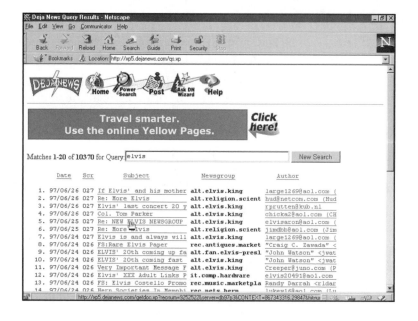

When I did this little search, I was surprised at what I found. I discovered information about a science-fiction conference at which I was to be a guest, and I found messages in which people recommended a book I'd written about PGP. I also discovered that there's a stunt man called Peter Kent (I found that in alt.cult-movies).

Deja News is not the only such service; you can find a list of these services at **http://www.yahoo.com/News/Usenet/Searching_and_Filtering/**. How about mailing lists? Well, there's Reference.com (**http://www.reference.com/**), which indexes many mailing lists, and some Web forums too. (You can even set up a service that searches automatically for you once a week or so, then e-mails you the result.) There's also **http://wais.sensei.com.au/**, though this catalogs only a few Macintosh-related lists.

I Was "Researching" at Hustler Online, and Now I'm Unemployed

This title is more than a joke. Some people really have been fired for viewing "inappropriate" Web sites during work hours. This seems quite unfair to me; companies give people Web browsers, often unnecessarily. They provide a temptation, then fire the people who succumb!

Of course, you can avoid such problems by staying away from the sites in the first place. But, if you really *have* to go there, practice safe surfing by clearing the cache when you finish! (We discussed the cache in Chapter 5.) When you visit a site, a copy of the Web page is saved on your hard disk in case you want to view it again at a later time. In effect, this creates a history of where you've been. And speaking of history, some browsers (such as Internet Explorer and Netscape Navigator 4) have excellent multisession history lists—which will also list every Web page you've seen!

> **It's Bugged!** You should also know that your boss can spy on your Internet activities using special software programs, whether you clear the cache and history list or not! So maybe you'd better just get back to work.

To cover your tracks, clear the cache to remove the offending pages. Then clear the history list (either clear it completely, or remove just the offending entries).

I Think Kevin Mitnick Stole My Credit Card Number!

Here's another Internet myth: shopping on the Internet is dangerous because your credit card number can be stolen. The second part of the myth is correct. Yes, your number can be stolen. But the first part is nonsense. Using your credit card on the Internet is not unsafe. Let me give you a couple of reasons.

First, credit card number theft is quite rare on the Internet. It can be done, but only by a computer geek who really knows what he's doing. But why bother? Credit-card numbers are not very valuable because it's so easy to steal them in the real world. For example, I handed over my credit card to a supermarket clerk the other day and then started bagging my groceries. The clerk put my card down while I wasn't looking. The woman behind me in the line moved forward and set her bag down on the counter. When I went to look for my card, it was gone. It wasn't until I (politely) asked her to move her bag that I found the card underneath. And from the look on her face, I'm sure she knew where it was.

This sort of theft is very common. When you give your card to a waiter, a grocery-store clerk, or someone at a mail-order company, you don't think twice about it. But for some reason people are paranoid about theft on the Internet. Banks know better, though. Internet-business author Jill Ellsworth found that credit card companies actually regard Internet transactions as safer than real-world transactions.

The second reason is that both Netscape and Internet Explorer, the two most-used browsers, have built-in data encryption. Many Web sites now use special Web servers that also have built-in encryption. When a credit card number is sent from one of these browsers to one of these secure servers, the data is encrypted and, therefore, unusable. The following figure shows how several different Web browsers indicate a secure Web site. Notice the little padlock in the lower-right or lower-left corner of the window? Both Internet Explorer and Netscape Navigator 4 use a locked padlock to indicate that a site is secure. Netscape 2 and 3 displays a key image in the lower-left corner for the same purpose; if the key is broken, the site is not secure.

When you see a locked padlock in the status bar, or a key, you can send your credit card without worry.

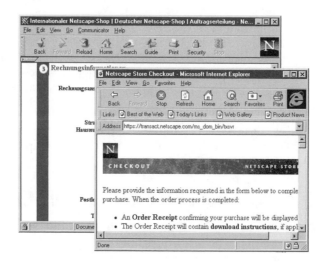

As for Kevin Mitnick, cyber-thief extraordinaire, there's a lot of confusion about what he did. He broke into systems and stole information en masse. (He didn't steal individual numbers as they flew across the Internet.) And no matter how you pass your credit card number to a vendor, the most dangerous time is *after* they've received the number—and there's little you can do about that.

My Wife Found My Messages in alt.sex.wanted

There are a lot of people saying a lot of odd things on the Internet. Undoubtedly, each day thousands of people with very poor judgment make millions of statements that could get them in trouble.

This little problem has long been recognized. And for some time now there's been an (almost) perfect way around it: you post messages anonymously. One way to do that is to configure your e-mail or newsgroup program with incorrect information (with another name and e-mail address, for instance). When you send the message, the header contains that incorrect information instead of the true data. That will fool most list members, but it's not completely safe; the header also contains information that allows the message to be tracked by a system administrator (or the police).

Another method is to use an anonymous remailer, a system that posts the messages for you, stripping out all information that can be used to track you down. In other words, you send the message to the remailer with information about which newsgroup it should be posted to, and the remailer sends the message on, sans identity.

You can find these services by searching for remailers at a search site (or go to a list of remailers, at **http://electron.rutgers.edu/~gambino/anon_servers/anon.html**, or Yahoo!'s Anonymous Remailers page: **http://www.yahoo.com Computers_and_ Internet/Security_and_Encryption/Anonymous_Mailers/**). They allow you to send both e-mail messages and newsgroup messages. But note that they are not perfect. They depend on the reliability of the person running the service and, in some cases, on that person's willingness to go to prison. If the police come knocking at his door, the administrator might just hand over his records. (In fact this has happened; at least one anonymous remailer has handed over records.) Of course, if you are trying to avoid embarrassment more than the law, an anonymous remailer might be just what you need.

Another Problem Who runs the anonymous remailers? If you were a smart computer cop, wouldn't it occur to you to set up your own anonymous remailer? It already has occurred to various police forces, so you can't be absolutely sure that the anonymous remailer you are using isn't merely a trick to track down people saying things that they "shouldn't" say.

Nothing's completely safe. Even using a genuine anonymous remailer can still leave you at risk; your e-mail could be intercepted between your computer and the remailer, for instance. As the *Frequently Asked Questions About Anonymous Remailers* document (**http://electron.rutgers.edu/~gambino/anon_servers/anonfaq**) says, "Hard-core privacy people do not trust individual remailers…[they] write programs that send their messages through several remailers…only the first remailer knows their real address, and the first remailer cannot know the final destination of the e-mail message."

I "Borrowed" a Picture, and Now They're Suing Me!

As you've seen throughout this book, grabbing things from the Internet is as easy as stealing from a baby—but there's none of the guilt. It's so easy and so guilt free that many Internet users have come to believe in a sort of "finder's keepers" copyright morality. If it's there, and if you can take it, you can use it.

Check This Out...

Can I Take It for Personal Use? In most cases, you probably can. When you connect to a Web site, all the things that are transferred to your computer end up in the cache anyway. However, some enthusiastic copyright lawyers claim that the use of a cache is in itself illegal—that even storing images and text on your hard drive goes against copyright law.

The law says otherwise, though. Here's a quick summary of copyright law: if you created it, it belongs to you (or to your boss if he paid you to create it). You can put it anywhere you want, but unless you actually sign a contract giving away rights to it, you still own the copyright. You don't have to register copyright, either.

Copyright law is quite complicated, however, and this summary misses many essential details. The important thing to understand is that it *doesn't* belong to you if you didn't create it! Unless something has been placed on the Internet with a notice explicitly stating that you can take and use it, you can take it for personal use but you can't use it publicly. You can't steal pictures to use at your Web site, for instance. (And even if there is a notice stating that the item is in the public domain, it may not be. After all, how do you know that the person giving it away really created it?)

Copyright law even extends to newsgroups and mailing lists. You can't just steal someone's poetry, story, ruminations, or whatever from a message and distribute it in any way you want. It doesn't belong to you. And of course, if you are concerned that your work will be taken from a newsgroup or mailing list and distributed, don't put it there!

I Downloaded a File, and Now My Computer's Queasy

Yes, you know what I'm talking about: computer viruses. These are nasty little programs that get loose in your computer and do things they shouldn't, like wipe your hard drive or destroy the directory information that allows your computer to find files on the drive.

First, my role as contrarian dictates that I inform you that much of the fuss about viruses is exaggerated—greatly exaggerated. When something goes wrong with a computer, a virus usually gets the blame. An example of how the virus threat is exaggerated is the famous Good Times virus. This virus never actually existed; it was myth from the start. The story was that an e-mail message containing a virus was being passed around the Internet. The story was obviously wrong because a plain e-mail message without a file attached cannot contain a virus.

Only files that "do things" can contain viruses. That includes program files, as well as document files created by programs that have macro languages. For instance, a variety of Word for Windows and Excel macro viruses just appeared in the last couple of years (what took them so long?). If a file can do nothing by itself—if it has to have another program to do something to it—it can't carry a virus. A plain text file (including text messages) can't do anything, and .GIF or .JPG image files cannot cause harm. (I'm just waiting for the next big hoax: someone will start a rumor that there's an image file used at many Web sites that contains a virus and that all you have to do is load the page with the image to infect your computer....)

Yes, viruses do exist. Yes, you should protect yourself. There are many good antivirus programs around, so if you plan to download software from the Web (not just images and documents from applications other than advanced word processors), you should get one. But no, it's not worth losing sleep over.

The Least You Need to Know

➤ Yes, there's sex on the Internet, but not as much as the press claims. Get a filtering and blocking program if you want to keep the kids away.

➤ E-mail can easily be stolen or forwarded. Don't write anything that you could be embarrassed by later.

➤ People on the Internet sometimes lie (just like in the real world). They may not be who they say they are (or even the sex they claim to be).

➤ Internet addiction? Snap out of it!

➤ You can search thousands of newsgroups at once with systems such as Deja News to see what people are saying about you.

➤ Your boss can find out what Web sites you are visiting, so watch out!

➤ Credit card transactions made on the Internet are safer than those made in the real world.

➤ Anonymous remailers can protect your identity in e-mail and newsgroups.

➤ You don't own what you find on the Internet; it's copyright protected.

➤ Viruses are relatively few and far between; but it's a good idea to protect yourself with an antivirus program.

Chapter 23

21 Questions:
The Complete
Internet FAQ

In This Chapter

➤ Shell accounts, finger, and winsocks

➤ Changing your password

➤ Why some programs won't run in Windows

➤ Getting rich on the Internet

➤ Slowdowns and connection problems

➤ Staying anonymous

In this chapter you will find answers to some questions you may have and a few problems you may run into—everything from the meaning of certain terms to solutions for certain problems.

What's a Shell Account?

You may remember me telling you (back in Chapter 2) that a few years ago most people dialing into a service provider were using dial-in terminal accounts. These are often known as *shell* accounts. And if you have a PPP or SLIP Internet account with a service provider, you probably also have a shell account. So you have a choice: you can connect to the Internet via the fancy graphical software, or you can connect using the bland command-line interface. Why bother with the command line when you can have the splashy graphics? Well, the next question will provide an example of why you would want to, and when you look at the *finger* command later in this chapter, you'll see another example.

Most service providers give you a free shell account when you sign up for a PPP account. Others have the nerve to charge extra for the privilege. You really shouldn't have to pay extra for it.

How Do I Change My Password If I'm Using a PPP Connection?

The fact that this is even a problem strikes me as a little strange. Most service providers don't provide a convenient way for you to change your password with a PPP or SLIP connection, yet they'll tell you that you should change your password frequently for security's sake. They *could* provide a Web form, but most don't. So how *do* you change your password?

Check This Out...

Not a Good Sign Some major service providers don't let you change your password at all. You have to call and ask them to do it for you, which is a *very* bad way to go about it!

If you are with an online service such as MSN, AOL, or CompuServe, there's probably some kind of menu option somewhere in the main program. But if you are with a service provider, you'll probably have to connect to their system with a terminal program. You need to get to the menu system used by people who are not fortunate enough to have a PPP or SLIP account. Find a menu option that says "Account Assistance" or something similar, and then look for one that says something like "Change Password."

But how do you get to the menu you need to use to change your password? One way is to connect using a simple serial-communications program (such as Windows 3.1's Terminal or Windows 95's HyperTerminal) or any commercial or shareware terminal program. You dial the phone number for your shell account and then log in; but you'll have to ask your service provider for information because the login instructions may be different. If you want more information about this you should see the first edition of this book; send e-mail to **ciginternet@mcp.com**, type the word **first** in the Subject line, and leave the body of the message blank. You'll get Chapter 7 in an e-mail response message. (For more information about using the e-mail responder, see Appendix C.)

The other way is to connect to the Internet in the manner you usually employ and then open a Telnet program (see Chapter 20). Connect to your service provider through Telnet, log on to your shell account, and then go to the change-password menu option. Call and ask your service provider which Telnet domain to use.

What's a Winsock?

Winsock is short for "Windows sockets," and it's the program used by Microsoft Windows to act as an interface between TCP/IP programs running on the computer and the Internet itself. Just as a printer needs a printer driver to interface between the programs and the printer, the Internet needs a "driver" to interface between the programs and the Internet. And in the Windows world, that's known as a Winsock.

In Windows 3.1, you have to acquire a Winsock program separately—it doesn't come with the operating system. Most service providers and online services now include Winsock with the software they provide you (you can install it yourself if need be; one of the most commonly used one is Trumpet Winsock, which you can find at many software archives; see Appendix A). In Windows 95 and NT Winsock is built in, so you don't need to get a separate program. (However, you may need an advanced degree in networking to figure out how to use it.) The easiest way to handle all this is to get an installation program from a service provider or an online service that installs and configures the Winsock for you.

Why Won't Netscape Run in Windows 95?

This problem is all too common these days. Say, for instance, that you are using Windows 95 and have connected to CompuServe or some other online service, or perhaps to a service provider that gave you Windows software to install. Then you go to the Netscape Web site to download the latest version of that navigator, or maybe you download the latest version of Internet Explorer. Which version do you pick? Why, the Windows 95 version, of course! That's the operating system you are using, after all. You install the program, and try it…but it doesn't work. What's going on?

The problem is that, although you are using Windows 95 (what's known as a 32-bit operating system), the Winsock program you are using is a 16-bit program. Remember, the Winsock is the "driver" that connects your programs to the Internet. The Winsock is installed when you install the software needed to dial into the Internet. And, in order for a 32-bit program (such as the Windows 95 versions of Netscape or Internet Explorer) to run, you must use a 32-bit Winsock! Yet many online services and service providers are still handing out old Windows 3.1 Winsocks. Thanks, online services!

This problem has almost (but not quite) disappeared as the online services and service providers have introduced 32-bit dial-in programs. If your service is still using an old 16-bit program, your only options are to stick with 16-bit programs (those created for

Windows 3.1), to find a service provider that will help you set up Windows 95's Dial-Up Networking software, or to install your own Winsock and configure it to work with the online service or service provider.

Anytime you run a 16-bit Winsock, you are stuck with 16-bit Internet programs. If you are trying to install a Windows 95 or Windows NT program and can't get it to work, start by checking to see if you have a Winsock designed for Windows 95 or NT.

How Do I Get Rich on the Internet?

Oh, that's easy. First, start a business selling some kind of Internet service or software. Run it for a few months on a shoestring, and then go public. It doesn't really matter what the intrinsic value of the company is—as long as it has the word "Internet" attached to it somehow, you'll get rich.

A year ago I thought perhaps that this Internet-investment hype was beginning to die out, but it appears to be alive and well. Just recently Amazon.com (an online bookstore) went public. The stock immediately followed the archtypical Internet-stock price; it soared to a level that has no direct relationship to the value of the company, creating a total stock value many, many times the value of the company. (It's not as if Amazon.com actually makes money, or is even likely to make money any time soon! As the President of Amazon.com, Jeff Bezos, reportedly said, "If we're profitable any time in the short term it'll just be an accident.")

Other Internet companies have used this get-rich-quick plan quite successfully, companies such as Yahoo!, Netscape, and Spyglass. Best-selling author James Gleick (he wrote the NYT bestseller *Chaos*), for instance, is worth around $25 million according to the Internet Millionaires list (**http://www.pulver.com/million/**). Not bad for less than two years of work building a small service provider, *The Pipeline*, which he later sold to a large national service provider, *PSINet*.

However, you may be a bit too late to get into this game. The market currently seems to be flooded, and more people are losing money on the Internet than are making it. Wait for the next big wave, though, and try to catch it early!

How Can I Sell Stuff on the Internet?

The second way to make money on the Internet is by selling stuff—real stuff, not other Internet services. The editors took a poll and told me they'd seen salad dressing, teddy bears (see the following figure), model horses, live horses, legal services, picture-scanning devices, Internet tutoring, and real estate for sale. There are also books, CDs, and videos …as well as hot sauce, pizza, a newsletter for writers of children's stories, and all sorts of other stuff. Of course this doesn't mean that all these people are actually making *money* doing this.

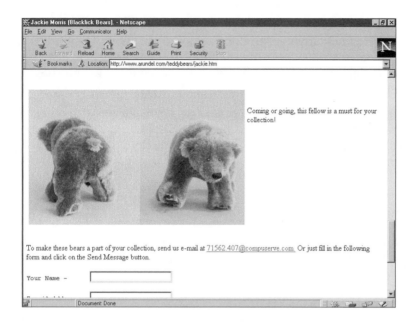

Yes, they really are selling teddy bears on the Internet.

But heed this warning. Very few people are actually selling things on the Internet, and much of the talk about what a wonderful market the Internet provides is marketing hype. (In fact, the high failure rate in Internet businesses is a joke among Internet insiders; when I told an executive at a major Internet-software company that I wanted to write a book about companies that have actually figured out how to make money on the Internet, he said, "Is anyone making money; I mean, we are, but is anyone else?")

If you really want to try it, you've got a lot to learn about the Internet—far more than I can ever explain here. Don't think you can just put up a few Web pages and then start taking orders. You'll also have to promote your Web site in newsgroups, mailing lists, online service forums, and so on. The odds are against you, so be prepared.

If I Have a Fast Modem, Why Are Transfers So Slow?

You've just installed a fancy new 33,600 modem, and still some Web sites are about as speedy as molasses on a hot day in Iceland. What's going on here? Your information has to pass through many different computer systems, along lots of different lines; hey, it may be coming from halfway across the world, after all.

Think of this transfer across the Internet as a relay race. The information you want is passed from person to person, maybe dozens of times, between the Web site and you. The last person in the chain is that speedy 33,600 modem you bought. But when you look at the others involved in the race, you see that some are as athletic as Roseanne, and others are as fast as your grandmother. Still others may be very fast, but they've got other jobs to do, too. They are actually involved in hundreds of relay races at the same time! So if you are at a very popular Web site, for instance, hundreds of other people just like you are trying to get information at the same time, and that relay runner might be having serious problems keeping up.

If it's any consolation (it probably isn't), those people are sitting at their computers in Alberta, Arizona, Austria and other places beginning with different letters, saying, "I just bought this 33,600 modem. Why did I bother wasting my money?" Why would anyone bother to get a fast modem? Because with a slow one, you'll be even slower. (And not *all* Web sites are slow—just the ones that everyone wants to go to.)

Will the Internet Kill Television?

No way. Using the Internet is active; using the television is passive. Remember, television was supposed to kill both movies and radio, but both seem healthy enough today. For that matter, movies were supposed to kill theater, and theater (if I remember right) was supposed to kill rock paintings.

Why Isn't Anyone Reading My Web Page?

I guess you heard the nonsense that "a Web page is a billboard that can be seen by millions," and you believed it. Well, let me put it this way. There are 250 million people in the United States. But if you put up a *real* billboard in the United States, will 250 million people see it? I won't bother answering that.

The Web is not a highway, and your page is not a billboard. If you want people to come to your Web page, you have to promote it. And don't believe all that "if you want people to come to your Web site it has to be compelling" nonsense either. A Web page has to serve a purpose; if it serves its purpose well and is well-promoted, it can do well (even if it doesn't use Java to display some pointless animation).

How Can I Remain Anonymous on the Internet?

Many people are concerned with keeping their privacy and anonymity on the Internet. In particular, women who like to spend time in chat rooms often feel the need to put up a protective wall between themselves and other members. If a relationship develops with someone online, they want to be in control of how much information about themselves they allow others to discover.

Well, there are degrees of anonymity on the Internet. The first level is easy to achieve.

➤ Get an account with an online service or service provider and obtain an account name that is nothing like your own name. If your name is Jane Doe, use an account name such as *HipChick* or *SusanSmith*.

➤ If you are with an online service, make sure your "profile" is empty; many online services allow you to enter information about yourself that others can view (in chat rooms, for instance).

➤ If you are with a service provider, you should also ask your provider to disable finger for your account. (finger is a service that other Internet users can employ to find information about you—see the next section.)

➤ Once you are actually on the Internet, be careful not to leave identifying information when you're leaving messages in newsgroups, working with mailing lists, and so on.

Although this doesn't ensure full anonymity, it's pretty good in most cases. In order to find out who HipChick or SusanSmith actually is, someone would have to persuade your service provider to divulge information. That's not impossible, but in most cases, it's unlikely (unless you're doing something to incite the interest of the police or the FBI).

Another form of anonymity is possible through *anonymous remailers*, systems that let you send anonymous messages to newsgroups via e-mail. You send a message to the remailer, and the remailer strips out identifying information and sends it on. (This is discussed in more detail in Chapter 22.)

You can also send anonymous messages from public e-mail connections. For instance, many libraries have Web browsers set up, and most Web browsers these days have e-mail programs. You can send messages from the browser and, in most cases, remain completely anonymous. (Libraries are getting a little more Internet savvy, these days, and sometimes disable e-mail.)

Getting a completely anonymous Internet account is probably more difficult. Most service providers require information that will identify you: a credit card, driver's license, and so on. With a little imagination, though, it's not impossible.

What's finger?

In the last section, I mentioned something called *finger*. This is a UNIX command that allows you to retrieve information about other people on the Internet if you have just a little bit of information. You can use this command in either of two ways:

➤ Log on to your shell account and get to the command line (you should find a menu option somewhere that will take you there; ask your service provider if you can't find it). At the command line, type **finger** and press **Enter** to run the command.

➤ Install an actual finger "client," a program that allows you to run finger from within your graphical user interface—from Windows or the Macintosh, for instance.

Here's how to use finger. Let's say you've seen the **HipChick@big.net** e-mail address and want to find out about HipChick. You use the finger command **finger HipChick@big.net** and press **Enter**. A request for information is sent to big.net. You *may* get such information as the account holder's real name, which is why I told you to make sure finger is disabled if you want to remain anonymous!

Some You Win, Some You Lose

Many service providers completely disable finger requests. Others disable certain types of requests. For instance, if you were to try a command like finger smith@big.net, some service providers would send a list of all the account holders called Smith, but some providers simply wouldn't respond.

Can Someone Forge My E-Mail?

A little while ago I saw a message in a mailing list from someone complaining that an e-mail message to the list was forged. Someone else had sent a message using this person's e-mail address. Another member of the list wrote a message telling her that she should be more careful. He said (a little bluntly) that if she left her computer unattended she should expect trouble. Thinking I'd play a little game, I sent a forged message to the list in *his* name. (No, I didn't know him, and I definitely didn't have access to his computer.) "That'll teach him, I thought...He should be more careful."

It's actually very easy to forge e-mail messages—so easy, in fact, that I'm surprised it doesn't happen more often. (It probably happens more often to people who spend a lot of time in newsgroups, mailing lists, and chat rooms—where it's easy to get into fights—than to people who use other services.)

A person can forge a message simply by entering incorrect configuration information into a mail program or, better still, the mail program of a public Web browser. However, before you run out and play tricks on people, I should warn you that this mail can still be traced to some degree. (It might be difficult, though, for anyone other than a police officer with a warrant to get the service providers to do the tracing for him.)

How can you avoid this problem? There's not much you can do really, except keep your head down and stay out of "flame wars" (which we'll discuss next). You *could* digitally sign all your messages, as discussed in Chapter 22, though that may be overkill.

What's a Flame?

I've heard it said that the Internet will lead to world peace. As people use the Net to communicate with others around the world, a new era of understanding will come to pass...blah, blah, blah....

The same was said about telegraph and the television, but so far, there hasn't been much of a peace spin-off from those technologies! But what makes me sure that the Internet will not lead to world peace (and may lead to world war) are the prevalence of flame wars in mailing lists and newsgroups.

A *flame* is a message that is intended as an assault on another person, an ad hominem attack. Such messages are common and lead to flame wars, as the victim responds and others get in on the act. In some discussion groups, flame wars are almost the purpose of the group. You'll find that the Internet is no haven of peace and goodwill—and I haven't even mentioned the obnoxious behavior of many in chat rooms.

I'm Leaving My Service Provider. How Can I Keep My E-Mail Address?

I currently have about eight Internet accounts. Over the past few years, I've had dozens, and that means I've had dozens of e-mail addresses. Although this is unusual, it's certainly not unusual for people to have a handful of different accounts as they search for the best one. Unfortunately, keeping your friends and colleagues up-to-date on your e-mail address is a real hassle. If only there was a way to keep the same address, even when you changed providers....

Well, there just might be. It is possible to register your own "domain name." You do this through InterNIC, and you can find instructions for doing so at the **http://rs. internic.net** Web page. It costs $100 for the first two years and $50 a year after that to keep the domain name. Many service providers will actually register a domain for you, but they may charge you an additional fee to do so.

You can set up a mail service (search for **e-mail service** at a search site such as Yahoo!), and assign the domain name to that service. Then all your e-mail addressed to that domain will be sent to the service, which will store it in your POP (Post Office Protocol) account. You'll use a mail program to download your mail from there. (When you register a domain name you have to already have chosen a service, because the e-mail service provider has to set up its computers to recognize the name.)

Once you are using an e-mail service, it doesn't matter which service provider or online service you use to get onto the Internet; you can change from one company to another, as many times as you like, and you'll still be able to get to your mail through the e-mail provider. And if you ever decide to use a different e-mail provider? Then find the new provider and transfer your domain to that company. Whether you change e-mail provider or change Internet service provider, you can always keep your e-mail address. (At the time of writing, InterNIC did not charge a fee for making a change.) These e-mail services start at around $5 a month.

Another way to keep your e-mail address is to sign up with a free or low cost e-mail service. There are a number of these around now (search at **http://www.yahoo.com/** for **free email service**). These services are usually free because they sell advertising that is shown when you get your mail. If you don't mind that, though, this is a good way to get and keep an e-mail address, regardless of how many times you change your service provider. One of these companies (MailBank: **http://mailbank.com/**) has bought up thousands of domain names based on people's last names, so for $5 a year you can have an address that uses your last name as the domain name: **john@kent.org**, **fred@smithmail.com**, and so on.

Why Can't I Get Through to That Site?

You'll often find that you cannot connect to sites that you've used before or that you've seen or heard mentioned somewhere. You might find Web pages that you can't connect to, FTP sites that don't seem to work, and Telnet sites that seem to be out of commission. Why?

The first thing you should check is your spelling and case; if you type one wrong character or type something uppercase when it should be lowercase (or vice versa), you won't connect. (The following figure shows the dialog box Netscape Navigator shows when you've typed the name incorrectly.) Another possibility is that the service you are trying to connect to might just be very busy, with hundreds of other people trying to connect; depending on the software you are using, you might see a message to that effect. Or it could be that the service is temporarily disconnected; the computer that holds the service might have broken or might have been disconnected for service. And finally, the service simply might not be there anymore.

Oops! I mistyped the URL, and my browser can't find the host.

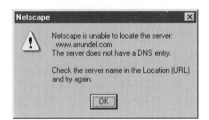

Trying again a few times often helps; you'll be surprised just how often you can get through to an apparently dead site just by trying again a few moments later. Also note that some software is a little buggy. For instance, some browsers seem to hang up and appear unable to transfer data from a site at times; but canceling the transfer and starting again often "jump starts" it.

Don't Place the Blame Too Quickly

Often it's your service provider, not the site you are trying to connect to, that's having problems. Try connecting to a variety of sites, and if you can't get through to any it's probably a problem with your connection to the service provider or with the provider's system. Try disconnecting and logging back on.

Why Won't This URL Work?

URLs are a special case because even if they don't seem to work, you may be able to modify them and get them to work. First, make sure you are using the correct case. If a word in the URL was shown as uppercase, don't type lowercase (if the URL doesn't work with some words uppercase, though, you might try lowercase).

Second, make sure you are using the correct file extension if there is one. If the URL ends in *.htm*, make sure you are not typing *.html*, for instance. If it still doesn't work, start removing portions of the URL. For instance, let's say you have this URL:

Remove the Period When you type a URL, don't type a period at the end. You may find URLs in books and magazines that appear to end with a period because they are used at the ends of sentences. But real URLs don't end with periods, so make sure you don't include the periods when typing.

> **http://www.big.net/public/software/macintosh/internet/listing.html**

You've tried using both "listing.html" and "listing.htm" at the end, and neither seems to work. So remove "listing.html" and try again. You may get a document with links to something you can use. If you still don't get anything, remove the "internet/" part (in other words, you are now typing just **http://www.big.net/public/software/macintosh/**). If that doesn't work, remove the next part, "macintosh/." Continue in this manner, removing piece after piece, and in most cases, you'll eventually find something useful.

Why Do So Many People Hate AOL?

It's an unfortunate truth that America Online members have a bad reputation on the Internet. You may run across rude messages in which people insult AOL members or treat them as if they are the scum of the earth.

Here's what happened. AOL, like all the online services, decided that it had better get Internet access in a hurry. So they started adding Internet services, and they added newsgroup access quite early. All of a sudden, about a gazillion AOL members flooded onto the Internet in a rush that would have the bulls at Pamplona running in the opposite direction. Millions of AOL members overwhelmed these discussion groups with questions such as "how do you download files from this group?" and "where are the pornographic pictures?" Of all the online services' members, AOL's members were probably the least computer literate. (AOL had targeted the "family" market, while CompuServe, for instance, had been a geek service for years.)

The Internet had been, until just a few months before, a secret kept from most of the world. All of a sudden, it was as busy as a shopping mall on a Saturday afternoon, and every bit as cultured. And there was an obvious scapegoat: all those people with @aol.com e-mail addresses! Unfortunately, you might still run across anti-AOL bias on the Internet.

My Download Crashed So I Have to Start Again. Why?

Most online services use file-transfer systems that can "recover" if the transfer is interrupted. For instance, if you are halfway through downloading a file from CompuServe when your three-year old kid decides he wants to see what happens when he presses the big red button on the front of your computer, all is not lost. After you reboot the computer and reconnect to CompuServe, you can begin the file transfer again. But you don't have to transfer the whole thing; instead the transfer begins in the middle.

However, that won't work on the World Wide Web, for the moment at least (Web browsers will eventually be able to resume interrupted downloads, but they can't yet). It *can* work on *some* FTP sites, with *some* FTP programs though, which is one reason that FTP can be so useful (see Chapter 14). If you prefer to use your Web browser for transferring files, though, you'll have to keep your kid away from the computer (or try covering the button with a piece of card).

Should I Start My Own Service Provider Company?

No.

Why Not?

One of the most common questions Internet writers get asked is, "how can I set up a business as an Internet service provider?" The easy answer is, "if you don't know, you shouldn't be trying." It's a very complicated—and currently very competitive—business. If you don't know what it takes, you probably don't know how little you know, and you shouldn't be trying. After all, over the next few years, thousands of Internet service providers will bite the dust as the big telecommunications companies get in on the act.

Why add your blood, sweat, and tears to the pile? You can run many other businesses with a better chance of success. Or, if you really want to bankrupt a business, pick one with lower intial costs.

Just One More Question...

You're going to come away from this book with lots of questions because the Internet is big, there are many different ways to connect, and there's a huge amount of strange stuff out there. I hope this book has helped you start, but I know you'll have many more questions.

Once you are on your own, what do you do? Try these suggestions:

➤ *Get the FAQs.* FAQ means "frequently asked questions," and it refers to a document with questions and answers about a particular subject. Many newsgroups and mailing lists have FAQs explaining how to use them, for example, and Web sites often have FAQ pages. Look for these FAQs and read them!

➤ *Continue your reading.* I've written about a dozen Internet books and really need to sell them, so continue buying (and reading them). Well, okay, there are other writers putting out Internet books too (you may have noticed a few). To become a real cybergeek you'll need to learn much more. So check out a few of these books.

➤ *Read the documentation.* There are literally thousands of Internet programs, and each is a little different. Make sure you read all the documentation that comes with your programs so you know how to get the best out of them.

➤ *Ask your service provider!* I've said it before, and I'll say it again: if your service provider won't help you, get another service provider! The Internet is too complicated to travel around without help. Now and again you'll have to ask your service provider's staff for information. Don't be scared to ask—and don't be scared to find another provider if they won't or can't answer your questions.

The Least You Need to Know

➤ A shell account is a dial-in terminal account. You may have a free shell account, and you may need to use your shell account to change your password.

➤ Getting rich on the Internet is a lot harder than it's been made out to be.

➤ You may have a fast modem, but if the Internet itself is busy, things will still move slowly.

➤ Use an e-mail service if you want to be able to switch between service providers without changing your e-mail address each time.

➤ You can be anonymous on the Internet—if you are careful.

➤ If your service provider won't answer your questions, you need another service provider!

Chapter 24

Ideas

In This Chapter

- ➤ What use is the Internet?
- ➤ Using the Internet for business and pleasure
- ➤ Finding information online
- ➤ Music and culture
- ➤ What else do you want to do?

Throughout this book, I've explained many of the services the Internet can provide. But you might now be wondering "What good are these things?" Unfortunately, until you get onto the Internet, get hooked, and forget that you have responsibilities out in the "real" world, it's difficult to understand what the Internet can do for you. (Imagine, for a moment, the Neanderthal thawed out of the ice and introduced to modern technology. "Okay, so I can use this soap stuff to remove the smell from my armpits, right? But why?")

This chapter gives you a quick rundown on just a few of the ways in which ordinary (and some not-so-ordinary folks) are incorporating cyberspace into their daily lives.

Keeping in Touch

The world has really shrunk over the last 18 months—at least for those of us in cyberspace. I hadn't spoken with my sister in a decade or two, but now that she's online I hear from her every week or two (every day or two if her computer's acting up). My brother lives a continent away, but I hear from him frequently via e-mail. An old school friend and I planned a trip to Iceland, using e-mail to swap lists of things we'll need. And just recently I got e-mail from someone I'd worked with a decade ago in another life. E-mail is a wonderful system—sort of like the U.S. Mail on amphetamines.

Meeting Your Peers

Many people use the Internet as a way to keep in touch with their peers. They can find out about job opportunities, new techniques and tools used in their business, or problems they've run into that they think *surely* someone else has experienced. The mailing lists and discussion groups provide a fantastic way to meet other people in your business field.

Business Communications

As I write this book, every now and then I have a question for the editor. I simply write the message and click a button, and off it flies. Later, when I finish this chapter, I can send the document file via e-mail, too. Then later still, after the chapter's been edited, the editor can send it back via e-mail. I'll change the edits back to what I originally wrote and then send it back yet again. (Editor's Note: yeah, that's what *he* thinks!)

Many businesses have discovered that the Internet provides a rapid communications tool. Why type a letter, memo, or report into a word processor, print it out, put it in an envelope, take it to a mailbox (or call FedEx), and wait a day or five for it to arrive, when you can send the same word processing document and have it arrive a minute or two later?

Product Information

We live in an instant gratification society, the entire purpose of which is to get toys into your hands faster and faster. Do you need information about that new car you want to buy, for instance? If so, go to **http://www.edmunds.com/** to check it out (you learned about Web addresses like this in Chapter 5). As you can see in the following figure, the page contains the car's specifications as well as a picture of it. You can drool over it—and even find out just how much the dealer pays for it.

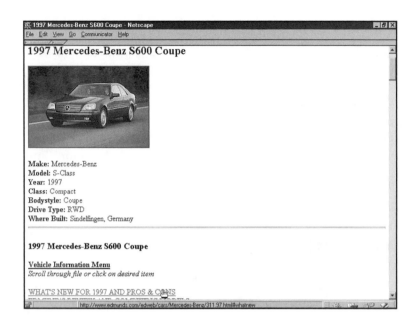

With what you'll save on this baby, you'll be able to buy Internet access for the rest of your life!

Product Support

There's a downside to the Internet of course: it's run by computers, which, as we all know, are the work of Satan. Still, the next time your computer does something weird or you need a new print driver, go online and find the fix or software you need. Many, perhaps most, computer and software companies now have an online technical support site.

A Testimony

Just the other day, I wanted to print something on Kinko's color printer for my son's science project. They had an Apple color printer; I use Windows 95. So off I went to the Apple site, from which I downloaded the Windows 95 driver for that printer. I then installed it, printed the page to a file, and took it to Kinko's. (And no, I haven't been paid a fee to say that.)

Getting Software

We're back to instant gratification. You know that program you just saw advertised in *Internet Windows Computing World* magazine? Want to try it out? Go online and download a demo right now! There's no more waiting. Pretty soon everybody will be buying software and transferring it straight to his or her computer.

You can use one of the Internet's great shareware libraries, too. (See Appendix A for more information.) The following figure shows the TUCOWS site. TUCOWS, The Ultimate Collection Of Winsock Software, is a library of shareware Internet programs for Windows. You can find it on the Web at **http://www.tucows.com**.

TUCOWS: The Ultimate Collection of Winsock Software (they have Macintosh and OS2 stuff now, too).

Research

If you are writing a school paper, researching a book, or planning a vacation, the Internet contains a cornucopia of illuminating tidbits. It's *not* a library (contrary to the nonsense of those in the Internet community who got a little carried away with their predictions), and it will be a long time before it can replace one. Still, it does give you access to huge amounts of useful information that's just waiting to be used.

For instance, suppose you are planning to visit, oh, I don't know, how about Iceland? Get onto the World Wide Web and search for Iceland (you learned how to search for stuff in Chapter 21). What do you find? A hundred or more sites with information about Icelandic travel, sports, culture, media, real estate (there's no way *I'm* actually moving there), news, and more.

Visiting Museums

I suppose you can't afford to visit the Louvre *and* the Smithsonian this year. What a shame. Still, you can get online and see what you are missing (see the following figure). Actually, the potential here is greater than the reality. Maybe someday most of the masterpieces in the world's great museums will be online; but right now, many just provide one or two pictures and information about which subway to take to get there.

*Visit the Louvre this summer, from the comfort of your own home (**http://www.louvre.fr**).*

Finding Financial Information

Want stock quotes? Information about competitors or about online banking services? You'll find it on the Internet. You can find links to great financial services at the search sites we discussed in Chapter 21. Or try Yahoo! Finance (**http://quote.yahoo.com/**) or InvestorGuide (**http://www.investorguide.com/**).

Music

If music is your passion, you'll be happy to know that you can hear some of the latest from the music world when you find it on the Internet. Try IUMA, the Internet Underground Music Archive (**http://www.iuma.com**). Would you prefer bagpipe music or film scores? Maybe you want to buy some CDs. Whatever you're looking for, you can find it on the Internet.

Magazines and 'Zines

You'll find thousands of magazines and 'zines online. (For the not-quite-so-hip among you, a *'zine* is a small magazine.) You'll find underground books and comics, as well as newsletters on almost anything you can imagine (and probably a few things you can't imagine).

Hiding from the Real World

There's a wonderful cartoon that is legendary in the computer world. It shows a dog in front of a computer terminal, and it has the caption "Nobody knows you're a dog on the Internet." Well, it's unfortunate that the need exists, but quite frankly, there are people who use the Internet to hide from the real world. For one reason or another they have trouble with face-to-face relationships, yet on the Internet they can feel safe and part of a community.

Shakespeare on the Net

Remember Your Old Friend, Chat? As you learned in Chapter 17, IRC is a "chat" system. You type a message, and it's immediately transmitted to all the other people involved in the chat session. They respond, and you immediately see what they have typed.

I met a fellow computer-book writer recently who stages Shakespeare plays in IRC (Internet Relay Chat). This chap (yes, chap, he's English), takes a play, modifies it slightly to his taste (he recently staged an updated version of *Macbeth*), and breaks it down into its individual character parts. He sends each "actor" his lines only, no more. Each line has a cue number, so the person playing the character will know when to type the lines. Then they start, each person typing his or her lines at the appropriate cue position. It's an act of discovery for all the "actors" because they don't know what the other characters will say until they say it. Strange, but strangely fascinating.

If You Can't Get Out

There are those among us who would love to have more face-to-face relationships but for some reason can't get out. Perhaps they are elderly or disabled or have been posted to the Antarctic. The Internet provides a link to the rest of the world for those times when you can't physically get somewhere.

Joining a Community of People with Common Interests

Suppose you have some, er, let's say unusual interests. You believe the U.S. government has been chopping up aliens for years—or maybe that it's in cahoots with aliens. Or suppose that, by chance, you are consumed with a hatred of purple dinosaurs (one in particular, anyway) or that you feel compelled to tell others of your latest experience in the air.

Now suppose that, in your neighborhood, there are few people who share your interests. Who do you share your thoughts with? Where can you find a sense of community? On the Internet, of course, in the newsgroups and mailing lists (see Chapters 11–13). (And yes, the examples suggested above are real examples.) You may be surprised at the sort of people you find online. It's not all techno-chat. I have a friend who's a member of a discussion group on the subject of renovating antique tractors, for instance!

You Don't Trust Your Doctor, So...

I must admit I don't have a lot of faith in doctors—Grandma was right, stay away from hospitals, they're dangerous! Many people go to the Internet in search of the answers their doctors can't provide. Whether you have a repetitive-stress injury, cancer, or AIDS, you'll find information about it on the Internet. Want to try homeopathy, acupuncture, or just figure out what leeches can do for you? Try the Internet.

Shopping

Yes, yes, you *can* shop online, although statistically speaking you probably won't for at least a couple of years. The press seems to think that the raison d'être for the Internet is for K-Mart and Sears to find another way to sell merchandise. Really, though, the more interesting things are elsewhere on the Internet. So Internet shopping has been grotesquely overrated—but yes, it is there.

Cybersex

The Internet provides a wonderful form of communication for those who seem to have trouble finding others with similar sexual proclivities. This is by no means a minor part of cyberspace; some commentators even claim that the sexual use of online services played a major part in their growth. You can get online and talk about things that your parents or spouse might consider *very* weird, with people who consider them quite normal.

Political Activism

As they say, political activism infects every form of human communication...or was that pornography? Well, the Internet is the latest frontier for political activities, providing militia groups a means of keeping in touch and providing Democrans and Republicats a place to seek votes.

Gore Vidal always did say it's a one-party system!

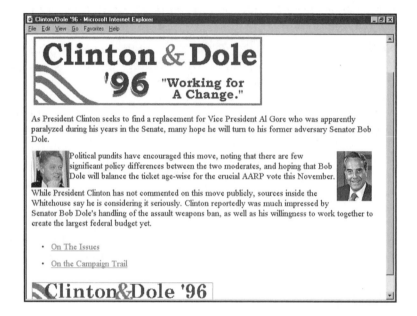

Subversion

The Internet provides a great way to subvert the political system in which you live. That's right, you too can publish information that your government doesn't want published, whether it's information about how Nutrasweet was created as part of a plot to take over our minds, or what was going on during the latest coup. Perhaps the most quoted such event was the last coup in Moscow, during which much information was "exported" via the Internet. Closer to home, the Internet has become a thorn in the side of the U.S. Government as it makes the distribution of encryption software so easy.

Looking for Work (and Help)

Thousands of people are looking for work on the Internet, and thousands more are offering both full-time and contract positions. Many professional associations have special mailing lists used for transmitting job leads. Do a little research and you could have dozens of leads arriving at your home every day.

Clubs and Professional-Association Information Servers

Are you running a large club or professional association? Why not set up a Web site? Your members can then check the Web site to find out when the next meeting is being held, search a database of fellow members, find out about the association's services, and more. Potential members can find out how to join, too.

Mating and Dating

Do people *really* meet online and get involved in romantic relationships of various kinds? Yes, they really do. I'd be inclined to make a joke about it, except that I have a friend who met a man online, and he eventually became her husband and the father of her child.

Long-Distance Computing

Being a computer geek comes with a real disadvantage: you always seem to be working. If you find yourself wishing you could get to the programs on your desktop computer while you are on vacation or are visiting relatives or clients, for example, you may have considered buying one of those remote control programs. You install the program on your laptop and then dial into your desktop machine. The program enables you to copy files between the computers and even run programs across the connection.

As you might guess, however, the long-distance phone calls can get very expensive. But now there's a new way to do it. Some of these programs actually let you make the connection across the Internet. So if you use a national service provider that has phone numbers throughout the U.S. (or even an international provider or an online service that has numbers throughout the world), you can dial into a local number and connect to your computer across the Internet and pay only a fraction of the long-distance charge.

Books

You can write books about the Internet. According to modern polls, there are now 5,357,131 people writing books about cyberspace, the Internet, and how we won't have to blow our noses ourselves 10 years from now because the Internet will do it for us. (Seriously, though, a recent survey found that more money is spent on books and magazines about the Internet than is actually spent buying things on the Internet! So much for the computer revolution killing off paper publications!)

What Did I Miss?

In addition to the ideas I've listed in this chapter, you could probably find a few thousand other uses or more. The Internet is huge, and it's diverse; it's whatever you make of it.

The beauty of the Internet is that although people begin as observers, they end up being real *participants*. They become active in discussion groups and perhaps even start their own groups. They often create their own Web sites (it's surprisingly easy, as you saw in Chapter 9).

Take a look at the Internet to see what's out there and how other people are using it. Who knows? You might soon find that it becomes part of your life. (Don't say I didn't warn you!)

Chapter 25

The Future of the Internet

In This Chapter

➤ Internet progress will slow down

➤ The future of high-speed connections

➤ Intercast PC/TV and $500 Internet boxes

➤ Multimedia

➤ The Internet backlash

➤ Open borders and free speech

➤ Software distribution

The nice thing about revising a chapter about predictions is that you can see if the predictions have come true. Or perhaps that isn't such a nice thing. As physicist Niehls Bohr once said, "Making predictions is very difficult, especially about the future."

Anyway, in this chapter I'm going to make some predictions, and look at how my predictions have fared since the last edition of this book. First, here are a few easy things to predict.

➤ The Internet will get bigger

➤ Many more people will begin using the Internet

➤ Many service providers are going to go out of business

➤ Lots of businesses are going to give up trying to make money on the Internet

➤ Eventually, the "let's get rich on the Internet" idiocy will subside; but we'll be left with plenty of good reasons to keep using it

Of all these things, I'm quite sure. In fact I believe that over the last year or so, since I first made these simple predictions, they've fared quite well. Of course the Internet got bigger, and more people are using it; anyone could have predicted that. Service providers have been merging, though we haven't yet seen a huge shakeout with a large proportion going out of business; that'll happen eventually, though.

Many businesses have lost money on the Internet, so although there's plenty of Internet hype to go around, I think perhaps it's subsiding a little, and we're seeing businesses use the Internet in useful ways, even if they don't make instant riches.

In the rest of this chapter I'm going to make some more predictions of which I'm, well, pretty sure.

Progress Will Slow Down

The rate of change on the Internet will slow down. Although the changes between 1993 and 1996 were phenomenal, this level of progress can't be maintained for two reasons.

First, most of the people who got on the Internet in the first few years of the boom were primed and ready to go. They were computer-literate, they had computers, and they had modems (or if they didn't, they could get them and install them). Few people went from being complete neophytes who had never used or owned a computer to Internet junkies. It will be difficult to continue the growth because newcomers to the Internet are likely to be new computer users as well as new Internet users, and therefore, they'll have bigger hurdles to jump. Getting the computerless and computer illiterate onto the Internet will be much more difficult than getting the already-computer-savvy up and running was.

Second, we appear to have seen great technological changes on the Internet in the past three years. But the changes have not been as dramatic as they first seemed. Most of the changes have come about as a result of companies taking existing technology and putting it together in a new way. For example, three years ago most people used some form of terminal account to access the Internet. Now they are using TCP/IP (SLIP and PPP) access, which allows them to use graphical-user-interface software. However, SLIP and PPP had been around for years; what made them popular was that a lot of companies wrote new software to take advantage of them. As another example, note that we went from considering the 14,400 modem the standard to the 28,800 modem being the standard. But the 28,800 modem was already in development, and anyway, it's just more of the same technology and not something radically different. Now we have the 33,600 modem, and coming up fast the 56k modems. But even these aren't so dramatically different. Modems are slow; the modem companies are just making them a little less slower.

Further improvements will be more difficult. Wiring up the world with super high-speed connections will take years (at least five years for the United States, maybe more). And until these fast connections become available, the Internet can't live up to the hype and potential.

Since I first made this prediction, I think I've been proven correct. Development on the Internet *has* slowed; fewer new users are signing up, and the technology isn't changing as fast as it did in the first few years of the boom.

High Speed Connections (Not Quite Yet)

Much of the hype about the Internet depends on high-speed connections to the Internet. Some pundits claim that Web sites need multimedia to make them more compelling. (This seems to be rather insulting to the average Internet user, who supposedly values form over function; it indicates that he is so shallow that a bit of glitz keeps him happy.) Without high-speed connections, though, this multimedia stuff is more of a nuisance than a real benefit. Java, video, and animations are all very nice, but if you are getting the goodies over a phone line, even with a fast modem, the novelty soon wears off.

Although the Internet will eventually have high-speed connections, it won't come overnight. A lot of technological problems must be overcome before cable, for instance, can handle large numbers of Internet users. And there are a number of financial and logistical reasons why the phone companies won't be able to provide high-speed connections for everyone (at a reasonable price) anytime soon.

The cable companies have been promising us Internet access since 1994; and they don't appear to be much closer now than they were then. And Microsoft Founder Bill Gates, in a recent interview, claimed that most people will be stuck with slow modem connections for another five years or so. Hey, I've been saying that for a long time, but would anyone listen to *me*?

The Web Comes Alive—More Multimedia

It's a foregone conclusion that the amount of multimedia (video, sound, animations, and such) on the Internet will increase. With the new tools becoming available—tools that make multimedia easier to create—it's inevitable. But there is still the slow-connection problem that will hold back multimedia for some time to come. Take a look at the online services; have they incorporated multimedia? Yes, a little. But not much because the connections most people have are simply too slow for multimedia to work well.

Multimedia on the Internet gets much more attention right now than it deserves based on its actual level of use. Very few Web sites use multimedia (that is, sound and video). The vast majority of Web pages contain nothing more than text and pictures. For all the talk of multimedia and "cool" stuff, only a tiny fraction of Web sites—perhaps less than 1 percent—use sound, and that's probably the easiest "multi-media" format to work with. Very few Web sites have video or animation.

Check This Out...

It's Not All That Common I was recently paid to put together a list of 50 Web sites that don't use sound (don't ask why, it's a long story!). And you know, it was laughably easy. Very few Web sights have sound or video, though they are the most popular forms of multimedia and the easiest to work with.

Intercast PC/TV

Eventually, the Web browser and TV will merge. Web browsers will be built into TVs, and the "Intercast" PC/TV may be one way that this will happen.

The Intercast system will merge data from the Internet with television signals. While watching a show on the TV, for instance, you may decide you want more background information on what you're watching. No problem. If you were watching something on the Discovery Channel, you could open the TV's Web browser and view the Discovery Channel Web site. From there you could find information about the program currently showing, perhaps in the form of a bibliography, of links to other Web sites related to the show's topic, of links to the store where you can buy products related to the show, and so on.

The Web information transferred to your TV would be transmitted between the lines of television data in the same way that captions for deaf viewers are already transmitted to TV sets in the U.S. It is also the means by which information for TeleText systems is transmitted in Europe (for news, TV listings, sports scores, and so on). Of course, another component is needed for this to work as planned: transmissions back from the TV to the Web site asking for particular pages. For now you'll have to wait for Intercast PC/TV, which will be available when the Internet cable-connection problem has been sorted out.

WebTV—A Relatively Small Niche

You've probably heard of WebTV. This system allows you to view the World Wide Web on your television screen. Think of it as a computer that does nothing more than download Web pages and display them on the TV. Because there's not a lot to it, it's relatively cheap (around $400). It has a modem used to connect to a service provider (many people seem to think WebTV uses the TV cable to access the Web, but it actually works with the phone lines), a remote control, and an optional keyboard.

WebTV is actually a brand name (it's from Sony and Philips/Magnavox), but it seems to me that it's turning into a generic term, WebTV meaning "a system that displays the Web on a television screen." And WebTV is not the only player in the game; for instance, there's a French system called NetBox.

Now for my prediction. WebTV, at least in its present form, won't catch on. Sure, they'll sell tens of thousands of these things, but many will be little used, and there will be plenty of dissapointed customers. Here's why. First, computer users won't, in general, want a WebTV. The WebTV has so many limitations when compared to a computer that it will be very frustrating to existing computer users. It's slow and awkward to use (as one reviewer put it, "it feels very much like using DOS or one of the old IBM 3270 terminals");

you can't download software; you can't use many other non-Web Internet services; you can't connect to any service provider you choose (you're limited to the service provided on the WebTV Network Service); the display is low-resolution, so you can't see much of a Web page without scrolling down; you can't save documents you find on the Web (though you can print them if you add a printer to the system); and on and on.

The problem is, this machine's trying to act like a computer without being a computer. Of course there are millions of people who don't have computers, and perhaps they'll want WebTV. Or perhaps they'll be disappointed. Another reason it won't catch on is that the Internet has been oversold. It's been shown to non-computer users as a kind of new TV channel, full of sounds and sites. You've seen the TV ads, haven't you, in which Internet pages always seem to have video and the video always seems to move very quickly? Well, it's hype, the Internet isn't a multimedia system, as many people who get WebTV will discover to their dismay.

The Internet Backlash

An Internet backlash is beginning as companies realize that making money on the Internet is not quite as simple as they were told. Web publishing is in trouble—no large Web magazine has yet figured out how to make money. Some book publishers are reducing their Internet presence to some degree, after realizing that they can't sell enough books online to make it worthwhile. You'll soon begin to see more stories in the press about Internet failures, as the press looks for a new "angle."

Is this bad, you wonder? No, it's probably good. Let's get rid of the Internet hysteria—of all the inflated claims about what the Internet can do—and start to focus on what it can really do. We need fewer people running get-rich-quick schemes on the Internet, and more people using the Internet in a rational, reasoned manner.

The Internet Will Open Borders

The Internet opens borders. As more of the world runs on software, more of the software will become the focus of argument. Although it's rare these days for software to be banned, some software is now and again censored; violent games and encryption software are the targets of legislation in some countries.

The problem is that software can slip across borders quickly and undetected when one's borders are punctured by the Internet. For instance, an organization of small telecommunications companies is trying to get the Federal Communications Commission to ban Voice on the Net programs (discussed in detail in Chapter 18). Let's say they are successful, and these programs are banned. Just how do you maintain such a ban? One of the best programs comes from Israel, and that company can continue to distribute the software across the Internet, perhaps without breaking any U.S. laws.

Check This Out...

Something to Think About... The idea of one country distributing software to a country in which it's banned brings up another issue that has to be dealt with by the courts: if you distribute something on the Internet, can you be held liable for the actions of people who download the software in countries in which your product is banned?

What can be done about this problem? The government could look for transmissions of this software and "bust" people who are caught using it. Or it could threaten Israel with sanctions if Israel didn't also ban the software. Or it could cut off the U.S. portion of the Internet from the outside world. In the next few years, you'll hear all three actions proposed in a variety of cases. The Internet crosses borders, and many people won't like that.

The Internet and the Fight for Free Speech

Here's another aspect of the borders issue—free speech. Some of the things you might say in the United States are unacceptable in, say, Indonesia. And some of the things a person might say in Holland would be unacceptable in, say, the United States. Speech (and images) that are perfectly legal in some areas of the world are illegal in others.

Because the Internet is an international system, regulating it is very difficult. I think there are three possible paths.

➤ A few countries may simply cut their connections to the Internet (though in a world of satellite communications, they won't be able to do that completely).

➤ Others may declare the Internet to be a sort of no-man's land, where communications have to be unregulated (or at least they may turn a blind eye).

➤ Others may try to regulate it the best that they can—if only to realize eventually that it can't be done. (However, China already controls Internet access, "filtering" information before it can enter the country; other nations will probably follow suit. Singapore is instituting tight controls on Internet access, too.)

And all over the world we'll continue to hear what a dangerous and evil place the Internet is, for the very reason that it can't be fully regulated.

Since I first made these predictions, problems have continued. France recently banned the use of Netscape Navigator, because it didn't like the idea of its citizens using encryption. (Netscape rushed out a special French version with the security features removed.) In Britain, a council tried to ban the distribution of a secret report about child abuse and satanism, only to find the report published at a number of Web sites across the world (they then tried threatening the people publishing the report with copyright law—it remains to be seen just how this case will end). Germany has been debating how to ban pornographic images coming into the country across the Internet, and is prosecuting a man for creating a link at his Web site to a foreign site that discusses how to sabotage trains. Canada periodically bans any mention of certain court trials in the press—but information is often available across the Internet. And Singapore is registering Internet users! The fight will continue.

Anarchy, or a battle for free speech? This site links to dozens of Web sites carrying a report that the owner, Nottingham County Council in the United Kingdom, has tried to suppress.

Schools Use the Internet; Test Scores Continue to Plummet

Some people say that the Internet will "save" our schools. Some go so far as to say that schools will no longer be needed, that our kids will learn at home through the TV.

To quote former Assistant Secretary of Education Dr. Diane Ravitch, "If Little Eva cannot sleep, she can learn algebra instead ... she'll tune in to a series of interesting problems that are presented ... much like video games." I don't know about your kids, but when mine can't sleep the last thing on their minds is algebra. Lewis Perleman (*School's Out*) says that we don't need schools anymore because information is plentiful outside schools (as if all that education is about is piping information into kids). Anyway, who's going to be looking after these kids? Oh, I forgot, we'll all be telecommuting by then, won't we?

Information is everything, these people think. All problems are a result of a lack of information, so if the information flows freely, all of our troubles will slip away. Put algebra on one channel and Power Rangers on another, and our children will make the "right" decision. If only life were so simple. Alan Kay, one of the founders of Apple Computer, says that problems schools cannot solve without computers won't be solved with them. He's dead right. Why would computers (and Internet connections) be a panacea? We've known how to educate kids well for centuries, so why would a sudden infusion of technology fix problems that have nothing to do with a lack of technology?

So my prediction is that computers with Internet connections will be found in greater numbers in schools. Yet, overall, it will make very little difference in whether or not kids succeed in school.

$500 Internet Boxes

Early in 1996 we heard a lot of talk about cheap Internet boxes—the "$500" Internet boxes you may have heard about. The theory is this: produce a box that allows people to connect to the Internet at a really low cost. The problem is this: you get what you pay for.

What won't these boxes do or have? Just take a look:

➤ They won't allow you to download shareware (because they don't have hard disks).

➤ They won't have good screens (although some will connect to a television).

➤ They won't let you use the software you want to use; you'll be limited to what you are given or whatever software you can run from your service provider's system (a subject I'll cover next).

➤ You won't be able to use the box for anything but connecting to the Internet. For example, you won't be able to install games from your local software store or track your household expenses. You really won't be able to do much at all except "cruise" the Internet. (Again, we're coming back to the misconception of what sort of person cruises the Internet: a mindless idiot who simply wants to be entertained by "cool" and "compelling" Web sites, and who doesn't actually want to do much. So why connect to the Internet when you can watch TV?)

Proponents of the $500 Internet box claim that you will be able to run whatever software you need directly over the Internet—that you won't need a hard disk. The important word there is will. Right now this is a pipe dream. Over the last year or so talk about $500 Internet boxes has subsided a little—partly because it looks like they're more likely to cost $1000. My prediction? Talk will subside even more.

Software Over the Internet

Eventually, a lot of software will be purchased from the Internet. Why take software, package it in hardware (disk, cardboard, plastic wrapper, and so on), put it in a store, and have people buy it there, just so they can take it home and load it? Why not just sell it over the Internet as an electronic product delivered electronically. Software can already be bought across the Internet: some sites sell software online, but it's often "light" or demo software (see the following figure). One day, however, the Internet may be a primary form of software distribution.

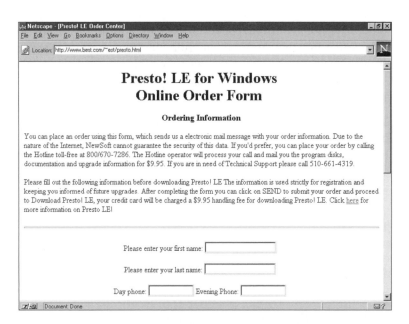

Fill out this form with your credit-card information, and then you can download the software.

Geeks versus Salespeople

Unfortunately, many geeks think that because something makes technological or financial sense, it will come to pass. They completely forget human nature, and consequently, their predictions are way off target. Most software packaging is already unnecessary from a purely utilitarian point of view (big boxes with a small book and a smaller disk rattling around inside), but it makes perfect sense from a marketing point of view! That's why software will continue to be sold in stores for years to come.

I don't believe some people's claims that software will eventually be run across the Internet. Many people are saying that you won't own software, you'll rent it. When you need it, you'll log onto the Internet and run it from another site. Although some software may be successfully distributed like this, I doubt that most will, for a few reasons.

➤ Storing software on a hard disk is very cheap. With prices around 10 cents a megabyte and dropping, hard-disk storage is a negligible cost. You pay $100 for a program, and 50 cents for the hard disk storage. If it's that cheap, why connect to the Internet to use it?

➤ "Why buy a program you can rent?" proponents ask. For those few programs you may want to use very occasionally, renting may be the way to go. But as you know from real world experience, if you use something frequently, it's almost always cheaper to buy than to rent.

321

➤ Connections to the Internet are unreliable and will be for a long time. Even voice phone connections are unreliable, and the telephone has been around for about 120 years. It's going to be a long time before we have very high speed and very reliable data connections to the Internet that are available at a cost that competes with the low cost of hard-disk storage.

➤ The more the Internet grows, the more traffic it will have to bear. A lot of traffic is unavoidable; the whole purpose of the Internet is communication after all. But if everyone was logging onto the Internet just to run programs that could run on their hard disks instead, the data that would have to be transferred would be immense. It's not necessary, so why do it? We won't.

Check This Out...

The LAN Example Do you have a network at work? How often is it down? How often is it sluggish because everyone's doing something at once? That's what the Internet will turn into if this idea ever becomes reality.

There are a lot of drawbacks and few real benefits to running software across the Internet. The next time you hear someone claiming this is what we are headed for, ask the question "Why?" I haven't heard a convincing answer yet.

On Predictions...

"The more things change, the more they stay the same" may be a cliché, but the more I look at failed predictions, the more it seems to make sense. The car, for instance, is 110 years old. Has it changed? A little. Cars are more comfortable, faster, and more fuel efficient. But it's more of the same. Do they hover or fly? No. Can they navigate themselves? No. We were promised these things decades ago. Do they have four wheels and a steering wheel? Why, yes. They had those things 110 years ago, and they still do.

The Internet has seen phenomenal change in the last few years, but remember one thing—most of the technology in use today was just sitting there waiting to be used. Some of the wild predictions depend on technology that doesn't yet exist and new technologies take a very long time to develop and become widely used. The Automated Teller Machine was introduced in 1965 in the United Kingdom, but it wasn't widely used in the U.S. until the mid-'80s. Twenty years for a relatively simple technology. The Internet is supposed to have far more dramatic effects—it's supposed to turn the world upside down. It might, but not anytime soon.

Here's my final prediction then: most of the predictions you hear about the Internet won't come to pass. (Not my predictions, of course; everything you read here is absolutely correct and most certainly *will* come to pass!) All the wild predictions about how the Internet will create a new world—how "nothing will ever be the same," how it will bring about world peace (seriously, some people are predicting this) and a new form of electronic democracy, and so on—all this is nonsense.

How do I know that? Because all-encompassing, far-reaching predictions are always wrong. The Green Revolution was supposed to end world hunger, antibiotics were supposed to eradicate infectious diseases, and the PC was supposed to lead to fantastic increases in productivity. True, the Green Revolution did raise crop yields, we did eradicate smallpox, and the PC allows ordinary people to do things they wouldn't have been able to afford before (such as create professional-looking business documents). But we still have world hunger, infectious diseases seem to be making a comeback, and economists have been unable to find more than negligible gains in productivity that are attributable to the PC.

Me, a cynic? Why, yes!

The Least You Need to Know

➤ Progress on the Internet will slow down. Whereas most of the initial development was just waiting to happen, future gains will be more difficult.

➤ We're still at least five years away from widespread, low-cost fast Internet connections in North America.

➤ Intercast PC/TV is one way that the Internet (specifically the Web) can be merged with TV; but we're still waiting for high-speed connections.

➤ WebTV won't catch on—it will remain a niche product.

➤ The Internet backlash is beginning: some businesses are no longer listening to the hype and are even, in some cases, "retreating" from the Internet.

➤ As the Internet opens borders, it will lead to fights over what may be distributed— and what may be said—across the Internet.

➤ Software will be more widely distributed across the Internet. However, we won't get rid of our hard disks and run programs over the Internet.

Part 4
Resources

Resources? You'll find reference information in this part of the book. I'll tell you where to find the software you need—programs to help you on your travels around the Internet, games, print drivers, and unlimited other things. I'll also give you some background information about picking a service provider, in case you don't have Internet access yet or you want to find a new one.

You'll also find out how to use the mail responder we've set up. And at the end of this part of the book is a glossary of Internet terms and a directory of hundreds of interesting Web sites you should visit.

All the Software You'll Ever Need

You've read about a lot of software in this book, and there's much more that hasn't been mentioned. Literally thousands of shareware, freeware, and demoware programs for the Macintosh, Windows 3.1, Windows 95, Windows NT, and all flavors of UNIX are available for you to download and use. "Where are they?" you ask. "How do I find all these programs?" It's easy to find software once you know where to look.

Check This Out...

Different Types of Software

Shareware is software that is given away for free, but which you are supposed to register (for a fee) if you decide to continue using it. *Freeware* is software that is given away with no fee required. *Demoware* is software that is generally free, but is intended to get you interested in buying the "full" program. There are many other related terms, such as *crippleware* (shareware that will stop working in some way—perhaps the entire program stops working, or maybe just one or two features—after the trial period is over)

The Search Starts at Home

You can always begin looking at home. If you use one of the online services you'll find stacks of software within the service itself; no need to go out onto the Internet. All the online services have Internet-related forums (or BBSs, or areas, or whatever they call them). These are good places to begin, and you can usually download the software more quickly from there than from the Internet. In addition, many online services have forums set up by software vendors and shareware publishers. These are good places to get to know, too.

If you are with a true Internet service provider, you'll often find that your service has a file library somewhere. The library will have a smaller selection than the online services do, but may be a good place to start nonetheless. On the other hand, you may want to go straight to the major Internet software sites, which will have a much greater range of programs.

The Software Mentioned

I've mentioned two programs in particular—Netscape Navigator and Internet Explorer— that you need to know how to find. You may already have one or the other of these. Many online services and service providers already provide one of them in the software package you get when you sign up. If you want to get the very latest version, or try the competing project, go to one of these sites:

> Netscape Navigator: **http://www.netscape.com/**

> Internet Explorer: **http://www.microsoft.com/ie/**

I've mentioned dozens of other programs throughout this book. Most of those programs can be found at the sites I discuss next.

The Internet's Software Libraries

The Internet is full of wonderful software libraries. Check out some of the following sites, but remember that there are more, which you can find using the links mentioned in the section "Finding More," later in this appendix.

TUCOWS (Windows)

TUCOWS originally stood for "The Ultimate Collection of Winsock Software," but these days they have software for the Macintosh and OS2, as well as Windows 3.1, 95, and NT. Go to the **http://www.tucows.com/** page (shown in the following figure).

The Consummate Winsock App Page (Windows)

Another excellent Windows software archive is at the **http://www.cwsapps.com/** or **http://www.cws.internet.com/** Web site.

Winsite (Windows)

You can find another good Windows archive at the **http://www.winsite.com/** Web site or at the **ftp.winsite.com** FTP site.

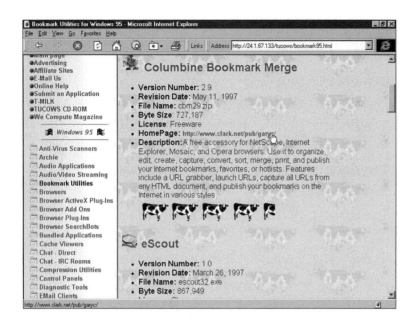

The TUCOWS site is an excellent place to find all sorts of useful Windows software. (The more cows a program's been awarded, the better it is.)

TopSoft (Windows, Macintosh, UNIX)

This is a relatively small site, but it has a nice selection of useful programs, and for each one you'll find a detailed description (many other sites have very simple descriptions, or none at all, for the programs they store). Go to **http://www.topsoft.com/**.

Keyscreen (Windows)

This unusual site (**http://www.keyscreen.com/**) provides pictures of many shareware programs, so you can see if you might like them before you bothering to download them.

ZDNets's Windows and Macintosh Archive

This site (**http://www.hotfiles.com/**) contains many Windows and Macintosh programs (more than 10,000 files). It's well organized, with detailed descriptions of the files.

ZDNet's Mac Download (Macintosh)

Go to **http://www5.zdnet.com/mac/download.html** to find a large Macintosh software archive.

Nonags (Windows 95 and NT; may add Macintosh eventually)

This site (**http://www.nonags.com/**) is dedicated to software that has "no nags, no time limits, no disabled features or any other tricks. Most are really free, a few are shareware…"

Shareware.com (Windows, Macintosh, UNIX)

This site (the **http://www.shareware.com/** Web page) contains a huge collection of software for all major operating systems. You can search for a keyword and come up with all sorts of interesting things here.

Jumbo (Windows, Macintosh, UNIX)

Another excellent site, Jumbo contains thousands of programs (they claim more than 200,000) for a variety of operating systems. To find it, go to the **http://www.jumbo.com/** Web page (shown here).

Keyscreen let's you see what you're downloading before you do so.

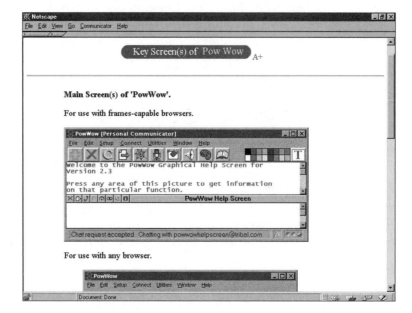

The University of Texas Mac Archive (Macintosh)

You can go to **http://wwwhost.ots.utexas.edu/mac/main.html** to find a good library of Macintosh software. It's not huge, but it's well-organized and helps you find the most important programs.

Info-Mac HyperArchive (Macintosh)

This is a large collection of Macintosh software at MIT **(http://hyperarchive.lcs.mit.edu/HyperArchive.html)**. It contains lots of files, but it's not very easy to work with.

The Ultimate Macintosh Site (Macintosh and Apple)

You'll find lots of information about the Mac, along with software, at the **http://www.velodrome.com/umac.html** Web site. You'll find links to Apple shareware sites, too.

Plug-Ins & Viewers

You can find many viewers at the software sites already mentioned, but you can also find them at a few sites specifically created for viewers and plug-ins. You can find links to viewers and plug-ins that will work in Internet Explorer at **http://www.microsoft.com/ ie/addons/**. A good place to find plug-ins for Netscape is at **http://home.netscape.com/ comprod/mirror/navcomponents_download.html**. For viewers, you can try **http:// home.netscape.com/assist/helper_apps/** or one of the following sites:

➤ **The NCSA Mosaic Home Page (http://www.ncsa.uiuc.edu/SDG/Software/ Mosaic)**; Select the appropriate operating system: Windows, Macintosh, or UNIX, and you'll find a link to viewers.

➤ **The WWW Browser Test Page (http://www-dsed.llnl.gov/documents/ WWWtest.html)**.

➤ **The IUMA Utilities Pages (http://www.iuma.com/IUMA-2.0/help/)** for audio and video utilities.

➤ **Browsers.com (http://www.browsers.com/)** has links to all sorts of browser-related software and information.

Finding More

New software archives appear online all the time, many of which are specialized. You can search for more at the search sites discussed in Chapter 19. For example, you can go to Yahoo's **http://www.yahoo.com/Computers_and_Internet/Software/** page and find links to all sorts of software sites. Another excellent source of information about software archives is the Dr. Shareware site at **http://www.rbi.com/~salegui/jim/download/**. It has a good collection of links to software download libraries for both the Macintosh and IBM-compatible PC. The Dr. Shareware site also contains a library of Macintosh games software. Also try **Pass The Shareware Please (www.passtheshareware.com)**, a site with loads of links to shareware sites.

Don't Forget Demos and Drivers

Thanks to the Internet, the distribution of demo software has increased greatly. Commercial software publishers often create versions of their software that they give away. Some of these programs are full working versions that just stop working after a while; others are "crippled" in some way from the very beginning (perhaps a few important features don't work). These offer a good way to find out if the company's product is worth buying, and in some cases, they even have enough features to make the demo itself worth having. You'll often see these demos advertised in the computer magazines with the URL of the company's Web page.

Looks Can Be Deceiving I've seen some demos that were obviously created by companies that seemed to think the way to make sales was to create a totally worthless demo that didn't even show what the full product could do. Sometimes you're better off working with shareware or freeware, rather than a demo.

Many companies also give away software such as drivers, a fact that came in handy for me recently when I wanted to print something on a color printer at a local copy store. The store had an Apple printer, so I went to the Apple Web site, dug around a little, and found the Windows driver for that printer. I was then able to print the page to a file using that print driver and take it to the copy shop.

Looking for Something Strange?

If you're looking for a program that you simply can't find at the popular software libraries, remember that you can always search for it using the techniques discussed in Chapter 21. It's amazing what those search sites can turn up sometimes! So if you're looking for something really obscure that the average library doesn't hold, don't give up too soon. You can even try Archie (see Chapter 15) to search for a file at an FTP site if you have a good idea of the file name.

The Least You Need to Know

➤ You can find thousands of programs for Windows, the Mac, and UNIX, scattered around the Internet.

➤ If you use an online service, start there. It's generally quicker to download from "home."

➤ There are a number of good software archives, such as TUCOWS, shareware.com, Jumbo, The University of Texas Mac Archive, The Ultimate Macintosh Site, Winsite, and so on.

➤ A number of sites hold only plug-ins and viewers.

➤ Don't forget demos and drivers—commercial software that's often very useful.

➤ You can also search the Web search sites or Archie to find more.

Finding a Service Provider

If you are reading this, either you don't have a service provider or you are considering changing the one you have. Let's deal with the first major question: Which is the best Internet service provider?

I Want the Best! Where Do I Get It?

Ah, so you want the best Internet account you can get. Well, if that's the case, be prepared to empty your bank account. You're going to need a special high-speed line from the phone company, a fast computer with special hardware to connect it to that line, a system administrator to set it up and maintain it...and on and on.

But for the rest of us, the ordinary Joe or Jane who wants to get hooked up to the Internet, what's the best way to do it? There's no easy answer to that, unfortunately. It's rather like asking "who makes the best spouse?" Needless to say, everyone has a different answer. A service that you think is good might prove to be a lousy choice for someone else.

Basically, what you need to do is pick a service provider that is cheap, helpful, and has a reliable and fast connection to the Internet and easy-to-install software. Of course, that's very difficult to find. I've had Internet accounts with a couple of dozen providers, and I haven't found one yet that I would rave about. They've ranged from pretty good to absolutely awful.

What's a Reasonable Cost?

Internet accounts vary quite a bit in cost. You might want to start out with an online service; there's no sign-up fee, and you'll probably get a trial period of 10 hours or so free. After that, it will cost approximately $10/month for the first five hours and $2.95 for each additional hour. Other plans might run, for example, $20 a month for 20 hours and

$2.95 for each hour after that. Online service prices have dropped dramatically over the past couple of years, thanks to intense competition from true Internet Service providers—there are thousands of companies vying for a slice of the Internet-access pie.

It's Getting Better

There was, for a while, a trend toward flat-fee services. This trend may reverse, as many companies are finding it very hard to make money using a flat-fee payment system. Still, although there are many "by-the-hour" services, flat-fee services have become more reliable, and many services that were originally "by-the-hour" now offer flat-fee plans (as America Online had to do a little while ago).

Service providers are usually cheaper, but they might charge a sign-up fee ($25 to $50), and they generally don't offer a free trial period (though some of the larger companies do give a few hours away). Rates usually average approximately $1 an hour: $10.95 for the first ten hours and $1.25 per hour after that, for instance. Some offer "unlimited" access for a flat fee that might range from $19.95 to $24.95 a month. This enables you to use as many hours as you want for a set fee. (Why quotation marks around the word *unlimited*? Because in many cases the service is unlimited only if you can actually get into it, and the busy signals may often thwart your attempts.)

Tips for Picking a Provider

Consider the following guidelines when you're trying to find an Internet service provider:

➤ The major online services often make it very easy to connect to the Internet: you just run the setup program, and away you go.

➤ On the other hand, the major online services are relatively expensive (though their prices have dropped greatly, and the difference is no longer so significant). Some of them also have a reputation for having very slow and unreliable connections to the Internet.

➤ There are a lot of low-priced Internet service providers (in Colorado, for example, there are about 70), and the competition is stiff!

➤ Unfortunately, many low-priced services have customer service that matches their prices: they are often not very helpful. To work on those services, you need more than a little of the geek gene inside you.

➤ Make sure the service has a toll-free or local support telephone number...you'll almost certainly need it!

➤ On the other hand, some of these services *are* very good and will help you hook up to the Internet at a very good price.

➤ A number of large national Internet service providers—such as WorldNet (owned by AT&T), EarthLink, and PSINet—often have very good prices ($20–25 a month for unlimited usage, for instance). In addition, in some areas, they might even have good service.

➤ Many small service providers also advertise "unlimited" access to the Internet for a flat fee. They are less likely to live up to the unlimited promise than are the big networks.

➤ There are no hard and fast rules! A service that is very good in one area may be lousy in another.

If you don't have an Internet account yet, but you want to find one, I can help. I'm going to give you a few ideas for tracking down service providers.

Finding a Service Provider

Here are a few ways to track down service providers:

➤ Look in your local paper's computer section; local service provider's often advertise there.

➤ Look in your city's local computer publication for ads.

➤ Check the Yellow Pages' "Internet" category.

➤ Ask at your local computer store.

➤ Check for ads in one of the many new Internet-related magazines.

➤ Look in a general computer magazine (many of which *seem* to have turned into Internet magazines).

➤ Ask your friends and colleagues which local service providers are good (and which to avoid).

➤ If you know someone who has access to the World Wide Web, ask him to go to **http://www.yahoo.com/Business_and_Economy/Companies/Internet_Services/ Internet_Access_Providers/**. Or, better still, say "Go to Yahoo and search for **'service provider'**"; you may not know what that means, but your friend probably will (check out Chapter 21 for more information). You'll find information about many service providers, and even some price comparisons. (You might also try using the Web at your local library; most libraries have Internet access these days.)

➤ Another good Web site to try is The List (**http://thelist.internet.com/**), a directory of over 5,000 service providers. Also, there's ISP Finder (2,500 service providers) at **http://ispfinder.com/**.

➤ If you can't get onto the Web, try ISP Finder by telephone. Dial **1-888-ISP-FIND** and follow the instructions; you'll be sent a list of service providers in your area.

335

Find a Free-Net

You might also want to look for a *Free-Net*. These are community computing systems. They might be based at a local library or college, and you can dial into the system from your home computer. And, as the name implies, they don't cost anything. (Well, some may have a small registration fee—$10, perhaps—but if it's not actually free, it's pretty close to it.)

Free-Nets offer a variety of local services, as well as access to the Internet. You may be able to find information about jobs in the area, or about local events and recreation. You may be able to search the local library's database, find course schedules for local colleges, or ask someone questions about social security and Medicare.

Free-Nets usually have a "menu" of options based on a simulated "town." There may be a Community Center, Teen Center, and Senior Center, for example. In addition, there might be an Administration Building (where you can go to register your account on the Free-Net), a Social Services and Organizations Center (where you can find support groups and local chapters of national organizations such as the Red Cross), and a Home and Garden Center (where you can find out about pest control). There might even be a Special Interests Center, where you can chat about UFOs, movies, religion, travel, or anything else. And Free-Nets also have a system that lets you send messages to other users.

Even without Internet access, Free-Nets are a great community resource, especially for home-bound people such as the elderly and handicapped. However, they have serious limitations. Not all Free-Nets will provide full access to the Internet. For security reasons, some may limit certain services. For instance, they may not want you to use FTP to bring possibly virus-laden files into their systems. And Free-Nets are often very busy and difficult to connect to.

Techno Talk

Free-Net or Freenet? You'll see the terms Free-Net, freenet, and FreeNet, and maybe even some other variations. All of these terms were service marks of NPTN (National Public Telecommuting Network), which preferred to use the term Free-Net. Note, however, that NPTN is bankrupt and will be out of business by the time you read this.

Most importantly, they are generally dial-in terminal connections, or shell accounts. You probably won't be able to use the fancy graphical software that makes the Internet so easy to use.

If you still want to find a Free-Net or other form of free access in your area, contact the Organization For Community Networks. They have a Web site (**http://ofcn.org/**), where you can find a listing of Free-Nets and other "community networks." (Again, take a trip to your library to use their Internet access, or find a friend with access.) You can also contact them at the following address:

Organization For Community Networks
PO Box 32175
Euclid, Ohio 44132
Phone: 216-731-9801

This organization does not have a full list of all the free Internet access systems available, though. Check your local computer paper, and ask at local computer stores (not the big chains, but the mom-and-pop type computer stores staffed by people who actually know what they are selling!).

Equipment You Will Need

You're going to need the following items to connect to the Internet:

➤ A computer
➤ A modem
➤ A phone line
➤ Software

Which computer? You know the story, the faster the better; the more RAM the better. Ideally, you need a computer that will run the nice graphical software, of which there are hundreds of programs for Windows and the Macintosh. If you don't have a computer that will run this sort of software, you can still access the Internet, but you'll have to use a dial-in terminal (shell) account. For instance, you'll probably want at least a 486, or better, if working in the PC world. You may be able to scrape by with a 386. But you'll find most software won't run well on a 286, if at all. (For a shell account, just about any machine is okay.)

A modem takes the digital signals from your computer and converts them to the analog signals that your phone line uses. You plug the phone line into the modem, and, if it's an external modem, you plug the computer into the modem, too. (If it's an internal modem, you install it in a slot inside your computer and the phone line connects to a socket on the edge of the card.)

When buying a modem, remember the rule of "the faster the better." Most service providers have 33,600bps connections these days, with many currently switching to 57,600bps. You can buy a good 33,600bps modem for $50 to $100.

Before you buy a 56.7?? modem, there are a few things you should understand. First, there are currently two rival techniques used for making modems transmit at this speed, and not all service providers can use both methods (in fact right now most service providers don't use this speed, though that will change soon). So before you buy a modem, check with your service provider to find out which ones will work with their system.

You Can Only Be So Tight

If you think $50(ish) for a 33,600bps modem is too much, you need to think long and hard before getting a slower modem. Even a 28,800bps modem will feel sluggish; anything less will be unbearable. (Actually, it's difficult to buy a *new* modem that is slower than 28,800, but you might find one secondhand—and you might regret your decision if you buy it.)

Secondly, note that although a modem will be rated at "56K," it can only transfer data at that speed one way. Transfers *from* the Internet will occur at 56??, but transfers *to* the Internet will go at the slower 33,600 bps rate. That's okay for most users, who are viewing information on the Web or downloading files.

Finally, even if you do get a 56?? modem, it may not transfer at that speed across some phone lines (if it can't reach top speed, it'll still be able to transmit at a lower speed). Most, but not all, of North America's phone lines can handle 56??.

Don't buy a modem from the *Acme Modem and Hiking Shoe Company* (or from any of the other hundreds of budget modem makers). Anyone can build and sell a modem; however, building a *good* modem is difficult. Modems are complicated things, and the cheap generic modems often do not connect reliably. Buy a modem from one of the well-known modem companies, such as US Robotics, Hayes, Practical Peripherals, or MegaHertz. (Look in a computer magazine, and you'll soon see which modems are being sold by most of the mail-order companies.)

You Want Something Faster

Yes, there are faster connections...for some of us. The following sections give a quick rundown of other possible types of connection that might be available in your area.

ISDN

This is an old Botswanan acronym for "Yesterday's Technology Tomorrow—Perhaps." ISDN phone lines are fast digital phone lines. This technology has been around for years, but the U.S. phone companies, in their infinite wisdom, figured that we really didn't need it. Of course, now they are scrambling to provide it, spurred on by the increasing number of people that use the Internet. Still, in some areas, if you call the local phone company and ask if you can have an ISDN line, you might hear something like "Sure, move to Germany."

Don't bother to get an ISDN line until you find a service provider who also has an ISDN connection; currently most don't. You'll be charged at both ends, by the phone company (who will charge to install and maintain the line) and the service provider (who will charge extra for the privilege of connecting to the Internet with it).

Not surprisingly, prices are all over the place. To use ISDN, you'll need a special *ISDN modem*, as they're known. That'll cost around $350–450, less soon. Then you pay the phone company to install the line (between $0 and $600—don't ask me how they figure out these prices), and you'll pay a monthly fee of $25 to $130. You'll have to pay both the phone company *and* the service provider an extra fee for this special service. I recently had ISDN installed, and discovered a few oddities about this technology. It requires that large holes be dug in your yard, generally by a small group of rotund men who stand around in front of your house staring at the hole. It may take a dozen visits from the phone company...they may even try to install it a couple of times after they've already installed it once. And it may also require the destruction of the neighbor's shrubbery.

> *Techno Talk*
>
> **ISDN Modem** An ISDN modem is not really a modem. The word "modem" is a contraction of two words "modulate" and "demodulate," which are the terms for the processes of converting digital signals to and from analog phone signals. Although they're called ISDN "modems," the signals are digital all the way; there's no modulating and demodulating there.

T1 Line

You could install this special type of digital phone line. It would be about 10 times faster than ISDN, but it would cost you a couple of thousand dollars. Although this is okay for small businesses who really need fast access to the Internet (very few really do), it's out of the price range of most individuals.

Satellite

You can connect to the Internet through a satellite dish. It would cost around $1,100 to install and $30 a month to maintain. The connection should be about 3–4 times faster than ISDN.

Cable

The cable companies have been promising Internet access for some time, even running ads implying that they were *already* providing Internet access. And one day they just might. But for the moment, don't hold your breath, or you'll turn blue long before you connect to the Internet via cable. It will be several years before Internet access is widely available through cable.

When this does become available, it will probably be about four times faster than ISDN— perhaps faster later on. It will probably cost $300–500 to install and $30 a month or so to maintain.

ADSL

This may be our best hope. It's a new telephone technology due to be introduced in some areas late in 1996. It will be very fast—perhaps even faster than cable—at approximately 10 times the speed of an ISDN line. Costs should be comparable to cable. Let's keep our fingers crossed.

For now, however, most of us are stuck with modems. With luck, they're 33,600bps modems, which are slow but affordable. But don't get too jealous of people using faster connections. The Internet can be very slow at times, and even if you have a very fast connection from your service provider to your computer, you may still find yourself twiddling your fingers. For instance, when you're using the Web or an FTP site, the server you've connected to might be slow. Or the lines from that server across the world to your service provider might be slow. Or your service provider's system might be clogged up with more users than it was designed to handle. So just because you have a fast connection…doesn't mean you have a fast connection.

For instance, as a recent ISDN user I should point out that you might be disappointed if you invest in that technology. It's okay sometimes—and at other times it's simply not worth the extra cost.

A neighbor said to me recently, "Won't it be great when the Internet runs fast, you know, a megabyte a second or whatever?" And I replied, "Sure, but won't it be great when the Internet runs at 28.8!"

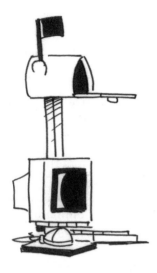

The E-Mail Responder

You can find additional information related to this book using a mail responder. The mail responder will automatically send you chapters from the first edition of *The Complete Idiot's Guide to the Internet* or a chapter from *The Complete Idiot's Next Step with the Internet*, in response to a special message from you.

Check This Out...

About the First Edition

Why might you want to see the first edition of this book. The book you are reading is completely different from the first edition. Back in 1993, when the first edition was written, most people were using the command-line interface to work with the Internet. Now most are using some kind of graphical user interface. But because some people are still stuck at the command line, we've bundled the first edition so that these people can get to all the funky little UNIX commands they're going to need.

Using the E-Mail Responder

Here's how to use the e-mail responder.

1. Send an e-mail message to **ciginternet@mcp.com**.

2. In the Subject line of the message, enter the appropriate command from the list below. When the e-mail responder receives your message, it automatically sends a message back to you containing the requested chapter.

3. When you receive the message, save it to your hard disk, and then open the chapter in a word processor or text editor. (Or simply read the chapter in your mail program if you wish.)

Don't bother to include any text in the message. Your message will be received by a computer—not an actual person—and whatever you write in the body of the message won't be read anyway. (If you want to contact QUE, see the contact information at the front of this book.)

With the e-mail responder, you can receive any of the following chapters from the first edition of *The Complete Idiot's Guide to the Internet* by typing the appropriate command.

Chapter	Command
5 Let's Get Physical: What You Need to Get Started	physical
7 Your First Trip to the Internet	first
8 Menus and Shells, Oh My!	shells
9 A UNIX Survival Guide	unix
10 Please Mr. Postman: An Intro to E-mail	email
11 UNIX Mail: Down to the Nitty Gritty	unixmail
12 Still More on Mail	moremail
10, 11, & 12 (Chapters 10, 11, and 12 together)	allmail
13 Return to Sender, Address Unknown	sender
14 Finding Folks with Fred and Whois	fred
13 & 14 (Both chapters 14 and 15 together)	who
15 Newsgroups: The Source of All Wisdom	wisdom
16 More on Newsgroups and Mailing Lists	maillist
15 & 16 (Both chapters)	news
17 Telnet: Inviting Yourself onto Other Systems	telnet
18 Grabbing the Goodies: Downloading Files with FTP	ftp
19 More Neato FTP Stuff	moreftp
18 & 19 (Both chapters)	allftp
20 Archie the File Searcher	archie
21 Digging Through the Internet with Gopher	gopher
22 Finding Your WAIS Around	wais
23 Think Global: World Wide Web	web

The autoresponder also has the following chapter from *The Complete Idiot's Next Step with the Internet*, which contains information about Internet Relay Chat:

1 Yak, Yak, Yak, Talking on the Net   irc

Finally, you can retrieve the OWNWEB.HTM file, mentioned in Chapter 9, "Your Very Own Web Page."

OWNWEB.HTM   ownweb

Speak Like a Geek: The Complete Archive

ActiveX   A new multimedia-authoring system for the World Wide Web, from Microsoft.

alias   A name that is substituted for a more complicated name, usually in an e-mail program. For example, you can use a simple alias (peterk) instead of a more complicated mailing address (pkent@arundel.com) for a mailing list.

America Online (AOL)   A popular online information system.

anchor   A techie word for an *HTML* tag used as a link from one document to another.

anonymous FTP   A system by which members of the Internet "public" can access files at certain *FTP* sites without needing a login name; they simply log in as anonymous.

Archie   An index system that helps you find files in more than 1,000 *FTP* sites.

archive file   A file that contains other files (usually compressed files). It is used to store files that are not used often, or files that may be downloaded from a file library by Internet users.

ARPAnet   Where the Internet began. The Advanced Research Projects Agency (of the U.S. Department of Defense) computer network, which was the forerunner of the Internet.

article   A message in an Internet newsgroup.

ASCII   Stands for American Standard Code for Information Interchange, which is a standard system used by computers to recognize text. An ASCII text file comprises the letters of the alphabet, the punctuation characters, and a few special characters. The nice thing about ASCII is that it's recognized by thousands of programs and many different types of computers.

backbone   A network through which other networks connect.

bandwidth   Widely used to mean the amount of information that can be sent through a particular communications channel.

baud rate   A measurement of how quickly a modem transfers data. Although, strictly speaking, this is not the same as bps (*bits per second*), the two terms are often used interchangeably.

BBS   See *bulletin board system*.

beta test   A program test based on the premise that "this program is virtually finished, but because we need a little help smoothing out the rough edges, we'll give it to a few more people."

BITNET   The "Because It's Time" network (really!). A large network connected to the Internet. Before the Internet became affordable to learning institutions, BITNET was the network of choice for communicating.

bits per second (bps)   A measure of the speed of data transmission; the number of bits of data that can be transmitted each second.

bookmark   A URL that has been saved in some way so that you can quickly and easily return to a particular Web document.

bounce   The action of an e-mail message being returned because of some kind of error.

bps   See *bits per second*.

browser   A program that lets you read *HTML* documents and navigate around the Web.

BTW   An abbreviation for By The Way; it's commonly used in e-mail and newsgroup messages.

bulletin board system (BBS)   A computer system to which other computers can connect so their users can read and leave messages or retrieve and leave files.

cache   A place where a browser stores Web documents that have been retrieved. The cache may be on the hard disk, in memory, or a combination of the two. Documents you "return to" are retrieved from the cache, which saves transmission time.

CDF   Channel Data Format, a system used to prepare information for *Webcasting*, that is, for retrieval by a *push* program.

CERN   The European Particle Physics Laboratory (CERN) in Switzerland is the original home of the World Wide Web.

chat   A system in which people can communicate by typing messages. Unlike e-mail messages, chat messages are sent and received as you type (like a real chat—only without the voice). The most popular Internet chat system is Internet Relay Chat. The best and most popular of all the chat systems, however, are on the online services.

CIX   The Commercial Internet Exchange, an organization of commercial Internet service providers.

client A program or computer that is "serviced" by another program or computer (the *server*). For instance, a Gopher client program requests information from the indexes of a Gopher *server* program.

compressed files Computer files that have been reduced in size by a compression program. Such programs are available for all computer systems (for example, PKZIP in DOS and Windows, tar and compress in UNIX, and StuffIt and PackIt for the Macintosh). Sometimes known as *archive* files, though the terms are not really synonymous; while an archive file may be compressed, it may not.

CompuServe A large online information service.

cracker Someone who tries to enter a computer system without permission. This is the correct term, though the term *hacker* is often mistakenly used in its place.

CSLIP (Compressed SLIP) See *Serial Line Internet Protocol (SLIP)*.

cyberspace The "area" in which computer users travel when "navigating" around on a network or the Internet.

DARPANET The Defense Advanced Research Projects Agency network, which was created by combining *ARPAnet* and *MILNET*. The forerunner of the Internet.

DDN The Defense Data Network is a U.S. military network that is part of the Internet. *MILNET* is part of the DDN.

dedicated line A telephone line that is leased from the telephone company and used for one purpose only. On the Internet, dedicated lines connect organizations to service providers' computers, providing dedicated service.

dedicated service See *permanent connection*.

dial-in direct connection An Internet connection that you access by dialing into a computer through a telephone line. Once connected, your computer acts as if it were an Internet host. You can run *client* software (such as Web browsers and *FTP* programs). This type of service is often called *SLIP*, *CSLIP*, or *PPP*. Compare to *dial-in terminal connection*.

dial-in service A networking service that you can use by dialing into a computer through a telephone line.

dial-in terminal connection An Internet connection that you can access by dialing into a computer through a telephone line. Once connected your computer acts as if it were a terminal connected to the service provider's computer. This type of service is often called *interactive* or *dial-up*. Compare to *dial-in direct connection*.

Dial-up service A common Internet term for a *dial-in terminal connection*.

direct connection See *permanent connection*.

DNS   See *Domain Name System.*

domain name   A name given to a host computer on the Internet.

Domain Name System (DNS)   A system by which one Internet host can find another so it can send e-mail, connect *FTP* sessions, and so on. The hierarchical system of Internet host domain names (domainname.domainname.domainname) uses the Domain Name System. The DNS, in effect, translates words into numbers that the Internet's computers can understand. For instance, if you use the domain name firefly.prairienet.org, DNS translates it into 192.17.3.3.

dot address   An informal term used for an *IP address*, which is in the form n.n.n.n, where each n is a number. For instance, 192.17.3.3.

download   The process of transferring information from one computer to another. You download a file from another computer to yours. See also *upload.*

e-mail or email   Short for electronic mail, the system that lets people send and receive messages with their computers. The system might be on a large network (such as the Internet), on a bulletin board or online service (such as CompuServe), or over a company's own office network.

EARN   The European network associated with BITNET.

EFF   See *Electronic Frontier Foundation.*

EFLA   Extended Four Letter Acronym. Acronyms are essential to the well-being of the Internet. See *TLA.*

Electronic Frontier Foundation (EFF)   An organization interested in social, legal, and political issues related to the use of computers. The EFF is particularly interested in fighting government restrictions on the use of computer technology.

emoticon   The techie name for small symbols created using typed characters, such as *smileys*— :).

encryption   The modification of data so that unauthorized recipients cannot use or understand it. See also *public-key encryption.*

etext   Electronic text: a book or other document in electronic form, usually simple ASCII text.

Ethernet   A protocol, or standard, by which computers may be connected to one another to exchange information and messages.

FAQ (Frequently Asked Questions)   A document containing a list of common questions and corresponding answers. You'll often find FAQs at Gopher sites, in newsgroups, and at *FTP* and Web sites.

Favorites   The term used by Internet Explorer for its *bookmark* list.

Fidonet An important network that is also connected to the Internet. Well-known in geek circles.

file transfer The copying of files from one computer to another over a network or telephone line. See *File Transfer Protocol*.

File Transfer Protocol A *protocol* defining how files transfer from one computer to another. FTP programs transfer files across the Internet. You can also use FTP as a verb (often in lower-case) to describe the procedure of using FTP, as in, "ftp to ftp.demon.co.uk," or "I ftp'ed to their system and grabbed the file."

Finger A program used to find information about a user on a host computer.

flame An abusive newsgroup message. Things you can do to earn a flame are to ask dumb questions, offend people, not read the FAQ, or simply get on the wrong side of someone with an attitude. When these things get out of control, a flame war erupts.

flamer Someone who wrote a flame.

form A Web form is a sort of interactive document. The document can contain fields into which readers can type information. This information may be used as part of a survey, to purchase an item, to search a database, and so on.

forms support A Web browser that has forms support can work with a Web form. Not all browsers can use forms (most recent ones can, though).

forum The term used by CompuServe for its individual bulletin boards or discussion groups (similar to Internet *newsgroups*).

frames Some Web pages are split into different frames (or panes); in effect, they create two or more independent subwindows within the main browser window.

Free-Net A community computer network, often based at a local library or college, which provides Internet access to citizens from the library or college or (sometimes) from their home computers. Free-Nets also have many local services, such as information about local events, local message areas, connections to local government departments, and so on.

freeware Software provided free by its creator. (It's not the same as *public domain* software, for which the author retains copyright.) See also *shareware*.

FTP See *File Transfer Protocol*.

gateway A system by which two incompatible networks or applications can communicate with each other.

geek Someone who knows a lot about computers, but very little about communicating with his fellow man—and, perhaps more importantly, with his fellow woman. (Vice versa if the geek happens to be a woman, although the majority of geeks are men.) Geeks spend more time in front of their computers than talking with real people. The term "geek" may have started as a derogatory term, but many geeks are proud of their geekness—and many have become very rich because of it. As Dave Barry (who got rich before becoming a computer geek) once said, "I'm a happy geek in cyberspace, where nobody can see my haircut."

GEnie   An online service owned by General Electric.

Gopher   A system using Gopher *clients* and *servers* to provide a menu system used for navigating around the Internet. Most Web browsers can act as Gopher clients. Gopher was started at the University of Minnesota, which has a gopher as its mascot.

gopherspace   Anywhere and everywhere you can get to using Gopher is known as gopherspace.

GUI (Graphical User Interface)   Pronounced "goo-ey," this is a program that provides a user with onscreen tools such as menus, buttons, dialog boxes, a mouse pointer, and so on.

hacker   Someone who enjoys spending most of his life with his head stuck inside a computer, either literally or metaphorically. See *geek* and *cracker*.

helper   See *viewer*.

history list   A list of Web documents that you've seen in the current session (some browsers' history lists also show documents from previous sessions). You can return to a document by selecting it in the history list.

home page   1. The Web document your browser displays when you start the program. 2. A sort of "main page" at a Web site. (Personally, I don't like this second definition, but there's not much I can do about it.)

host   A computer connected directly to the Internet. A service provider's computer is a host, as are computers with permanent connections. Computers with *dial-in terminal connections* are not; they are terminals connected to the service provider's host. Computers with *dial-in direct connections* can be thought of as "sort of" hosts: they act like hosts while connected.

host address   See *IP address*.

host name   The name given to a *host*. Computers connected to the Internet really have *host numbers*, but host names are easier to remember and work with. A host name provides a simpler way to address a host than using a number.

host number   See *IP address*.

hotlist   A synonym for *bookmarks*, URLs of Web documents you want to save for future use. You can return to a particular document by selecting its bookmark from the hotlist.

HTML (HyperText Markup Language)   The basic coding system used to create Web documents.

350

HTTP (HyperText Transfer Protocol)   The data-transmission *protocol* used to transfer Web documents across the Internet.

hyperlink   See *link*.

hypermedia   Loosely used to mean a hypertext document that contains, or has links to, other types of media such as pictures, sound, video, and so on.

hypertext   A system in which documents contain links that allow readers to move between areas of the document, following subjects of interest in a variety of different paths. With most browsers you use the mouse to click a link to follow the link. The World Wide Web is a hypertext system.

HYTELNET   A directory of Telnet sites. A great way to find out what you can do on hundreds of computers around the world.

IAB   See *Internet Architecture Board*.

IAP   Internet Access Provider; another term for service provider.

IETF   See *Internet Engineering Task Force*.

IMHO   An abbreviation for In My Humble Opinion, which is used in e-mail and newsgroup messages.

index document   A Web document that lets you search some kind of database.

index server   A special program, accessed through an index document, that lets you search some kind of database.

inline images   A picture inside a Web document. These graphics must be .GIF, .JPG, or .XBM format files, because those are the formats browsers can display.

Integrated Services Digital Network (ISDN)   A digital telecommunications system that everyone's been waiting for but that the telephone companies seem unable to get installed in a decent time. ISDN allows voice and data to be transmitted on the same line in a digital for-mat—instead of the normal analog—and at a relatively high speed.

interactive service   See *dial-in terminal connection*.

internet   Spelled with a small i, this refers to networks connected to one another. "The Internet" is not the only internet.

internet address   See *IP address*.

Internet Architecture Board (IAB)   The "council of elders" elected by ISOC; they get together and figure out how the different components of the Internet will all connect together.

Internet Engineering Task Force   A group of engineers that makes technical recommenda-tions concerning the Internet to the IAB.

351

Internet Explorer   A Web browser from Microsoft. It's one of the two best browsers around, giving Netscape Navigator a run for its money.

Internet Protocol (IP)   The standard protocol used by systems communicating across the Internet. Other protocols are used, but the Internet Protocol is the most important one.

Internet Relay Chat (IRC)   A popular *chat* program. Internet users around the world can chat with other users in their choice of IRC channels.

Internet Society   The society that, to some degree, governs the Internet; it elects the Internet Architecture Board, which decides on technical issues related to how the Internet works.

InterNIC   The Internet Network Information Center. Run by the National Science Foundation, this provides various administrative services for the Internet.

IP   See *Internet Protocol*.

IP address   A 32-bit address that defines the location of a host on the Internet. Such addresses are normally shown as four bytes, each one separated by a period (for example, 192.156.196.1). See *dot address*.

IRC   See *Internet Relay Chat*.

ISDN   See *Integrated Services Digital Network*.

ISOC   See *Internet Society*.

ISP   An abbreviation for Internet Service Provider that's much loved in geekdom. See *service provider*.

Java   A new programming language from Sun Microsystems. Programmers can create programs that will run in any Java "interpreter," so a single program can run in multiple operating systems. There are now two browsers with built-in interpreters: Netscape Navigator and Internet Explorer.

JavaScript   A sort of subset of Java; JavaScript is a scripting language that's simpler to use than Java. Both Netscape Navigator and Internet Explorer can run JavaScripts.

JPEG   A compressed graphic format often found on the World Wide Web. These files use the .JPG or .JPEG extension.

JScript   Microsoft's version of *JavaScript*; it contains as much of JavaScript as Microsoft can manage to add (Netscape develops JavaScript, so they're always ahead of Microsoft), plus some JScript-specific commands.

Jughead   Jonzy's Universal Gopher Hierarchy Excavation And Display tool. A Gopher search tool that's similar to *Veronica*. The main difference between Veronica and Jughead is that Jughead searches a specific Gopher server whereas Veronica searches all of gopherspace.

KIS   See *Knowbot Information Service.*

Knowbot   A program that can search the Internet for requested information. Knowbots are in an experimental stage.

Knowbot Information Service (KIS)   An experimental system that helps you search various directories for a person's information (such as an e-mail address).

LAN   See *Local Area Network.*

leased line   See *dedicated line.*

link   A connection between two Web documents. Links are generally pieces of text or pictures that, when clicked upon, make the browser request and display another Web document.

linked image   An image that is not in a Web document (that's an inline image), but is "connected" to a document by a link. Clicking the link displays the image. Often known as an external image.

LISTSERV list   A *mailing list* that is handled by the popular LISTSERV mailing-list program.

Local Area Network (LAN)   A computer network that covers only a small area (often a single office or building).

log in   The procedure of *logging on* or logging in. Also sometimes used as a noun to mean the ID and password you use to log on.

logging off   The opposite of *logging on* or logging in; telling the computer that you've finished work and no longer need to use its services. The procedure usually involves typing a simple command, such as exit or bye.

logging on   Computer jargon for getting permission from a computer to use its services. A "logon" procedure usually involves typing in a username (also known as an account name or user ID) and a password. This procedure makes sure that only authorized people can use the computer. Also known as logging in.

lurker   Someone involved in *lurking.*

lurking   Reading newsgroup or mailing list messages without responding to them. Nobody knows you are there.

mail reflector   A mail program that accepts e-mail messages and then sends them on to a predefined list of other e-mail addresses. Such systems provide a convenient way to distribute information to people.

mail robot   An e-mail system that automatically carries out some sort of procedure for you.

mail server   1. A program that distributes computer files or information in response to e-mail requests. 2. A program that handles incoming e-mail for a host.

mailing list   A list of e-mail addresses to which a single message can be sent by entering just one name as the To address. Also refers to discussion groups based on the mailing list. Each message sent to the group is sent out to everyone on the list. (*LISTSERV* groups are mailing list groups.)

MB   Abbreviation for *megabyte*.

MCImail   An e-mail system owned by MCI.

megabyte   A measure of the quantity of data. A megabyte is a lot when you are talking about files containing simple text messages, but it's not much when you are talking about files containing color photographs.

The Microsoft Network   A major online service (the fastest growing service in history); it was launched in 1995 when Windows 95 was released. Also known as MSN.

MILNET   A U.S. Department of Defense network connected to the Internet.

MIME (Multipurpose Internet Mail Extensions)   A system that lets you send computer files "attached" to e-mail. Also used to identify file types on the Web.

mirror site   A copy of another site. (There are FTP mirrors and Web mirrors.) Every so often the contents of the other site are copied to the mirror site. The mirror site provides an alternative location, so that if you can't get into the original site, you can go to one of the mirror sites.

modem   A device that converts digital signals from your computer into analog signals for transmission through a phone line (modulation), and converts the phone line's analog signals into digital signals your computer can use (demodulation). (So-called "ISDN modems" are not true modems; they don't modulate and demodulate.)

Mosaic   The first popular *GUI Web browser*, from the *NCSA*. This was the first graphical browser; some of the original Mosaic programmers helped to found Netscape Communications, the publisher of Netscape Navigator.

MPEG   A computer video format. With the right software and, in some cases, hardware, you can play MPEG video files on your computer.

MUD   A type of game popular on the Internet. MUD means Multiple User Dimensions, Multiple User Dungeons, or Multiple User Dialogue. MUDs are text games. Each player has a character; characters communicate with each other by the users typing messages.

navigate   Refers to "moving around" on the Web using a browser. When you jump to a Web document, you are navigating.

navigator   A program that helps you find your way around a complicated online service. Several navigator programs are available for CompuServe, for instance. Navigators can save you money by letting you prepare for many operations (such as writing mail) offline, and then go online quickly to perform the operations automatically.

NCSA   (National Center for Supercomputing Applications) The people who make the *Mosaic* World Wide Web browser.

netiquette   Internet etiquette, the correct form of behavior to use while working on the Internet and in *USENET* newsgroups. These guidelines can be summarized as "Don't waste computer resources, and don't be rude."

Netnews   See *USENET*.

Netscape Communicator   A suite of programs based on *Netscape Navigator*; it contains Navigator (a *Web browser*), Messenger (*e-mail*), Collabra (*newsgroups*), Netcaster (a *push* program), Conference (a *chat* and *VON* program), Composer (Web-page creation), IBM-Host-on-Demand (*tn3270*), and Calendar (a scheduling program).

Netscape Navigator   The Web's most popular browser, created by some old NCSA programmers who started a company called Netscape Communications.

Network Information Center   A system providing support and information for a network.

Network News Transfer Protocol (NNTP)   A system used for the distribution of *USENET newsgroup* messages.

newbie   A new user. The term may be used to refer to a new Internet user, or a user who is new to a particular area of the Internet. Since everyone and his dog is getting onto the Internet, these loathsome creatures have brought the general tone of the Internet down a notch or two, upsetting long-term Internet users who thought the Internet was their own personal secret.

news server   A computer that collects newsgroup data and makes it available to *newsreaders*.

newsgroup   The Internet equivalent of a *BBS* or discussion group (or "*forum*" in CompuServe-speak) in which people leave messages for others to read. See *LISTSERV lists*.

newsreader   A program that helps you find your way through a *newsgroup's* messages.

NIC   See *Network Information Center*.

NNTP   See *Network News Transfer Protocol*.

NOC   Network Operations Center, a group that administers a network.

node   A computer "device" connected to a computer network. That device might be an actual computer, or something else—a printer or router, for instance.

NREN   The National Research and Education Network.

NSF   National Science Foundation; the U.S. government agency that runs the *NSFNET*.

NSFNET   The National Science Foundation network, a large network connected to the Internet.

Offline browser   A program that automatically collects pages from Web sites and then makes them available for viewing *offline*.

online   Connected. You are online if you are working on your computer while it is connected to another computer. Your printer is online if it is connected to your computer and ready to accept data. (Online is often written "on-line," though the non-hyphenated version seems to be gaining acceptance these days.)

online service   A commercial service (such as *CompuServe*, *The Microsoft Network*, and *America Online*) that provides electronic communication services. Users can join discussion groups, exchange e-mail, download files, and so on. Most such services now have Internet access, too.

packet   A collection of data. See *packet switching*.

Packet InterNet Groper (PING)   A program that tests whether a particular host computer is accessible to you.

packet switching   A system that breaks transmitted data into small *packets* and transmits each packet (or package) independently. Each packet is individually addressed, and may even travel over a route different from that of other packets. The packets are combined by the receiving computer.

permanent connection   A connection to the Internet using a leased line. The computer with a permanent connection acts as a host on the Internet. This type of service is often called *direct*, *permanent direct*, or *dedicated service*, and is very expensive to set up and run. However, it provides a very fast high *bandwidth* connection. A company or organization can lease a single line and then allow multiple employees or members to use it to access the Internet at the same time.

permanent direct   See *permanent connection*.

personal certificate   An electronic certificate containing *encryption* data used to encrypt and sign e-mail or computer files, or to identify the owner to a Web site. See also *public-key encryption*.

PING   See *Packet InterNet Groper*.

plug-in   A special type of *viewer* for a *Web browser*. A plug-in plays or displays a particular file type within the browser's window. (A viewer is a completely separate program.)

point of presence   Jargon meaning a method of connecting to a service locally (without dialing long distance), often abbreviated *POP*. If a service provider has a *POP* in, say, Podunk, Ohio, people in that city can connect to the service provider by making a local call.

Point-to-Point Protocol   A method for connecting computers to the Internet via telephone lines; similar to *SLIP*, though a preferred, and these days more common, method.

POP   See *point of presence* and *Post Office Protocol*.

port   Generally, "port" refers to the hardware through which computer data is transmitted; the plugs on the back of your computer are ports. On the Internet, "port" often refers to a particular application. For instance, you might telnet to a particular port on a particular host. The port is actually an application.

Post Office Protocol (POP)   A system for letting hosts get e-mail from a server. This is typically used when a dial-in direct host (which may only have one user and may only be connected to the Internet periodically) gets its e-mail from a service provider. The latest version of POP is POP3. Do not confuse this with *point of presence* (POP).

posting   A message (article) sent to a newsgroup, or the act of sending such a message.

postmaster   The person at a host who is responsible for managing the mail system. If you need information about a user at a particular host, you can send e-mail to postmaster@hostname.

PPP   See *Point-to-Point Protocol*.

private key   The "key" or code used, in a *public-key encryption* system, which must be kept secure. (Unlike the public key, which may be freely distributed.)

Prodigy   An online service founded by Sears.

protocol   A set of rules that defines how computers transmit information to each other, allowing different types of computers and software to communicate with each other.

public domain software   Software that does not belong to anyone. You can use it without payment, and even modify it if the source code is available. See *shareware* and *freeware*.

public key   The "key" or code, used in a *public-key encryption* system, which may be freely distributed. (Unlike the private key, which must be kept secure.)

public-key encryption   A system that uses two mathematically related keys, a *private key* and a *public key*. Information that has been encrypted using one key can only be decrypted using the associated key. The private key is used to digitally sign an electronic document or decrypt files that were encrypted using the public key.

push   A push program periodically retrieves data from the Internet and displays it on the user's computer screen. A push program is a sort of automated *Web browser*. See also *Webcasting*.

RealAudio   A well-known streaming audio format.

reflector, mail   Messages sent to a mail reflector's address are sent automatically to a list of other addresses.

reload (or refresh) A command that tells your browser to retrieve a Web document even though you have it in the cache. Microsoft uses the term refresh in its Internet Explorer browser; this term has a different meaning in Netscape Navigator.

remote login A BSD (Berkeley) UNIX command (rlogin) that is similar to Telnet.

rendered An *HTML* document has been "rendered" when it is displayed in a Web browser. The browser renders it into a normal text document. You don't see the codes, just the text that the author wants you to see. An unrendered document is the source *HTML* document (with codes and all).

rlogin See *remote login*.

rot13 (Rotation 13) A method used to "encrypt" messages in newsgroups so that you can't stumble across an offensive message. If you want to read an offensive message, you'll have to decide to do so—and go out of your way to decode it.

router A system used to transmit data between two computer systems or networks using the same protocol. For instance, a company that has a permanent connection to the Internet will use a router to connect its computer to a leased line. At the other end of the leased line, a router is used to connect it to the service provider's network.

RTFM Abbreviation for (Read the F***ing Manual), which is often used in reaction to a stupid question (or in response to a question which, in the hierarchy of nebwies and long-term Internet users, is determined to be a stupid question).

Serial Line Internet Protocol (SLIP) A method for connecting a computer to the Internet using a telephone line and modem. (See *dial-in direct connection*.) Once connected the user has the same services provided to the user of a permanent connection. See *Point-to-Point Protocol*.

server A program or computer that services another program or computer (the *client*). For instance, a Gopher server program sends information from its indexes to a Gopher client program.

service provider A company that provides a connection to the Internet.

shareware Software that is freely distributed, but for which the author expects payment from people who decide to keep and use it. See *freeware* and *public domain software*.

shell account Another name for a simple *dial-in terminal* account.

signature A short piece of text transmitted with an e-mail or newsgroup message. Some systems can attach text from a file to the end of a message automatically. Signature files typically contain detailed information on how to contact someone: name and address, telephone numbers, Internet address, CompuServe ID, and so on—or some strange little quote or poem.

Simple Mail Transfer Protocol (SMTP)   A *protocol* used to transfer e-mail between computers on a network.

SLIP   See *Serial Line Internet Protocol*.

smiley   A symbol in e-mail and newsgroup messages used to convey emotion or simply for amusement. Originally the term referred to a symbol that seems to "smile," but the term now seems to refer to just about any small symbol created with text characters. You create smileys by typing various keyboard characters. For example, :-(means sadness. Smileys are usually sideways: turn your head to view the smiley. The correct term for a smiley is *emoticon*.

SMTP   See *Simple Mail Transfer Protocol*.

source document   An *HTML* document; the basic ASCII file that is rendered by a browser.

stack   See *TCP/IP stack*.

Start Page   A term used by Microsoft in its Internet Explorer browser to refer to the *home page*.

streaming   In the old days, if you transferred an audio or video file, you had to wait for it to be transferred to your computer completely before you could play it. Streaming audio and video formats allow the file to play while it's being transferred.

tags   The codes inside an *HTML* file.

talk   A program that lets two or more Internet users type messages to each other. As a user types a character, that character is immediately transmitted to the other user. There are several common talk programs: talk, ntalk, and YTalk. Similar to *chat*, though chat systems are intended as "meeting places," while talk programs are "private."

tar files   Files *compressed* using the UNIX tape archive program. Such files usually have file names ending in .tar.

TCP/IP (Transmission Control Protocol/Internet Protocol)   A set of *protocols* (communications rules) that control how data transfers between computers on the Internet.

TCP/IP stack   The software you must install before you can run TCP/IP programs across a dial-in direct connection. You might think of the TCP/IP stack as an Internet driver. In the same way you need a printer driver to send something from your word processor to your printer, you need the TCP/IP stack to send information to (and receive information from) your dial-in direct programs.

Telnet   A program that lets Internet users log in to computers other than their own host computers, often on the other side of the world. Telnet is also used as a verb, as in "telnet to debra.doc.ca."

telneting   Internet-speak for using Telnet to access a computer on the network.

TLA (Three Letter Acronym)   An acronym for an acronym. What would we do without them? See *EFLA*.

tn3270   A Telnet-like program used for remote logins to IBM mainframes.

Trojan Horse   A computer program that appears to carry out a useful function but which is actually designed to do harm to the system on which it runs. See *virus*.

UNIX   A computer operating system. Many—probably most—hosts connected to the Internet run UNIX.

upload   The process of transferring information from one computer to another. You upload a file from your computer to another. See *download*.

URL (Universal Resource Locator)   A Web "address."

USENET   The "User's Network," a large network connected to the Internet. The term also refers to the *newsgroups* distributed by this network.

UUCP   UNIX to UNIX copy program, a system by which files can be transferred between UNIX computers. The Internet uses UUCP to provide a form of e-mail, in which the mail is placed in files and transferred to other computers.

UUCP network   A network of UNIX computers connected to the Internet.

UUDECODE   If you use UUENCODE to convert a file to ASCII and transmit it, you'll use UUDECODE to convert the ASCII file back to its original format.

UUENCODE   The name given a program used to convert a computer file of any kind (sound, spreadsheet, word processing, or whatever) into an ASCII file so that it can be transmitted as a text message. The term is also used as a verb, as in "uuencode this file." There are DOS, Windows, UNIX, and Macintosh UUENCODE programs. In Windows, there's a program called Wincode that can UUENCODE and UUDECODE files.

VBScript   A scripting language from Microsoft, which is similar in concept to *JavaScript*.

Veronica   The Very Easy Rodent-Oriented Net-wide Index to Computerized Archives, a very useful program for finding things in *gopherspace*.

viewer   A program that displays or plays computer files that you find on the Web. For instance, you need a viewer to play video files you find. These are sometimes known as *helpers*.

virus   A program that uses various techniques for duplicating itself and traveling between computers. Viruses vary from simple nuisances (they might display an unexpected message on your screen) to serious problems that can cause millions of dollars' worth of damage (such as crashing a computer system and erasing important data).

Voice-On-the-Net   Also known as VON, this is a new service by which you can talk to other Internet users. You need a sound card, microphone, speakers, and the right software; then you can make Internet "phone calls." They're warbly, but very cheap.

VON See *Voice-on-the-Net*.

VT100 The product name of a Digital Equipment Corporation computer terminal (DEC). This terminal is a standard that is emulated (simulated) by many other manufacturers' terminals.

W3 See *World Wide Web*.

WAIS See *Wide Area Information Server*.

Web Pertaining to the *World Wide Web*.

Webcasting Distributing information via *push* programs.

Web forum A discussion group running on a Web site.

Web-hosting company A company that sells space on a Web server to people who want to set up Web sites.

Web server A computer system—a computer running special server software—that makes *Web* documents available to *Web browsers*. The browser asks the server for the document, and the server transmits it to the browser.

Web site A collection of *Web* documents about a particular subject on a host.

Webspace The area of cyberspace in which you are traveling when working on the *Web*.

WebTV A system used to display Web sites on a television. A box containing a *modem* is connected to a TV; the signals from the Internet are transmitted on the phone lines (not along the TV cable line), and displayed on the TV screen. WebTV is manufactured by Sony and Philips/Magnavox (and recently bought by Microsoft), though the term is also widely used to describe the technology in generic terms.

White Pages Lists of Internet users.

Whois A UNIX program used for searching for information about Internet users.

Wide Area Information Server (WAIS) A system that can search databases on the Internet for information in which you are interested.

Winsock A *TCP/IP stack* for Microsoft Windows.

World Wide Web A hypertext system that allows users to "travel through" linked documents, following any chosen route. World Wide Web documents contain topics that, when selected, lead to other documents.

WWW See *World Wide Web*.

X.500 A standard for electronic directory services.

XBM   X Bitmap graphics format, a bitmap from the UNIX X Window system. These are simple images, one of only three types that can be used as inline graphics; the others are .GIF and .JPG. They're rarely seen on the Web these days, though.

XML   Extended Meta Language, the *HTML*-like tags used by *CDF*.

Online Glossary

Introduction

The World Wide Web is chock-full of interesting places to visit; there are Web sites covering everything from UFOs to personal finance. The following directory is designed to provide you with a guide to some of the most exciting and informative Web pages.

You will find that the Web can be interesting, serious, and a great deal of fun, and when you find your way to a Web page that's really your cup of tea, remember to add it to your Favorites list on your Web browser.

"A"

Alternative Medicine

Ask Dr. Weil

http://www.drweil.com

You've seen this guy's face all over *Time* and *Life* magazines and now he's taken the Web by storm with his Ask Dr. Weil site. Each day Dr. Weil posts a new alternative medicine topic dealing with everything from AIDS, cancer, and arthritis to the common cold, dry skin, and headaches, all generated through questions sent into the site from readers. In addition to Dr. Weil's daily topic, viewers can browse the site for FAQs, previous topic discussions, optimum health recipes, a searchable database of diseases, treatments and remedies, and a referral page with links to professional organizations.

New Age

http://www.newage.com/

A companion to the popular health magazine, *New Age* features a Holistic Health Forum where readers can search for topics, books, clinics, and schools online. The Holistic Health Directory can also help you find a practitioner in your state specializing in any one of over a 100 areas of alternative medicine from acupressure to yoga therapy.

Mother Nature's General Store

http://www.mothernature.com/

If you're looking for alternative medicine products, Mother Nature's General Store stocks it all including aromatherapy, hair and skin care, vitamin, homeopathy, and herbal products. In addition to being a great source for actual alternative medicine product, this site also provides resourceful forums and a comprehensive online research library.

Health Trek

http://www.healthtrek.com/

Visit the Health Trek Shopping Mall for the best health products and foods, search for books on dozens of health topics, or drop in and read the monthly newsletter. Whether you are exploring the Botanical Reference, visiting the online Doctor's Office, browsing the Treatment Library or stopping by the Learning Center, Health Trek is the definitive online resource for "exploring the alternatives."

Alternative Medicine Digest

http://www.alternativemedicine.com/

This site provides one-stop shopping for information on alternative medicines and cures. The Digest tracks the latest and greatest in medical research of an alternative bent and then summarizes the information in their online journal. This site also provides links to alternative medicine books, alternative medicine radio programs and an online chat area.

HealthWorld Online

http://www.healthy.net/

Offering a map of "HealthWorld Village" as a navigational tool, this site has information on nutrition, fitness, and other wellness issues. You can click on the "Nutrition Center" map icon and peruse a variety of topics including the use of herbs in the kitchen and vegetarian cooking.

A bookstore offers the online purchase of alternative medicine book titles and a health food store gives you access to various "healthy" food products. The site is dedicated to "self managed care" offering resources so everyone can participate in the maintenance of their own wellness.

Acupuncture

http://www.acupuncture.com/

This site is by far the most informative and diverse site in terms of alternative therapies and medicines. Focusing on traditional Chinese therapies including acupuncture, herbology, Qi Gong, Chinese nutrition, Tui Na, and Chinese massage, this site offers valuable information and treatment for three focused audiences: consumer, student, and practitioner.

Animals

ASPCA

http://www.aspca.org/

Whether it's your average family pet or the beautiful American bald eagle, the American Society for the Prevention of Cruelty to Animals is the animal world's biggest friend. On this Web site you'll find everything from pet care tips to animal services to newsletters devoted to the animal lover. This is a complete Animal lover's site with information from overpopulation to a calendar of events geared toward pet lovers and people who just love to study animals. You also can join the ASPCA and find e-mail links to other animal organizations.

PETA

http://www.envirolink.org/arrs/peta/

This page offers a list of tips to help you take care of your pet and a guide to proper treatment of all animals. It's a must-see for any animal lover.

Holistic Health

http://www.cyberark.com/animal/

This is a great page to learn about products and services that help you take care of animals. It's one of the most complete sites on the Web dedicated to home care of animals.

Animals, Animals

http://www.pacificablue.com/animals/

If you're interests lies in learn about animals from all over the world then this site is the place to visit. It also includes sound bites and video clips of various animals.

Animal Species

http://www.fws.gov/%7Er9endspp/mammals1.html

This site offers a complete listing of all endangered wildlife and fish residing in the United States. Each description also provides links for more information.

Auto Racing

RaceZine

http://www.primenet.com/~bobwest/

If you're looking for the fastest auto racing news around, then RaceZine is the answer. This site features news on all the major racing organizations plus sound bites and archived pictures of some of the top teams in the world. This site isn't a rehash of wire service stories, but offers an in-depth look at various teams in NASCAR, CART, and the NHRA. The site also offers trivia contests and links to some of the other top racing sites on the Web. However, don't come here looking for the latest race results. This site is more focused on features and the history of auto racing then it is on offering the most complete list of results. There are, however, plenty of links to sites that do offer up-to-the-minute race results.

SpeedNet

http://www.starnews.com/speednet/

From the auto racing capitol of the world comes the most informational racing-related page on the Net. The *Indianapolis Star*'s SpeedNet page features complete results and news of all the major racing organizations in the world.

NASCAR

http://www.nascar.com/

If NASCAR is your thing, then the NASCAR home page is a dream come true. This page offers up-to-date results, a history of the sport and features on top drivers.

CART

http://www.cart.com/

Championship auto racing is one of the fastest forms of racing in the world, and this page is up to speed with results on all races and features on all CART drivers.

IRL

http://www.indyracingleague.com/

A league fighting for survival has one of the top pages on the Net, featuring news from the Indianapolis Motor Speedway and links for both IRL and NASCAR events.

"B"

Baseball

Major League Baseball Bat

http://www.majorleaguebaseball.com/

This is the official home of the Boys of Summer on the Web. From here you can link to all of the Major League teams as well as their minor league affiliates. At the right time of year, you can participate in voting for the All-Star Game. There's a Virtual Ballparks tour that takes you to the park even if you can't get away from your computer. There are special sections and events for young fans and everyone will enjoy special treats like the tribute to Jackie Robinson in the 1997 season. Look for trivia contests and giveaways all over the site including the This Week In Baseball (TWIB) area. And if you are in a shopping mood, browse the Clubhouse Shop for apparel from all of your favorite teams.

Classic video clips from baseball history and current highlights await at the video section of @Bat. You'll have to install some extra software to see these (it's free and are instructions included) but once you do you'll have your pick of great plays like "The Catch" and highlights from every week of the current season.

Fastball

http://www.fastball.com/

This site features incredibly detailed coverage of the Major Leagues as well the minors. You won't miss a single story with their baseball news directly from the A.P. wire. There are chats with players and personalities from the game and you can join the action with interactive fun and games.

Instant Sports

http://www.instantsports.com/

Don't tell my boss but this site is one of my favorite ways to waste time on a summer day at the office. With Instant Ballpark at Instant Sports you can see an animated version of every game. Every 30–90 seconds the animation is updated showing the progress of the game.

Baseball Statsweb

http://www.baseballstats.com/

This site is the ultimate source for settling any bet on baseball stats. Every stat for every pitcher, batter, and team in the modern era is here. Ty Cobb's lifetime batting average: .366. There's a million more where that came from.

Major League Rotisserie Baseball

http://www.fantasysports.org/

Hundreds of Web sites offer fantasy baseball leagues so it's hard to pick just one that will appeal to everyone. But I'll recommend Major League Rotisserie Baseball. Be sure to check out some of the other sites listed here and the sites in the sports news section as many of them also have fantasy leagues.

Basketball

NBA.com

http://www.nba.com/

The NBA season and playoffs may only run 8 months a year, but the NBA.com Web site is available to you 24 hours a day, 365 days a year to provide you with your pro hoops fix. During the season, you'll find highlights, scores, game summaries, previews, interviews, and more basketball news than you could possibly read. In the off-season, be sure to check here for draft news, player trades and signings, as well as news from the training camps. If you want to join the action, you'll find a variety of interactive forums including chats with other fans (even players and coaches stop in some times).

On Hoops

http://www.onhoops.com/

This site is a self-proclaimed alternative NBA site. The proprietors are hardcore fans and want to provide a Web site with a different view of the NBA. Take a look and see what you find and then you can be the judge of who's site is better.

College Hoops Insider

http://www.collegehoopsinsider.com/

For my money, the best basketball isn't played by guys with multimillion dollar contracts but on the floors of college halls around the country. If you want the most complete scores, stats, and news on every Division 1 A basketball program, this is the best site bar none.

National Wheelchair Basketball Association

http://www.nwba.org/

Basketball is a game that almost anyone can play, especially with some determination. If you are looking for a local wheelchair league, or just more information about wheelchair basketball in general, the NWBA is the premier organization. They have leagues for men, women, and youth at all levels of play.

WNBA.com

http://www.wnba.com/

You've seen the commercials, you know they've "got next." Women's professional basketball is one of the fastest growing pro sports and with the backing of the NBA, it looks like a sure hit. This site looks very similar to the NBA site and you'll find a lot of similar features here.

Beauty

Redbook Beauty and Style

http://homearts.com/rb/toc/00rbbec1.htm

Redbook has taken the information and advice from the magazine world and upgraded it to a virtual beauty community. The *Redbook* Beauty and Style site provides visitors with tips, advice, forums, and bulletin boards to help every woman become more beautiful. This site is not just a take-off of its magazine or a high-tech advertising teaser: it is a full information center. It provides real information for women of all ages. *Redbook* knows that not everyone has time to spend hours in the beauty salon, so they update the site with new articles on how to save time and still look great. *Redbook* also covers other topics such as how to look your best though the upcoming weather, finding the perfect scent for your personality, how to care for your clothes, and how to rescue your hair from a bad hair day.

@ Hairnet

http://www.hairnet.com/html/home.html

Get the latest news on the hair and salon industry at the Hairnet site. This site reviews the latest hair styles, the best hair products, and connects you to the best salons in your area. This is a must see before you visit your salon!

Beauty Spot

http://www.beautyspot.com/

Beauty Spot is a great online beauty store which helps you pick the best product and then gets it to your door without having to leave your computer. The best part is that Beauty Spot serves both women and men with great advice and products.

Paula Begoun—The Cosmetics Cop

http://www.cosmeticscop.com/

Before you buy any more cosmetics, make sure you visit Paula Begoun's site. Begoun is know as the "Cosmetics Cop" because she exposes the cosmetics industry's secrets to help beauty consumers make the wisest buying decisions. She posts many reviews of new beauty products as well as large excerpts from her books including "Don't go to the Cosmetics Counter Without Me."

Cover Girl

http://www.covergirl.com/

Cover Girl's beautifully designed site helps its visitors become customers by providing them with the latest news, tips, and makeup advice. You can fill in a questionnaire and the "beauty advisor" will tell you which Cover Girl colors and products will work the best for you and your lifestyle.

Beer

All About Beer Online

http://www.allaboutbeer.com/

All About Beer Magazine sponsors this Web site which contains a wealth of information about the beer industry and a generous sampling of columns and feature articles from the printed magazine. There are large sections of beer tasting notes, advice on the art of homebrewing, what food to eat with which beers, and how to cook food with the ingredients you normally find in beer. One of the best columns is "Jackson's Journal," in which famed beer expert Michael Jackson (not the pop musician) details his trips throughout the world looking for the perfect beer. *All About Beer* online also contains international news about the beer industry, information on beer-related stocks, and keen insights into beer advertising campaigns.

The Beer Info Source

http://www.beerinfo.com/

The Beer Info Source has a rich collection of links to Web sites that deal with all aspects of the beer industry, from beer tasting clubs and homebrew organizations to magazines, books, and retailers. You can also search their virtual library for listings of brew pubs and beer festivals around the world.

Brew Your Own

http://www.byo.com/

This Web site contains select articles from current and back issues of *Brew Your Own* magazine. If you're looking for beer recipes, articles on the beer industry, or answers to tough questions like "What's the difference between Laaglander and klages dry malt?" look here.

BrewCrafters

http://www.brewcrafters.com/

BrewCrafters has everything you need to make your own homebrew, from brewpots and cookers, yeast and hops, to bottles, caps, and rubber stoppers. You can order everything online via e-mail or call their toll free number.

breWorld

http://www.breworld.com/

BreWorld is the largest European Internet site devoted to beer. It contains information on international beer festivals, meetings, and breweries. You can also find tips and recipes for brewing other alcoholic beverages like hard cider and perry.

Books

BookWire

http://www.bookwire.com/

The man who does not read good books has no advantage over the man who can't read them.

—Mark Twain

This incredible site offers everything a book lover could possibly want, whether your taste is for mysteries, non-fiction, "fine literature," poetry, or even computer books. BookWire is a rich and well organized resource where you can consult hundreds of book reviews, read hundreds of complete books they have online, and check to see if your favorite author will appearing soon in a bookstore near you. BookWire also has a lot of publishing news, including a link to *Publishers Weekly* magazine (referred to by those in the know as simply "*PW*"), a comprehensive list of awards, and critics' choices.

New York Times Book Review

http://www.nytimes.com/books/home

The New York Times book review has ruined more aspiring writers than a mean-spirited high school writing teacher. It's also made many writers. The Web site contains over 50,000 book reviews from the past 17 years. You'll have to subscribe to the Web version of the *The Times* before you use it, but subscriptions are free.

The Literary Web

avery.med.virginia.edu/~jbh/litweb.html#rev

The Literary Web contains hundreds of links to Web sites that deal with literary fiction and poetry. It is well organized and covers a lot of ground, from online books to book clubs, journals, and writers' resources.

Publishers Weekly Interactive

http://www.bookwire.com/pw/pw.html

This site is sponsored by the leading magazine for the publishing industry—*Publishers Weekly*. The magazine and the Web site specialize in publishing industry news, early reviews of upcoming books, the *PW* bestseller's list, and classified ads for publishing jobs.

Amazon.com

http://www.amazon.com/

If you want to buy a book online, you can't beat Amazon.com. Search their database of more than 2.5 million titles, read descriptions and reviews, and then order your book at a discount.

"C"

Camping

CampNet America

http://www.campnetamerica.com/

As the ultimate camping resource on the Web, CampNet America can tell you the best places to camp, how to get there, what to do once you get there, and much more! With more than 12 areas focusing on all your camping needs including an RV Parks and Campground Locator, a complete listing of National and Public Parks, Camping and Outdoor Supplies, Log Cabin Rentals, Travel Clubs and Associations, the CampNet Traveler's Journal, and the Campfire Forum and Recipes, you can plan your next camping adventure right from your desktop. With cool links to AAA's Map 'N' Go (an online trip router), USA Today's Weather site, and First Aid Online, CampNet America is your one-stop-shop for all your camping needs.

Wrolin Camping 'Round the World

http://www.wrolin.com/campindx.htm

Should your camping adventures lead out of the country, the Wrolin Camping 'Round the World site can help you find campgrounds in virtually any country in the world. From the rustic outback of Australia to the sunny beaches of the Virgin Islands, you'll find some of the best and beautiful camping the world has to offer.

Coleman

http://www.coleman-eur.com/

Let the oldest and most trusted name in camping outfit your next camping trip. Coleman camping supplies brings you a complete catalog of camping and hiking paraphernalia including tents, lanterns, coolers, sleeping bags, camping stoves, and more.

Harvest Foodworks

http://www.harvest.on.ca/

So roasting weenies and marshmallows over the fire can get a little boring…spice up your camping menu with zesty, healthy recipes and products from Harvest Foodworks. You'll find a complete index of recipes for breakfast, snacks, lunch, dinner, and desserts, and a complete product line of healthy alternative camping meals.

Intercamp: Summer Camp & Resource Directory

http://www.intercamp.com/

Parents take note…you can't pass this one up! With a listing of more than 2,000 summer camps searchable by price, location, specialty, and Web sites, Intercamp can help you solve your child's summertime blues. You'll also find convenient chat rooms and a special section on summer camp gear for your kids.

Car Buying

Edmund's

http://www.edmunds.com/

Edmund's knows the automobile industry—they've been publishing automobile buying guides since 1966. So if you're in the market for a new or used car, don't even think about stepping on to a dealer's lot without first visiting the Edmund's Web site. For new cars they list the base price, prices for all the options, and most importantly, what the dealer really paid for the car. You'll also find exact details on the car's interior and exterior dimensions, safety features, performance data, fuel efficiency, warranties, and how much it costs to insure it. Once you've found the car you want, Edmund's will even help you locate a dealer near you.

AutoVantage

http://www.cuc.com/

AutoVantage is a free service; they work with over 2,300 car dealers to give you a pre-negotiated discount on a new car. Simply fill out their online form and AutoVantage will tell you what dealer to go to for a good deal.

Yahoo! Classifieds

http://classifieds.yahoo.com/auto.html

Search for cars, trucks, and motorcycles that are for sale anywhere in the US by individual owners and dealers. You can even print out a map that tells you how to get there.

Consumers Car Club

http://www.carclub.com/

Consumers Car Club membership is free when you apply on their Web site. Members get access to special automobile pricing information, financing programs, and insurance discounts.

AutoSeek

http://www.autoseek.com/

If the thought of negotiating with a car dealer makes you break out in hives, then check out AutoSeek. This is a free service that will locate the car you want, and negotiate the purchase or lease amount that you want to pay.

Comics

VR-1 Digital Comics

http://www.vr1.com/comics/

As one of the first online comics to hit the Internet, VR-1 Digital Comics has several series to interest the diehard comics junkie. Stories run from serious to silly; all the while taking full advantage of all that modern Internet technology can offer.

Doonesbury Electronic Town Hall

http://www.doonesbury.com/

If your tastes run a little more mainstream, visit Mike, Zonker, and the rest of the crew from Walden Puddle. Here you'll find Flashbacks to comic strips past with a short list of what happened in the real world on that day, all the way back to the strip's inception in 1977. After getting hit with a heavy dose of nostalgia from the Flashback, you may want to test your knowledge of Doonesbury trivia or buy your own memories with a bit of Doonesbury paraphanalia.

The Dilbert Zone

http://www.unitedmedia.com/comics/dilbert/

This is the center of the *Dilbert* universe where you can get as close to "Nerdvana" as possible without leaving the safety your cubicle. Here you'll find sage advice from the Dogbert Oracle, micromanagement tips straight from Dilbert's boss, and many other daily time wasters. You'll also get your daily *Dilbert* comic fix as well.

Calvin and Hobbes

http://www.uexpress.com/ups/comics/ch/

United Press Syndicate, publishers of *Calvin and Hobbes* have devoted a entire section of their Web site to the child in all of us, Calvin and his pal Hobbes. You'll find information about the strip's creator Bill Waterson, his creations Calvin and Hobbes, letters to Bill and links to some Web pages created by some of the comic's many fans.

This Modern World

http://www.well.com/user/tomorrow/

This popular alternative comic strip is often seen on the online literary magazine *Salon*. At the creator's (Tom Tomorrow) site, you'll have access to an archive of interview and articles giving you insight in what goes into the creation of each weeks strip as well as links a vast library of *This Modern World*'s episodes.

Celebrities

People Online

http://www.people.com/

No other celebrity site focuses more on famous people than—you guessed it—*People* Online. The interface design is modeled after the design of the printed magazine and there are plenty of photos and cool graphics as well as intriguing articles and daily updates. You'll find some of your familiar *People Magazine* features such as "Picks and Pans," and you'll be able to check out back issues without ever having to subscribe or sort through the newstand or library! Of course if you would like to subscribe you can do that at the site too. Look through the People Online "Peephole" to get a sneak peak at the latest activities of your favorite celebs.

Mr. Showbiz!

http://www.mrshowbiz.com/

Need information about the hottest celebs? Ask Mr. Showbiz! Catch daily exclusive stories on your favorite celebrities, Hollywood's top headlines, TV, video, movie reviews, and daily updated featured photos. Go to "Star Bios" to find biographies, real names, astrological signs, credits, and educational backgrounds. There's even a Star Bios Top Ten list of the week's most accessed celebrities at Mr. Showbiz!

Celebsite

http://www.celebsite.com/

Find your favorite star at Celebsite. Celebsite is a Mr. Showbiz site and you can link to Celebsite from Mr. Showbiz or link to Mr. Showbiz from Celebsite. Use the search engine to type in the names of the celebrities you'd like to locate or browse alphabetically or by category. Get recent news and birthday information on your favorite celebrities, check out your horoscope, send fan mail, or find out more about a featured celebrity.

Celebrity Four11

http://www.four11.com/

Go to **http://www.four11.com/** and choose *celebrity* to link to e-mail and mailing addresses for your favorite celebrities. If you are looking for a quick, easy way to contact an actor, author, business leader, entertainer, government politician, model, sports star, or other celebrity, this is the quickest way to get in touch with the star of your choice.

Sports Celebrity Network

http://www.sportspin.com/

Whether you like football, basketball, baseball, hockey, golf, autoracing, or tennis, if you want intense coverage of your favorite sports celebrities you can't miss the sports celebrity network. The site provides daily updates of athlete news and articles feature your favorite sports personalities.

Community Service

Peace Corp

http://www.peacecorps.gov/

The Peace Corps site is loaded with information about the work done by this organization. There is a complete list of the countries that the Corps has helped or is helping. Many of the countries in the list have links detailing the kinds of work that is being done in those countries. You can read all about the Peace Corps volunteer programs and how you can become a volunteer. Links here describe the various work that volunteers do and the areas of expertise that are needed. The complete application process is detailed online.

Habitat for Humanity

http://www.habitat.org/

You don't have to be Bob Villa to help the Habitat for Humanity build homes. At this site, find out how to get involved with the Habitat for Humanity in your area. An online search engine will help you find a local affiliate in any of the 50 states and 53 other countries.

United Way of America

http://www.unitedway.org/

At this site you can find out about the many United Way programs. You can find your local United Way by state and see what new things the United Way is doing. Football fans will certainly be interested in the NFL and the United Way section describing the long standing efforts of the NFL for this organization.

Idea List

http://www.idealist.org/

This is provides a huge directory of Web sites of over 10,000 non-profit groups. They also have a section on tools for non profits describing ideas for fundraising, using computers and the Internet, non profit management, and more.

Rotary International

http://www.rotary.org/

Use this Web site to understand the mission of the Rotary club and search for a club that meets in your area. The history of the organization, current news, and their relationships with other organization are some of the many other topics to explore here.

Chat

Talk City

http://www.talkcity.com/

Started a couple of years ago by some members of Apple's *e-world*, Talk City has carried the tradition of community started on that online service to the World Wide Web. There's literally something for everyone here, with chat rooms covering topics of all kinds from politics to music.

Talk City stresses the safety of their community, providing "clean well lighted places for conversation on the Internet." What that means is that all chat area are moderated by community standard advisors who maintain a family friendly atmosphere.

Finding others who share your interest is easy at Talk City. A click on the Communities button brings up a list of all the communities on Talk City with a description of what they cover.

Yahoo! Chat

http://chat.yahoo.com/

Yahoo! isn't just a search engine. At Yahoo! Chat you use the iChat plug-in, Java, or html and your Web browser to chat with others over the Internet. There are 10 general subject areas to choose from with several rooms in each area dealing with specific topics. Users can create their own rooms as well.

State of Insanity

http://soi.hyperchat.com/

The chat here is not insane as the name of the site suggests. This online community has rooms created and moderated by its users. Think of it as sort of cybercommune that's open to the public. There's plenty to experience here and some of the conversation is really meant for the ears and eyes of adults.

Chat Central

http://chat.nstate.net/

Chat Central is another online community run by folks who want to keep the site safe for chatting. The sponsor of the site makes it clear that no vulgarity or other inappropriate behavior will be tolerated. The one downfall of this site is that occasionally you may find that you may be banned from Chat Central because of the actions of someone else using your ISP.

World League of Air Traffic Controllers

http://www.geocities.com/CapeCanaveral/1140/

Not all chatting on the Internet is done through communities like Talk City. The World League of Air Traffic Controllers is a group of…air traffic contollers. They meet monthly at Yahoo! Chat to discuss the concerns of their industry. This site provides a meeting schedule and agendas.

Children's Toys

Dr. Toy's Guide

http://www.drtoy.com/

Dr. Toy's online guide to children's toys is jam-packed with information on the latest toys on the market. This site comes complete with descriptions of the newest toys available as well as lists of the top toys from previous years. It has a list of summer activities to help keep your kids occupied during the long summer days. This site is a must-see for parents with children ranging in ages from 2 to 14.

Learning

http://www.difflearn.com/

This page specializes in learning materials and educational toys geared toward children with special challenges, but any parent will enjoy the material described here.

Legos

http://www.lego.com/

What child doesn't enjoy the creativity of building and the fun that comes with playing with Legos? This site has all the new Lego products complete with pictures.

Yo-Yo

http://www.socool.com/socool/yo-yo.html

No childhood is complete without a yo-yo. This page teaches all those cool yo-yo tricks and has a complete listing of yo-yo products.

Games Kids Play

http://www.corpcomm.net/~gnieboer/gamehome.htm

From *Red Rover, Red Rover* to *Flashlight Tag*, this site offers complete descriptions on all those wonderful childhood games that makes you want to stay young forever.

Cigars

Cigar Aficionado

http://www.cigaraficionado.com/

Whether you're a seasoned cigar connoisseur or looking for a good first smoke, your first stop should be *Cigar Aficionado* magazine's Web site. Here you'll find an incredible wealth of information that is as easy to access as lighting a match. Their database lists over 1,000 cigars with ratings, tasting notes, and prices. You can find restaurants around the world that are cigar-friendly, and tobacco shops complete with address and phone numbers. Learn how cigars are made and how to store them so they'll last. But that's just the beginning. *Cigar Aficionado* has links to articles on art, music, fashion, fine jewelry, drinks, and everything else that's needed to live in the high life.

Cigar.com

http://www.cigar.com/

Cigar.com features a wide-range of articles on how to pick a good cigar, the legendary men who make cigars, and the famous people who enjoy cigars. You'll also find a great collection of links to places where you can smoke cigars and buy cigar accessories.

The [Internet] Smoke Shop

http://www.thesmokeshop.com/

Now that cigars are in vogue again, you may order your favorite smoke and end-up on a long backlist—but not at The [Internet] Smoke Shop. You can see exactly what they have in-stock and order appropriately. Best of all, freshness is guaranteed.

Smokerings.com

http://www.smokerings.com/

If there were a secret password to get into Smokerings.com, it would probably be "fun". This site is full of great quotes about cigars, jokes, trivia contests, and interesting facts. Don't pass this one by!

ALT.SMOKERS.CIGARS FAQ

http://www.cigargroup.com/faq/

The best source on the Web for answers to all your technical questions about tobacco, how cigars are made, how to choose a cigar, how to store it, and how to enjoy it.

Computers

ZDNet

http://www.zdnet.com/

ZDNet is a great comprehensive computer resource on the Web. ZDNet has all of the news about the newest hardware and software, product reviews and recommendations, and links to downloading software. A favorite area for shoppers here is the ratings of PC hardware and software vendors for quality, customer satisfaction, service and repair, technical support, and other key measures. If you are thinking about buying a new PC anytime soon, look here to see how fellow consumers rate the products. Check out the Healthy PC area for tips on keeping your PC running in tip-top shape and for troubleshooting advice when something goes wrong.

Que

http://www.quecorp.com/

The Que Web site is where to go to get information about computer books on every computing topic. The entire contents of many books may be previewed online.

c\net

http://www.cnet.com/

This is another complete computer news site, this time from the makers of the c\net TV shows. There are reviews of hundreds of software and hardware products here. The "How To" section has a great collection of tips and tricks for getting the most out of your software and making your own hardware upgrades.

Dell

http://www.dell.com/

If you've ever thought about ordering a PC online, Dell's site is a great place to put those thoughts to work. You can completely customize any Dell offering on this site and get an exact price quote for your new system. Then order it online or call them and talk to a sales rep.

TuneUp

http://www.tuneup.com/

Try this service for 60 days for free. You can find answers to thousands of frequently asked computer questions at this site. It also features one-on-one answers to your specific questions from trained PC technicians. After the 60-day free trial, the service costs a few dollars a month.

Conspiracies

60 Greatest Conspiracies of All Time

http://www.conspire.com/

Feeling paranoid? Then hop over to the online version of this popular book (Citadel Press Book, $18.95). You'll find several chapters of the book online for a sneak preview. The site is rich in conspiracies including UFOria, Paranoia, Madness, and Subversion. You'll find sections detailing the most up-to-date "bizarreness," as well as archives. You can also check out the Rant-O-Rama for weird articles, from the late David Koresh of Waco fame to Lyndon LaRouche, the perennial Presidential candidate who always has several conspiracy theories up his sleeve.

The Conspiracy Pages

http://w3.one.net/~conspira/

Voted by Hotwired as a "Netizen Fresh Link" this conspiratorial site talks about the genocide of native Americans and the Biblical Rapture Index. Site tends to focus on government covert conspiracies.

Gonzo Links—Your Online Guide to Millennia

http://www.capcon.net/users/lbenedet/

Gonzo is a powerful site with hundreds of links to indepth conspiracy information. You'll find a section on "current news" conspiracies as well as UFOs. The Spooks section related to the National Security Agency and the CIA is rich with critical stories. And for the "sky is falling" set, there is a Panic Culture site filled with apocalyptic links.

disinformation

http://www.disinfo.com/

Think the world is ruled by a handful of capitalistic elites? If you answer yes, then cruise over to the disinformation site. They maintain that your 6:00 news is dictated by powerful corporate interests and it is up to the disinformation site to give you the *real* news, from genetic altering to mind control.

Art Bell

http://www.artbell.com/

Art Bell is the premier late night radio talk host of UFOs and other extraterrestrial matters. Although you can hear his show in selected cities in the wee hours of the night, you can always here him whenever you want by using Real Audio on his Web site. You can tune in to his show live or go back and listen to the archived shows at your leisure. Bell interviews many of the leading UFOlogy experts of the day, including Richard C. Hoagland, former NASA scientist, who is a proponent of life on Mars.

Contests, Sweepstakes, and Lotteries

Sweepstakes Online

http://www.sweepstakesonline.com/

Because Web sites and Web pages change every day in some cases, the contests that are here today are likely to be gone tommorow. So the best place to start when you are looking for contests and sweepstakes is a site that lists and reviews them all. Sweepstakes Online has links to hundreds of contests as well as some special contests of their own. They also have a sub-scription available for an email newsletter with up-to-the minute news for sweepstakes fans.

Publisher's Clearing House

http://www.pch.com/

Save yourself a stamp and enter the famous Publisher's Clearing House Sweepstakes online. You can enter once a day and there are additional Internet-only prizes. And yes, you can subscribe to the magazines while you are entering.

Prizes.com

http://www.prizes.com/

Once you register and set up an account here, you can play lots of free "scratch-and-win" type games. Prizes range from tokens that you can exchanges for real prizes to cash. Some games require payment.

PLUS Lotto

http://www.pluslotto.com/

As with most lotteries, this is a contest you have to pay to enter. If you are playing from the U.S., be sure to read the prize amounts in U.S. dollars, not some foreign currency. And be sure you are familiar with the rules and comfortable giving out your credit card number to enter.

Lottery News Online

http://www.lotterynews.com/

Lottery players don't have to play games on the Internet to get some use out of the Web. With Lottery News Online you can get results from several state lotteries and PowerBall. It also has a good list of links to other sites with other lottery results and "official" lottery pages.

Cooking

Cookbooks On/Line

http://www.cookbooks.com/

If you don't have space for a shelf full of cookbooks, Cookbooks On/Line is the site for you. Over one million recipes await you in an easy to use searchable database. Access to the database is free, but you must register for your user id and password.

The Food Network's CyberKitchen

http://www.foodtv.com/

The companion Web site to cable's Food TV network offers all the variety of the network's programming. Here you'll find recipes, food news, and, of course, information about your favorite Food TV shows. You can get your cooking questions answered by the Cyberchef and go to the Cybermarket gift show, if all the browsing has made you hungry.

The Dinner Co-op Home Page

http://dinnercoop.cs.cmu.edu/dinnercoop/

The Dinner Co-op is about 15 people, all Carnegie-Mellon graduates who love food. The Co-op home page has an extensive collection of recipes, menus, links to stores, farmer's market directories, and their very own downloadable cookbook.

387

Judy's Flavors of the South

http://www.ebicom.net/~howle/

If you want a little spice in your cooking visit Judy's Flavors of the South. The emphasis here is the chile pepper: As Judy points out, "variety is not the spice of life…Chile is!" There are special recipes here and tons of links to other homespun cooking pages.

foodwine.com

http://www.foodwine.com/

Home to the electronic Gourmet Guide (eGG), foodwine.com has recipes and much more. Interviews with nationally recognized chefs give you help in the kitchen and monthly columns help with meal planning and provide insight to the world of food and wine.

"E"

Education—Colleges and Universities

CollegeEdge

http://www.collegeedge.com/

What do you need to prepare for your future? Whatever you need, you can find it at the award-winning CollegeEdge Web site. Use the advanced college search feature to explore colleges to find the one most suitable to you. This is available through AT&T's WorldNet service for only $19.95 per month. With the convenience of the CollegeEdge Web Apps feature you can apply to colleges and universities electronically! And there's no need to worry about life after college, since you can also explore employment opportunities and acquire advice on careers, as well as academic majors. Perhaps the greatest deal of all at this Web site is the opportunity to add $1,000.00 to your college fund. So hurry to apply for the CollegeEdge scholarship.

Resource Pathways College Information Community

http://www.collegeguides.com/

If you're looking for a great resource suitable for your academic and financial needs, visit Resource Pathways on the Web. Only the best college choices, admissions, and financial aid resources make their recommendations list. This site provides current, comprehensive data. The prices of available resources vary, but are well worth the money.

CollegeNET

http://www.collegenet.com/

Get ready to soar through the skies with CollegeNET, rated one of Lycos' top 5%. Whatever your college search needs are, you can rest assured that you'll be fine in flight with CollegeNET. You can directly apply to 34 of 38 universities listed at this site. Check out the 3-D VRML tour while you're visiting.

U.S. News

http://www.usnews.com/usnews/edu/home.htm

The U.S. News site is great for college-bound students and parents. Acquire detailed information about choosing and applying to colleges, and available financial aid. An even greater value is the information on jobs and careers after graduation. The post-graduate student can access information on the GRE, GMAT, LSAT, and so on.

Purdue University

http://www.purdue.edu/

I couldn't let you slip through this Web directory without showing you an example university site! Purdue, home of the Big Ten Boilermakers, sports a site full of the details you need to check out the various disciplines and the application process. Contact students, faculty, and find out more about the great campus life in West Lafayette.

Education—K-12

Discover Learning

http://www.discoverlearning.com/

Here's a site that meets the needs of parents, teachers, and students. From the catchy section area names like Student Skull Camp and Parent Brain Dump to the feature articles, this site is interesting to look at and to read. There is a community forum for speaking your mind on educational topics, an area devoted to facilitating the creation of online learning sites, and a large set of links to other interesting educational resources. My favorite part is "Free Speak" where students can answer a creative question like "If you were asked to make a 'Top Ten' list of the people you regard as the all-time greatest people, whom would you rank first and why?" and see the answers that other students have given.

The Jason Project

http://www.jasonproject.org/

The Jason Project Web site allows students and teachers to participate in an annual scientific expedition via the Web. Logs and highlights of past expeditions to sites including hydrothermal vents in the Mediterranean sea and a lava flow in Hawaii are also online.

Federal Resource Center for Special Education

http://www.dssc.org/frc/

This Web site has information about conferences and technology for parents and teachers of students in special education programs. There are links to resources about disabilities defined under the Individuals with Disabilities Education Act as well as links to many other types of special educational needs.

AskEric

http://ericir.syr.edu/

Through AskEric, teachers, administrators, and other educators can educational information and receive a personalized response researched by a real person. Users can also search the Eric databases, which include lesson plans and infoguides.

Family Education Network

http://www.families.com/

Parents with Web access have no excuse for not being involved in their children's educations. This site has suggestions for ways parents can get involved at school and also features home-schooling resources. There are opinion polls, chat areas, and other interactive features on the Web site itself.

Encyclopedias and Reference

Britannica Online

http://www.eb.com/

If you have school-age children, this site is the replacement for any printed encyclopedia you may have ever considered buying. There's a seven-day free-trial period before you have to pay a yearly subscription to use this. But you'll probably find that the subscription price is a small one to pay for the wealth of information here. The site is loaded with high-quality reference material, articles, pictures, and multimedia. And best of all, it's all constantly updated and added to.

Grolier Multimedia Encyclopedia Online

http://gme.grolier.com/

This is the Web home of the popular CD-ROM based Grolier Multimedia Encyclopedia. All of the pictures, sounds, and other multimedia that you would expect to find are here. As with the Britanica site, there is a subscription fee and a free-trial period.

The Electric Library

http://www.elibrary.com/

Electric Library is a huge collection of searchable current reference materials. They have the complete text of thousands of books, newspapers, magazines, and other sources online in a searchable format. This is a great source of the most current and accurate information available on the Web. Try the free trial and see if this is for you or your family.

The World Factbook

http://www.odci.gov/cia/publications/nsolo/wfb-all.htm

The CIA publishes this yearly electronic World factbook containing a huge amount of reference information about other countries. Maps, flags, population, natural resources, government, economy, and much more are detailed for every country.

Knowledge Adventure Encyclopedia

http://www.adventure.com/encyclopedia/

This site isn't intended to compete with the comprehensive commercial Web encyclopedias. What it offers is a smaller selection of very fun and interesting on topics of interest to kids including dinosaurs, bugs, and space.

"F"

Finding People

1-800-U.S. Search

http://www.1800ussearch.com/

1-800-U.S. Search is a fee-based service, charging from $29.99 to $59.95 to locate someone for you. All you need is the person's name that you want to locate, although the more information you have (previous address, telephone number, social security number, and so forth) the better your chance of locating them. 1-800-U.S. Search uses a wide variety of public records, including Post Office information, lists of telephone numbers, magazine subscription lists, marketing databases, driver's license records, and voter registration information. If you have a credit card, you can fill out a search form online and submit your query immediately. 1-800-U.S. Search does not use a secure server, however.

Four11

http://www.four11.com/

Four11 can help you contact someone by finding the person's e-mail address for you. This is a free service although it is not as reliable more thorough services like 1-800-U.S. Search.

Find-It!

http://www.iTools.com/find-it/

Find-It! can help you locate lots of different things on the Internet, including someone's name, e-mail address, service provider, and video phone listing.

Internet Address Finder

http://www.iaf.net/

This service is similar to Find-It! except that you can enter a user's e-mail address into the Internet Address Finder in order to get information about the person.

Info Space

http://www.accumail.com/iui/

Info Space enables you to search for government resources, businesses, and individuals. It can tell you someone's Web site address, e-mail address, phone number, and street address.

Fishing and Hunting

Fish and Game Finder

http://www.fishandgame.com/

Fish and Game Finder Magazine offers one of the best fishing and hunting sites on the Net. This site offers complete up-to-date news, fishing reports, hunting information, and a market place where you can find any fishing or hunting equipment around. The best part of this site is how easy everything is to locate and how complete the monthly fishing reports are. The site also offers information on fishing tournaments throughout the country and feature articles from their magazine. Whether you are a weekend angler or a more serious hunter, this site provides everything you need to make the experience more enjoyable.

The Fishing Hole

http://www.roanoke.infi.net/~dolores/fish.html

If you are looking specifically for fishing information, this page offers state-by-state fishing reports, the latest in fishing news, and all the equipment you'd ever need. A must-see for all fisherman.

Sporting Adventures

http://www.spav.com/

This site is geared toward informing and educating hunters and fishermen about the various conservation groups that help look out for their interests. It also offers a complete fishing guide.

Tackle Towne

http://www.saint-james.com/captain.html

Capt'n Mike's Tackle Towne site is one of the best sites to visit when you're looking for the latest and greatest fishing and hunting equipment.

Outdoors Online

http://www.ool.com/

This is a great site to visit for the serious outdoorsman. This site offers fishing and hunting information as well as legislative news geared toward hunters.

Food

Epicurious

http://food.epicurious.com/

Epicurious is the site "for people who eat." Actually it's more than eating; it's drinking and playing with your food as well. You'll find everything from tips for outdoor grilling, with a grill guide and over 150 recipes to directions to dozens of festival round the country where you can sample your favorite food and drink.

Los Angeles Times Food News

http://www.latimes.com/HOME/NEWS/FOOD

Los Angelenos have benefited from the *LA Times* food section for generations, now the online version shares that information with everyone. Not only will you find detailed reviews of area restaurants (handy for your next trip to LA), you'll also find recipies, cooking tips, and helpful articles covering everything from spices to Kiwi fruit.

PastaNet

http://www.pastanet.com/

You'll find everything you've ever wanted to know about pasta at PastaNet. From its history (yes, it did come from China) to its composition (anything from wheat to seaweed), this entertaining and informative site is certainly one to add to a food lover's bookmark list. You'll even find 10 rules for making better pasta, so you'll no longer have an excuse for cooking soggy noodles!

Godiva Chocolates

http://www.godiva.com/

This is the chocolate center of the Internet universe. Godiva's Web site is a treasure chest of things cocoa. You'll find recipes and descriptions of everything in Godiva's line. If you're daring you'll want to try the Chocolate Meter to see how much you really love chocolate. And after you're done cruising around their pages, you can order some chocolate of your own.

Insect Recipes

http://www.ent.iastate.edu/Misc/InsectsAsFood.html

Insects, as this page cheerfully tells us, can be delicious and nutritious. While eating insects may be unthinkable to many, the folks at Iowa State have come up with dozens of ways to serve our creepy crawly friends as your next meal. In addition to the recipes, you'll find detailed nutritional information about some of the more popular insects, links to more insect "treats" at the University of Kentucky, and a link to a place where you can buy your very own chocolate covered crickets.

Football

NFL.com

http://www.nfl.com/

Every pro football fan will want to start his exploration of football on the Web at the National Football League's NFL.com site. This site has complete news from the NFL year-round, statistics for teams and individual players, and chat areas for fans to communicate with each other. In season you'll find up-to-the minute scores on game day and TV times and schedules for coverage. There are areas of the site devoted to the playoffs and to the big finale—the SuperBowl.

Dick Butkus Football Network

http://www.dickbutkus.com/

One of the NFL all-time greats has taken to the Web at this site. Look for his inside perspective and commentary to give this site a unique slant.

Collegeball.com

http://www.collegeball.com/

Here's your chance to get involved in one of the longest running college football "office pools" on the Internet. Pick your teams each week and see how you stack up against the competition. Ranking the games by order of your confidence in your picks makes for an additional challenge.

The College Football Hall of Fame

http://collegefootball.org/index.shtml

Check out this site for a virtual tour of the College Football Hall of Fame. You can view information about all of the Hall of Famers, search for them by category or accomplishment, and find out about events scheduled around the Hall of Fame.

"G"

Games

The Game Cabinet

http://www.gamecabinet.com/

With all the video and computer games on the market you might wonder if there's room in this world for an old fashioned game of Chess or Checkers. The *Game Cabinet*, a monthly e-zine, gives you all the information you may want about all those games that don't require microchips and a television set. The site has regular features covering everything from the latest in gaming news to a "Stump the Net" section where the *Cabinet's* editors challenge you to identify obscure games or solve scenarios encountered in games such as Chess, Okey (a Turkish card game), or Carom (a wooden board game).

Social Recreation Resources

http://www.pacifier.com/~shaffer/games/games.html

Some games aren't much fun if played alone or with one other person; occasionally you need a crowd to get your game going. This site, which started as a BYU class project, deals specifically with "social" or party games. If you wanted more information on "Duck, Duck, Goose" or "Dragon Tail Tag," this is the place to go.

Chess Space

http://www.chess-space.com/

One of the oldest and more popular strategy games in the world, Chess is one game that most of us have played at least once in our lives. *Chess Space* is one site that every chess aficionado should visit. With an easy-to-use search utility, visitors can find tons of information about this popular game, and where they can play it on the Internet.

The WWW Backgammon Page

http://www.statslab.cam.ac.uk/~sret1/backgammon/main.html

The WWW Backgammon *Page* is the most popular Backgammon site on the Internet and has mirror sites in the US, Greece, Portugal, South Africa, and Russia, in addition to it's home site in the UK. Everything from Backgammon rules, book reviews, and a list of Backgammon clubs can be found here.

The Scottish Tiddlywinks Association

http://www-groups.dcs.st-and.ac.uk:80/~ben/tiddlywinks

The home of the alt.games.tiddlywinks newsgroup FAQ and promoters of the modern game of Tiddlywinks, The Scottish Tiddlywinks Association's home page is the center of Tiddlywinks information on the Internet with everything from tournament listings to rules of the game. You'll get to rediscover that game that you loved as a child (and perhaps, still do).

Gardening

Garden Escape

http://www.garden.com/

With so many stunning photographs, valuable gardening information, and great products, *Garden Escape* is simply a gardener's online paradise. Sponsored by *Garden Escape* magazine and chock full of the best and most innovative gardening information available online, this site is bound to hold your attention for hours and keep you coming back for all your gardening concerns. Search from the hundreds of flowers, vegetables and herbs available online or just tiptoe through the tulips at your own speed. Whether you need to buy plants and flowers, start a garden from scratch, tend a dying plant, or landscape a yard, or just want to keep abreast of gardening news, talk to fellow gardeners, check out the gift store, or read the online magazine, Garden Escape is your one-stop shop for all your gardening needs.

The Great Exotic Seed Company

http://www.gen.com/exoticseeds

Move over boring old beets and marigolds and make room for some of the most exotic seeds available from around the world. Choose from fragrant flowers, nuts and fruits, cacti, rainforest plants, and even natural insect repellent plants, all available for online ordering. And you'll be surprised by the low, low prices too.

GardenTown

http://www.gardentown.com/

Whether you want to brag about your six-foot sunflowers or commiserate about your herb garden that went to the dogs, GardenTown is the place to go for garden chat. Pull up your watering can and choose from several types of chat and forums. And don't forget to visit the Town Library and the GardenTown Gallery.

Plant of the Week

http://www.lclc.com/plantof.htm

This is great site to bookmark and visit every once in a while to check out the Plant of the Week. Each week you'll find a new plant, complete with picture, botanical and common names, size, description, uses, and other comments. You can also look up past Plant of the Week features.

Better Home & Gardens

http://www.bhglive.com/gardening/index.html

As a long and trusted household and garden name, *Better Home & Gardens* offers a wide variety of gardening resources including Garden Features where you can get tips, hints and suggestions from the *Better Homes and Gardens* gardening editors, Garden Talk where you can join reader discussions, Garden Map where you check out the most detailed plant hardiness maps on the Internet and much more.

Government

Thomas

http://thomas.loc.gov/

If you're a C-Span junkie, a political activist, or just want to be a knowledgeable citizen, then aim your browser at Thomas, the legislative tracking service provided by the Library of Congress. Named after Thomas Jefferson, this service tracks bills before the U.S House of Representatives and the U.S. Senate. You can search for bills, sorted by topic, title, and number, and follow the bill of your choice through the various committees that have jurisdiction over it. The Web site also contains historical documents like the Constitution and Federalist Papers. Thomas supplies Congressional member names complete with phone numbers and office addresses.

United States Government Printing Office

http://www.access.gpo.gov/

On the surface the Government Printing Office doesn't sound too exciting (you might say that about government in general), but this site is chock-full of government documents ranging from the latest Food and Drug Administration regulations to full text of the U.S. Government budget. Check out the latter and see where your tax dollars are going.

The White House

http://www.whitehouse.gov/

Well what's a tour in government without a stop at the White House? Here you will find not only what Bill and Al are up to but the entire executive branch as well. All sorts of government information including access to social security, student aid, small business assistance, and countless other federal programs can be accessed from this Web site. Don't forget to read some of the transcripts of White House press briefings; they can be pretty funny.

National Air and Space Museum

http://www.nasm.si.edu/

One of the more popular Washington tourist sites is the National Air and Space Museum of the Smithsonian Institute. The same exhibits that you can see live are now at this Web site. Find great color pictures (fast downloading time) of aircraft from the early Wright Brothers years to modern day space flight.

Guns

The National Rifle Association

http://www.nra.org/

Guns and The National Rifle Association(NRA) are almost synonymous. The word "gun" stirs up many different emotions—both pro and con. The NRA site is the definitive site to find out the latest news on gun safety, legislation, and national statistics. The site also includes a page covering the laws of every state related to owning and carrying a firearm. The NRA site always contains links to the latest news stories from around the nation and world covering gun ownership and use. The site goes much further than gun ownership and contains information about crime prevention programs in general. The NRA page is a great place to start for anyone who owns a gun or is thinking of purchasing a gun.

Doug's Shooting Sports Interest Page

http://www.users.fast.net/~jasmine/

This site is an excellent place to find out about all types of shooting sports. This site covers Olympic shooting sports, trap and skeet shooting, and others. If you are interested in any type of shooting, this is the Web page for you.

Women's Firearm Network

http://www.amfire.com/wfn.html

Women are becoming a larger percentage of gun buyers. In fact, gun manufacturers are offering handguns made specifically for women. This page is tailored to the specific issues related to women using firearms. This site contains helpful information related to women carrying and using a firearm.

The Gun Page

http://www.prairienet.org/guns/

The most important issue with using any type of firearm is SAFETY FIRST! This page contains the universal safety rules all gun owners should observe. This page says it best: "A gun never 'goes off' unless something causes it to do so." This site contains a list of the most important gun safety rules that must become second nature of all gun owners.

National Shooting Sports Foundation

http://www.nssf.com/

If you are interested in shooting sports of any type, the National Shooting Sports Foundation(NSSF) is the organization for you. The NSSF is for the hunter as well as the serious competition target shooter. This organization was formed from business leaders in firearms and hunting industries.

"H"

Men's Health

Men's Fitness

http://www.mensfitness.com/

Men's Fitness magazine has one of the most comprehensive sites online dealing with men's health issues. In addition to select feature articles from the magazine, this site also includes information about the best sports equipment on the market, nutritional information, tips on how to improve your health, and an excellent interactive forum. The site also has a tip of the day that focuses on everything from exercise to the political information. This is a great site to visit for men interested in improving their health and getting the most out of their bodies.

Men's Health

http://www.menshealth.com/

Men's Health magazine covers this topic in great detail. This site is more geared toward subscriber's but still offers complete coverage of key issues.

Prostate Cancer

http://www.prostate-online.com/

Prostate cancer is one of the most serious health issues for men and this site covers the topic in great detail. This is a must-visit for men of all ages.

Ask the Dietitian

http://www.dietitian.com/

This site is complete with tips on how to improve your diet and what foods to stay away from. It also has a listing of the affects of alcohol (just in case you haven't figured them out yet).

Fertility

http://www.dash.com/netro/nwx/tmr/tmr0595/fertility0595.html

Fertility problems is one of the most worrisome problems facing couples. This site explores fertility issues from the man's perspective.

Health—Women's

Women's Wire

http://www.women.com/body/

The Women's Wire is one of the top sites dealing with women's health issues. The site contains a top news article each day dealing with anything from skin cancer to profiles on healthy diets. The site also contains tons of information from sex experts to nutrition experts that will help keep any women in tune with her body. One of the best parts of the site, however, is an interactive page where you can talk directly with doctors in the field.

OBGYN.net

http://www.obgyn.net/

This site is for everyone from medical professionals to women just wanting information on women's health. This site is provided by physicians, so you definitely get the health field perspective on this site.

Women's Health

http://www.nytimes.com/women/

The New York Times offers a comprehensive page dealing with 29 topics of special concerns to women. The women's health forum on this page is of special interest.

Women's Health Interactive

http://www.womens-health.com/

This site is an interactive learning environment geared toward the exchange of ideas and advice. It also has a great health assessment page.

Healthgirl

http://www.nethealthgirl.com.au/

This is an extremely fun page on a serious topic. Women of all ages will get a kick out of how the page deals with all types of health and beauty concerns.

Herbs

Algy's Herb Page

http://www.algy.com/herb/

The most comprehensive site available for information on planting herbs, cooking with herbs, healing with herbs, and decorating with herbs, Algy's Herb Page features special sections including herbal products, herbal news, and a complete herbal library. Take a walk through

The Garden and discover helpful gardening tips or visit The Store for herbal oils, art, soaps, plants, seeds, and books. Feeling hungry? Sit a spell in The Kitchen to explore the culinary uses of herbs and exchange recipes online. Not feeling up to par? Visit The Apothecary and find an herbal remedy for whatever ails you. Explore The Potting Shed where you can exchange seeds with other readers or stop in The Greenhouse to join a live online chat.

The Herb Finder

http://www.woodny.com/garden/herbfinder.html

This searchable database sponsored by Ithaca Gardens can help you locate the name of virtually any herb in existence. Or if you just want to browse, use the alphabetical listing to find sizes, uses and pictures of all the herbs in the database.

Herbal Information Center

http://www.kcweb.com/herb/herbmain.htm

The Herbal Information Center and Vitamin Directory will provide you with a complete listing and detailed summary of the most popular medicinal herbs available including Feverfew, Echinacea, Ginseng, St. John's Wort, and many more. You'll also find a General Store for online ordering and an Herbal Book Shoppe.

Seeds of Change

http://www.seedsofchange.com/

Order the best in organic traditional, heirloom, and antique flower, herb, and vegetable seeds from Seeds of Change's online store. Search the database for hundreds of seed varieties grown by certified organic farmers.

American Botanical Council

http://www.herbalgram.org/

Stay abreast herbal news by checking out what the American Botanical Council is up to. Read about current education and research projects, subscribe to the HerbalGram (The Journal of the American Botanical Council and Herb Research Foundation), or browse current book reviews.

History

The History Channel

http://www.historychannel.com/

This Web site is sponsored by The History Channel cable television channel. Like the television channel, the Web site brings together images, video, and descriptions of historical events to teach you about the world in a fun and engaging way. The Exhibits section is full of rich, multimedia displays that usually focus on a historical place like Ellis Island and Jerusalem. The Classroom section has free classroom materials, study guides, and videos. The Events Calendar lists historical reenactments, special museum exhibits, conferences, and other events happening in the US and UK. The TV Listings is a convenient way to check The History Channel's programming schedule so that you don't miss your favorite shows. If you want to read more about the things you've learned here, check out The History Store, which sells books, videos, and authentic historical documents.

Exploring Ancient World Cultures

http://eawc.evansville.edu/

This site focuses on ancient history from the Uruk culture (3450 BCE) to medieval Europe. Here you'll find complete ancient texts, a useful chronology, maps, images, and descriptive text. There is also a great collection of links to other ancient history Web sites.

Military History

http://www.thehistorynet.com/MilitaryHistory/

This Web site is sponsored by *Military History* magazine and focuses on famous wars and battles throughout history. You'll find articles and book reviews from the current magazine and four years' worth of back issues.

Art History Resources on the Web

http://witcombe.bcpw.sbc.edu/ARTHLinks.html

The name of this Web site does not do it justice—it contains an incredible wealth of images, history, and analysis of artwork from prehistoric cave paintings to Greek pottery, medieval manuscripts, Gothic architecture, Barouque paintings, and 20th century pop art.

The History Net

http://www.thehistorynet.com/

The History Net contains a diverse collection of historical information, from the usual types of images and descriptive text to recorded speeches, eye-witness accounts, and interviews with the people who lived through historical events.

Hobbies

CraftSearch

http://www.craftsearch.com/

CraftSearch is really four sites in one, combining online catalogs of craft, hobby, quilting, and sewing sites. If you want to find a craft or hobby site quickly, this is the site to visit. CraftSearch has a total of 3,200 sites to choose from and they can be searched two ways. First, you can search their pages by zip code. By entering the first three digits of a zip code, CraftSearch will bring up a listing of all the sites that have those three digits in their zip code. This is a great way for finding hobby supplies in your area.

Nerd World Hobbies

http://www.nerdworld.com/nw565.html

Don't let the title scare you. This listing of hobby sites covers everything that CraftSearch doesn't. You'll find links to sites that deal with yo-yo tricks, slot car racing, and model railroads just to name a few topics. Nerd World's hobby page makes a great companion to CraftSearch.

Hobby Craft Network

http://www.hobby-craft.com/

It seems there are cable networks for everything these days. This companion site to the upstart Hobby Craft Network (HCN) has information about their programming and links to other hobby resources. Tune in to HCN's Web site and look for it on a cable system near you.

National Model Railroad Association on the Web

http://www.mcs.net/~weyand/nmra/

The home page of the National Model Railroad Association (NMRA) has everything for the novice or veteran model railroader. You'll find tips for creating a new layout, a detailed reference library and links to magazines and Web sites world wide.

CyberSlot

http://www.cyberslot.com/

This is the site for hardcore slot-car enthusiasts. You'll find a catalog of custom-built engines and engine parts, in addition to links to model car raceways. And if you want to see some model racing in person, directions are given to their store in Cleveland, Ohio.

Hockey

NHL Open Net

http://www.nhl.com/

Where better to get information about the NHL than from the NHL? For the latest news about what is going on in the NHL, from wins and losses to trades and firings, this the site. You can read the headlines on the main page and follow the links to the full stories. If you are interested in hockey gear, stop by The Store, where you can purchase gear online over a secure connection. You can also find links to every NHL team, where you can find that team's statistics and records and a link to the official team's site outside of the NHL Web site. Want to see that great shot that won the game? Take a look at the Cool Shots Video page. When does your team play? You can see that as well, including if the game will be televised. No site has more to offer about the big league of hockey.

Le Coq Sportif: Guide to Hockey

http://www.canadas.net/sports/Sportif/

This magazine's official online site is packed full of information. You can read some of the featured articles from the current issue as well as investigate back issues. Here you can find pages for injured players, box scores, player salaries, schedules, and game odds. You name it, it is here.

Joe Tremblay's WWW Hockey Guide

http://www.hockeyguide.com/

This site provides over 1,000 links to other hockey-related Web sites. You can find links to the NHL, IHL, ECHL, and other hockey leagues. Additionally, worldwide hockey, amateur hockey, goal tender, and trivia sites are easily found. If you don't know where to go to find WWW hockey sites, start here.

The Exploratorium's Science of Hockey

http://www.exploratorium.edu/hockey/

The Exploratorium is a science museum in San Francisco. If you have ever had questions about what the announcers and players are talking about, this site probably has your answer. Find answers to such questions as, "Why is ice slippery?" "What is the difference between good and bad ice?" and "Just what does the Zamboni do?" Real science with some great information.

The Hockey News Online

http://www.thn.com/

This is the official site for *The Hockey News*, one of the premier hockey rags around. Ask the writers about the upcoming draft as well as read some of the featured articles in the current issue of the newspaper. You can also find the nearest hockey summer camp or school.

Holidays

Kaplan's Holiday Fun and Games

http://www.kaplan.com/holiday/

Procrastinator's Anonymous should put a warning label on this site. Kaplan test preparation center built this "Festive Study Break" site that is a creative and humorous, yet educational, site for anyone taking a break from life. Visit this site and send mom a Mother's Day card, learn how to untangle those Christmas Tree lights, and learn a new creative prank to play on Halloween. This is not only a place with links to interesting places…finding out where they are leading you is half the fun! (Clicking on "Trick or Treat" will lead you to the government's site on Extortion.)

World Wide Holidays and Events

http://www.classnet.com/holidays/

This searchable site helps you find holidays happening all over the world. Search for holidays by name, date or country. A different holiday is highlighted each day with explanations of its purpose, place of celebration, and history. This site will also link you to many different holiday sites of your choice.

Christmas 'Round the World (Wide Web)

http://www.auburn.edu/~vestmon/christmas.html

This site will point you to anything that you want to know about Christmas. It covers not only the serious side of Christmas, but traditions and humor of the season as well. You can even do your Christmas shopping here while you are in the Christmas mood.

Happy Birthday America

http://citylink.neosoft.com/citylink/usa/

Experience Independence Day through USA Citylink's site devoted to the sounds, history, and events surrounding the Fourth of July. Find local fireworks displays throughout the U.S., read a copy of the Declaration of Independence, or just get in the spirit by reading quotes from famous Americans.

Groundhog's Day

http://www.groundhog.org/

This award-winning site brings you to the town of Punxsutawney where Groundhog's Day isn't just another holiday—it's a way of life. This well-designed and information-packed sight tells you everything from Groundhog's Day history to upcoming events. Find out which years "Punxsutawney Phil" (the groundhog) predicted the coming of spring correctly, or play groundhog games during your virtual visit.

Home Improvement

Better Homes and Gardens Home Improvement Encyclopedia

http://www.bhglive.com/homeimp/docs/

Whether you are a home improvement wanna-be or and old pro looking to brush up on some long forgotten skill, *Better Homes and Gardens* is a great starting place on line. Their encyclopedia is organized into categories by type of repair. There's a basics section for those just getting started and plenty of in-depth information about specific types of repairs, procedures, and tools for do-it-yourself types of any skill level.

Home Ideas

http://www.homeideas.com/

Here's a great place to help you decide what home improvements you want to make and what supplies to make them with. The site will send you any of the hundreds of product brochures they have, and you'll also find neat applications for estimating materials and costs for your projects.

Remodeling Online

http://www.remodeling.hw.net/

This is a great site for ideas for remodeling your house. Or, if you aren't a do-it-yourselfer but would like to find a good remodeler, search their online database of over 1,000 remodelers.

HouseNet

http://www.housenet.com/

In addition to a good selection of "how to" material to help you with your home improvement projects, this site has a couple of nice unique features. The family fun area shows some simple projects that the whole family can get involved with. And there's a section devoted to new products.

Builder's 411

http://www.builders411.com/

This is a large online directory of builders and contractors. If you need to find a professional to do the job, it's a great place to start your search.

Humor and Jokes

Funny Town

http://www.funnytown.com/

Funny Town satisfies even the hardest-to-please funny bone. This site not only serves jokes but also funny stories, satire, quotations, and real life humorous happenings. You can read the featured funny articles, pick one of several joke categories, or even access the joke archives of past years. If you would rather receive your jokes automatically, sign up on the mailing list for jokes to be sent to you via e-mail. Have you ever heard a really good joke and couldn't remember exactly what the punch-line was? Funny Town comes to your rescue by making their site searchable. The best part is that you can also post new jokes to the message board and read postings from other Funny Town visitors. This vast collection includes jokes about the most teased people such as John Tesh and Bill Clinton. You can also read up on odd facts or even rare jokes about flesh-eating albino chickens.

Mefco's Random Joke Server

http://www.randomjoke.com/topiclist.html

If your friends have heard all of your jokes, visit the Random Joke Server. You can browse the 6,000 jokes from 17 categories such as one liners ("Help Wanted: Telepath. You know where to apply."), jokes for nerds ("Ethernet is what you use to catch the Ether Bunny."), politics, lightbulb jokes, and quotations.

Laugh Web

http://world.std.com/~joeshmoe/laughweb/lweb_ns.html

No matter what you find humorous, you will find a good laugh at Laugh Web. This site not only has the usual political and computer humor, its jokes also cover popular topics like Redneck humor, Windows 95, Star Trek, and Barney. You can even subscribe to "Laugh of the Day" to have a joke e-mailed to you daily.

The Late Show with David Letterman

http://www.cbs.com/lateshow/

If you missed Letterman last night, you can catch up on everything from Dave's crazy quotes to the Top Ten List at CBS's Late Show homepage. This site has a complete archive of every Top Ten List since the show aired on CBS in 1993. You can also order tickets, browse the photos of Dave with visiting celebrities, or find out who is scheduled to appear on the show.

The Daily Muse

http://www.cais.net/aschnedr//muse.htm

Get a fresh look at the news through the eyes of a hilarious cynic at The Daily Muse. This site is updated daily with the latest news, pictures, and the laugh-out-loud commentary to go with it.

"I"

Insurance

Insure Market

http://www.insuremarket.com/

The insurance industry has caught on to two of the big features of the Web that people really like—timely and easy information. The Insure Market Web site is an example of many insurance sites that can provide you with real-time quotes on a variety of insurance needs. There's no need to talk with an agent and the companies that provide quotes through this are all nation-wide and easily recognized firms including AllState, MetLife, and State Farm. The "risk evaluator" is a neat way to find out things like how likely your model of car is to be stolen and how your area ranks for hit-and-run and drunk-driving accidents.

Insurance Information Institute

http://www.iii.org/consumer.htm

Buying and understanding insurance can be confusing. The Insurance Information Institute has this useful Web site that will help you find answers and information about common insurance questions and provide tips about purchasing insurance coverage.

InsWeb

http://www.insweb.com/

InsWeb is another site that offers online insurance quotes. Their quotes include auto, life, health, and other services. Some are given real time. Other participating companies will send you a quote by e-mail or mail.

Net Quote Insurance Shopper

http://www.netquote.com/

Here's one more source for online insurance quotes. NetQuote offers quotes for auto, health, home, and life insurance. The quotes aren't provided over the Web but you will get competitive quotes from several agents via fax, phone, or mail.

Insurance New Network

http://www.insure.com/

This is another good site for consumers to brush up on their insurance knowledge. It provides a glossary of insurance terms, information about vehicle safety, and current news that could affect your insurance coverage.

"J"

Job Searching and Employment

The Monster Board

http://www.monster.com/

They don't call it The Monster Board for nothing. This site is busting at the seams with more than 50,000 U.S. and International job postings. You can search the site for specific careers or just choose the Personal Job Search Agent to do the work for you. The Monster Board lists thousands of jobs in virtually every area possible including both trade and non-trade positions. You'll find listings by location, discipline, and keywords guaranteed to save you hours of digging through the classifieds or making cold calls.

The Monster Board also boasts some unique features including Online Open Houses and a complete calendar of Career Fairs coming to your area. Still not convinced that finding a job on the Web is possible or respectable?; check out the testimonials under Success Stories. The Monster Board will also help you create a résumé online. You provide the content and they'll take care of the rest.

CareerPath

http://www.careerpath.com/

With almost 200,000 job wanted ads from across the country, CareerPath is an excellent source for helping you find the right job. Searchable by newspaper, job, or keywords, this complete database of jobs not only provides you with the most up-to-date information but also offers tips on how to interview and build your resume.

e-span

http://www.espan.com/

espan is unique from the other career and employment sites because it not only provides you with jobs but also helps companies find candidates for their job openings. espan works with some of the big boys, like Microsoft, GTE, and Ameritech. And don't forget to check out the Hot Jobs list and the online Salary Calculator.

Cool Jobs

http://www.cooljobs.com/

Forget the stuffy corporate jobs, this site is for the daring and adventurous. With an out-of-the-ordinary list of jobs that change daily, you'll find job opportunities with NASA, Walt Disney, ClubMed, MTV, and Jeopardy. You say you want to join Cirque du Soleil? Check out the very cool job description and submit your resume online.

JobVault

http://www.jobvault.com/

Looking for a job with a big company or just a company with a big name? The JobVault has job postings with Nike, Sun Microsystems, Eastman Kodak, Ford Motor Company, Gateway, Netscape, Proctor & Gamble, Hallmark, Phillip Morris, and oh-so-many more. Submit your resume online, get career advice, and check out the cool Exclusive Interviews from celebrities about their jobs.

"L"

Languages

Berlitz World

http://www.berlitz.org/

Over the past 115 years Berlitz International has taught 31 million people to speak a second language. Berlitz publishes it's own books, runs it's own courses, and has now started the Berlitz World Web site. The Web site contains a lot of practical information, like the 25 phrases (in four different languages) that you need when dining out. You can also find tips for how to conduct yourself in foreign countries, and how to do business. On the lighter side, there's the Faux Pas section that contains funny and true stories of people who have mixed up their foreign vocabulary and embarrassed themselves. There's also a Bulletin Board where visitors to the Web site can debate the importance of various languages and the best ways to learn them.

Foreign Languages for Travelers

http://www.travlang.com/languages/

To use this site you simply pick which language you speak, which language you want to learn, and what area you want to focus on (names of food, numbers, and so on). You not only see how to spell the foreign words, but you'll hear the proper pronunciation!

Squeal Empire Learn-a-Language

http://www.kaiwan.com/%7Eslayer/squeal/free.html

The Learn-a-Language site contains links to other places on the Web that have full, sophisticated tutorials for more than 40 languages. The owners of this site have checked over each link to make sure that the language tutorial is high quality.

A Web of Online Grammars

http://www.bucknell.edu/~rbeard/grammars.html

If you want a more academic approach to learning a language, try A Web of Online Grammars which has links to online grammar books for over 40 languages, including "dead" languages like Latin. There are also links to online dictionaries, morphologies, and other learning materials.

Animated American Sign Language

http://www.feist.com/~randys/index1.html

This creative and unique Web site teaches the American Sign Language (ASL) by using animated graphics that show you exactly how to move your hands to spell the words. There are also many links to other language resources and articles about the deaf community.

Legal

Lawyers Online International

http://www.global-villages.com/lawyers/

All of us sometimes have legal questions that could be answered rather quickly, and therefore, we don't want to enlist the services of a lawyer who may feel compelled to charge us for his or her time. Well, given the wonderful world of technology, sites such as the Lawyers Online International, home of the Harvard Legal Team are now available to you. You can e-mail this team of attorneys with your legal questions 24 hours a day. Wait, there's more. Other key features of this Web site include a segment on how to select a lawyer and legal news. Some of the legal news topics include the latest Supreme Court decisions and major new Federal legislation. You may also want to check out the Do-It-Yourself legal forms.

West's Legal Directory

http://www.wld.com/

You really don't have to go far to learn about lawyers, law firms, and other legal entities since the West Legal Directory is available to you at the click of a button. If you're an attorney, you can even add your contact information at this site.

Martindale-Hubbell Lawyer Locator

http://www.martindale.com/locator/home.html

Need a lawyer? Looking for a particular law firm? Don't know where to begin your search? The Martindale-Hubbell site is a good resource to start looking. Find comprehensive listings for 900,000 lawyers and law firms around the world.

Yahoo!

http://www.yahoo.com/Business_and_Economy/Companies/Law/

For your convenience, the Yahoo! search engine has a comprehensive directory presented by area of law. For an attorney to handle estate planning, try the Estate and Probate link. If you need an attorney for an International business venture, try the International Law link. A wealth of legal resources at your fingertips!

USA Law Resources

http://www.laws.com/usgen.html

This Legal section has primarily focused on obtaining legal services. However, if you simply want to do some legal research or just find out about different legal organizations, then the USA Law Resources site is the place to be. Check out various law libraries, court opinions, and other legal information.

Libraries

The Library of Congress

http://lcweb.loc.gov/

The most famous library in all of history is the ancient Library of Alexandria. The Library was built to house all the knowledge of mankind, and to be a place where scholars could freely exchange ideas. The Library contained some 400,000 scrolls when it was accidentally destroyed by Julius Caesar in 48 BC. Our modern equivalent is the Library of Congress which contains over 17 million books stored on 532 miles of shelves. It's mission is "to sustain and preserve a universal collection of knowledge and creativity for future generations." The Library of Congress is a research library, which means you cannot wander through the book stacks, and you cannot checkout books—you can, however, view any book in the Library's reading room. You can also use the Web to search their complete catalog listing for detailed information on any book the Library owns.

The New York Public Library

http://www.nypl.org/

The New York Public Library is the largest library in the world where you can actually checkout books and take them home. The research library has many fine exhibits of books and artwork that you can view online.

The Internet Public Library

http://www.ipl.org/

The Internet Public Library has the text of over 12,000 books, magazines, newspapers, and other written material online. You can search by author, title, Dewey decimal number, or topic. They also have some permanent and rotating art and book exhibits.

Pick

http://www.aber.ac.uk/~tplwww/e/history.html

Pick is a Web site devoted to the history of learning, libraries, books, reading, and everything to do with the written word. They have links to library societies and associations and an active mailing list.

Carrie

http://www.ukans.edu/carrie/carrie_main.html

The Carrie electronic library was started in England in 1993. They now have full electronic text for thousands of books, from ancient writers to 19th century poets. The site is very easy to use and contains a wealth of literature.

"M"

Magazines

Pathfinder

http://www.pathfinder.com/

This is easily one of the largest and most well known sites on the Web and certainly the best starting point to explore magazines. Pathfinder is run by Time Warner, publisher of over a dozen of the world's best-known magazines. This site is a central jumping-off point for access to all of their magazines that are available online, including *People*, *Money*, *Time*, *Sports Illustrated*, *Fortune*, and *Life*. In addition to providing links to the magazine the main site itself keeps track of news and current events in many topics. With each of the magazines expect to find, at the very least, headlines and sample stories from the print edition. With most you'll also find additional features such as stories not available in print, daily (or more frequent) updates, and archives of past issues.

Ziff Davis Magazines

http://www.zdnet.com/findit/mags.html

If you love to read the latest news and product reviews that the computer industry has to offer, look no further than ZDNet's magazine page. The is a collection of sites for Ziff Davis's impressive collection of computer magazines including *PC Magazine*, *Computer Life*, *Computer Shopper*, and over a dozen other magazines.

The Electronic Newstand

http://www.enews.com/

If you are looking for a magazine's Web site and can't find it here, it either doesn't exist or isn't worth reading. With links to over 2,000 magazines, this is one of the largest general magazine reference sites there is.

Hearst Magazines

http://www.hearstcorp.com/mag.html

This is another publisher's "super site," this one for the family of Hearst magazines. It includes links to their popular publications including *Cosmopolitan*, *Esquire*, *Good HouseKeeping*, *Popular Mechanics*, and *Redbook*. There's enough variety here to satisfy almost any reader.

National Enquirer

http://www.nationalenquirer.com/

With the incredible circulation that this publication has, it's impossible to leave this section without mentioning it. So, while you won't find all of the stories from this week's issue on their site, you will find enough tibdits to satisfy your craving until you can pick up a copy at the supermarket.

Movies

The Internet Movie Database

http://us.imdb.com/

The Internet Movie Database was one of the very early major sites on the Web that you could actually do something with. It's grown from a humble labor of love to a major force in the online entertainment world. So what's here? Just a completely searchable database of facts and figures for nearly every movie ever made. Not interested in who played the T1000 character in Terminator 2? Are reviews of current theatrical releases and new videos more what you need? They're all here too. And they've got movie and Hollywood news, links to local movie theater schedules, and you can even buy tickets online from participating theaters.

Cinemania

http://cinemania.msn.com/

Microsoft's Cinemania CD-ROM is one of the favorite CD's of many movie fans. On this Web site they've built an online version of the movie database as well as current news and interviews. You'll also find other staples such as local movie times, news, and gossip.

Movie Finder

http://www.moviefinder.com/

If you find yourself constantly missing movies on TV, this site is at least part of the answer. You search their database of movies to find showing times by location. If you don't know exactly what you want to see but you need to find out when a good love story is on, you can search by genre, rating, and other criteria.

MovieLink

http://www.movielink.com/

This site provides a useful way to check movie times for theaters in your area. You can search by city name or zip code to find the theaters and what they are showing. You can order tickets from some of the theaters. The downside is that the number of cities covered is limited. But it's still a great start.

Hollywood Online

http://www.hollywood.com/

You would expect a site about Hollywood to be full of glitz and this doesn't disappoint. In addition to a movie guide, show times, and other standard fare for movie sites, be sure to check out their *Buzz* forums for fun online chat with other movie fans.

Movie Studios

Paramount

http://www.paramount.com/

The major movie studios have all taken to the Web in a big way and Paramount is no exception. Home to blockbuster hits like *Mission Impossible* and the entire series of *Star Trek* movies, this is a fun site to visit for movie fans. Look for sound clips, videos, and even interactive games relating to new releases and to blockbuster favorites. There's a whole additional offshoot of this site for fans of the Star Trek movies. And since Paramount is into television as well, be sure to look for parts of the site related to their great shows including *Duckman* and, of course, the current Star Trek series.

Fox Film

http://www.fox.com/movies.html

Another major studio with a first-class site is Fox. Most of this site centers around current releases so the content here will certainly change by the time you see this. (At least I hope *Speed 2* isn't still current several months from now!) So be sure to check this site often for what's new.

Disney Pictures

http://www.disney.com/DisneyPictures/index.html

This is one that you and your kids will enjoy. There are lots of games and downloadable snippets from many Disney favorites here. (My favorite, *Toy Story*, actually has it's own site and address at **http://www.toystory.com**.) This will provide hours of family fun.

Universal Pictures

http://www.mca.com/universal_pictures/

Universal has certainly had their run of good luck lately with *Liar Liar* and *The Lost World*. At this site, catch up on current as well as coming attractions from this major Hollywood player. You can also check out the syndicated television hits offered by Universal such as *Hercules: The Legendary Journeys* and *Xena, Warrior Princess*.

Warner Bros.

http://www.movies.warnerbros.com/main.html

Warner Brothers was one of the "classic" film studios of the 30s and 40s and is also the home of the cartoon favorite Bugs Bunny and friends. In addition to current movies from Warner Brothers, this site offers links to the part of their site about movies out on home video and the Warner Brothers television offerings on their new network.

Museums

The Metropolitan Museum of Art

http://www.metmuseum.org/

The Metropolitan Museum of Art in New York has over 2 million pieces that span 5,000 years of human culture. The Web site has images and historical notes on thousands of pieces of art from Ancient Egyptian, Greek, Roman, Asian, African, Islamic, and Medieval Europe to more modern Italian Renaissance, Baroque, and the 19th and 20th centuries. You can also use this Web site to visit some of the museums current special exhibits which contain detailed histories, critiques, a timeline, and a glossary of terms to go along with images of the artwork. There is also a link to the Cloisters, a medieval museum located in a beautiful park on the northern side of Manhattan. The Cloisters Web site contains a wide collection of medieval artwork, including the famous Unicorn tapestries.

The Vatican Museum

http://www.christusrex.org/www1/vaticano/0-Musei.html

The Vatican Museum specializes in ancient, medieval, and Renaissance artwork. The Web site contains hundreds of images of Egyptian, Greek, Roman, Etruscan, and Italian Renaissance sculpture; medieval paintings and sculpture; and tapestries, books, and maps.

The Smithsonian Institute

http://www.si.edu/newstart.htm

The Smithsonian Institute in Washington DC owns over 140 million artifacts that are housed in 16 museums and galleries. Getting lost can be a real problem, but not on the Web site. Simply pick a tour that sounds interesting, and the Web site will guide you around the museums.

Museum of Modern Art (MoMA)

http://www.moma.org/

The MoMA is located in New York and specializes in 19th and 20th century art. The museum has over 100,000 paintings, sculptures, and architectural models; 14,000 films; and 120,000 books.

The Rock-and-Roll Hall of Fame and Museum

http://www.rockhall.com/

The Rock-and-Roll Hall of Fame and Museum has built a substantial Web site that shows off some of their great collections. You can listen to songs and read the lyrics, view videos of your favorite rock stars, and watch the footage from when they were inducted. New exhibits arrive all the time, so check back often.

Music

MTV Online

http://www.mtv.com/

The world's first music-video network is online with all the flash and style that comes through televisions worldwide. MTV's site is *the* place for the latest in what's happening in the world of popular music.

Classical Net

http://www.classical.net/

If you want to build your own Classical music library or need help in finding that perfect recording of Mahler's 4th Symphony, Classical Net is the place to go. In addition to this site's extensive resources, there are links to over 2,000 other Classical music related pages.

House of Blues

http://hob.com/

B.B. King and other Blues greats live online at House of Blues Online. This is the ideal place to get the latest Blues news and concert information. There are links that take you to LiveConcerts.com if you want to experience some music right now, or if you'd like get a job at one of the many House of Blues locations around the country.

Sony Music Online

http://www.music.sony.com/

Most of the major record labels have Web pages, usually featuring some of their more popular offerings. Sony Music lets you sample their entire catalog from Classical to Country. Virtual Press conferences let you talk to your favorite recording artists and afterwards you can sample their wares online with Music On Tap.

JAZZ Online

http://www.jazzonln.com/

If you want a laid-back, cool Web page to visit, go to JAZZ Online. You'll get to talk to your favorite Jazz performers, get help in distiguishing the difference between Be-Bop and Swing, and even pick up a few CDs through **JOL@Cdnow** to listen to at home after you've completed your education.

"N"

News

USA Today

http://www.usatoday.com/

Experts predicted *USA Today* would not last long on newsstands when the paper first published in the early 1980s. Not only has it survived and thrived, but now it has a Web site that continues to break news. You'll find the familiar four-colored sections NEWS, SPORTS, MONEY, and LIFE, just like the morning paper but these sections are updated 24 hours a day on the Web. Track your stocks, read up-to-the-minute sports scores, and plan trips with the Travel Extra Bonus Section. Follow weather developments in the special Yellow Weather section. Teachers can enroll in the Classline feature designed to make today's headlines relevant to students. *USA Today* even reports winning lottery numbers for every state that plays to win.

The Washington Post

http://www.washingtonpost.com/

If you want more national and international news than your local paper provides, go to The *Washington Post* for excellent in-depth coverage of the White House, Congress, and the rest of the federal government. Participate in Talk Central with Washington Post reporters and columnists on topics ranging from business, style, technology and, of course, public policy.

MSNBC

http://www.msnbc.com/

This is the Web site associated with the Microsoft/NBC cable channel that is aiming to steal some of CNN's thunder. You'll receive up-to-the minute coverage of sports, news, politics, science, health, and the usual suspects, but you'll also hear audio clips of newsmakers and NBC's star reporters and anchors. You can also join MSNBC chat rooms to sound off on the issues of the day.

USNews Online

http://www.usnews.com/

One of the more substantive news magazines, *U.S. News and World Report* brings the same quality to its Web site. You'll find in-depth coverage of topical national and international news as well as business and technology developments. Don't forget to check out the college and career center, which stores information such as college rankings, financial aid, and career guidance.

Drudge Report

http://www.drudgereport.com/

If you want screaming tabloid headlines, bookmark The Drudge Report. Matt Drudge won't dazzle you with Java applets and animated plug-ins, but he is a "grassroots reporter" who has the New York-Washington DC chattering class talking. Based out of Los Angeles, the Drudge Report scoops the national press sometimes with stories that usually fall into the following categories: politics, Hollywood gossip, technology, and earthquakes (hey, he lives in California). You can even sign-up for his free e-mail updates, which are a hoot. He supplies hotlinks to nearly every major news organization and columnist on the Web today.

"O"

Olympics and Amateur Sports

The Olympic Movement

http://www.olympic.org/

The Olympics are the most watched and participated sporting events there are. The International Olympic Committee has done a topnotch job of presenting their efforts on the Web. This site describes the purpose and mission of the Olympics as well as how they are organized and managed. Sections about the organizing committee's activities and news related to the Olympics are worth a look. And be sure to check out the pages for each of the upcoming game sites for both Winter and Summer games in the next few years.

NCAA Online

http://www.ncaa.org/

Whether you are a sports fan looking for information about any NCAA sanctioned sports or a college-bound student-athlete looking for eligibility and enrollment guidelines, you'll want to check out this site. It make lack a little in flash, but it sure makes up for it with great information.

NJCAA

http://www.njcaa.org/

The NCAA isn't the only collegiate sports governing body. The NJCAA administers the activities of junior college sports. This is a great site that does a nice job providing information about the events and sports sanctioned at it's member schools.

International Amateur Athletic Federation

http://www.iaaf.org/

Track and field is one of the highest profile amateur sports there is. The IAAF is the governing body for this sport and their Web site is the best place to get the latest news from the sport. For each event the site includes descriptions and significant milestones and records.

Team USA

http://www.olympic-usa.org/

The best features of this site are the sport-by-sport descriptions and links to biographies of the 1996 US athletes. If you are looking for Team USA merchandise, it also features an online store full of all your favorite goodies.

Online Games

Internet Gaming Zone

http://www.zone.com/

For years playing games online usually meant hours setting up your modem so you could play Doom with your friend across the country. It was a tedious and expensive proposition at best. Now Microsoft has joined a half dozen other companies to bring you the thrill of playing some of your favorite games over the Internet.

Kali

http://www.kali.net/

Kali is one of the best values on the Internet today. While most online game companies have a "pay per play" policy, Kali has a one-time, $20 registration fee. For $20 you get to play dozens of different games over their network and free upgrades of their software. Some of the games you'll be able to play on Kali include: Diablo, Quake, Duke Nukem 3D, Command and Conquer, and X Wing vs. Tie Fighter.

Total Entertainment Network

http://www.ten.net/

One of the largest online game providers, Total Entertainment Network provides a safe haven where you and your closest friends can blow each other away in games such as Blood. For the less violent among you, NASCAR Racing Online give you the chance to be the next Jeff Gordon. TEN has varying rate plans ranging from five hours per month at $9.95 to unlimited time per month at $19.95.

DWANGO

http://www.dwango.net/

A pioneer in the online gaming industry, DWANGO started out as a network of servers around the country where folks could dial-in and play DOOM and DOOMII. Today, DWANGO is on the Internet with 24 games to choose from including Big Red Racing, Decent, and G-nome.

Engage Games Online

http://www.engage.net/

Engage already provides games to online services such as Compuserve, Prodigy, and America Online. Their selection on the 'net is very extensive, ranging from trivia games to strategy games like Castles II to shooting games like Shattered Steel. Engage has a no monthly subscription fee, you pay only for the time you spend playing a game.

"P"

Parenting

ParentSoup

http://www.parentsoup.com/

We all grow up with chicken noodle soup, vegetable soup, and alphabet soup. Did you ever imagine such a thing as "parent soup?" Well, neither did I, but this site, Parent Soup, truly leaves a warm feeling in your heart just as the above-mentioned favorites left a warm feeling in your young tummy. Join this group of parents over a cup of coffee to share joy and laughter, words of wisdom, and love at "the neighborhood's favorite kitchen table." You're sure to have peace of mind about your parenting woes after spending time chatting with some of the other members of this popular site. In addition to taking the opportunity to ask questions of other parents, you can also share your perspective on parenting. It's a great way to learn what others like yourself are doing in the world of parenting, and to meet people and make friends.

Parenthood Web

http://www.parenthoodweb.com/

Find out information on a variety of topics at the Parenthood Web site's pick-of-the-week topics. To name a few, there may be topics on children's health or behavioral issues, early childhood mental and physical development, or even family-related matters. Be adventurous.

babyonline

http://www.babyonline.com/main.html

Check out comprehensive information on pregnancy, parenting, prenatal, postnatal, and other related issues. Take the virtual tour of the site to discover the various offerings you could have access to as a member of the site. Also, take advantage of such information as updates on the best baby products currently available to consumers.

ParentsPlace.com

http://www.parentsplace.com/

Welcome to a place you can call your own. Well, sort of. This site offers information on topics like children's health, pregnancy, and family fun and activities. You can't go wrong with a pit stop to ParentsPlace.com. You're sure to learn something or teach something to someone else during a chat session with other parents.

Disney's FAMILY.COM

http://www.family.com/Categories/Parenting/

Everybody loves Disney! Well, almost. Check out this site, which provides information on topics of interest to old parents and new parents alike. So what exactly do you do to prevent spoiling your child? If you "spare the rod," does that impact your child's disposition? Find the answers to this and other current parenting topics.

Personal Finance

Money Online

http://www.pathfinder.com/money/

Looking for information on personal finance. Check out the *Money Magazine* Web site to get everything you need to enhance and improve your personal finances. If you're into the stock market, Money can tell you about the status of the Dow Jones Index and other financial markets. Learn to establish a personal investment portfolio. Also, get some help with setting financial goals for college savings, home purchasing, retirement planning, savings and borrowing, and managing your taxes. Other great features of this Web site include a wealth of information on various companies, savings and investment opportunities, and financial news. In addition to learning about some of the best places to live in America, you can also obtain advice from Money's editors.

Consumer Credit Counseling

http://www.pe.net/market/cccs/

It may be difficult to budget your money. You can get help through the Consumer Credit Counseling Service. Manage your debt by consolidating your bills in a single monthly payment with lower interest rates. The best part is that you can learn to use cash, instead of credit, and balance your personal budget effectively.

The Personal Finance Mailing List

http://www.bcs.org/Groups/cad/personal_finance.html

If you're having difficulty managing your finances, the Personal Finance Mailing List is a good networking tool for you. Get online with experts such as financial planners, accountants, and attorneys to get solid, applicable advice. Credit card usage, debt management, and estate planning are a few topics you can learn about.

BizWeb Personal Finance

http://www.bizweb.com/keylists/finance.personal.html

This is a great tool for finding financial information resources to meet your every need. For example, check out the Center for Financial Independence, which presents financial performance ideas and tools, and provides assistance for businesses and individuals. You may also be interested in the Cyber CPA for free tax- and financial-planning services.

CNN Financial Network

http://www.cnnfn.com/

Your personal finance directory is incomplete without the CNN Financial Network. Get stock quotes and pricing and performance data on mutual funds. Visit the Reference Desk for government resource connections like the Federal Finance Information Network and the Small Business Administration. Don't miss the Web Connection for credit and tax information, and emerging business resources.

Politics

Roll Call Online

http://www.rollcall.com/

"Hill Rats" who can't get enough of Congress go to Roll Call's Web site to share in its insiders' reporting on Capitol Hill. Roll Call takes you behind the usual headlines to what is really going on behind closed doors in the House of Representatives and Senate. Get a ringside seat on who is fighting whom (often within the same political party) for power. You'll find news scoops, commentary, policy briefings, and other roll-call files.

The Republican Party

http://www.republicanweb.com/

If you want the party line, come to the Republican Party cyber-headquarters to get the latest in GOP strategy, issue papers, and news on GOP activities in your state. You can also join the political discussion chats and link to other conservative Web sites.

The Democratic Party

http://www.democrats.org/

Well, this is not much different from the Republican Web site (is there much difference between the two *parties*, either?). You'll find press releases, news, how to get active in the Party, and links to other liberal Web sites.

free-market.com

http://www.free-market.com/

A pro-free-enterprise site containing public policy discussions such as "Privatizing Social Security" and the role of government in a free society. Download "freedom" images to add to your Web page. Follow links to other libertarian pages and sign up for the free e-mail update: "The Daily Outragem," a brief update highlighting bureaucratic follies and government corruption.

Turn Left

http://www.turnleft.com/

Liberals should flock here to learn tactics in "fighting the right" as well as take part in interactive newsgroups. Read policy papers and follow links to other liberal magazines and pundits.

"R"

Radio

Timecast

http://www.timecast.com/

Half a century ago our grandparents gathered around the radio and listened to President Franklin Roosevelt's fireside chats, heard reports from WWII battlefields, and listened to shows like *The Shadow*. Now you can do the same thing while using your computer. With the ingenious Real Audio Web browser plug-in (**http://www.realaudio.com/**), you can listen to live sporting events and concerts, as well as archived shows right from your cozy computer room or laptop. For the *TV Guide* of radio programming, go to TIMECAST. This handy viewer's guide has links to live programming, news briefings from ABC, FOX, and others, as well as a directory organized by topics much like Yahoo!.

NetRadio

http://www.netradio.net/

NetRadio specializes in over a hundred music and information links ranging from jazz, classical music, celebrity news, vintage rock, and New Age music. Don't forget to whip out your wallet and go to Valuevision, which is NetRadio's version of the home shopping network.

CNET Radio

http://www.news.com/Radio/?ctb.radio

If you want the latest scoop on the latest Web browser beta from Netscape and Microsoft, Apple's latest operating system, and other computer industry news, then aim your browser at CNET Radio. You can listen to daily industry reports, live reports from shows like Comdex, as well as seminars. Most of these reports are archived for easy access.

Atlantic Broadcasting System

http://www.abslive.com/

An incredibly in-depth site for financial market junkies. You'll get live updates every half hour on the NYSE, NASDAQ, and the Chicago Futures Pits. Expert analysts will also give you the inside scoop on market ups and downs. You can also sign up for the free e-mail market updates.

LiveConcerts.com

http://www.liveconcerts.com/

Forget about listening to your favorite group's CDs or listening to tunes on a FM station, go to the liveconcerts lobby and find out which bands are playing live! Listen to interviews with your favorite performers and if you happen to miss a live show, the site contains archives so you don't miss a thing.

Religion

The Vatican

http://www.vatican.va/

One of the most intriguing sites on the Web in *any* category, "The Holy See" is a well-designed blending of the traditional Roman Catholic experience and modernity. This site uses a clever, hidden, three-frame layout available in English, French, German, Italian, Latin, Polish, Portuguese, and Spanish. Completely searchable, you can research papal history and documents, hear the latest news from Rome and view historic art from the Vatican in a seamless, easy-to-navigate interface. Remember, where there is love, there is hope—and where there is link, there is Pope.

Gospel Communications Network

http://www.gospelcom.net/

The multilingual and meta-searchable Bible Gateway is just one of dozens of GCN's member ministries. Other affilated sites range from Arab World Ministries and The Calvinist Cadets to The Fellowship Of Christian Magicians and Christian Computing Magazine. All these resources make this site practically omnipotent!

BuddhaNet

http://www2.hawkesbury.uws.edu.au/BuddhaNet/

The path to enlightenment never had so many worldwide connections—and you won't have to meditate while you wait for it to load. This interactive site will enable you to chat with other Buddhists; study Karma art; Buddhist art, and architecture; read in-depth articles, and practice meditation techniques—there is even a page for kids. The site's graphics are clean and quick, too.

JCN (Jewish Communication Network)

http://www.jcn18.com/

With an interactive Torah study, daily feature stories and news, an online mall, Jewish personals, and an excellent site-review page to locate other Jewish Web sites. JCN is a one-stop online hub on the Web for Judaism.

435

Spirit-WWW

http://www.spiritweb.org/

In addition to channeling, you can explore new and modern religious concepts in detail, including altered states of consciousness, reincarnation, yoga, and theosophy among others. The site also includes an image gallery with 15 different categories of images, from "animals" to "vedic deity."

"S"

Searching the Web

Yahoo!

www.yahoo.com

At some point you'll want to find something on the Web that isn't listed in this book and that you won't find by following a link from another page. That's when you'll turn to a directory or search page to find things on the Web. Probably the best known of these is Yahoo!. Yahoo! isn't the biggest, but it is one of the best. Yahoo! has a huge directory style list of categories with hundreds of thousands of Web sites listed. If you are looking for a Web site about a certain topic, this is a great place to start. To use Yahoo!, just click a link for one of the category topics and this will open a page with a list of subcategories and Web pages for that topic.

Excite

www.excite.com

While Yahoo! is based mainly on a directory of sites that are handpicked and entered into categories, Excite is a huge database of sites that you can search. Excite has an automated program that visits Web pages and catalogues them into a database. When you search Excite, it may return a list of hundreds or even thousands of sites that match your topic.

Lycos

www.lycos.com

Lycos is another site that runs off a huge (10's of millions) database of Web pages that it has automatically searched and indexed. Type in what you want to look for and click search. All of the sites like Lycos and Excite return long lists of possibly macthing sites with the most likely matches first.

HotBot

www.hotbot.com

There are dozens of these sites that act as databases of Web sites. Everyone who uses the Web a lot has a personal favorite. HotBot is mine. I make a living knowing about the Internet and the Web, and this site is always helpful to me when I need to find something.

SuperSeek

www.mcp.com/superseek/index.cgi

With so many search sites on the Web, you may wish there was just one place you could go to search them all. In fact, there are several of them including SuperSeek. Type what you want to find at the SuperSeek site and it searches several other search sites for you and returns results from all of them.

Shopping

America's Choice Mall

http://www.choicemall.com/indexnl.html

America's Choice Mall is an exciting place to shop with over 1,300 stores and services from which to choose. If you're shopping for a doctor or dentist, or if you're shopping for clothes, this is a good place to start. You can begin your search by region at the 60 regional malls. The stores are also listed by category. Other great features of this site include customer contests, shopping sprees, and even reviews for the latest movies. If you're looking to buy or sell a home, you can even do a bit of real estate shopping at this site.

World Shopping Directory

http://worldshopping.com/director.html

Why limit yourself to shopping at the local malls, or even to shopping in the Continental United States? Shop online and you can shop the world. The World Shopping Directory can take you virtually anywhere at any time, and you never have to leave the house.

Access Market Square

http://www.icw.com/ams.html

Access Market Square is great place for your every shopping need from clothes, jewelry, and specialty products to audio/video, toys, and finance. This site has claimed more than nine awards as a top shopping site. Be sure to check out the World Trade Center classifieds and business opportunities while you're visiting.

The Internet Mall

http://www.internet-mall.com/

This is truly the world's largest shopping mall with over 27,000 stores. Choose from items such as books and media, travel, household items, personal services, professional services, and much more.

The All-Internet Shopping Directory

http://www.all-internet.com/

If you're shopping for something, but nothing in particular, the All-Internet Shopping Directory is a good place to begin your journey. This directory has connections to anything and everything you're looking for with it's extensive database search tools.

Software

Download.com

http://www.download.com/

The Internet is home to thousands of pieces of software that you can download and use for free. Some, you try and pay for if you keep (shareware). Others are free for as long as you use

438

them (freeware). Download.com is one of the biggest directories of downloadable software on the Web. If you want to look for software for almost any use, this is the place to start. Software is sorted by application category and by operating system, which makes it very easy to find the software you need. The site also includes reviews and ratings as well as lists of the most frequently downloaded programs.

Microsoft

http://www.microsoft.com/

Come to this site to get the latest news about any Microsoft software product. You can download many free products including the Internet Explorer Web browser and download updates and extras for other popular programs like the Microsoft Office suite of applications and Windows.

Netscape

http://home.netscape.com/

This is the home of the Netscape Web browser, which made this company famous in record time. Read about their other products and services here. You can buy copies of their software online or download them for a free trial.

Stroud's Consummate Winsock Apps

http://cws.internet.com/

This is another site listing hundreds of pieces of software that you can download. This site specializes in software for use with the Internet such as browsers, plug-ins, and add-ons. Stroud has been reviewing Internet software as long as anyone and this is considered to be one of the best lists around.

Symantec

http://www.symantec.com/

Symantec is the company that makes the popular Norton anti-virus software. Stop by their site to download monthly updates for your virus definitions to keep your PC virus free. You'll also want to read about their Norton Secret Stuff program for keeping email private and download it for free.

Space

NASA (National Aeronautics and Space Administration)

http://www.nasa.gov/

You shouldn't be too surprised that the world's oldest and largest active space agency has not only a Web site but a comprehensive one at that, possibly the most comprehensive site on the Web. The site has almost as many links as the night sky has stars, including an immense number of downloadable movies, images, and sounds. All of NASA's latest missions are updated daily, including countdowns to shuttle launchings, and their well-honed site design will have you light-clicking your way through as you explore areas like Aeronautics, Space Science, Human Space Flight, and Education.

Hubble Space Telescope

http://www.stsci.edu/

In addition to the latest Hubble Telescope pictures, you can track the current position of the telescope, view live video from its video components, and explore highly technical, as well as more viewer-friendly research about Hubble and how it works.

The Nine Planets

http://seds.lpl.arizona.edu/nineplanets/nineplanets/nineplanets.html

Currently mirrored on 37 different sites in over 30 countries, The Nine Planets guides you through the history, mythology, and science behind each of the planets and moons in our solar system. Images and comprehensive technical data download quickly so you won't have to wait and many of the pages have sounds, movies, and a complete set of links to related information.

The Planetary Society

http://planetary.org/

Become a voluntary space explorer, read daily headlines, find out about conferences, sign up for workshops, and keep up with the Mars Pathfinder spacecraft mission. Founded in 1980 by Drs. Carl Sagan, Bruce Murray, and Louis Friedman this site focuses on the exploration of our solar system and the search for extraterrestrial life.

The Deep Space Network

http://deepspace1.jpl.nasa.gov/dsn/

Managed and operated for NASA by the Jet Propulsion Laboratory, this site will take you to the heart of interplanetary spacecraft missions, such as the Galileo mission to Jupiter and its moons and the Cassini mission to Saturn and its moon Titan. The DSN page supports the international network of antennas that makes it all possible.

Sports News

ESPNet SportsZone

http://espnet.sportszone.com/

Fans of all sports will want to make "The Zone" one of their first bookmarks. If you are looking to catch up and keep up on all the scores, they've got it with a constantly updated scoreboard with all the scores of games and events in progress. (You can even put it on your desktop so that you don't have to keep their Web page open.) But this site is about more than just scores. All the sports news, all the inside scoop, interviews with players and coaches, its all here. But I don't need to tell you that. If you watch ESPN on TV, you know they are the leader in television sports and their Web site is *en fuego* too!

The Sporting News

http://www.sportingnews.com/

The Sporting News is the definitive sports paper for serious sports fans. The site offers a lot of the same type of content as ESPN, but all with a different flavor. So if you just can't get enough sports, or prefer a different style, check out the Sporting News.

CBS SportsLine

http://cbs.sportsline.com/

CBS Sports on TV and radio hosts some of the premier sporting events in the world including the NCAA Men's Basketball Championships. Their Web site draws from their long time experience with some of the Web broadcasters and reporters in the game to bring you scores, stories, fantasy sports leagues, and more.

Sports Illustrated

http://cnnsi.com/

Yes, they have some shots from the swimsuit issue here but that's not what this site is about. When you are looking for a site that goes beyond the headlines and scores, SI Online is a great choice. The in depth style of the magazine is preserved in this first class online site.

Audio Net Sports Guide

http://www.audionet.com/sports/

With the right additional software installed (and you can get it here) you can listen to almost any major sporting event on your PC from the links at this site. It no longer matters that your favorite team's games don't make it to where you live, you can bring them home live with AudioNet.

stock quotes

The Nasdaq Stock Market Home Page

http://www.nasdaq.com/

Nasdaq's Web site lets you research and track not only the over-the-counter stocks that are traded on the Nasdaq exchange, but also stocks traded on the New York and American exchanges. You can search for up to 10 separate stocks or mutual funds to gauge their daily performance. The Nasdaq 100's performance is updated constantly during the day so you can see the market's performance at a glance.

PC Quote Online

http://www.pcquote.com/

PC Quote is one of the few sites that display all the major market indices at a glance and with a click of your mouse button you can watch their progress through a trading day. If you're an Office97 user, you can use PC Quotes modules built into Excel97 to track up to 20 different stocks.

The American Stock Exchange

http://www.amex.com/

While not as comprehensive as some of the other stock quote sites, The American Stock Exchange offers a useful Dictionary of Financial Risk Management. This is invaluable resource, provides essential tips for anyone trading securities whether they be a bull or a bear. The site also provides charts tracking the exchange's performance, offers up to the minute financial news and offers career options for professional traders.

NETworth Quote Server

http://quotes.quicken.com/investments/quotes/

A service offered though Quicken FN, the NETWorth quote server works with your Quicken software to track investments and initiate trades. For those of you without a copy of Quicken, the site offers a quick look into your stocks performance as well as some handy information about investment basics and other resources to help you make informed investment decisions.

CNNfn-Quote Search Service

http://cnnfn.com/markets/quotes.html

Drawing on the vast resources of CNN, the CNNfn Stock Quote service offers instant quotes of any stock, mutual, or money market fund regardless of on which exchange they're traded. After you've received your quotes, click on the CNNfn logo to get the latest in business news.

"T"

Taxes

The IRS

http://www.irs.ustreas.gov/

This is a site you almost have to see to believe. The same folks who give us beautiful and fun literature like the 1040 and Schedule C can't be responsible for a truly great Web site. Right? But they are. The IRS has shed its stodgy pain-inflicting image and built a Web site that actually helps taxpayers. There are tax tips and hints from the real masters themselves, all of the current year's forms online in a format you can download and print for use (you'll need to install the free Adobe Acrobat plug-in for your Web browser to use any of these), and much more. But beyond that, the site is actually fun, well presented, and has a sense of humor. This should be every taxpayer's first stop on the Web.

SecureTax

http://www.securetax.com/

This site takes the concept of Tax software one step further by making it all Web-based and online. You fill out all of your tax forms online, check them, and then, if you want to send the return to the IRS, pay a small fee and submit it. I used it this year and it was fast, accurate, and cheaper than any tax software I've seen.

1040.com

http://www.1040.com/

You'll want to bookmark this site if for no other reason than their links to all of the state tax forms and instructions online. In addition, there is a good variety of tax help and advice.

Tax Help Online

http://www.taxhelponline.com/

When it comes to tax tips and advice, my philosophy is that the more you can find out, the better off you are. So here's another site with a good collection of tips and advice for preparing your return, avoiding problems, and paying as little as is legal.

TaxWeb

http://www.taxweb.com/

If you still haven't found enough tax help, TaxWeb is one more good place to look. And they have a list of links to other sites with even more help for federal and state taxes. If the answer to your tax questions exists, you'll find it at one of these sites.

Teaching

Teachnet

http://www.teachnet.com/

This is a site with lots of class: the lesson plans and ideas in Art, Music, Language Arts, Math, Science, Social Studies, Physical Education, and even the Internet itself are well worth the field trip. But there's much more to learn: gain ideas on how to fill up five minutes of empty classroom time, get help with decorating your classroom, and find techniques for better class organization and management. An active forum for teachers and news about current events affecting teachers will keep you informed between bells, too.

PedagoNet

http://www.pedagonet.com/

PedagoNet gives you instant access to learning resource materials in over 50 subjects—and you can post your own to share with other teachers. The site also has active chat and discussion areas.

Teachers.net

http://www.teachers.net/

Like over 14,000 other teachers before you, you can create your own Web page with The Teachers.Net Homepage Maker, in addition to a chatboard, lesson exchange board, and a fully functioning reference desk which has online links to dictionaries, maps, calculators, encyclopedias, and more.

NSTA (National Science Teachers Association)

http://www.nsta.org/scistore/

The best in science education materials (over 300 products reviewed according to NSTA standards) are available to you through the Science Store for grades K-6, 5-9, and 9-College. Titles are indexed by subject, alphabetically, and you can search for a specific product.

Math Forum Elementary Teachers' Place

http://forum.swarthmore.edu/teachers/elem/

For grade school teachers this site has brainteasers, math problems, and math projects to help you keep the subject exciting (and not so hard), as well as a new math problem every week. You can also browse a special career area (in case those puzzles and projects don't do the trick) that includes links to workshops, discussion groups, publications and professional organizations.

TV Networks

NBC.com

http://www.nbc.com/

NBC.com is a "must-see-TV" Web site rich in graphics yet surprisingly easy to download. The site contains direct links to MSNBC Online News and NBC Sports sites, a homepage layout similar to a magazine cover with featured links, and a directory of important links within the site, such as online programs with information about the show and excerpts. You can shop, search, send e-mail, check out a site map, and even chat. NBC.com is effective in using their brand recognition to attract your attention by using recognizable marketing slogans (such as "must-see-TV"), the network mascot, the NBC peacock, and music also used in their television network promos.

ABC

http://www.abc.com/

The ABC site provides more comprehensive coverage of their programming, focusing on the prime-time line-up, spotlighting individual programs, and providing new season previews. The homepage changes daily, featuring a specific show that airs that particular day. The site also includes a gallery of candid photos of network celebrities.

FOX

http://www.fox.com/

The Fox site gives you instant access to updates of special programming, new video releases, movies, television listings, and history. The most impressive part of the site is Fox Interactive, which uses Shockwave to take you on an interactive adventure and show you excerpts of your favorite episodes.

CBS

http://www.cbs.com/

CBS presents an eye-catching directory on its homepage, which makes it easy for you to find updates of CBS News, CBS Sports, The CBS Store, Daytime, CBS Kids, Specials, Primetime, and the popular program, *The Lateshow with David Letterman*, and a featured in-depth news report (*The Class of 2000*). You can use the RealAudio Player to hear the CBS theme, catch movie reviews, and go to the David Letterman link to see famous Top Ten Lists.

PBS

http://www.pbs.com/

The PBS site will take you on electronic field trips and help you find teacher connections. You can also find instructional television, adult learning, and a business channel. Since PBS is well known for its excellent children's programming, you won't be surprised to see the several links dedicated to its most popular children's shows, such as *Sesame Street*, *Mr. Rogers*, and *Shining Time Station*.

"u"

UFOs

SETI Institute

http://www.seti-inst.edu/

Are we alone in the Universe? The SETI (Search for ExtraTerrestrial Intelligence) Institute's Web site wants to help you answer that question with in-depth articles and details on the exisistence (or lack thereof) of extraterrestrial life; up-to-the-minute reports of signals from Pioneer 6, Pioneer 10, and Voyager 2 spacecrafts; and an online version of the SETI Newsletter.

Ufomind

http://www.ufomind.com/

Greatly evolved from its beginnings a couple of years ago as the The Desert Rat, this site is one of the most comprehensive and critical sources of UFO information on the Web, including definitive coverage of Area 51 that won't leave you stranded in the New Mexico desert. You'll click for days just to get through the site's Master UFO Index, an exhaustive link structure leading to practically every UFO site on the Web with over 1,896 links and 322 people.

The Enterprise Mission

http://www.enterprisemission.com/

UFO researcher Richard Hoagland's brainchild, The Enterprise Mission, contains a wealth of information about NASA's official (and unofficial) investigations (and denials) of the UFO phenomenon. You can study the the face on Mars, the mystery of Europa, and moon artifacts, as well as the latest NASA and UFO conspiracy theory in detail.

Sightings

http://www.scifi.com/sightings/

Post your own paranormal experiences (and read others), listen to Sightings on the Radio six nights a week via RealAudio, and follow the show itself (from the SciFi Channel) with weekly news about UFO's, ghosts, reincarnation, and everything eerie.

"W"

Weather

Intellicast

http://www.intellicast.com/

The Web is a great place to get all kinds of weather and meteorological information, and one of the best sites around is Intellicast. Intellicast is easy to navigate and has clear maps that are updated frequently from a variety of satellites, seismographs, and Doppler radar data. More adventurous, scientific types looking for hard-core meteorological data should check out the Space Science and Engineering Center listed on the following page. Intellicast enables you to zoom in on any part of the world to get detailed current weather conditions and anticipated low and high temperatures. Want more? Check out where the jetstream is, get a surface analysis, or get a 24- to 48-hour forecast. If you're a real weather buff, check out the Dr. Dewpoint section, which has articles on a variety of topics from summaries of past weather patterns to the effects of sunspots on global temperatures.

The Weather Channel

http://www.weather.com/

Cable TV's Weather Channel sponsors this Web site. It has clear, accessible weather maps and forecasts, but the thing that separates it from the rest is that travelers can check to see if their flights are delayed anywhere due to weather.

Space Science and Engineering Center

http://www.ssec.wisc.edu/

The University of Wisconsin at Madison sponsors this site, and it's not for the weak of heart. If you're tired of pretty pictures and want preciptable water vapor levels, lifting indexes, cloud top pressure, and need to distinguish among temperature, dewpoint temperature, and sea surface temperature, look here.

Weather Imagery and Data

http://urbanite.com/web/imagery/home.htm

Like many of the weather Web sites, Weather Imagery and Data gives you a quick and easy snapshot of temperatures and weather around the world. What sets this site apart is that it enables you to check current tornado and severe thunderstorm warnings, and view recent seismological data.

The Weather Shops

http://www.intellicast.com/wxshops/

Want to understand more about weather or try your hand at forecasting? The Weather Shops has everything you need, from books and videos, to all kinds of instruments and gauges for measuring weather.

Weddings

Island Weddings

http://www.rsabbs.com/islandweddings/

Paradise Island, Disney World, Barbados, and Puerto Rico are a few places that make your mouth water and your heart melt when you think of beginning your happy wedding bliss there. Take a trip with In the Mood to Cruise and check out the beautiful locations where you could have your special day. Your every wish could come true if you just believe and dare to venture into the unknown and never-before imaginable. Don't be afraid to leap into adventure, romance, and everlasting memories for your wedding endeavor. You should enjoy your day and be able to cherish it for a lifetime. In the Mood to Cruise can help you get there with careful planning and consulting expertise. Give them a try and you could be one of the couples you see in these pictures.

Wedding Tips

http://www.weddingtips.com/wttips.html

If you need assistance with your wedding plans, Wedding Tips Online is a great place to start your search. They provide a wealth of resources from photography, to entertainment, to wedding and reception sites, to beauty tips. Don't miss out.

Wedding Experts

http://www.weddingexperts.com/

The Wedding Experts National Bridal Service can provide for your every need. Don't waste any time getting to them for bridal fashions, jewelry, accessories, and more. While you're there, take time to listen to the music to which you'll soon be marching down the aisle.

Bride's Do-It-Yourself Wedding Planners

http://www.horncreek.com/winmark/

You can plan your own wedding and save yourself a great deal of money. I planned my own wedding and established my own budget for what I wanted to spend and how to spend it. I came out $7,000.00 cheaper than many of my friends. Don't be shy, see what this site has to offer.

Nation-Wide Services

http://www.bridalnet.com/states/nation_wide.htm

Don't feel limited in any way when you can take advantage of these nationwide wedding services. Your wedding plans are at your finger tips at the click of a button.

Wine

Wine Spectator

http://www.winespectator.com/

Wine Spectator magazine sponsors this extensive Web site devoted to all aspects making and enjoying wine. The Web site is updated daily—in the Daily Report section you'll find a featured wine, news of the wine industry, a thought-provoking question or short editorial, and live stock updates. The Wine Library contains articles from *Wine Spectator* dating back to the beginning of 1994, and an excellent introduction to buying, storing, serving, and enjoying all types of wine. In the Wine Forums you can participate in scheduled chats with industry experts and post topics for discussion. Traveling soon or looking for a restaurant near you that serves good wine? Checkout the Travel and Dining sections. The Events section lists wine tastings, exhibits, and auctions around the world.

UC Davis Department of Viticulture and Enology

http://wineserver.ucdavis.edu/VEN5b.HTML

The University of California-Davis has the best program in the US for learning the art of making wine. The information on this Web site will give you a great start down the road towards making your own vino.

World Wine Web

http://www.winevin.com/

The World Wine Web site is a comprehensive wine encyclopedia that contains information about all the areas around the world that make wine. You get maps of the countries, lists of the varieties or appellations they produce, the types of grapes they use, and links to wineries in the area.

Winebid.com

http://www.winebid.com/

If you can't travel to New York, California, or France at the drop of a hat but still want to have a shot at obtaining a premium wine, then check out Winebid.com. They have monthly auctions featuring a variety of fine wines.

Virtual Vineyards

http://www.virtualvineyard.com/

Virtual Vineyards was one of the first wine stores on the Web and it has grown substantially in the last few years. Not only do they carry a wide selection of wines, but they also have books, glasses, bottle openers, and every other accessory you need.

"V"

Video Games

VideoGameSpot

http://www.videogamespot.com/

If there's one place on the Web to get the latest scoop on the latest video game releases it's VideoGameSpot. An offshoot of the Ziff-Davis' popular GameSpot site, VideoGameSpot offers the die-hard platform gamer with news, tips, tricks and previews for games available on the popular video-game platforms including Sony PlayStation and Nintendo64.

BradyGAMES Strategy Guides

http://www.bradygames.com/

The homepage of one of the leading publishers of video and computer game strategy guides offers more than just an advertisement for their books. At the BradyGAMES Web site, gamers can find an extensive library of cheat codes for all video game platforms. Oh, and if you see something you like, you can even buy one of their books in their online bookstore.

Next Generation

http://www.next-generation.com/

If you still crave more video game news after visiting VideoGameSpot, point your browser to the online version of *Next Generation Magazine*. Each day *Next Generation* has the latest game industry news, plenty of video clips to see what's coming up, and links to *NextGeneration's* sister magazines. There's plenty here to keep the most ardent gamer happy.

Playstation Homepage

http://www.playstation.com/

Sony's page in support of their popular PlayStation video game system is more than just a billboard for their product. You can get information about existing and upcoming games and get codes to help you past some of those rough spots. There's also detailed information about their NetYaroze program that will let you create your own PlayStation games.

Nintendo Power Source

http://www.nintendo.com/

Named for their magazine, Nintendo's home page is home to Mario, Luigi, Donkey Kong, and everything you want to know about games for the classic Super Nintendo Entertainment System and the increasingly popular Nintendo64. You'll find tips to popular games, like Super Mario 64 and preview of upcoming Nintendo offerings.

Index

Symbols

\ (backslash, directory names), 72
/ (forward slash, directory names), 72
1-800-U.S. Search Web site, 392
1040.com Web site, 444
128-bit
    encryption, breaking, 53
    software
        downloading, 53-54
        exporting, 53
3-D
    images
        scanning, 10
        VRML, 99
        WWW, 99
    plug-ins, 99
    viewers, 99
3270 software (telnet), 260-262
60 Greatest Conspiracies of All Time Web site, 385

A

ABC Web site, 446
Access Market Square Web site, 438
accessing
    Archie, 188-197
    dial-in direct connections, 15
    directories (Archie), 190
    Gopher
        browsers, 201
        servers, 202
    Internet
        altruism, 192
        availability, 9
        methods, 12
        online services, 15
accounts
    acquiring, Internet, 14
    command-line, 19
    costs, 333
    e-mail, 46
        account names, 26
        POP (HTML mail), 46
    types, 14
Active Desktop
    availability, 128
    channels, adding, 128-132
ActiveX, 91-94
Acupuncture Web site, 365
addiction (Center for On-Line Addiction), 281
adding
    channels to Active Desktop, 128-132
    information to FTP site manager, 182
    text to Web pages, 112
address books (e-mail), 38
addresses
    e-mail, 25-26
        Internet addresses, 31-32
        retaining, 297
    Gopher, typing, 202
    LISTSERV, 162-169
    types, 5
    VON, 236-240
ADSL connections, 340
AK-Mail Web site, 25
alcohol Web sites (beer), 371-372
Algy's Herb Page Web site, 403
aliases, 38
All About Beer Online Web site, 371
All-Internet Shopping Directory Web site, 438
alt. groups, reading, 145
ALT.SMOKERS.CIGARS FAQ Web site, 383
alternative medicine Web sites, 363-365
Alternative Medicine Digest Web site, 364
Amazon.com Web site, 373
America Online, see AOL
American Botanical Council Web site, 404
American Stock Exchange Web site, 443
America's Choice Mall Web site, 437
anchor tags ((HTML), 115-116
Animal Species Web site, 366
Animals, Animals Web site, 366
animated icons, 89-94
Animated American Sign Language Web site, 416
animations, 101
anonymous, 294
    FTP (File Transfer Protocol), 173
    remailers, 285
    posting messages, 285
AOL (America Online), 13
    chat, 214-227
    services, 13
applications
    Java Web sites, 90
    renting, Internet, 91

Archie
accessing, 188-197
client/server, 188-197
clients
acquiring, 193
browsers, 189
commands
e-mail, 197
servers, 196
directories, accessing, 190
e-mail, 194-195
forms, 189
gateways, 189
mail, 188
options, 191-197
searching
cancelling, 190
descriptions, 196
methods, 189
procedures, 189
speed, 189
types, 192-197
whatis, 196
servers
finding, 195
types, 195-197
services, 11
Web sites, 189
archives
files, 247-252
self-extracting, 249-252
shareware, 6
software, Internet, 5, 328
telnet programs, 254
Art Bell Web site, 386
Art History Resources on
the Web Web site, 405
articles, 149
Ask Dr. Weil Web site, 363
Ask the Dietitian Web
site, 402
AskEric Web site, 390
ASPCA Web site, 365
associations, 311
Atlantic Broadcasting System
Web site, 434
attachments, newsgroups
displaying, 153
overview, 152
procedures, 152-155
Audio Net Sports Guide Web
site, 442
authoring Web pages, 93-94
auto racing Web sites,
366-367
automation, FTP (File
Tranfer Protocol), 173
automobile Web sites,
375-376

AutoSeek Web site, 376
AutoVantage Web site, 375
avatars Web site chats, 218
images, scanning, 10
setting up, 220
see also chats

B

babyonline Web site, 430
backgrounds, saving, 78
backlash (Internet), 317
backslash (directory
names), 72
BackWeb push Web
sites, 130
Baseball Statsweb Web
site, 368
baseball Web sites, 367-368,
388-389
basketball Web sites, 369-370
BBSs (bulletin board systems),
134
beauty Web sites, 370-371
Beauty Spot Web site, 370
beer Web sites, 371-372
Beer Info Source Web
site, 371
Berlitz World Web site, 415
Better Home & Gardens Web
site, 399
Better Homes and Gardens
Home Improvement Web
site, 410
BinHex, 35
BizWeb Personal Finance Web
site, 432
bookmarks
features, 62
Gopher, 203
searching, 273
URLs (Uniform resource
Locators), finding, 117
windows, 63
books, 311
Web sites, 372-374
BookWire Web site, 372
Boolean operators, Gopher,
206-210
BradyGAMES Strategy Guides
Web site, 453
breaking encryption
(128-bit), 53
Brew Your Own Web
site, 372
BrewCrafters Web site, 372
breWorld Web site, 372

Bride's Do-It-Yourself Wedding
Planners Web site, 451
Britannica Online Web
site, 391
browsers
Archie clients, 189
buttons, displaying, 60
choosing, 59-68
documents
searching, 191
viewing, 4
file formats, handling, 95
FTP (File Transfer
Protocol)
copying information,
181
disadvantages, 180-185
incorporating, 174
Gopher, accessing, 201
graphics, 67-68
HTML files, opening, 71
market share
Microsoft, 58
Netscape Navigator, 57
multiple windows, opening,
70-71
paragraphs, 116
saving Web items, 77-79
search sites, 269-274
security, 85
servers, choosing, 61
shortcut menus, 77
types, 58
URLs (Uniform Resource
Locators), entering,
64, 66-68
viewers, 96
Web pages, displaying, 60
browsing directories, 272
BuddhaNet Web site, 435
bulletin board systems,
see BBSs
business
Internet, 304
selling, 292
starting an ISP, 300
ventures, 292
buttons
displaying, 60
Refresh, 112

C

clnet Web site, 384
cable connections, 339
caches, 72-75
clearing, 283-287
configuring, 73-75

copying files from, 79
copyright laws, 286
Netcaster, setting, 125
options, 75
Reload command, 75-76
Calvin and Hobbes Web
  site, 377
camping Web sites, 374-375
CampNet America Web
  site, 374
Capture commands, 218
CareerPath Web site, 414
Carrie Web site, 418
car Web sites, 375-376
CART Web site, 367
Castanet push Web sites, 130
CBS Web site, 447
CBS SportsLine Web site, 441
CDA (Communications
  Decency Act), 277
CDF (Channel Data
  Format), 131
celebrities, Web sites,
  377-378
Celebrity Four11 Web
  site, 378
Celebsite Web site, 378
censoring newsgroups, 136
Center for On-Line
  Addiction, 281
certificates, *see* personal
  certificates
Change Profile
  commands, 217
Channel Data Format,
  see CDF
Channel Finder
  procedures, 124
channels
  adding to Active Desktop,
    128-132
  displaying, 125
  levels, 126
  listing, 223
  procedures, 127
  push, choosing, 123
  updating, 124
  Web pages, 127
chat
  addiction, 281-287
  AOL, 214-227
  commands, 217-227
  CompuServe, 215-227
  deception, 281-287
  disadvantages, 213-227
  e-mail, comparing,
    212-227
  MSN, 215
  online services, 213-227

overview, 211
purpose, 225-227
services, 10
sex, 213
types, 213-227
voices, 212
see also IRC
Chat Central Web site, 381
chats, 5
  connecting, 234
  discussion groups, compar-
    ing, 220
  Web site avatars, 218
  see also avatars
Chess Space Web site, 397
children, protecting from
  pornography, 276-287
choosing
  avatars, 218
  browsers, 59-68
  directories, 243-252
  newsreaders, 144
  plug-ins, 97
  push channels, 123
  servers, 61
  viewers, 97
  Web page channels, 127
Christmas 'Round the World
  Web site, 409
Cigar Aficionado Web
  site, 382
Cigar.com Web site, 383
cigar Web sites, 382-383
Cinemania Web site, 420
Classical Net Web site, 424
classified ads, 310
clearing caches, 283-287
Client pull, 92
clients
  acquiring, Archie, 193
  Archie, 188-197
    browsers, 189
  definition, 57
Clipboard
  copying images to, 78
  URLs, saving, 78
clubs, 311
CNET Radio Web site, 434
CNN Financial Network Web
  site, 432
CNNfn-Quote Search Service
  Web site, 443
Coleman Web site, 374
College Football Hall of Fame
  Web site, 396
College Hoops Insider Web
  site, 369

Collegeball.com Web
  site, 396
CollegeEdge Web site, 388
CollegeNET Web site, 389
colleges, Web sites, 388-389
colors (links), changing, 61
combining commands
  (LISTSERV), 166
comics, Web sites, 376-377
command-line accounts, 19
command-line, FTP, 173
command-line users
  Gopher, 200
  information, 172
  IRC, 221
  people, finding, 266
commands
  Archie, 196-197
  chat, 217-227
  combining, LISTSERV, 166
  Find, 76
  IRC, writing, 223
  reload, frames, 88
  Reload command, 75-76
  searching, Gopher,
    207-210
  super reload (Netscape
    Navigator), 76
  Veronica, 209-210
  Word for Windows Protect
    Document, 49
Communications Decency Act,
  see CDA
community services, Web sites,
  379-380
Components page
  (Netscape Navigator), 96
Compose window (e-mail),
  29-31
compression
  files, 247-252
  FTP sites, 179
  utilities, downloading, 249
CompuServe
  chat, 215-227
  online services, 13
  telnet programs, 254
Computer Decency Act,
  see CDA
computers, Web sites,
  383-384
Conference directories, 235
configuring
  cache, 73-75
  e-mail systems, 27-29
  LISTSERV, 165-169
  Netscape Messenger,
    27-29

457

connections
  ADSL, 340
  cable, 339
  enabling, 19
  Free-Nets, 336
  FTP sites, 174, 181
  high speed, 315
  Internet, 238-240
  ISDN lines, 338
  satellites, 339
  servers
    IRC, 222
    news servers, 145
    phone lines, 230
  see also dial-in direct
    connections
  see also dial-in terminal
    connections
  T1 lines, 339
  telnet procedures, 255
  video, 99
  VON chat rooms, 234
  see also mail connections;
    permanent connections
conspiracies, Web sites,
  385-386
Conspiracy Pages Web
  site, 385
Consumer Credit Counseling
  Web site, 431
Consumers Car Club Web site,
  376
content
  FTP sites, 172
  WWW (World Wide Web),
    66-68
contests, Web sites, 386-387
conventions
  FTP directories, 178
  newsreaders, 148
converting
  images, newsreaders, 153
  systems, newsreaders, 153
Cookbooks On/Line Web site,
  387
cooking, Web sites, 387-388
Cool Jobs Web site, 414
copies, e-mail, 48
copyright law, 286-287
correspondences mailing lists,
  167-169
costs
  Internet accounts, 333
  VON, 230
Cover Girl Web site, 371
CraftSearch Web site, 406
crashing during
  download, 300

creating
  home pages, 59
  links, 112
  Web pages
    examples, 110-118
    overview, 109-118
    purpose, 114-118
    responding, 110
credit cards
  Internet, 5
  stealing, 283-287
CuteFTP, 182-185
cybersex, 309
CyberSlot Web site, 407

D

Daily Muse Web site, 412
data formats, push
  (Microsoft), 131
dating, 311
Deep Space Network Web site,
  441
DejaNews newsgroups,
  searching, 273
Dell Web site, 384
Democratic Party Web
  site, 433
demoware, 327, 331
destinations, WWW
  (World Wide Web), 61
dial-in direct connections
  accessing, 15
  features, 16
  procedures, 19
  software, 16
dial-in terminal accounts, 24
dial-in terminal connections
  disadvantages, 17
  features, 16
  procedures, 19
  WWW (World
    Wide Web), 56
Dick Butkus Football Network
  Web site, 396
digests, mailing lists, 164
digital signatures
  automatic, 51
  e-mail, 280
  public-key encryption, 51
Dilbert Zone Web site, 377
Dinner Co-op Home Page Web
  site, 387
directories
  accessing, 190
  browsing, 272

Conference, 235
  definition, 242
  download, 242
    choosing, 243-252
  finding, 268
  FTP (File Transfer
    Protocol)
    conventions, 178
    names, 178
    viewing, 176
  Gopher, URLs, 203
  hard disks, 242
  subdirectories, 242
  telnet
    HYTELNET, 255
    Web sites, 257
  WWW types, 266-274
Discover Learning Web
  site, 390
discussion groups, 4, 10
  addiction, 281-287
  comparing, 220
disinformation Web site, 385
Disney Pictures Web site, 422
Disney's FAMILY.COM
  Web site, 430
displaying
  attachments,
    newsgroups, 153
  buttons, 60
  plug-ins, 96
  push channels, 125
  Web pages, 60
distribution (software), 320
documents
  format types, 98-107
  Gopher, 203
  searching, 191
  viewing, 4
domain names, 26
  registering, 297
Doonesbury Electronic Town
  Hall Web site, 376
Doug's Shooting Sports
  Interest Page Web site, 400
download directories, 242
  choosing, 243-252
Download.com Web site, 438
downloading
  compression utilities, 249
  crashing, 300
  drivers, printing, 305
  games, telnet, 260
  software, 306
    128-bit, 53-54
    VON software, 233-240
  viruses, 286-287

Dr. Toy's Guide Web
site, 381
drivers, printing, 305
Drudge Report Web site, 426
DWANGO Web site, 429

E

e-mail
accounts, 46
address books, 38
addresses, 25-26, 297
Internet addresses,
31-32
aliases, 38
Archie, 194
commands, 197
responses, 195
attached files, sending
across the Internet,
34-37
choosing e-mail systems,
24-25
communication guidelines,
39-40
comparing, 212-227
copies, 48
digital signatures, 280
emoticons, 40-41
encryption
Web sites, 280
see also encryption
file-filtering, 38
forging, 296
forwarding e-mail, 38
IMAP (Internet Message
Access Protocol), 25
incoming e-mail, 32-33
mailing lists, 37
online shorthand, 41-42
overview, 3
POP (Post Office
Protocol), 25
public-key encryption
features, 49-54
procedures, 50-54
quoting (replies), 33
responders, 19, 341-342
security, 279-287
sending messages, 29-32
between online services,
31-32
Compose window,
29-31
services, 10

signing, 51
system setup, 27-29
vacation messages, 38
writing, 195
see also mail
e-span Web site, 414
editors, see text editors
Edmund's Web site, 375
education, 319
museums, 307
research, 306
Web sites, 388-391
teaching, 445-446
Electric Library Web site, 391
electronic mail, see e-mail
Electronic Newstand Web site,
419
embedded objects, 96
emoticons, 40-41
employment, 310
Web sites, 413-415
emulating terminals
(telnet), 258
enabling connections (Internet), 19
encryption
breaking, 128-bit, 53
e-mail, Web sites, 280
messages (newsreaders),
150-155
overview, 43
PGP, 47-54
purpose, 48-54
systems security, 52
see also private-key
encryption; public-key
encryption; security
Engage Games Online Web
site, 429
Enterprise Mission Web
site, 448
Epicurious Web site, 394
equipment, VON, 231-240
ESPNet SportsZone Web
site, 441
Eudora Web site, 25
Exact searches, 192
Excite Web site, 436
Exploratorium's Science of
Hockey Web site, 408
Explorer, see Internet Explorer
Exploring Ancient World
Cultures Web site, 405
exporting software
(128-bit), 53
Extended Meta Language,
see XML
extensions (file), 244-252

F

failed URLs (Uniform Resource
Locators), 299
Family Education Network
Web site, 391
FAQs (Frequently Asked
Questions), 301
see also Web sites
Fastball Web site, 368
Federal Resource Center
for Special Education
Web site, 390
Fertility Web site, 402
file formats
browsers, handling, 95
HTML, 115
types, 101-107
File Transfer Protocol, see FTP
file-filtering (e-mail), 38
files
archives, 247-252
self-extracting, 249-252
availability, 10
categories, 79-80
compression, 247-252
formats, 248-252
versus archiving, 248
extensions, 244-252
.HTM, 72
.HTML, 72
finding, 177
formats
compression, 248-252
examples, 245-252
plug-ins, 247
types, 244
FTP (File Transfer
Protocol)
index, 183
text, 177
zipped, 179
HTML (HyperText Markup
Language), 114
opening, 71-72
saving, 80-81
searching, FTP, 173
sending across the Internet,
34-37
BinHex, 35
choosing e-mail systems,
35-36
MIME (Multimedia
Internet Mail Exten-
sions), 35, 37

online service
  systems, 35
  uuencoding, 34, 36
  types, 241
  viruses, 251
filtering tools, 277
  mailing lists, 167
financing Web sites, 431-432
Find (on this page)
  command, 76
Find command, 76
Find-It! Web site, 393
finding
  directories, 268
  files, FTP, 177
  HTML Mail, 44-54
  mailing lists, 158-169
  newsgroups, 136-142
  people, 266-274
  pornography, 276-287
  servers, 195
  URLs, 117-118
finger, 295
firearms, Web sites, 400-401
Fish and Game Finder Web
  site, 393
fishing Web sites, 393-394
Fishing Hole Web site, 393
fitness Web sites, 401-403
flaming, 296
food Web sites, 394-395
Food Network's CyberKitchen
  Web site, 387
foodwine.com Web site, 388
football Web sites, 395-396
Foreign Languages for
  Travelers Web site, 415
forging e-mail, 296
formats
  documents, 98-107
  files
    compression, 248-252
    examples, 245-252
    plug-ins, 247
    types, 244
    .VIV, 100
  multimedia samples, 102
  sounds
    MIDI, 98
    playing, 97
forms, Archie, 189
forums, 134
forward slash (directory
  names), 72
forwarding e-mail, 38
Four11 Web site, 392
FOX Web site, 447

Fox Film Web site, 422
frames, 88
free-market.com Web
  site, 433
Free-Nets, 336
freeware, 327
FTP (File Transfer Protocol), 4
  anonymous, 173
  automation, 173
  browsers
    copying information,
      181
    disadvantages, 180-185
    incorporating, 174
  command-line, 173
  directories
    conventions, 178
    names, 178
    viewing, 176
  Web sites, 174
  files
    finding, 177
    index, 183
    searching, 173
    text, 177
    zipped, 179
  history, 172
  links
    functions, 176
    Web pages, 175
  permissions, 172
  programs
    graphical, 173
    types, 181-185
  searching, 274
  services, 11
  site manager, 182
  sites
    compressed, 179
    connecting, 174, 181
    contents, 172
    features, 175
    global, 184-185
    indexing, 187
    logging in, 175
    names, 174
    private, 176-185
    time restrictions, 173
    Web pages, 178
    see also Archie
full-duplex cards, 232
Funny Town Web site, 411
future of the Internet,
  314, 322
futzing, push, 122-132

G

Game Cabinet Web site, 396
games
  downloading, telnet, 260
  Web sites, 396-397,
    428-429
    video, 453-454
Games Kids Play Web site, 382
Garden Escape Web site, 398
gardening Web sites, 398-399
GardenTown Web site, 398
gateways, Archie, 189
global FTP sites, 184-185
Godiva Chocolates Web
  site, 395
Gonzo Links—Your Online
  Guide to Millennia Web site,
  385
Gopher, 4, 200-210
  accessing, 201
  addresses, typing, 202
  bookmarks, 203
  command-line users, 200
  documents, 203
  history, 200-210
  menus, searching, 203
  popularity, 201
  searching, 274
    Boolean operators,
      206-210
    commands, 207-210
    wild cards, 206-210
  servers
    accessing, 202
    links, 203
    procedures, 203
    search tools, 204
  services, 11
  URLs (Uniform Resource
    Locators), 203
Gopherspace, searching, 204
Gospel Communications
  Network Web site, 435
government Web sites,
  399-400
graphical FTP programs, 173
graphical interfaces, 19
Graphical User Interface,
  see GUI
graphics, 67-68
Gravity newsreaders, 141
  Web sites, 143
Great Exotic Seed Company
  Web site, 398

Grolier Multimedia
Encyclopedia Online
Web site, 391
Groundhog's Day Web
site, 409
groups
LISTSERV
examples, 160-169
features, 159-169
see also discussion groups
growth of the Internet, 314
GUI (Graphical User
Interface), 16, 20
Gun Page Web site, 401
guns Web sites, 400-401

H

Habitat for Humanity Web
site, 379
half-duplex cards, 232
Handle commands, 217
Happy Birthday America Web
site, 409
hard disks, 242
hardware
Internet, 4
requirements, 337
Harvest Foodworks Web
site, 375
health Web sites, 401-403
Health Trek Web site, 364
Healthgirl Web site, 403
HealthWorld Online Web site,
364
Hearst Magazines Web
site, 420
Herb Finder Web site, 404
Herbal Information Center
Web site, 404
herbs, Web sites, 403-404
hierarchies (newsgroups),
138-142
high speed connections, 315
histories
FTP, 172
Gopher, 200-210
Internet, 7
lists, 63
URLs, finding, 117
Web sites, 405-406
WWW, 62, 199
History Channel Web site, 405
History Net Web site, 406
hits, 188
hobbies, Web sites, 406-407

Hobby Craft Network Web site,
406
hockey Web sites, 407-408
Hockey News On-Line Web
site, 408
holidays, Web sites, 408-409
Holistic Health Web site, 365
Hollywood Online Web
site, 421
Home Ideas Web site, 410
home improvement, Web sites,
410-411
home pages, 59
promoting, 294
Web pages, 112-118
see also start pages
HotBot Web site, 437
House of Blues Web site, 424
HouseNet Web site, 410
.HTM file extension, 72
HTML (Hypertext Markup
Language)
files
features, 114
formats, 115
opening, 71-72
rendering, 114
source documents,
saving, 78
tags
anchor, 115
definition, 111
line breaks, 116
links, 115
types, 115-118
text editors, 114
Web pages, 111
.HTML file extension, 72
HTML Mail
appearances, 44
POP accounts, 46
programs
capabilities, 46-54
finding, 44-54
requirements, 44
standards, *see* Inbox Direct
Hubble Space Telescope
Web site, 440
humor Web sites, 411-412
hunting Web sites, 393-394
hypertext, 56
navigating, 62
systems, 4
Hypertext Markup Language,
see HTML
HYTELNET
directories, telnet, 255
links, 256

I

icons, animated, 89-94
Idea List Web site, 379
Ignore commands, 217
images
3-D
VRML, 99
WWW, 99
converting, newsreaders,
153
copying to Clipboard, 78
saving, 78
scanning, 10
IMAP (Internet Message Access
Protocol), 25
Inbox Direct, 46
registering, 47
incoming e-mail, 32-33
indexing (FTP files), 183
Info Space Web site, 393
InfoSeek search engines,
270-274
Insect Recipes Web site, 395
installing
plug-ins, 102-107
software, 20
viewers, 103-107
Internet Explorer,
105-107
Netscape Navigator,
103-107
Instant Sports Web site, 368
insurance Web sites, 412-413
Insurance Information
Institute Web site, 412
Insurance New Network Web
site, 413
Insure Market Web site, 412
InsWeb Web site, 413
Intellicast Web site, 449
interactive Web pages, 84-94
Intercamp: Summer Camp &
Resource Directory Web site,
375
Intercast, 316
interfaces, GUI (Graphical User
Interface), 16, 19-20
International Amateur Athletic
Federation Web site, 427
international issues
(Internet), 317
International Traffic in Arms
Regulations, *see* ITA
Internet
accessing
altruism, 192
availability, 9

methods, 12
online services, 15
accounts, acquiring, 14
applications, renting, 91
backlash, 317
business uses, 304
connections, enabling, 19
dangers, 5
definition, 3
e-mail, *see* e-mail
future considerations,
314-315, 322
hardware, 4
history, 7
international issues, 317
national borders, 317
online services, 13
phones
connecting, 238-240
features, 230
legal issues, 231
protocols, 65-68
services, 10
software archives, 5
Internet Address Finder
Web site, 393
Internet Explorer
cache, configuring, 74-75
Find (on this page)
command, 76
HTML files, opening, 71
locating online, 328
market share, 58
multiple windows, opening,
70-71
QuickLinks, 61
saving files, 81
shortcut menus, 77
viewers, installing,
105-107
Internet Gaming Zone Web
site, 428
Internet Mall Web site, 438
Internet Millionaires list Web
site, 292
Internet Movie Database Web
site, 420
Internet Public Library Web
site, 418
Internet Relay Chat, *see* IRC
Internet Service Providers,
see ISPs
Internet Underground Music
Archive, *see* IUMA
interpreters (Java), 90
Invite commands, 217
IRC (Internet Relay Chat), 5
channels, 223
command-line users, 221
commands, writing, 223

conversations, 225
features, 224
nicknames, 222
overview, 221-227
participants, 224
servers, connecting, 222
software, 222
IRL Web site, 367
IRS Web site, 443
ISDN lines, 338
Island Weddings Web
site, 450
ISPs (Internet Service Providers), 15
e-mail addresses, 297
Free-Nets, 336
rates, 334
selecting, 334-335
starting up, 300
ITAR (International Traffic in
Arms Regulations), 53
IUMA (Internet Underground
Music Archive), 307

J

Jason Project Web site, 390
Java, 90, 254
JavaScript, 91-94
JAZZ Online Web site, 425
JCN (Jewish Communication
Network) Web site, 435
job searches, Web sites,
413-415
JobVault Web site, 414
Joe Tremblay's WWW Hockey
Guide Web site, 408
jokes, Web sites, 411-412
Judy's Flavors of the South
Web site, 388
Jughead
case-sensitivity, 205
features, 204
procedures, 205-210
wild cards, 206
see also Gopher

K

Kali Web site, 428
Kaplan's Holiday Fun and
Games Web site, 408
key servers, 50, 52
Kick or Ban commands, 218
Knowledge Adventure
Encyclopedia Web site, 392

L

languages, Web sites,
415-416
Late Show with David
Letterman Web site, 412
Laugh Web Web site, 411
Lawyers Online International
Web site, 416
Le Coq Sportif: Guide to
Hockey Web site, 407
Learning Web site, 381
legal issues
Internet, 231
Web sites, 416-417
Legos Web site, 382
libraries
software, 328
Web sites, 417-419
Library of Congress
Web site, 417
line breaks, HTML tags, 116
links
appearances, 60
colors, changing, 61
creating, 112
FTP
functions, 176
Web pages, 175
Gopher servers, 203
HYTELNET, 256
tags, HTML, 115
URLs , finding, 117
lists
histories, 63
mailing lists, *see* mailing
lists
LISTSERV
addresses, 162-169
commands, 166
configuring, 165-169
groups
examples, 160-169
features, 159-169
peered mailing lists, 159
subscribing, 163-169
unsubscribing, 164-169
see also mailing lists
Literary Web Web site, 373
live objects, 96
Live3D plug-ins (Netscape
Navigator), 99
LiveConcerts.com Web
site, 434
Log commands, 218
logging in
FTP sites, 175
telnet sites, 257-262

logging off telnet
programs, 259
Los Angeles Times Food News
Web site, 394
lotteries, Web sites, 386-387
Lottery News Online Web site,
387
Louvre Web sites, 307
Lycos Web site, 437

M

Macmillan Web sites, 112
magazines, 308
Web sites, 419-420
mail
Archie, 188
connections, 18
see also e-mail; HTML Mail
mailing lists
correspondences, 167-169
e-mail, 37
features, 158-169
filtering tools, 167
finding, 158-169
flaming, 297
LISTSERV, peered, 159
manually administered,
166-169
messages
digests, 164
sending, 165
searching, 274
services, 12
types, 159-169
Web sites, 158
see also Majordomo
Major League Baseball Bat Web
site, 367
Major League Rotisserie
Baseball Web site, 368
Majordomo
subscribing, 166-169
see also mailing lists
marking messages
(newsgroups), 148-155
Martindale-Hubbell Lawyer
Locator Web site, 416
Math Forum Elementary
Teachers' Place Web
site, 446
medicine (alternative) Web
sites, 363-365
Mefco's Random Joke Server
Web site, 411
Men's Fitness Web site, 401
Men's Health Web site, 402
menus, searching, 203
message boards, 134

messages
mailing lists, 164
newsgroups
accessing, 146
listing, 146
marking, 148-155
reading, 147
saving, 148-155
newsreaders
conventions, 148
encryption, 150-155
moving, 149-155
printing, 150
retrieving, 149
saving, 150
sending/responding,
150-155
posting, anonymously, 285
searching newsgroups, 273
sending, 165
Metropolitan Museum of Art
Web site, 423
Microsoft
Active Desktop, *see* Active
Desktop
browsers, 58
push data formats, 131
Web site, 439
Microsoft Network, *see* MSN
MIDI formats, 98
Military history Web site, 405
MIME (Multipurpose Internet
Mail Extensions), 35, 37
Web sites, 106
modems, slow transfer
rates, 293
moderated newsgroups, 138
Modern World Web site, 377
money (business
ventures), 292
Money Online Web site, 431
Monster Board Web site, 413
MOOs, 260-262
Mother Nature's General Store
Web site, 364
Movie Finder Web site, 421
MovieLink Web site, 421
movies
studios, Web sites,
421-422
Web sites, 420-421
moving messages
(newsreaders), 149-155
Mr. Showbiz! Web site, 378
MSN (Microsoft Network), 13
chat, 215
purpose, 14
services, 13
MSNBC Web site, 426

MTV Online Web site, 424
MUCKs, 260-262
MUDs (Multi-User Dimen-
sions), 260-262
multimedia
formats, 102
Web pages, 96
WWW, 315
overview, 93-94
multiple windows, opening,
70-71
Multipurpose Internet Mail
Extensions, *see* MIME
Museum of Modern Art
(MoMA) Web site, 423
museums, 307
Web sites, 423-424
music, 307
Web sites, 424-425

N

names
FTP (File Transfer
Protocol)
directories, 178
sites, 174
newsgroups, 138-142
telnet sites, 255
NASA (National Aeronautics
and Space Administration)
Web site, 440
NASCAR Web site, 367
Nasdaq Stock Market Home
Page Web site, 442
Nation-Wide Services
Web site, 451
National Aeronautics and
Space Administration,
see NASA
National Air and Space
Museum Web site, 400
national borders
(Internet), 317
National Center for
Supercomputing
Applications, *see* NCSA
National Enquirer Web
site, 420
National Model Railroad
Association on the Web Web
site, 407
National Rifle Association Web
site, 400
National Science Teachers
Association, *see* NSTA
National Shooting Sports
Foundation Web site, 401

National Wheelchair
Basketball Association
Web site, 369
navigating
hypertext, 62
Web pages, 60, 62-68
Navigator, *see* Netscape
Navigator
NBA.com Web site, 369
NBC.com Web site, 446
NCAA Online Web site, 427
NCSA (National Center
for Supercomputing
Applications), 58
Nerd World Hobbies Web site,
406
Net Nanny, 277
Net Quote Insurance Shopper
Web site, 413
Net Search, 61
Netcaster
caches, setting, 125
push Web sites, 123-132
NETdelivery push Web
sites, 130
NetRadio Web site, 434
Netscape
bookmarks, 63
Inbox Direct, *see* Inbox
Direct
software, 128-bit versions,
53-54
viewers, installing,
103-107
Web site, 439
Netscape Messenger
configuring, 27-29
PGP, 48
Netscape Navigator
browsers, 57
cache, configuring, 73-74
Components page Web
sites, 96
HTML files, opening, 72
locating online, 328
multiple windows, opening,
70-71
plug-ins (Live3D), 99
saving files, 80
setting up, 104-107
shortcut menus, 77
super reload command, 76
Windows 95, 291
NETworth Quote Server Web
site, 443
New Age Web site, 364
New York Public Library Web
site, 418

New York Times Book Review
Web site, 373
news
definition, 135
Web sites, 425-427
sports, 441-442
news servers, 134
connecting, 145
public, 135
newsgroups, 134
addiction, 155
articles, 149
attachments
displaying, 153
procedures, 152-155
censoring, 134, 136
examples, 135-142
finding, 136-142
flaming, 297
hierarchies, 138-142
levels, 139-142
messages
accessing, 146
listing, 146
marking, 148-155
reading, 147
saving, 148-155
searching, 273
moderated, 138
naming, 138-142
numbers, 134
searching, 282-283
services, 12
sources, 137-142
starting, 136
subscribing, 134, 145
threads, 147
Web sites, 139
see also alt. groups
newsreaders
choosing, 144
converting, 153
definition, 134
features, 140-142, 154-155
Gravity, 141, 143
images, converting, 153
messages
conventions, 148
encryption, 150-155
moving, 149-155
printing, 150
retrieving, 149
saving, 150
sending/responding,
150-155
setting up, 144-155
UNIX, 141

Next Generation Web
site, 453
NFL.com Web site, 395
NHL Open Net Web site, 407
nicknames, IRC, 222
Nine Planets Web site, 440
Nintendo Power Source Web
site, 454
NJCAA Web site, 427
NSTA Web site, 445

O

OBGYN.net Web site, 403
objects, *see* live objects;
embedded objects
Olympic Movement Web site,
427
On Hoops Web site, 369
online services
chat, 213-227
comparing, 13
Internet, accessing, 15
profiles, 280
sending
e-mail between online
services, 31-32
files across the Internet,
35-37
opening
HTML files, 71-72
multiple windows, 70-71
operators, *see* Boolean
operators
Outdoors Online Web
site, 394
ozines, 308

P-Q

panes, *see* frames
paragraphs, browsers, 116
Paramount Web site, 421
Parenthood Web site, 430
parenting Web sites, 429-430
ParentSoup Web site, 429
ParentsPlace.com Web
site, 430
passwords
changing, 290
protection (user
profiles), 87
Web sites, 86-94
PastaNet Web site, 395

Pathfinder Web site, 419
Paula Begoun—The Cosmetics
    Cop Web site, 371
PBS Web site, 447
PC Quote Online Web
    site, 442
PC/TV (Intercast), 316
Peace Corp Web site, 379
PedagoNet Web site, 445
peered mailing lists
    (LISTSERV), 159
Pegasus Web site, 25
people, finding, 266-274
People Here commands, 217
People Online Web site, 377
permanent connections
    advantages, 16
    procedures, 18
    TCP/IP, 15
permissions (FTP), 172
personal certificates, 52
    Web sites, 52-54
Personal Finance Mailing List
    Web site, 431
PETA Web site, 365
PGP (Pretty Good Privacy)
    encryption, 47-54
    Netscape Messenger, 48
    Web sites, 52
phones
    connecting to
        Internet, 238-240
        servers, 230
    Internet
        features, 230
        legal issues, 231
        services, 11
Pick Web site, 418
pictures, *see* graphics
Planetary Society Web
    site, 440
Plant of the Week Web
    site, 398
playing sounds, 97
Playstation Homepage
    Web site, 453
plug-ins
    3-D, 99
    animations, 101
    availability, 96
    choosing, 97
    displaying, 96
    file formats, 247
    installing, 102-107
    locating online, 331
    Netscape Navigator
        Live3D, 99
    purpose, 96
    video, 100
PLUS Lotto Web site, 387

Point-to-Point Protocol,
    see PPP
PointCast push Web
    sites, 130
police, anonymous
    remailers, 285
political activism, 310
politics, Web sites, 432-433
POP accounts (HTML
    mail), 46
pornography on Web
    children, protecting from,
        276-287
    cybersex, 309
    finding, 276-287
    Internet, 5
    prevalence, 276-287
    restricting, software,
        277-287
    Web sites, 276
Post Office Protocol
    (POP), 25
posting messages
    anonymously, 285
PPP (Point-to-Point
    Protocol), 16
    see also dial-in direct
        connections, 16
Preferences commands, 218
prefixes
    Internet protocols, 65-68
    Web site security, 86
printing
    drivers, downloading, 305
    messages (newsreaders), 150
    Web documents, 78
private FTP sites, 176-185
private-key encryption,
    49-54
Prizes.com Web site, 386
products
    push
        Netcaster, 123-132
        overview, 122-123
        voice-on-the-net, 5
    VON
        types, 236-240
        Web sites, 233
Profile commands, 217
profiles
    online services, 280
    see also user profiles
programs
    FTP, 173, 181-185
    HTML Mail
        capabilities, 46-54
        finding, 44-54
    push, 12
    talk, 226

telnet
    archives, 254
    Compuserve, 254
    features, 254-262
    logging off, 259
    records, 259-262
    transferring viruses, 251
    WWW, 89
promoting home pages, 294
Prostate Cancer Web
    site, 402
Protect Document
    commands (Word for
    Windows), 49
protocols
    definition, 16
    prefixes, Internet, 65-68
public news servers, 135
public-key encryption
    digital signatures, 51
    e-mail
        features, 49-54
        procedures, 50-54
    functions, 49
    problems, 50
    software requirements, 53
Publisher's Clearing House
    Web site, 386
Publishers Weekly Interactive
    Web site, 373
publishing Web pages,
    56, 117-118
pull, *see* client pull
Purdue University Web
    site, 389
push
    channels
        choosing, 123
        displaying, 125
        updating, 124
    data formats
        (Microsoft), 131
    functions, 121
    futzing, 122-132
    overview, 4, 121
    products
        Netcaster, 123-132
        overview, 122-123
    programs, 12
    starting, 122
    systems, 130-132
    Web sites, 130-132
    see also server push;
        Webcasting

Que Web site, 384
QuickLinks (Internet
    Explorer), 61
quoting e-mail (replies), 33

R

RaceZine Web site, 366
radio Web sites, 433-434
rates (ISPS), 334
reading
    alt. groups, 145
    newsgroup messages, 147
RealAudio, 97
Record commands, 218
Redbook Beauty and Style Web
    site, 370
Refresh buttons, 76, 112
Regex searches, 192
registering Inbox Direct, 47
religion, Web sites, 435-436
reload commands, 75-76, 88
Reload Frame command, 76
remailers, 285
Remodeling Online Web
    site, 410
remote access, 311
rendering HTML, 114
renting applications, 91
Republican Party Web
    site, 432
requirements
    HTML Mail, 44
    Java, 90
    software public-key
      encryption, 53
research, 306
Resource Pathways College
    Information Community
    Web site, 389
resources, WWW, 268-274
responding to messages,
    150-155
restricting pornography
    software, 277-287
retaining e-mail
    addresses, 297
retrieving messages, 149
right-clicking (mouse), 77
Rock-and-Roll Hall of Fame
    and Museum Web site, 424
Roll Call Online Web
    site, 432
Rotary International
    Web site, 380

S

satellite connections, 339
saving
    files, 80-81
    messages
      newsgroups, 148-155
      newsreaders, 150

Web items, 77-79
Web pages, 112
scanning images, 10
Scottish Tiddlywinks
    Association Web site, 397
search sites, 269-274
searching
    Archie, 189, 196
      cancelling, 190
      descriptions, 196
      procedures, 189
      speed, 189
      types, 192-197
    bookmarks, 273
    documents, browsers, 191
    engines
      direcories, finding, 268
      InfoSeek, 270-274
      procedures, 270-274
    files, FTP, 173
    Gopher servers, 204
      Boolean operators, 206,
        207-210
      commands, 207-210
      menus, 203
      wild cards, 206-210
    Gopherspace, 204
    newsgroups, 282-283
      messages, 273
    resources, WWW, 268-274
    Veronica, 209-210
    Web documents, 76
    WWW topics, 273
secondary windows, 87-94
SecureTax Web site, 444
security
    anonymity, 294
    e-mail, 279-287, 296
    encryption, 52
    passwords, changing, 290
    Web sites, 85-94
    see also encryption
Seeds of Change Web
    site, 404
selecting ISPs, 334-335
self-extracting archives,
    249-252
sending messages
    mailing lists, 165
    newsreaders, 150-155
Serial Line Internet Protocol,
    see SLIP
server push, 92
servers, 57
    accessing, 202
    Archie, 195-197
    choosing, 61
    commands, 196
    connecting, 222
    finding, 195

Gopher
    links, 203
    procedures, 203
    search tools, 204
key, 50, 52
phone lines,
    connecting, 230
VON, 236
WWW, 57
see also client/server
service providers
    definition, 15
    see also ISPs
services, *see* online services
sessions, telnet, 258-262
SETI Institute Web site, 448
setting up
    avatars, 220
    caches, 125
    e-mail systems, 27-29
    Netscape Navigator,
      104-107
    newsreaders, 144-155
sex
    chat, 213
    VON, 234
    see also pornography
Shakespeare, 308
shareware, 327
    archives, 6
    locating online, 327
    WWW sites, 328
shell accounts, 24, 290
    see also dial-in terminal
      connections
shopping, 309
    Web sites, 437
shortcut menus, 77
Sightings Web site, 448
signatures, *see* digital signa-
    tures
site manager (FTP), 182
sites, *see* Web sites
SLIP (Serial Line Internet
    Protocol), 16
slow transfer rates
    (modems), 293
smileys, 40-41
Smithsonian Institute Web
    site, 423
Smoke Shop Web site, 383
Smokerings.com Web
    site, 383
SMTP (Simple Mail Transfer
    Protocol) server, 28
Social Recreation Resources
    Web site, 397
software
    archives, 328
      Internet, 5
    demoware, 327, 331

dial-in direct
    connections, 16
distribution, 320
downloading, 53-54, 306
exporting, 53
freeware, 327
GUI, dial-in direct
    connections, 16
installing, 20
Internet, 4
IRC, 222
libraries, 328
locating online, 327
pornography, restricting,
    277-287
requirements, 53
shareware, 327
spying, 283
telnet, 260-262
VON, 232-240
    downloading, 233-240
    procedures, 233-240
    types, 232
Web sites, 438-439
WWW sites, 331
Sony Music Online Web
    site, 425
sounds
    cards, 232
    formats, 97-98
Space Science and
    Engineering Center
    Web site, 449
space Web sites, 440-441
SpeedNet Web site, 366
Spirit-WWW Web site, 436
Sporting Adventures Web site,
    394
Sporting News Web site, 441
sports, Web sites
    baseball, 367-368,
        388-389
    basketball, 369-370
    fishing/hunting, 393-394
    football, 395-396
    hockey, 407-408
    news, 441-442
    Olympics, 427-428
Sports Celebrity Network Web
    site, 378
Sports Illustrated Web
    site, 442
spying software, 283
Squeal Empire Learn-a-
    Language Web site, 415
Squelch commands, 217
start pages, 60
    see also home pages

starting
    newsgroups, 136
    push, 122
starting an ISP business, 300
State of Insanity Web
    site, 380
stealing credit cards, 283-287
stock quotes, Web sites,
    442-443
streaming video, 101
StreamWorks, 97
Stroud's Consummate
    Winsock Apps Web
    site, 439
Sub searches, 192
Subcase searches, 193
subdirectories, 242
subscribing to
    LISTSERV, 163-169
    Majordomo, 166-169
    newsgroups, 134, 145
Substring searches, 193
subversion, 310
super reload command
    (Netscape Navigator), 76
SuperSeek Web site, 437
Sweepstakes Online Web
    site, 386
Symantec Web site, 439

T

T1 lines, 339
tables, 83-94
Tackle Towne Web site, 394
tags (HTML), 44
    anchor, 115
    definition, 111
    line breaks, 116
    links, 115
    types, 115-118
talk
    features, 212
    programs, 226
Talk City Web site, 380
targeted windows, 88
Tax Help Online Web
    site, 444
taxes, Web sites, 443-444
TaxWeb Web site, 444
TCP/IP (Transmission Control
    Protocol/Internet Protocol), 15
Teachers.net Web site, 445
teaching Web sites, 445-446
Teachnet Web site, 445
Team USA Web site, 428
technical support, 305
telecommuting, 311

television, 294, 316
telnet, 5, 253-262
    3270 software, 260-262
    connections, 255
    directories
        HYTELNET, 255
        Web sites, 257
    games, downloading, 260
    Java Web sites, 254
    programs
        archives, 254
        Compuserve, 254
        features, 254-262
        logging off, 259
        records, 259-262
    resources, 256
    searching, 274
    services, 11
    sessions, 258-262
    sites
        logging in, 257-262
        names, 255
    terminals, emulating, 258
text
    adding to Web pages, 112
    FTP files, 177
    saving, 77
text editors
    HTML, 114
    Web pages, creating, 110
Thomas Web site, 399
threads, 147
Timecast Web site, 433
titles of Web pages, 111
tools
    filtering, 277
        mailing lists, 167
    searching, 204
    Web pages, navigating,
        62-68
Total Entertainment Network
    Web site, 428
toys, Web sites, 381-382
transfer rates, modems
    (troubleshooting), 293
transferring program
    viruses, 251
Transmission Control
    Protocol/Internet Protocol,
    see TCP/IP
TrueSpeech, 97
TUCOWS, 6
    Web site, 80
TuneUp Web site, 384
Turn Left Web site, 433
TV networks Web sites,
    446-448
typing URLs, 299

U

U.S. News .edu Web site, 389
UC Davis Department of
  Viticulture and Enology Web
  site, 452
Ufomind Web site, 448
UFOs, Web sites, 448-449
United States Government
  Printing Office Web
  site, 399
United Way of America Web
  site, 379
Universal Pictures Web
  site, 422
universities, Web sites,
  388-389
UNIX
  finger, 295
  newsreaders, 141
unsubscribing LISTSERV,
  164-169
updating push channels, 124
URLs (Uniform resource
  Locators)
  dissecting, 64-68
  entering, 64, 66-68
  failure to connect, 299
  finding, 117-118
  Gopher directories, 203
  prefixes, Internet
    protocols, 65-68
  saving to Clipboard, 78
  typing, 299
  Web pages, 65
USA Law Resources Web
  site, 417
USA Today Web site, 425
Usenet newsgroups, 138
  searching, 273
user profiles, password
  protection, 87
USNews Online Web
  site, 426
uuencoding, 34, 36

V

Vatican Museum Web site, 423
Vatican Web site, 435
Vcards, 50
Veronica
  commands, 209-210
  features, 204
  procedures, 208-210

searching, 209-210
  see also Gopher
video
  connections, 99
  games, Web sites, 453-454
  plug-ins, 100
  streaming, 101
  viewers, 100
  VON, 239-240
  WWW, 99-107
VideoGameSpot Web site, 453
viewers
  3-D, 99
  animations, 101
  availability, 96
  choosing, 97
  installing, 103-107
    Internet Explorer,
      105-107
    Netscape, 103-107
  locating online, 331
  purpose, 96
  video, 100
viewing documents, 4
  FTP directories, 176
Virtual Vineyards Web
  site, 452
viruses
  downloading, 286-287
  files, 251
  overview, 184-185,
    250-252
  precautions, 251-252
  programs, transferring, 251
  types, 250-252
VON (Voice on the Net)
  addresses, 236-240
  chat rooms,
    connecting, 234
  costs, 230
  disadvantages, 231-240
  equipment, 231-240
  products, 233, 236-240
  servers, 236
  sex, 234
  software, 232-240
    downloading, 233-240
    procedures, 233-240
  video, 239-240
  Web pages, 239
  white boards, 238
VR-1 Digital Comics Web
  site, 376
VRML images (3-D), 99

W-X

wallpaper images, 78
Warner Bros. Web site, 422
Washington Post Web
  site, 426
weather Web sites, 449-450
Weather Channel Web
  site, 449
Weather Imagery and Data
  Web site, 450
Weather Shops Web site, 450
Web browsers, *see* browsers
Web files
  categories, 79-80
  saving, 80-81
Web forums, 157
  procedures, 168-169
  Web sites, 158, 168
Web of Online Grammars Web
  site, 415
Web pages
  authoring, 93-94
  channels, 127
  creating, 109-118
    purpose, 114-118
    responders, 110
  displaying, 60
  FTP, 178
  home pages, 112-118
  interactive, 84-94
  links
    creating, 112
    FTP, 175
  multimedia, 96
  navigating tools, 62-68
  posting, 56
  publishing, 117-118
  saving, 112
  searching, 76
  text, adding, 112
  titles, HTML, 111
  URLs, 65
  VON, 239
Web sites
  1-800-U.S. Search, 392
  60 Greatest Conspiracies of
    All Time, 385
  1040.com, 444
  ABC, 446
  Access Market Square, 438
  Acupuncture, 365
  AK-Mail, 25
  Algy's Herb Page, 403
  All About Beer Online, 371
  All-Internet Shopping
    Directory, 438

ALT.SMOKERS.CIGARS FAQ, 383
alternative medicine, 363-365
Alternative Medicine Digest, 364
Amazon.com, 373
American Botanical Council, 404
American Stock Exchange, 443
America's Choice Mall, 437
Animal Species, 366
animals, 365-366
Animals, Animals, 366
Animated American Sign Language, 416
Archie, 189
Art Bell, 386
Art History Resources on the Web, 405
Ask Dr. Weil, 363
Ask the Dietitian, 402
AskEric, 390
ASPCA, 365
Atlantic Broadcasting System, 434
Audio Net Sports Guide, 442
auto racing, 366-367
AutoSeek, 376
AutoVantage, 375
avatars, 218
babyonline, 430
baseball, 367-368, 388-389
Baseball Statsweb, 368
basketball, 369-370
beauty, 370-371
Beauty Spot, 370
beer, 371-372
Beer Info Source, 371
Berlitz World, 415
Better Home & Gardens, 399
Better Homes and Gardens Home Improvement, 410
BizWeb Personal Finance, 432
books, 372-374
BookWire, 372
BradyGAMES Strategy Guides, 453
Brew Your Own, 372
BrewCrafters, 372
breWorld, 372

Bride's Do-It-Yourself Wedding Planners, 451
Britannica Online, 391
BuddhaNet, 435
Builder's 411
c|net, 384
Calvin and Hobbes, 377
camping, 374-375
CampNet America, 374
CareerPath, 414
Carrie, 418
cars, 375-376
CART, 367
CBS, 447
CBS SportsLine, 441
celebrities, 377-378
Celebrity Four11, 378
Celebsite, 378
Chat Central, 381
Chess Space, 397
Christmas 'Round the World, 409
Cigar Aficionado, 382
Cigar.com, 383
cigars, 382-383
Cinemania, 420
Classical Net, 424
CNET Radio, 434
CNN Financial Network, 432
CNNfn-Quote Search Service, 443
Coleman, 374
College Football Hall of Fame, 396
College Hoops Insider, 369
Collegeball.com, 396
CollegeEdge, 388
CollegeNET, 389
comics, 376-377
community service, 379-380
computers, 383-384
conspiracies, 385-386
Conspiracy Pages, 385
Consumer Credit Counseling, 431
Consumers Car Club, 376
Cookbooks On/Line, 387
cooking, 387-388
Cool Jobs, 414
Cover Girl, 371
CraftSearch, 406
CyberSlot, 407
Daily Muse, 412
Deep Space Network, 441
Dell, 384
Democratic Party, 433

Dick Butkus Football Network, 396
Dilbert Zone, 377
Dinner Co-op Home Page, 387
Discover Learning, 390
disinformation, 385
Disney Pictures, 422
Disney's FAMILY.COM, 430
Doonesbury Electronic Town Hall, 376
Doug's Shooting Sports Interest Page, 400
Download.com, 438
Dr. Toy's Guide, 381
Drudge Report, 426
DWANGO, 429
e-mail encryption, 280
e-span, 414
Edmund's, 375
edmunds, 304
education, 390-391
Electric Library, 391
Electronic Newstand, 419
employment, 413-415
Engage Games Online, 429
Enterprise Mission, 448
Epicurious, 394
ESPNet SportsZone, 441
Eudora, 25
Excite, 436
Exploratorium's Science of Hockey, 408
Exploring Ancient World Cultures, 405
Family Education Network, 391
Fastball, 368
Federal Resource Center for Special Education, 390
Fertility, 402
financing, 307, 431-432
Find-It!, 393
Fish and Game Finder, 393
Fishing Hole, 393
food, 394-395
Food Network's CyberKitchen, 387
foodwine.com, 388
Foreign Languages for Travelers, 415
Four11, 392
FOX, 447
Fox Film, 422
free-market.com, 433
FTP, 174
Funny Town, 411
Game Cabinet, 396

games, 396-397, 428-429
Games Kids Play, 382
Garden Escape, 398
gardening, 398-399
GardenTown, 398
Godiva Chocolates, 395
Gonzo Links—Your Online
  Guide to Millennia, 385
Gospel Communications
  Network, 435
government, 399-400
Great Exotic Seed
  Company, 398
Grolier Multimedia
  Encyclopedia
  Online, 391
Groundhog's Day, 409
Gun Page, 401
guns, 400-401
Habitat for Humanity, 379
Happy Birthday
  America, 409
Harvest Foodworks, 375
health, 401-403
Health Trek, 364
Healthgirl, 403
HealthWorld Online, 364
Hearst Magazines, 420
Herb Finder, 404
Herbal Information Center,
  404
herbs, 403-404
history, 405-406
History Channel, 405
History Net, 406
hobbies, 406-407
Hobby Craft Network, 406
Hockey News On-Line, 408
holidays, 408-409
Holistic Health, 365
Hollywood Online, 421
Home Ideas, 410
Home Improvement,
  410-411
HotBot, 437
House of Blues, 424
HouseNet, 410
Hubble Space
  Telescope, 440
humor, 411-412
Idea List, 379
Info Space, 393
Insect Recipes, 395
Instant Sports, 368
insurance, 412-413
Insurance Information
  Institute, 412
Insurance New

Network, 413
Insure Market, 412
InsWeb, 413
Intellicast, 449
Intercamp: Summer
  Camp & Resource
  Directory, 375
International Amateur
  Athletic Federation, 427
Internet Address
  Finder, 393
Internet Gaming
  Zone, 428
Internet Mall, 438
Internet Millionaires
  list, 292
Internet Movie
  Database, 420
Internet Public Library, 418
IRL, 367
IRS, 443
Island Weddings, 450
IUMA, 307
Jason Project, 390
Java applications, 90
JAZZ Online, 425
JCN (Jewish
  Communication
  Network), 435
job searches, 413-415
JobVault, 414
Joe Tremblay's WWW
  Hockey Guide, 408
jokes, 411-412
Judy's Flavors of the South,
  388
Kali, 428
Kaplan's Holiday Fun and
  Games, 408
key servers, 52
Knowledge Adventure
  Encyclopedia, 392
languages, 415-416
Late Show with David
  Letterman, 412
Laugh Web, 411
Lawyers Online
  International, 416
Le Coq Sportif: Guide to
  Hockey, 407
Learning, 381
legal issues, 416-417
Legos, 382
libraries, 417-419
Library of Congress, 417
Literary Web, 373
LiveConcerts.com, 434
Los Angeles Times Food
  News, 394

Lottery News Online, 387
Louvre, 307
Lycos, 437
Macmillan, 112
magazines, 419-420
mailing lists, 158
Major League Baseball Bat,
  367
Major League Rotisserie
  Baseball, 368
Martindale-Hubbell Lawyer
  Locator, 416
Math Forum Elementary
  Teachers' Place, 446
Mefco's Random Joke
  Server, 411
Men's Fitness, 401
Men's Health, 402
Metropolitan Museum of
  Art, 423
Microsoft, 439
Military history, 405
MIME, 106
Modern World, 377
Money Online, 431
Monster Board, 413
Mother Nature's General
  Store, 364
Movie Finder, 421
movie studios, 421-422
MovieLink, 421
movies, 420-421
Mr. Showbiz!, 378
MSNBC, 426
MTV Online, 424
Museum of Modern Art
  (MoMA), 423
museums, 423-424
music, 307, 424-425
NASA, 440
NASCAR, 367
Nasdaq Stock Market Home
  Page, 442
Nation-Wide Services, 451
National Air and Space
  Museum, 400
National Enquirer, 420
National Model Railroad
  Association on the
  Web, 407
National Rifle
  Association, 400
National Shooting Sports
  Foundation, 401
National Wheelchair
  Basketball Association,
  369
NBA.com, 369
NBC.com, 446

NCAA Online, 427
Nerd World Hobbies, 406
Net Nanny, 277
Net Quote Insurance
    Shopper, 413
NetRadio, 434
Netscape, 439
Netscape Navigator, 96
NETworth Quote
    Server, 443
New Age, 364
New York Public
    Library, 418
New York Times Book
    Review, 373
news, 425-427
newsgroups, 139
newsreaders, 143
Next Generation, 453
NFL.com, 395
NHL Open Net, 407
Nine Planets, 440
Nintendo Power
    Source, 454
NJCAA, 427
NSTA, 445
OBGYN.net, 403
Olympic Movement, 427
On Hoops, 369
Outdoors Online, 394
Paramount, 421
Parenthood Web, 430
parenting, 429-430
ParentSoup, 429
ParentsPlace.com, 430
password protected, 86-94
PastaNet, 395
Pathfinder, 419
Paula Begoun—The
    Cosmetics Cop, 371
PBS, 447
PC Quote Online, 442
Peace Corp, 379
PedagoNet, 445
Pegasus, 25
People Online, 377
personal certificates,
    52-54
Personal Finance Mailing
    List, 431
PETA, 365
PGP, 52
Pick, 418
Planetary Society, 440
Plant of the Week, 398
Playstation
    Homepage, 453
plug-ins, 331
PLUS Lotto, 387

politics, 432-433
pornography, 276
Prizes.com, 386
Prostate Cancer, 402
public news servers, 135
Publisher's Clearing House,
    386
Publishers Weekly
    Interactive, 373
Purdue University, 389
push, 130-132
Que, 384
RaceZine, 366
radio, 433-434
Redbook Beauty and Style,
    370
religion, 435-436
remailers, 285
Remodeling Online, 410
Republican Party, 432
Resource Pathways College
    Information Community,
    389
Rock-and-Roll Hall of Fame
    and Museum, 424
Roll Call Online, 432
Rotary International, 380
Scottish Tiddlywinks
    Association, 397
SecureTax, 444
security, 85-94
    prefixes, 86
Seeds of Change, 404
SETI Institute, 448
shareware, 328
shopping, 437
Sightings, 448
Smithsonian Institute, 423
Smoke Shop, 383
Smokerings.com, 383
Social Recreation Resources,
    397
software, 331, 438-439
    Netscape, 53-54
Sony Music Online, 425
space, 440-441
Space Science and
    Engineering Center, 449
SpeedNet, 366
Spirit-WWW, 436
Sporting Adventures, 394
Sporting News, 441
sports
    fishing/hunting,
        393-394
    football, 395-396
    hockey, 407-408
    news, 441-442
    Olympics, 427-428

Sports Celebrity
    Network, 378
Sports Illustrated, 442
Squeal Empire Learn-a-
    Language, 415
State of Insanity, 380
stock quotes, 442-443
Stroud's Consummate
    Winsock Apps, 439
SuperSeek, 437
Sweepstakes Online, 386
Symantec, 439
Tackle Towne, 394
Talk City, 380
Tax Help Online, 444
taxes, 443-444
TaxWeb, 444
Teachers.net, 445
teaching, 445-446
Teachnet, 445
Team USA, 428
telnet
    directories, 257
    Java, 254
Thomas, 399
Timecast, 433
Total Entertainment
    Network, 428
toys, 381-382
TUCOWS, 80
TuneUp, 384
Turn Left, 433
TV networks, 446-448
U.S. News .edu, 389
UC Davis Department
    of Viticulture and
    Enology, 452
Ufomind, 448
UFOs, 448-449
United States
    Government Printing
    Office, 399
United Way of
    America, 379
Universal Pictures, 422
USA Law Resources, 417
USA Today, 425
USNews Online, 426
Vatican, 435
Vatican Museum, 423
video games, 453-454
VideoGameSpot, 453
viewers, 331
Virtual Vineyards, 452
VON products, 233
VR-1 Digital Comics, 376
Warner Bros., 422
Washington Post, 426
weather, 449-450

Weather Channel, 449
Weather Imagery and Data, 450
Weather Shops, 450
Web forums, 158, 168
Web of Online Grammars, 415
Wedding Experts, 451
Wedding Tips, 450
weddings, 450-451
West's Legal Directory, 416
White House, 400
wine, 451-453
Wine Spectator, 451
Winebid.com, 452
WNBA.com, 370
Women's Firearm Network, 401
Women's Health, 403
Women's Health Interactive, 403
Women's Wire, 402
World Factbook, 392
World League of Air Traffic Controllers, 381
World Shopping Directory, 438
World Wide Holidays and Events, 409
World Wine Web, 452
Wrolin Camping 'Round the World, 374
WWW Backgammon Page, 397
Yahoo!, 417, 436
Yahoo! Chat, 380
Yahoo! Classifieds, 376
Yo-Yo, 382
ZDNet, 383
Ziff Davis Magazines, 419
Webcasting, 122
Websprite, 130
Webtop, 128
Wedding Experts Web site, 451
Wedding Tips Web site, 450
West's Legal Directory Web site, 416
whatis, searching Archie, 196
white boards, VON, 238
White House Web site, 400
Who commands, 217
wild cards
  Gopher, searching, 206-210
  Jughead, 206
windows
  bookmarks (Netscape), 63
  targeted, 88

Windows 95 Netscape Navigator, 291
Windows wallpaper, 78
wine, Web sites, 451-453
Wine Spectator Web site, 451
Winebid.com Web site, 452
WinPGP, 47-48
Winsock, 291
WNBA.com Web site, 370
women, health Web sites, 402-403
Women's Firearm Network Web site, 401
Women's Health Web site, 403
Women's Health Interactive Web site, 403
Women's Wire Web site, 402
Word for Windows commands, Protect Document, 49
word processors, creating Web pages, 110
World Factbook Web site, 392
World League of Air Traffic Controllers Web site, 381
World Shopping Directory Web site, 438
World Wide Holidays and Events Web site, 409
World Wide Web, *see* WWW
World Wine Web Web site, 452
writing
  e-mail, Archie, 195
  IRC commands, 223
Wrolin Camping 'Round the World Web site, 374
WWW (World Wide Web), 4
  addiction, 281-287
  browsers
    purpose, 57
    security, 85
  chats, 220-227
  content, 66-68
  definition, 4
  destinations, 61
  dial-in terminal accounts, 56
  directories, 266-274
  frames, 88
  graphics, 67-68
  history, 199
  home pages, promoting, 294
  hypertext, 4
  images, 3-D, 99
  multimedia, 93-94, 315

navigating, 60
overview, 55-68
programs, 89
publishing, 56
searching
  resources, 268-274
  topics, 273
servers, 57
services, 11
sites, *see* Web sites
tables, 83-94
television, 316
video, 99-107
WWW Backgammon Page Web site, 397

XML (Extended Meta Language), 131

Y-Z

Yahoo!
  Chat Web site, 380
  Classifieds Web site, 376
  newsgroups, 273
  people, finding, 268
  Web site, 417, 436
Yo-Yo Web site, 382

ZDNet Web site, 383
Ziff Davis Magazines Web site, 419
zipped FTP files, 179